Safety Net

Blanche D. Coll

SAFETY NET

Welfare and Social Security
1929–1979

Rutgers University Press
New Brunswick, New Jersey

Library of Congress Cataloging-in-Publication Data

Coll, Blanche D.
    Safety net : welfare and social security, 1929–1979 / Blanche D.
Coll.
        p.   cm.
    Includes bibliographical references (p.   ) and index.
                    ISBN 0-8135-2159-9
    1. Public welfare—United States—History.   2. Social security—
United States—History.   I. Title.
HV91.C66   1995
361.973–dc20   94-32737
                                                              CIP

British Cataloging-in-Publication information available

To Genevieve W. Carter

and to the memory of Frederic C. Lane

Contents

Acknowledgments

I HAVE BEEN PLOTTING this history of modern public welfare in the United States for many years. My first job, as a stenographer at the southern district office of the Baltimore Family Welfare Association (FWA) began in 1936, about a year after passage of the Social Security Act. The FWA, a Community Chest agency, had only recently transferred relief to the needy to the city's Department of Public Welfare. Mary E. Richmond (1861–1928), a Baltimorean and the author of *Social Diagnosis* (1917), a leading text, had started out in this very office building. By my day the trend toward psychoanalytically based counseling and verbatim recording of interviews with clients had taken hold.

As an undergraduate at Goucher College and later at the College for Teachers, Johns Hopkins University, I commanded the highest clerical rate from the National Youth Administration, the agency that Lyndon Johnson headed in Texas. Always the writer at heart, I dipped into memories of problem families to produce, for example, a tearjerker about juvenile delinquency that attracted favorable attention from the student marker in English 1. My senior paper, "Basic Concepts in American Charities," helped me qualify for a graduate tuition scholarship in the Hopkins history department.

As a graduate student I was the lone historian among economists working part-time preparing a subject index and critique of some fifty official publications selected from the extensive Hopkins collection dating back to the organization of national unions and federations. *Trade Union Publications* (1944) got my name in print, and, as a huge bonus, an introduction to lifelong friends.

Veering away from charities into labor history brought me my first job in the federal government. In 1946, Frederic C. Lane, on leave from the Hopkins history department, hired me to research and write first drafts on labor issues for his forthcoming *Ships for Victory: A History of Merchant Shipbuilding in World War II* (1951). I became one of three collaborating authors. Subsequently I became principal author of *The Corps of Engineers: Troops and Equipment* (1958), in the U.S. Army in World War II series.

Meanwhile, my "Baltimore Society for the Prevention of Pauperism" (*American Historical Review*, October 1955) called attention to the importance of American charities as a field of study. This article was a major entrée to the Department of Health, Education and Welfare where I transferred in 1964. *Perspectives in Public Welfare: A History,* with an introduction by Robert H. Bremner, was published by HEW in 1969. It has been widely used in schools of social work and provides basic background information for *Safety Net.*

My deep gratitude is extended to the National Endowment for the Humanities (NEH) which granted me a fellowship for calendar year 1980 (# FA-*0025-80), and to the American Council of Learned Societies (ACLS) which approved a grant-in-aid for the year beginning May 1, 1987. To my referees for these grants—Edward D. Berkowitz, Genevieve W. Carter, Clarke A. Chambers, Gerald N. Grob, and Kathryn Kish Sklar— go my thanks for yet another demonstration of their sustaining interest.

In making final revisions I am again indebted to Ed Berkowitz and Gerry Grob. Prior to the final stage, Jonathan P. Lane generously applied his writing skills, insider's knowledge of social research, and statistical expertise to improve clarity in content and presentation.

My interviews with policymakers will be placed on permanent deposit in appropriate archives and open for use in the near future. These interviews, cited in the text, are as follows: Robert M. Ball, February 2, 1988; Jules H. Berman, August 20, 1987; Eveline Burns, July 1, 1985; Wilbur J. Cohen, October 19, 1985; Mary Flynn, May 9, 1986; Alvin L. Schorr, June 11, 1987; Elizabeth Wickenden, May 28, 1986; and Ellen B. Winston, September 13, 1982.*

For answers to queries and comments on my paper, "Public Assistance: Reviving the Original Comprehensive Concept of Social Security," in *Social Security: The First Half Century,* ed. Gerald D. Nash, Noel H. Pugach, and Richard F. Tomasson (Albuquerque: University of New

*The interview with Winston was obtained through the Women in the Federal Government project under the auspices of the Schlesinger Library for the History of Women in America.

Mexico Press, 1988) and the *Safety Net* manuscript, I am grateful to David L. Arnaudo, Eloise Bittel Cohen; Brian Grattan; Jonathan Grossman; Louis B. Hays; Dorothy A. Mohler; Maurine Mulliner; Mollie Orshansky; Wayne D. Rasmussen; David B. Smith; Martha Swain; and Elizabeth Wickenden. For sources in Chapters 10 and 11, I am indebted to J. Kenneth Maniha, who turned over his valuable collection of final reports of research grants, together with his own and Howard M. Iams's analysis and evaluation of these grants.

As an old civil servant myself, I may be prejudiced, but it seems to me that librarians and archivists went far beyond their job descriptions in attending to my needs. Specifically, Peter Galley and Anthony Meis served me well professionally at the Library of Congress, and skillfully at the weekly bridge game on the Hill. At the National Archives, Washington, D.C.; and at the National Archives Records Center, Suitland, Maryland; I was pampered by John Howarton, Aloha South, and Maryellen Trautman. At the Franklin D. Roosevelt Library, Hyde Park, New York, I was greeted by Director William R. Emerson, a friend from military history days, who turned me over to a student of Bob Bremner who would help me into the papers of Harry Hopkins, John Winant et al. Efficient service was also forthcoming at the John F. Kennedy Library, Boston, Massachusetts, and, by long distance, from the Lyndon B. Johnson Library, Austin, Texas. At the Social Welfare History Archives, University of Minnesota, David Klaassen was on target in 1994 as he was in 1980.

Although the bibliography contains references to those historians who are pioneers in social welfare history, it is a pleasure to repeat their names and seminal publications here, the cut-off date for inclusion being about 1970 when the flood began: Robert H. Bremner, *From the Depths: The Discovery of Poverty in the United States* (New York: New York University Press, 1956); Clark A. Chambers, *Seedtime of Reform: American Social Service and Social Action, 1918–1933* (Minneapolis: University of Minnesota Press, 1963); Ralph E. Pumphrey and Muriel W. Pumphrey, eds., *The Heritage of American Social Work: Readings in Its Philosophical and Institutional Development* (New York: Columbia University Press, 1961); James Leiby, *Charity and Correction in New Jersey: A History of Welfare Institutions* (New Brunswick, N.J.: Rutgers University Press, 1967); Roy Lubove, *The Professional Altruist: The Emergence of Social Work as a Career: 1880–1930* (Cambridge: Harvard University Press, 1965) and *The Struggle for Social Security, 1900–1935* (1968); and Walter I. Trattner, *Crusade for the Children: A History of the National*

Child Labor Committee and Child Labor Reform in America (Chicago: Quadrangle Books, 1970).

Ralph, a trained historian, and Muriel, a trained social worker, were among the founders of the Social Welfare History Group (1956–   ). The annual bibliography appearing in the Group's Newsletter, and scholarly presentations at annual conferences of historians and/or social workers became focal points for a lively organization.

The movement for recognition of modern public history—hitherto referred to as "current events"—made its formal debut at the 1952 annual meeting of the American Historical Association. The title of the session, "Clio Goes to Washington," caused Sidney Painter, the author of *French Chivalry* (1940) to wonder: "Was she raped?" Whatever the answer, it was some twenty-five years before the Society for History in the Federal Government (1979–   ) was founded. Both the Social Welfare History Group and the Society for History in the Federal Government have served me as essential professional anchors.

Virginia Boman, Evelyn and Fred Peel, Harold Schwartz, Charlotte Gillmor, Gene and Daniel Mack, Virginia T. Sandifer, Dorothy Alford, Oliver and Patricia Moles, and Sue Whitman, all old friends, know how much they have contributed over the long haul, and I thank them.

New friends, as if to reaffirm my good fortune, came along with a change of address in 1987. Max Holland, a fellow writer, and Corinne Whitlatch, a seeker of peaceful change in the Middle East, have responded to nighttime alarms and daytime malaise with transportation, with food, and above all, with stimulating discussions.

Having been around for a while, I've had my share of good doctors, not a few of whom wrote the text under which they were practicing. I name only two. Dr. Lex B. Smith and Dr. Stephen W. Peterson, at different places and different times, held the safety net taut for me.

My editors at Rutgers University Press—Marlie Wasserman, who initiated the contract and guided my effort through the acceptance process; Karen Reeds, the science editor; and Marilyn Campbell, the managing editor—have shepherded *Safety Net* to the printer with the efficient and tactful assistance of Elizabeth Gretz, the copy editor, who sharpened her pencil on other public welfare studies.

While hesitating to identify living persons as if they were machines, I have been referring to "my word processor, Michael Weeks," for some time now. Weeks is only the last in a series of word processors that began with Carolyn Prencipé who was obtained through a former colleague and friend Maria Candamil. Linda Willis Tyler, my secretary of twenty-five years ago, word processed my application to NEH. Susanne Lane helped put some of my interviews in shape and also referred me to Judy Buckelew, who was Weeks's immediate predecessor. Cheers!

Having presented a mile-long list of helpers, I do firmly assert that I did most of the work myself, and do affirm that I am solely responsible for *Safety Net,* including any errors of commission or omission.

Blanche D. Coll
November 15, 1994

Safety Net

"OUR POSITION is that you take assistance as the safety net, the court of last resort, for those people who fall through the insurances, who do not fit in any single category, and that you make this program a catch-all, a last resort for any needy person who finally has to come to the assistance agency."

Elizabeth Wickenden, representing the American Public Welfare Association at Hearings before the House Ways and Means Committee, 1949

"THOSE WHO, through no fault of their own, must depend on the rest of us—the poverty stricken, the disabled, the elderly, all those with true need—can rest assured that the social safety net of programs they depend on are exempt from any cuts."

President Ronald Reagan, Address before the Joint Session of the Congress on the Program for Economic Recovery, February 18, 1981

1

This Business of Relief

THE STOCK MARKET collapse on October 24, 1929, signaled the end of the prosperous 1920s and the beginning of ten years of economic depression. Contemporaries failed to see the crash as a sign of what was to come. The most recent downturn in the economy, a deflation following World War I, had been over in eighteen months. The most recent major depression had occurred before the turn of the century, beginning in 1893 and lasting four years.

Boom and Bust

As early as 1927, the economy showed some signs of weakness. Home construction, automobile production, purchase of consumers' durable goods, and new investment in producers' durable goods all declined. In the summer of 1929 a little noticed, but serious, downturn set in. The Federal Reserve index of industrial production peaked at 126 in June, falling to 117 by October. By September-October, a recession was already under way. By the end of the year, all aspects of American business and finance were on the skids.

At its lowest point, in 1933, the gross national product (GNP) stood at $56 billion, just about half its value in 1929. Not until 1937 did the GNP reach $95 billion, only to drop sharply in the recession of that year. The Depression years saw industrial production fall by almost one-half, bankruptcy of one-third of the nation's railroad mileage, and widespread mortgage foreclosure, particularly of farms. During 1929–1933 alone, more than one-third of the country's banks suspended operations. Behind the staggering figures lay a mass of human suffering—physical, mental, and moral. At the depth of the Depression, nearly thirteen million persons were unemployed—24.9 percent of the labor force. In 1937, when unemployment reached the lowest point of the Depression decade, an average of eight million persons were still out of work. That translated to 14.3 percent of the labor force. A lower figure was not reached until 1940. Among nonfarm workers, unemployment was a great deal worse, reaching 37.6 percent in 1933 and still extremely high at 21.3 percent in 1937.[1]

President Herbert C. Hoover, a Republican elected in a landslide that gave his party control of both houses of Congress in November 1928, had been in office less than a year when the stock market crashed. A highly successful engineer and businessman, Hoover had served as secretary of commerce since 1921, during the Harding and Coolidge administrations. Hoover had spent most of his life outside the United States, living long periods of time in Australia and England. In London, he had watched from his club as World War I veterans lined up week after week for their "dole," their unemployment compensation, even though jobs were presumably available.

Not only a successful businessman, President Hoover was an expert in modern methods of efficient management. He was also a Quaker who took his religion seriously. His reputation as an outstanding humanitarian had been gained as head of the vast effort to deliver food and other necessities of life to Europe's civilian victims of World War I. In such enterprises Quaker and manager joined to attain admirable results.[2] Aside from a modest increase in federal public works, the Hoover administration's major action to combat the Depression was the formation of a federal lending agency, the Reconstruction Finance Corporation (RFC), chartered by Congress in January 1932. Thus the RFC entered the picture very late, more than two years after the crash and almost two years after the economy had turned downward. The agency concentrated its attention on banks, other financial institutions, and railroads, saving many from failure. No interest was shown in the average person with a small business in jeopardy or a home threatened by foreclosure. The Hoover administration's seeming preoccupation with big business came to be referred to as the "trickle down" cure for the Depression, a term coined by Will Rogers, the cowboy philosopher, and remembered by the citizenry with anger and scorn.

Nothing contributed more directly to the growing dislike and distrust of Hoover than his failure to deal forthrightly with relief—food, clothing, shelter—for the needy unemployed. The President turned instinctively toward a voluntary effort on a local level, and he clung to this idea long after it became clear that the sources of voluntary giving had dried up. When Hoover finally conceded the necessity for some local public financing of relief, he assumed these funds would be administered through private agencies. After most local tax bases had eroded, Hoover reluctantly looked to the states to raise additional money. On February 3, 1931, he promised to "ask the aid of every resource of the federal government," if the needy would otherwise suffer hunger and cold. But the following week he dug in his heels, stating his convictions in characteristic laissez-faire fashion: "The Federal Government has sought to do its part by example in the expansion of employment, by affording credit to drought sufferers for rehabilitation, and by cooperation with the community, and thus to avoid the opiates of government charity and the stifling of our national spirit of mutual self-help."[3]

By this time popular disillusion with Hoover was widespread. The Democratic party captured the House, having gained more than fifty seats in the mid-term elections of November 1930, while in the Senate, the Republicans retained a plurality of only one.[4]

It is difficult to remember, even to imagine, the vulnerability of the American worker to economic depression. The families of the unskilled, even though both parents often worked, had incomes that barely met or fell below the Department of Labor's standard of decency level. Even in good times, such families were thrown upon charity when illness, accident, or temporary layoff occurred. Skilled workers had more resources for an emergency—savings, some equity in a home, greater credit available. Still, though sufficient for the proverbial rainy day, such resources could not sustain a family over a long haul. Moreover, many working-class families, as well as those in the middle- and higher-income groups, had accumulated considerable debt as installment buying became widespread in the 1920s. Investment in stocks was not nearly so universal as supposed. Less than thirty million families were in the market. In short, for the vast majority of Americans, a job was both the beginning and the end of their livelihood and that of their families.

It is also often forgotten that once an individual's job and savings were gone, that was the end of the line. No insurance protected savings in the failed bank. Except for a small number of workers in a few states, no public or private unemployment compensation replaced a portion of wages. Housing was all but universally in private hands, with no safe-guards against dispossession or eviction. If payments owed could not be met, furniture could be seized without compensation for the amount previ-ously paid on installment. Once all was lost the unemployed had but one recourse, charity, be it from relatives, friends, or as was often the case, a public or private agency.[5]

No One Shall Starve

Public agencies established under local poor laws have existed since colonial times. The profession of social work, which dates from the late nineteenth century, originated in protest against the administration of the poor law. The organizers of private charities feared that charity in public hands would be claimed as a right and would result in pauperization of large portions of the citizenry. They also feared political corruption—that votes would be bought with grocery orders—votes from both grocer and pauper. The realities of the Great Depression modified but did not eradi-cate these attitudes.

The private charities that nurtured the social work profession were not necessarily averse to accepting public money, but they preferred public money to be dispersed by private charities or, at the very least, through social casework methods of investigation and supervision used by private charities. Social casework evolved out of earlier assumptions that the ap-plicant for charity was at fault and therefore must be changed in some way. As casework came under the influence of the mental hygiene move-ment and psychoanalytic theories in the early twentieth century, relief (as charity was now designated) given by private agencies was often made conditional upon the recipient's willingness to come to grips with his or her inner conflicts. In this context, relief became a "tool in treatment."

Although the drive by national federations of private agencies to abolish public relief except within alms- or workhouses fell short of its goals, considerable success was had in large cities. During the progressive era, however, a countermovement began. In 1911, Illinois passed the first mother's pension law, focusing on unskilled widows wih young children; in 1914, Arizona passed the first law establishing old age pensions. By 1933, forty states had mother's pensions and about thirty had pensions for the elderly.[6]

Actually, so far as relief-giving was concerned, public activities had already been greatly extended and were on the increase. By 1928, in seventeen of twenty-one cities where both public and private agencies dispensed outdoor relief, public expenditures accounted for more than half the total. In eight cities, relief from the public agency made up at least two-thirds of the total. The public share averaged 72 percent. Everywhere mother's pensions raised the level of public expenditures appreciably.

During the 1920s fund-raising took on New Era business methods—consolidation, advertising, salesmanship—as private agencies joined together to make one united appeal annually through a specialized agency called the Community Chest. By the 1930s all the large and most medium-size cities had established welfare departments to administer the provisions of the poor law—institutional care, outdoor relief (relief outside of an institution), placement of orphaned or neglected children—and often such modern additions as pensions for needy mothers and the aged. These departments were staffed with experienced persons who worked full time. Even in cities such as Philadelphia and Baltimore, where outdoor relief remained in the exclusive control of private family welfare agencies, the staff of the public agency was also experienced and full time. The public welfare worker in these agencies was more apt than not to follow the lines of social investigation and social diagnosis elaborated by Mary Richmond, the founder of social casework. Case records included some detailed information about the family and the cause of its dependency. These public welfare workers thought of themselves as social workers and were so regarded by the community.

In the small towns and county seats surrounded by farms and pasture, it was another story. All over the countryside, countless numbers of persons dispensed relief and other social services—child placement, for example. Like the city welfare workers, these workers' statutory base was the poor law. But unlike city workers, rural poor law officials did not think of themselves as social workers. And no wonder. For them administering the poor law was often merely a sideline performed on a part-time basis by someone elected or appointed to a more important or comprehensive position, such as justice of the peace. The responsible body of officials varied from place to place: it could consist of county commissioners, county courts, grand juries, township trustees, or specially named overseers of the poor or poor commissioners.[7]

Although the poor laws and their administrators were, and continued to be, criticized by social reformers for sustaining harsh attitudes toward dependents and for using humiliating means to deter applicants for assistance, by the 1930s pauper oaths, denials of suffrage, and similar anachronisms had all but faded from the scene, even the rural scene. In various historical surveys and reports made at this time, poor law officials are most often pictured as well-meaning, doing the best they knew how, even kindly disposed. In these publications, poor law administration is commonly summed up as "haphazard." In a misguided faith in community knowledge, applicants were often taken at their word instead of receiving a thorough investigation and continued follow-up. Record keeping was crude: family case records were nonexistent and proper financial accounts hard to find. Because the overriding concern of poor law officials was to keep a tight rein on expenditures, the amounts of assistance are consistently referred to as "pittances" by the authors of these studies. There are a good many references to petty graft and buying votes with the "dole." Also included are the not-uncommon accounts of relatives continuing to collect a dead man's pension, and of checks being forwarded to pensioners long after they had left the state. Many reports deplored the absence of any attempt to "rehabilitate" dependents or to collect support from responsible relatives.[8] After reviewing a 1934 study of poor relief administration in Pennsylvania, the sponsoring committee expressed in its foreword what can be taken as the general tenor of opinion nationwide:

'While the evidence reveals that the State's 425 Poor Boards constitute an outmoded, inefficient, and uncoordinated system of relief, it should be remembered that there are certain boards which stand out as exceptions. In particular phases of administration a minority of boards have maintained highly creditable standards. Again, while there have been many instances of incapacity and a few of dishonesty among directors of the poor, the members are in a sense the victims of the system, which is no longer adapted to present conditions.'[9]

In the process of combining relief-giving with social services, the Family Welfare Associations and their predecessor agencies had waged unremitting war on indiscriminate charity. In this category were placed all manner of handouts—giving money to beggars, establishment of soup kitchens, or providing free lodging or meals without a work test. Especially to be deplored was anything smacking of the English dole—the regular government payment made to the unemployed that Hoover had observed with such repugnance. The Family Welfare Associations believed strongly in an individual case-by-case approach with the amount of relief determined on the basis of standards of decency. Needy families should be helped to bridge temporary distress in privacy and dignity.[10]

As the unemployed continued to increase in the fall and winter of 1930—five million in September, seven million in December—personal distress became highly visible. Many individuals, some with their families, began to travel from one place to another seeking work. Unsuccessful more often than not, they ran out of money in unfamiliar places. Numbers of beggars appeared on city streets—not just the same old bums, but the type of person described in "Brother, Can You Spare a Dime?" those who had built the country and gone to war for it.[11] Breadlines, long, long breadlines, stretching for blocks, became commonplace. Dreadful improvised shelters, put together with box crates and other discards, made their appearance on the outskirts of cities and towns, each cluster of shanties yet another "Hooverville." To compound the misery, a series of crop-destroying droughts settled over much of the nation's farmland, first in 1930, and again in 1931. Thus farmers and farm laborers, usually able to manage somehow during a depression, suffered losses comparable to those of town and city dwellers.[12]

It was in dealing with the effects of the drought that Hoover first showed his preference for private agencies and his opposition to federal grants. At a conference called by the President, governors of the drought states recommended federal loans, public works, lowering railway rates for shipping food, and relief through the Red Cross. The Red Cross had dealt efficiently with many disasters, but in this instance the agency procrastinated and pussy-footed about, holding up relief pending the arrival of official forms and otherwise behaving as if nothing much needed to be done. With $5 million in hand, the Red Cross had spent only $1 million by January 1931. Although Hoover asserted there was little real suffering in the drought areas, he nevertheless asked Congress to appropriate funds for loans to the states for the purchase of seed and feed for animals. George Norris, a progressive Republican senator from Nebraska, expressed the farmers' anger when he intoned: "Blessed be those who starve while the asses and mules are fed, for they shall get buried at public expense." Congress, with Hoover's encouragement, later appropriated money for agricultural rehabilitation loans of money that could be used to buy food for people. On the grounds that acceptance of public money would violate its principles of voluntarism, the Red Cross would have none of it. The Department of Agriculture then assumed responsibility, but held on to the money appropriated so that little food reached the neediest groups. Doubtless state governors were at least as culpable as the Hoover administration. So long as funds for drought relief had to be borrowed when their own tax revenues were shrinking, they tended to perceive less need than actually existed. In April 1931 Hoover announced the drought over.[13]

Meanwhile, Hoover had responded, albeit weakly, to the worsening unemployment situation. In October 1930 he established the President's Emergency Committee for Employment (PECE). Essentially a center for public relations and a clearinghouse, PECE exhorted local communities to get on with public and private construction and called upon business and industry to spread the work, stabilize wages, and provide assistance for needy laid-off employees. Reliance on private agencies through Community Chests and Red Cross fund-raising efforts was stressed.[14]

Upon the resignation of its frustrated chairman in April 1931, leadership of PECE passed to Fred C. Croxton, an able administrator, who pledged that no one asking for help would starve. The focus upon local responsibility and private agencies began to blur as the possibility of using state revenues was discussed. Acknowledging the public welfare sector for the first time, Croxton now included in the committee's counsels the federal Children's Bureau and the American Association of Public Welfare Officials. The Association of Community Chests and Councils and the Family Welfare Association of America, representing the private welfare sector, had been included all along.[15]

Public and private welfare professionals were growing closer together. Linton B. Swift, executive secretary of the Family Welfare Association of America, challenged both the truth and the implications of Hoover's repeated assertions that private charity constituted the American way of relief to the unemployed. The fact was, Swift reminded an audience of social workers, that at least 70 percent of relief was ordinarily funded by public taxes.[16]

The 1932 Community Chest campaign brought in more money than ever before, but nowhere near enough to meet expected demands. Local public funds were drying up. Some cities were already bankrupt; others on the edge of becoming so. Chicago and Detroit could not pay their schoolteachers. Using their wider tax base, some states began to appropriate unemployment relief money for local communities. In August 1931, Governor Franklin D. Roosevelt of New York called the state legislature into special session. In his message to the lawmakers, Roosevelt emphasized the government's duty to care for the destitute:

While it is true that we have hitherto principally considered those who through accident or old age were permanently incapacitated, the same responsibility of the State undoubtedly applies when widespread economic conditions render large numbers of men and women incapable of supporting either themselves or their families because of circumstances beyond their control which make it impossible for them to find remunerative labor. To these unfortunate citizens aid must be extended by government— not as a matter of charity but a matter of social duty.[17]

In the next few months six industrial states—New Jersey, Pennsylvania, Rhode Island, Wisconsin, Illinois, and Ohio—followed New York in appropriating unemployment relief funds. The amounts were huge, rendering minuscule the $35 million pledged nationally to the Community Chest: New York, $40 million; New Jersey, $10 million for six months; Pennsylvania, $10 million. Surveys and special studies laid the basis for sums appropriated; later reports showed that needs had not been exaggerated.[18]

Beginning in December 1931, the "third winter of distress" in the words of Senator Edward P. Costigan of Colorado, several bills authorizing federal intervention were introduced in Congress. They included provision for grants to the states for unemployment relief, for additional public works, for a nationwide system of employment offices, and for relief for transients. Senators Costigan and Robert M. LaFollette, Jr., of Wisconsin, sponsors of similar bills for unemployment relief, assembled what seemed to them incontestable evidence to prove widespread suffering and the inability of state and local governments to deal with it unassisted. The evidence derived from testimony by those closest to the problem, social workers affiliated with public and private agencies, labor leaders, and, to a lesser extent, city and county officials. Representatives of business groups and the Hoover administration acknowledged the gravity of the situation, but continued to resist federal action as a dangerous and unnecessary intrusion into state and local affairs.

They argued that federal expenditures for unemployment relief would impair the government's credit and prevent attainment of a balanced budget, thus retarding economic recovery. Further government borrowing or increased taxation would have an adverse effect on much-needed investment and capital expansion. Federal relief funds would perforce be administered by a cumbersome and meddlesome bureaucracy.

Perhaps most telling in measuring the degree of support for federal assistance was the absence of testimony on the part of those destined to be most affected. With few exceptions, governors and state legislatures failed to press for federal aid. This inaction on the part of the states followed a pattern visible a few months previously. Of forty governors polled by Senator Hiram Bingham in 1931, thirty-nine believed relief could be managed within their state. Most of the nation's mayors expressed a similar opinion to a newspaper poll. It is therefore hardly surprising that the LaFollette-Costigan bill first died in committee. When combined, reintroduced, and brought to a vote on February 16, 1932, the bill was defeated 48 to 35, Democrats joining Republicans in making up the majority. The opponents of federal action also prevailed in defeating legislation in aid of public works, relief for transients, and a federal employment service.[19]

But the idea of federal intervention would not die. A later questionnaire sent to mayors showed a marked change in attitude as many confessed their cities faced bankruptcy. Everyone knew, however, that federal aid through outright grants to states invited a presidential veto that would be impossible to overturn. In February 1932 Senators Robert J. Buckley of Ohio and Robert F. Wagner of New York joined Representative Henry T. Rainey of Illinois in sponsoring a bill devised to avoid a veto. Instead of offering grants to states, the federal government would be authorized to make loans, upon certification by a state governor that these were necessary for emergency relief. The fiction of state-local responsibility could thus be preserved and the creation of a federal bureaucracy avoided. Despite the ingenuity of the bill, Congress showed no disposition to act hastily. Debate continued through the third winter of distress and on into the spring and early summer.

Despite Croxton's pledge that "no one would starve," some did. Many more were hungry. Hunger, compounded by exposure from lack of clothing and fuel, by the shutoff of gas and electricity, by repeated evictions, brought people into the streets in hunger marches and into at least one serious riot. In a desperate effort to help more and more of the needy unemployed, relief agencies divided up what money they had into smaller and smaller portions. Finally, in some places, nothing remained to divide. Then the leading citizens, the chambers of commerce, the business interests joined the social workers in a plea for federal aid.[20]

In June 1932 Silas H. Strawn, president of the U.S. Chamber of Commerce, joined other leading citizens of Chicago in a telegram to their senator, Otis F. Glenn:

For many months the Illinois Emergency Relief Commission has been taking care of 111,000 families, or about 600,000 of the destitute. The $10.5 million fund contributed by the citizens and the $12.5 million additional, being the proceeds of the State of Illinois notes, in all $23 million are exhausted. Accordingly, the relief stations in Chicago have been notified by the Illinois Emergency Relief Commission that all available funds having been exhausted, the stations must close tomorrow night. The undersigned, representing the business interests in Chicago, are meeting in an effort to raise sufficient funds to temporarily prevent this catastrophe until federal aid can be made possible.[21]

Such pleas finally tipped the scale. A revised Wagner-Rainey bill passed both houses of Congress and was sent to the President. The bill authorized the RFC to advance money to states and make loans to local governments for unemployment relief. More than $300 million was also earmarked for public works. Hoover, objecting that the amount for public works put a balanced budget in jeopardy with consequent burdens on the taxpayers, vetoed the bill. But the President, like the nation's business leaders, now stood ready to approve federal aid to the states through the RFC. So anxious was he "to secure the relief bill . . . with these very vital provisions in relief of distress, employment, and agriculture," Hoover explained, that he signed a virtually identical bill, with the offending sum for public works intact, within two weeks of his veto, on July 21, 1932.

The Emergency Relief and Construction Act made $300 million available to the RFC for advances to states or territories and loans to cities and counties. Yet the Hoover administration did not intend to give anything away. Money advanced at 3 percent interest was to be repaid through deductions from future federal highway construction funds. Loans were to be secured according to current practice. Fred Croxton transfered to the RFC to take charge of its newly established Emergency Relief Division.[22]

Despite the cries of desperation that preceded passage of the act, money moved out very slowly. Applications from a few states, Illinois among them, came in immediately and were acted upon promptly. Many states held back, however, some forced to await legislative action relaxing constitutional limitations, others because they were reluctant to pledge rural highway funds to help urban areas, others because they were determined to keep relief-giving on a local level. Only $30 million, about 25 percent of the total fund, had been released by December 31, 1932.

By May 1933, when administration of the emergency funds ended, $280 million had been disbursed, all but $19.6 million through advances to states. Municipalities had reached their limit on borrowing. Forty-two states and two territories received some federal money. Predictably, about 60 percent of the total went to seven populous industrial states—California, Illinois, Michigan, New York, Ohio, Pennsylvania, and Wisconsin. Six states—Connecticut, Delaware, Massachusetts, Nebraska, Vermont, and Wyoming—and the District of Columbia and the territories of Alaska and the Virgin Islands did not apply for funds. Much of the money was handed out in dribs and drabs, often only enough to cover a month's requirements. This practice inhibited state and local planning and hampered orderly administration. In most communities relief continued on a hand-to-mouth basis, with many needs unmet. Congressional intent would seem to have been violated. The progressive Republican Hiram Johnson of California complained that RFC relief money failed to reach the needy quickly enough or in sufficient amounts.[23]

Those wise in the ways of politics assumed that once money was transferred from federal to state and local coffers it would never be repaid. They were right. The Federal Highway Act of 1934 contained a waiver on deductions to repay state obligations. In 1938 the entire debt was canceled.[24]

Even had the RFC program been more effective, it would probably have come too late to restore President Hoover's image as a great humanitarian. Pessimistic and uncommunicative, Hoover was unable to project his sympathy for the unemployed and their families, much less to assure them that their government would not forsake them. Too often, and for too long a time, Hoover and his aides spoke as if they didn't believe the distress was real. In September 1931 the President declared unemployment "exaggerated." Even when he acknowledged a problem, Hoover seemed grudging, as in October 1930 when he announced: "As a nation we must prevent hunger and cold to those of our people who are in honest difficulties." If he had left out "honest," the President could have expressed an appealing sentiment. Why was the criterion of need so frequently placed at the line of starvation? "No one is actually starving," asserted the President in 1932, as if citizens of the world's wealthiest nation should be content to renounce their standards of health and decency.[25]

On July 1, 1932, the Democratic party had named Franklin D. Roosevelt, age fifty, its nominee for President. A country gentleman from Hyde Park, New York, a Harvard graduate, and trained as a lawyer, Roosevelt had been active in politics since 1910. During World War I he had been assistant secretary of the navy. His wife, Eleanor, was a gracious woman, a cousin from the Theodore Roosevelt side of the family. She was just as interested in politics as he. Franklin, though severely crippled by the polio he contracted at age thirty-nine, nevertheless returned to public life, winning the governorship of New York in 1930. He had a warm, outgoing personality, an air of confidence born of inner security, and an outstanding capacity to communicate with others, be the audience small or large. Although he approached serious issues in a serious way, he gave the impression of optimism, a sense that problems could be solved, improvements made, and above all, action taken. He set the tone for the campaign in his acceptance speech to his party, using a phrase that came to characterize an era: "I pledge you, I pledge myself, to a new deal for the American people."[26]

Roosevelt led the Democrats to a landslide victory in November. He won by a popular vote of twenty-eight million over Hoover's sixteen million, and victory in the Electoral College of 472 to Hoover's 59, capturing every state but Maine, Vermont, New Hampshire, Connecticut, Pennsylvania, and Delaware. Congress was solidly Democratic. In the Senate, the Democrats held 60 seats to the Republicans' 35 and Farmer-Labor's 1; in the House of Representatives, the Democrats held 310 seats, the Republicans, 117, and Farmer-Labor, 5.[27]

But these being the days of the long lame-duck session, it would be four months before the newly elected assumed office. The winter of 1932–33, the Depression's worst, was got through somehow. Undoubtedly RFC loans to the states helped reduce human suffering, but administration of relief remained uncertain and tentative, with responsibility divided between public and private agencies and little or no unified policy, even though the number of persons receiving relief and the sums expended reached unprecedented heights.

In the absence of a national statistical series it cannot be known precisely how many persons received relief or at what cost during 1929–1932, the Hoover years. Through the use of several restricted but reliable studies, however, a good general picture of relief-giving in this period can be estimated. During the first quarter of 1929, a special study by the Bureau of the Census found that the number of families receiving relief averaged about 334,000 per month. By the first quarter of 1931, an average of more than one million families a month were on relief, an increase of more than 100 percent. During the first quarter of 1933, the numbers on relief averaged more than four million (4,070,933 families and 432,400 single persons) per month, altogether about eighteen million men, women, and children.[28] The increase in relief expenditures and the public-private share is shown in data collected from 120 urban areas by the Children's Bureau:[29]

Year	Total (million $)	Public funds (million $)	Private funds (million $)
1929	43.7	33.4	10.2
1930	71.4	54.7	16.6
1931	172.7	123.3	49.4
1932	308.1	251.1	57.0

Federal Emergency Relief

Although the Democratic platform contained words pledging federal funds for public works and relief for the unemployed, it left the specifics to future legislation and administration. For the most part, candidate

Roosevelt was content to run on this generalized statement. When he became more specific, he sounded very much like Hoover: the federal government should step in only when state and local funds had run out.
Emphasizing the need for a balanced budget, FDR saw the presence of
hunger and cold as the only justification for federal deficits. But FDR's
record looked more liberal than his speeches sounded. Roosevelt had been
the first governor to disburse state funds to cities and counties to help them
finance unemployment relief.[30] When told that some needy persons were
ashamed to apply for assistance, he encouraged them to do so: "I take this
opportunity to urge all who have such hesitancy about applying for home
relief to realize that home relief is in no sense charity. Home relief is being
given to individuals to whom society will have failed in its obligations if it
allows them to suffer through no fault of their own."[31]

For his actions to combat the miseries of the Depression and for his
ideas to soften the effects of future economic crises, Roosevelt was indebted to Frances Perkins, his state industrial commissioner. Born in Boston in 1880, Perkins graduated from Mount Holyoke with a physics major,
taught science for a while, then gradually shifted into social reform. She
was greatly influenced by the sociologist Simon Patten, of the University
of Pennsylvania, who argued that the abundance resulting from modern
industrial production should be more equitably divided—not along socialist lines but through improvements in economic planning and the regulation of capitalism. If Perkins's commitment to social reform needed
sealing, it was provided by the Triangle Shirtwaist Company fire, which
occurred in New York City in 1911. She witnessed the fire in which nearly
150 young women and children perished, many leaping from the flames to
their deaths. For the next half-dozen years, Perkins worked for pay and as
a volunteer in a variety of causes—women's suffrage, maximum hour
laws, industrial safety legislation. She retained her birth name after marriage and motherhood, and for most of the years after 1918 she was the
principal provider for a depressive husband who spent much of his life in
institutions.

Perkins became increasingly active in the Democratic party and closely
associated with the like-minded reformer Governor Alfred E. Smith.
Smith appointed Perkins to the New York State Industrial Board, where
she successively took an active hand in the mediation and arbitration of
strikes, oversaw factory inspection, and administered the Workmen's
Compensation Act. In 1926 Smith elevated her to head the Industrial
Board. When Roosevelt kept her in this job for his terms as governor,
Perkins used her strategic position to challenge Hoover's unrealistic state-

ments on the volume of unemployment and to attack his failure to exert leadership to surmount the relief problem.

Never content just to criticize, Perkins turned to Roosevelt with constructive ideas for the state to pursue in its own effort to deal with the Depression. She talked of insurance against unemployment and pensions for the aged. She helped establish the New York State Temporary Emergency Relief Administration (TERA). She organized a conference of neighboring governors at Albany to discuss possible solutions for common problems. She called in academics, including the liberal economist Paul Douglas of the University of Chicago and the labor economist Leo Wolman from the New School for Social Research. At a time when Hoover had closed his doors to all but those who agreed with him, Roosevelt was opening his mind to new concepts and proposals for change. While still governor, Roosevelt began to speak approvingly of a government role in economic planning and experiment.[32]

President-elect Roosevelt's choice of Perkins for secretary of labor broke precedent in a big way. For the first time, a woman would serve in the Cabinet. Moreover, owing to the desperate situation of the nation's workers, this secretary of labor was expected to shoulder greater responsibilities than her predecessors.

For the short run, until the economy recovered, Perkins called for immediate federal action to assist the unemployed. Federal money must go to the states, not as loans, but as outright grants to help finance relief. Jobs must be created through a public works program. For the long run, in order to raise living standards, preserve jobs for adults of suitable age, and provide protection during future economic downturns, Perkins advocated minimum wage and maximum hours laws, abolition of child labor, creation of a federal employment service, and social insurance protection against unemployment and old age.

Ten weeks after his inauguration, on May 12, 1933, President Roosevelt signed the Federal Emergency Relief Act into law. The act embodied the ideas of Senator Robert Wagner as well as Senators Costigan and LaFollette, of Perkins, and, last but not least, of Harry L. Hopkins, head of the New York State TERA. When, on May 22, Roosevelt appointed Hopkins head of the Federal Emergency Relief Administration (FERA), it could be said that Hopkins had written his own ticket.[33]

The Federal Emergency Relief Act of 1933 authorized grants to the states on a matching basis—$1 of federal money for every $3 of public money spent for unemployment relief by the state itself or its local governments. One-half of the total $500 million was earmarked for matching purposes. Most of the remaining $250 million was placed in a discretionary fund—for additional grants to states that could not otherwise carry the relief burden, for the relief of transients, and for assistance to cooperatives and self-help organizations. The needy would be assisted, according to local custom, through cash, service, materials, or commodities. The administrator of FERA was accorded immense power. In addition to final approval of the federal matching monies and management of the large discretionary fund, Hopkins could order a federal takeover of any state relief administration he judged ineffective or inefficient, and his was the final say as to the purpose of any expenditure.[34]

At forty-two, Hopkins had several successful social work ventures behind him. He was born in Iowa and lived there through most of his childhood and youth. His father was a salesman and sometime storekeeper, his mother a schoolteacher before her marriage. Hopkins attended Grinnell College in his home town, graduating in 1912. His favorite subjects were political science and sociology. He did well in these subjects and in extracurricular activities, showing marked ability to win friends and class elections. Eager for new sights and experiences after graduation, Hopkins snapped up an opportunity for a job in New York City, though it paid next to nothing.

The job involved assisting with recreational activities in a settlement house on the Lower East Side. He earned a little spending money by moonlighting in the tough waterfront districts making investigations for a private relief agency. During World War I, Hopkins worked for the American Red Cross Home Service, rising to become director of the South Atlantic Region. In 1924 he became executive director of the New York Tuberculosis Association. In this position he showed his exceptional talents for empire building and spending money. When he took a leave of absence in October 1931, the Tuberculosis Association had become the New York Tuberculosis and Health Association, attesting to Hopkins's leadership in broadening its base of activities. Along the way, Hopkins had converted a treasury surplus of $90,000 into a deficit of $40,000.

So far as money was concerned, it was ever thus. Hopkins himself never accumulated any. In a sense he continued to moonlight all his life, selling a magazine article now and then and betting on the horses. He took a large cut in pay, from $15,000 to $8,000, when he left New York for Washington, D.C. Yet Hopkins always had enough to live decently. He was shocked and repelled by poverty and disease, and convinced that America should guarantee its underprivileged citizens a better life. Although he was dead serious in his convictions and indifferent to opposition, he wasn't one to preach or boast.

Because of a serious digestive disorder that was not identified until after his premature death in 1946, Hopkins was extremely thin. A detached retina rendered him blind in one eye. He was a nervous type, chain smoking and drinking coffee; in appearance hastily put together; inclined to slump in his chair, reaching for the phone rather than the pen. At the same time a cheerful, optimistic personality, straightforward and candid, Hopkins exuded confidence. In conference or impromptu speech, his concise, colorful expressions commanded attention and respect. His language was liberally punctuated with slang and mild profanity. He enjoyed telling a good story but held back in a press conference because "the women reporters cramp my style." He could blast away at critics, combining sarcasm and insult with a generous use of "damn" and "God damn," and a minute later, encourage a reporter to continue his question, confessing, "I am not really mad." Above all, Hopkins loved his work in Washington— "a fascinating experience. It is worth any amount of money to have a ringside seat at this show." He worked very hard, showing—in Perkins's estimate—his unusual "capacity to organize in a field where there wasn't anything, or where there was a little something but tremendous additions were needed, bringing in all elements of the population . . . and getting people to cooperate."[35] Once sworn in at FERA, Hopkins lost no time putting his power to work. On May 22, his first day on the job, he answered the pleas of seven governors, agreeing to grant them a total of $5 million on hearing their relief funds were exhausted.

That same day, Hopkins set about gathering his top staff. He turned first to Frank Bane, who knew more about state and local public welfare than anyone in the country. A native of Virginia and a 1914 graduate of Randolph-Macon College, Bane had entered the welfare field through the public side. After a few years in county education, he became secretary of the Virginia State Board of Charities and Corrections. In 1920 he moved to Knoxville, Tennessee, as director of public welfare. Bane's boss in Knoxville was the newly appointed city manager, Louis Brownlow, leader in the movement for reform of local public administration. Three years with Brownlow greatly enhanced Bane's abiding interest in the attainment of efficient public administration.

When the Depression began, Bane was back in Virginia heading its Department of Public Welfare. He was one of a small group who founded, in 1930, the American Public Welfare Association (APWA), signaling by this action a role distinct from that of the private agencies. In September 1931, a five-year grant from the Laura Spelman Rockefeller Memorial Fund facilitated employment of a paid staff, and Bane was chosen director of the APWA. After authorization of loans to the states through the RFC, APWA's work accelerated as its field staff worked closely with Croxton's field representatives in preparing states for their new responsibilities. When approached by Hopkins in May 1933, Bane agreed to help get the federal relief program started.[36]

With Bane's blessing, the APWA staff was thoroughly decimated, at least four of its professionals joining FERA. Among them was Aubrey Williams, who first worked as a field representative in his native south and later became Hopkins's deputy administrator. Despite his well-deserved reputation for spending money freely, Hopkins maintained a very lean agency. Antibureaucratic and impatient of red tape, Hopkins ran "this show," as he referred to it, with 125–400 dedicated professionals working long hours for low pay.[37]

During 1933, FERA staff was organized in the immediate office of the administrator and in three divisions: the Division of Relations with States; the Division of Research, Statistics, and Finance; and the Work Division. Their major functions are self-evident. The Division of Relations with States constituted the main line of communication with state relief representatives. The division was the conduit and interpreter of federal policy and the advisor on methods of organization and administration to the states. Assessment of conditions within the states—needs, resources, administrative adequacy—formed a necessary supplement to reports from state authorities, giving the federal agency a feel for the actual situation and consequently improving the chances of sound decisions in distributing funds.

Essential additional information came from monthly statistical reports, now required of state agencies for the first time. After three years of depression and heavy federal monetary contributions, the government finally had a count of the numbers of persons receiving relief and the amount of money spent in their behalf. Such figures also provided data for comparative purposes—a national profile of relief needs and expenditures. From routine reporting and special studies, the Division of Research, Statistics, and Finance analyzed the demographic, economic, and social characteristics of relief recipients. When these findings were compared with characteristics of the population as a whole and with economic data, attention was called to problem areas and groups needing special programs. Corrington Gill, the division's head, came to FERA from the Federal Employment Stabilization Board.[38]

The early designation of the Work Division underscored Hopkins's determination to avoid direct relief and to offer work to the unemployed to the greatest extent possible. Direct relief, "the dole," required no work from the recipient. Work relief had a long history of use during previous economic crises, and local work relief projects had become common during the Hoover years. Consequently the Work Division picked up the oversight of numerous ongoing projects and began by early summer 1933 to plan for expansion. Jacob Baker, who had been president of the Emergency Exchange Association in New York City, became chief of the Work Division.[39]

Despite the social workers' claim that expertise in direct relief was their exclusive province, a full year elapsed before the FERA accorded any formal recognition to the profession. In April 1934, following an outburst of charges that relief rolls were swollen with loafers and cheaters, a Social Service Section headed by Josephine C. Brown was established within the Division of Relations with States.[40]

Brown graduated from Bryn Mawr College in 1913. She initially taught at an exclusive girls' school, but soon, in 1920, began a long career in social work, first with the United Charities of St. Paul (Minnesota), then as executive secretary of the Dakota County (Minnesota) Welfare Association. She got some formal training along the way by attending an Institute on Social Casework given at the New York School of Social Work.

Moving to the Southeast in 1923, Brown became associate field director or consultant in charge of eight states for the Family Welfare Association of America. She was fast becoming a pioneer in rural social work, which she maintained should be represented by "generalists" rather than by psychologically trained city caseworkers. Brown was called to the Social Science Research Council to represent social work among economists and sociologists who were studying problems peculiar to agricultural occupations. In 1933 the Family Welfare Association of America published her first book, *The Rural Community and Social Case Work*. Brown had known Hopkins and Aubrey Williams when they were with the American Red Cross in the South. Her rural specialization appealed to them, for it was in rural areas, where courthouse politics dominated administration of the poor law, that most difficulties were expected. Industrialized areas with their large cities had long ago adopted modern methods—not just in social casework, but also in accounting, record keeping, and so on.

Brown's appearance was deceiving. At age forty-seven, her long straight hair pulled back in a bun, she wore "sensible" shoes and nondescript clothing. She was modest and unassuming, somewhat of a curiosity in an agency well endowed with prima donnas and hyperactive types. Yet Brown was perfectly suited to her job. She was, first of all, friendly and kind—virtues of considerable merit in one whose main job was to supervise the twenty or so field workers who were supposed to keep the states in line with FERA rules and regulations. Their jobs were not easy. Brown could hold their hands at the same time that she held firm to FERA's rules. Above all, Brown was creative. She was able to take the sharp criticism that her originality aroused with an equanimity born of basic self-confidence and persistence.[41]

Federal-State Administration

The magnitude of the task assumed by the FERA in May 1933 would be hard to exaggerate. Huge sums of money had been placed in its trust. At stake was the very existence of millions of citizens. Success in the enterprise depended largely on engaging forty-eight states in an honest and efficient effort to channel the money in proper amounts, when and where needed. Although by this time some states had improved their organization and staffing to handle public welfare, most were unprepared to assume supervision of and accountability for the performance of local agencies where relief was applied for and disbursed.

As to funding the relief program, Hopkins was surprised to discover that RFC "loans" were covering some 80 percent of expenditures in the spring of 1933. At the time, over 4 million families and almost 500,000 single individuals—a total of 19 million persons—were on relief. One family in six and a total of 16 percent of the population was dependent. If the federal government continued to absorb such a large percentage of these expenditures, which amounted to more than twice that allotted under the matching formula, the FERA would run completely out of money before the fiscal year ended on June 30, 1934.

Convinced that many of the states were "lying down on this job," Hopkins announced his intention to fight the tendency to shift the burden to Washington. The President stood firm with his administrator. Speaking to a conference of state representatives on June 14, 1933, Roosevelt emphasized the cooperative nature of the relief program, insisting that "the states and local units of government do their fair share," while the federal government financed "a reasonable proportion of the total." By "total," the President meant the amount spent for relief of the unemployed. States were expected to continue to meet their ordinary welfare bills—bills for the care of dependent persons in institutions, for children in foster care, for old age or mother's pensions—without federal assistance. So the states were notified on May 31.[42]

In accepting federal money and assuming a fair share of overall costs, a state presumably entered a cooperative relationship to assure timely, sufficient relief to the needy unemployed. To that end, the federal government expected competent, businesslike administration, free from partisan politics. Such efficient administration, evident at the state level, must be made to flourish also in local communities, through state supervisory and auditing staff.[43]

State Emergency Relief Administrations (SERAs) confronted far more complicated organizational problems at the local level than those presented to the FERA by the states themselves. Local relief agencies existed in various sizes and shapes, conformed to no set geographical pattern, and often contained an unpredictable mixture of public and private sponsorship. Adhering to the lines of traditional political organization, local welfare units were set up by county, city, town, or some mixture of the three. A mixture was present in many states, where the larger towns often had welfare units independent of the county unit that was otherwise in charge. In New England the township unit prevailed; in the South, the county dominated. Large areas of the country, perhaps two thousand counties, had no welfare agency as such, simply a local official who handled charity cases.[44]

Poles apart from the petty politicians grouped around county courthouses were the social workers and board members of private agencies. Bane and his field representatives in the APWA had long preached the equation: public funds = public agency. How else assure accountability to the taxpayers? Private agencies continued to dispense public funds throughout the period of RFC loans, however, even though under the formal control of public and county emergency boards. The mixture of responsibility between public and private agencies was most pronounced in the large cities, the very places where the relief load was greatest. In 71 cities in 32 states, 175 private agencies were disbursing public funds when the FERA entered the scene.

As Hopkins's advisor in such matters, Bane pushed the APWA position: the FERA should insist on public administration of public funds. He argued that Hopkins should come down strong on the public side and announce this position to the audience likely to be most affected, the National Conference of Social Work, which was to assemble in Detroit for its annual meeting on June 11, 1933. Hopkins worried about taking this stand. He was reluctant to offend his former colleagues, conscious of the early effort made by the private agencies to carry the relief load, and aware that he must depend on the support of social work professionals. Nevertheless he followed Bane's advice, announcing his policy to administer public funds through public agencies, while adding:

> This policy obviously must be interpreted on a realistic basis in various parts of the United States. Hundreds of private agencies scattered throughout the land have freely and generously offered their services in the administration of public funds. It would be a serious handicap to relief work if the abilities and interests of these individuals were lost. But these individuals should be made public officials, working under the control of public authority.[45]

The FERA issued a formal notice to this effect on June 23, 1933, giving states until August 1 to bring emergency relief administration under public state and local agencies. Public relief was henceforth to be funded entirely by public money, the salaries of all individuals working for the relief agency were to be paid out of public money, and such individuals were to be supervised by public authorities. In sum, "the unemployed must apply to a public agency for relief, and this relief must be furnished direct to the applicant by a public agent."[46]

State participation in relief funding, efficient public administration—to these a third key policy was added: the quest for higher standards of relief. With few exceptions, the standard set earlier had been measured along the "no one shall starve" scale. In fairness, however, it must be remembered that in ordinary times a "tideover" of food was often all a family needed to meet a temporary crisis. The landlord could wait a bit; clothing on hand would last a while. After prolonged unemployment the food-only standard became untenable, but relief agencies were slow to adjust their practices to the unprecedented situation, particularly when faced with a shortage of money. After Pennsylvania began to receive loans from the RFC in October 1932, its SERA allowed a limited amount for fuel. The following December, issues of shoes were added; many months later, clothing. Rent payments were *never* allowed in Pennsylvania. Whatever was given, in Pennsylvania or elsewhere, was given in the form of orders on merchants or "in kind" through commissaries. Relief recipients got no cash.

Hopkins, who needed no persuading of the necessity to raise relief standards to a decency level, minced no words in his speech at the National Conference of Social Work: "The Federal Relief Administration does not intend to subsidize miserably low wages. We do not intend to permit anybody to use relief funds to reduce the standard of living lower than it is now. We are not going to allow relief agencies to starve people slowly to death with our money."[47]

In less dramatic but no uncertain terms, SERAs were notified on July 11 of their obligation to assure the needy "sufficient relief to prevent physical suffering and to maintain minimum living standards." The amount allowed a family was to be derived from an estimated budget that included: (1) food, the amount to be determined by the number, ages, and needs of individual members of the family in accordance with standard food schedules; (2) shelter; (3) fuel and other utilities; (4) household supplies; (5) clothing; and (6) medicine and medical visits in the home. Any income or other resources available to the family were to be subtracted from the budget estimate. The resulting deficiency could be made up through cash, orders on merchants, or in kind.

The decision to grant relief or to withhold it must be preceded by a businesslike investigation, to be carried out by employees of the local public relief agency. This was the *means test,* an inquiry to determine the applicant's eligibility for assistance. The means test outlined by the FERA for local agencies as a "minimum investigation" took the identical form followed by leading private agencies. Under the recognized method, the investigator gathered basic facts about the applicant's situation in an office interview. Additional knowledge came through observation of the family and its standard of living in a visit to the home. Resources were looked into by examination of bank books, deeds of property, and insurance policies. References from employers were obtained. Relatives, friends, churches, and other possible sources of assistance were contacted. Where state law made family or relatives liable for support, this aspect must be explored. Once a family had been accepted for relief, the investigator was supposed to maintain contact, visiting the home at least once a month and conducting a complete reinvestigation from time to time.[48]

Since this was the way social workers handled investigations of applicants for relief, the obvious sequence was to hire social workers to carry out this part of the relief agency's work. But by no stretch of the imagination could this be done. Even under the broadest possible definition of social worker—a person with some previous attachment to a social work agency—the gap between the numbers of social workers available and the numbers of investigators required could not be bridged. The American Association of Social Workers (AASW) had about five thousand members. Ultimately state and local emergency relief agencies employed some forty thousand persons, most of them social investigators and their supervisors.

The FERA acknowledged the shortage from the beginning, settling for social workers at the supervisory level. Regulations called for at least one trained and experienced investigator on the staff of each local agency, and not less than one trained and experienced supervisor for every twenty investigators.[49]

As Hopkins expected, many social workers transferred to state and local public relief administration from private welfare agencies. This was particularly true in heavily populated industrial areas of the country that had developed comprehensive social service systems in response to long-existing social problems—the Northeast, the Pacific Coast, the upper tier of midwestern states, and Alabama, Florida, and Louisiana in the South. In other areas, particularly in rural counties, social workers were not available even for the supervisory positions. The rank and file, the thirty thousand social investigators, were predominantly young, many just out of college. Their job, though calling for tact and stamina, was far from complex. In agency after agency, its elements were successfully learned through in-service training on the job.[50]

During its brief existence, a mere two-and-a-half years, the FERA passed through four distinct phases. In the first phase, from May to December 1, 1933, direct relief and work relief predominated, the work relief consisting largely of projects carried over from RFC days. The second phase, which ran from December 1933 through March 1934, was dominated by the existence of a special public works program carried out under the Civil Works Administration (CWA), a separate agency also under Harry Hopkins. Following the abolition of the CWA, from April 1, 1934, through June 1935, the FERA program again focused on direct relief and work relief, with work relief receiving the greater emphasis. The fourth and final phase, which occurred during the last six months of 1935, was a period of winding down as the needy unemployed were transferred to jobs funded by the Works Progress Administration (WPA), an agency formally established on April 8, 1935, again with Hopkins as its head. The FERA issued its last grants to the states during November and December 1935.[51]

Such frequent shifts in program emphasis produced in FERA an erratic operational pattern analogous to a taxi proceeding crosstown in Manhattan. Yet the shifts cannot be considered arbitrary. A common thread—a decided preference for work relief over direct relief—runs through the history of FERA. To some degree also, the FERA partook of the experimental aspects of the New Deal, as shown in Roosevelt's willingness to try first one approach, then another, in an effort to move the country out of the Depression. In other respects, the FERA responded and adjusted to the failure of the administration's effort to bring about a real upturn in the nation's economy as quickly as anticipated. In no small measure, FERA policy reflected Hopkins's inventive mind, powers of persuasion, and ability to pick up any loose change he found lying around. Nevertheless money constraints occupied an important place in the several factors influencing the agency's course of operations.

Signs that funds for relief might be less than anticipated occurred early, threatening to undermine FERA's drive for higher standards. Adequacy of funds hinged on the success of the federal-state-local partnership in which each would contribute its "fair share." Except for half a dozen states in the Northeast, state governments had done little heretofore except to borrow from the RFC. Although it was assumed that some very poor states would be unable to do much if anything, the FERA expected to apply the one-third matching formula in most cases. Once the states began to kick in, federal money would make a real difference.[52]

The FERA combined exhortation and threats and hired experts to figure state and local fiscal capacity in an effort to extract contributions from laggard states with resources in the high or middle range. Laggard states in this category were located in all areas of the country except the Northeast: in the South and Southwest, West Virginia, Kentucky, Tennessee, and Louisiana; in the Midwest, Ohio, Illinois, Michigan, and Missouri; in the West, Colorado, California, and Oregon. At first, state response seemed encouraging. Michigan assumed some responsibility in June, and by August, California, Colorado, Ohio, and Texas had either authorized bond issues or voted relief money. In Illinois, Missouri, and Oregon the situation was expected to improve in the fall of 1933. Prospects remained uncertain or poor in Kentucky, Tennessee, West Virginia, and Louisiana.[53]

Ultimately the federal government picked up by far the greater share— much closer to two-thirds than the projected one-third (see Table 1.1). Expenditures for the three-year (1933–1935) FERA program of direct and work relief totaled $4.1 billion. Of this amount the federal share represented 70.9 percent, with states contributing 12.6 percent, and localities, 16.6 percent. During the course of the program, the federal share rose from 62.2 percent in 1933 to 74.0 percent in 1935. The state share remained about the same, but the local input, which was 24.8 percent in 1933, dropped to 13.7 percent in 1935. These total figures mask the very large federal contributions necessary to keep some states going. Eleven states in the South and Southwest received over 90 percent of their emergency relief funds from Washington.[54]

Unofficial watchdogs tended to agree that the FERA had remained

TABLE 1.1.   Percentage of Relief Funds Supplied by FERA to States (January 1933 through December 1935)

Percentage	No. of states	States (includes local funds)
Under 35	11	Maine, Vermont, Massachusetts, Connecticut, Rhode Island, New Jersey, Delaware, Maryland, Wyoming, Nebraska, District of Columbia
35–54	5	New York, Pennsylvania, Minnesota, North Dakota, California
55–74	11	New Hampshire, Virginia, Ohio, Indiana, Wisconsin, Missouri, Iowa, Kansas, South Dakota, Idaho, Nevada
75–94	13	North Carolina, Florida, Kentucky, Illinois, Michigan, Oklahoma, Colorado, New Mexico, Utah, Arizona, Montana, Washington, Oregon
95–100	9	West Virginia, Tennessee, Texas, Arkansas, Louisiana, Mississippi, Alabama, Georgia, South Carolina

SOURCE: Derived from Josephine Chapin Brown, *Public Relief: 1929–1939* (1940; reprint, New York: Octagon Books, 1971), 204–206.

remarkably free of political pressure. Edith Abbott, dean of the University of Chicago's School of Social Service Administration, long a friend of public welfare free of political manipulation, praised FERA's "courageous and resolutely non-political course." Good results were evident in community after community where leaders had become convinced that "ability, integrity, and professional skill are necessary for relief work," Abbott testified. Only in 1935, as the FERA began to wind down, did columnists for *The Survey* magazine express fears that the agency's long "immunity from political pressure may be nearing its end."[55] In its financial management, moreover, the relief program remained free of graft and corruption.

To rise above petty politics and show balanced accounts might well have satisfied most minds that efficient administration had been attained. Not so the leaders of FERA. In their minds, efficient administration must include delivery of an acceptable service, in this case, relief to the needy in amounts sufficient to maintain health and decency—at least at a minimum level and if possible, somewhat higher. Also present was the desire to treat all the needy in the same way. Federal money appropriated for the benefit of citizens of the United States should be dispensed according to the same rules, not according to an assortment of rules developed independently by state and local officials. The FERA never questioned the state's authority to fix relief standards either through a statewide scale or by delegating its power to local authorities. But the FERA believed that uniform rules and regulations applied nationwide would encourage uniform treatment of applicants for, and recipients of, relief, which would, in turn, encourage relief standards to rise.

Other grant-in-aid programs to states, for higher education or highway construction, offered no model for the pursuit of FERA's goals. Typically, states dispensed the federal grant under some previously approved plan, reported progress periodically, and consulted occasionally with a federal representative. To a degree unprecedented in federal grant-in-aid programs, the FERA amplified the basic law under which it operated by laying down specific policy and practice. Not far behind the written rule and regulation was the field representative or other federal official ready to interpret and explain to state officials how best to conform to Washington's wishes.

The FERA, though insisting on a measure of local responsibility, assumed the dominant position. During the first months of the program when experience was spread thin, guidance from Washington was welcomed, even sought for, down to the last detail. As the passage of time brought knowledge and experience to state and local staffs, dependence on Washington diminished. On the whole, however, emergency relief agencies looked to the national, rather than the state, capital.[36]

Hopkins had little cause to exercise his authority to assume complete control of state relief programs. Action to "federalize" was taken in a few states, but no state remained under federal operation from beginning to end. Five states in the south-southwest region were subjected to "virtual control" through federal dictation of appointments and unusually close federal supervision. These states were either bankrupt or close to it.

During 1934 and 1935 six states were federalized. In Massachusetts, federalization resulted from legal technicalities that prevented equitable distribution of monies to the townships administering work relief. The governors of Oklahoma, Louisiana, and Georgia invited a takeover by refusing federal money unless they were free of federal rule and regulation. In North Dakota, evidence of assessment for political contributions in the state relief office precipitated action.[57]

All of these instances offered politicans and bureaucrats alike opportunities for public statements, usually colorful, sure to attract attention from press and radio. But for the story that had it all, nothing compared to the storm over Ohio. Politics, money, federal domination, social workers—these were the issues. In a long letter to Hopkins dated March 4, 1934, the newly elected governor, Martin L. Davey, a conservative Democrat, poured forth his complaints, concluding with a request for federalization. The relief system was so "wasteful and inefficient," "loaded with red tape and unnecessary reports," he argued, that "many worthy people are left without prompt attention, many chiselers are permitted to secure relief money . . . and many worthy folks in need are subjected to humiliation and distress." Young, immature graduates of "welfare colleges" rather than citizens of intelligence, character, and mature judgment made the important decisions. Davey was not inclined to support such a system by additional taxes to make up Ohio's $2 million share of the $10 million monthly expenditure. Charges that he was playing politics with the relief system, he said, were lies. Even though he claimed that members of his party had been discriminated against by the outgoing Republican regime, Davey disavowed interest in opening up jobs for Democrats. Finally:

You know, as well as I do, that all the policies for the relief program in this state are determined in Washington and supervised by your agents in Columbus.

This creates an anomalous situation. The state of Ohio is charged in the public mind with the responsibility. And yet we have absolutely nothing to say about it. We do not want anything to say. For my part, I wish merely to have the responsibility rest where it belongs, on the Federal authorities, and not on the state.

Hopkins shot back a brief note, refusing to take over the Ohio relief programs and threatening to withhold federal funds if Ohio failed to contribute its fair share.

A week later the Ohio relief program was federalized. Hopkins acted on what he termed "incontrovertible evidence" that Davey's campaign committee had engaged in a shakedown of Ohio businessmen who sold goods to the state ERA. The President, who had to authorize the takeover, did so with apparent gusto, urging Hopkins to follow up on the investigations and "let the chips fall where they may." Hopkins announced that he was turning over his evidence to the Ohio attorney general (a Republican). Davey countered by filing a criminal libel suit against Hopkins.[58] Nothing ever came of these theatrical charges and threats. Federalization presumably saved Ohio from politicizing relief. The episode was highly suggestive, however, of increasing dissatisfaction with federal dominance and with social work dominance on the part of state and local officials and other community leaders.[59] In successfully fostering efficient administration, the FERA left a legacy ranging from discontent to resentment of the heavy federal hand.

Relief Standards and Caseload Dynamics

Adding fuel to these negative feelings was the FERA's partial success in raising relief standards. FERA leaders determined early in 1934 to maintain the morale and work habits of the unemployed and keep some distance, however small, between the emergency relief program and the dole. As the White House press release put it: "Direct relief as such, whether in the form of cash or relief in kind, is not an adequate way of meeting the needs of able-bodied workers. They very properly insist upon an opportunity to give to the community their services in the form of labor in return for unemployment benefits."[60] The projects to be pursued would not be "public works" in the usual sense of that term. And the wages paid would no more than satisfy the weekly relief budget of worker and dependents.[61] Yet it was partly through work relief that standards were raised. In families being supported by work relief or in families where low earnings were supplemented, the budget could be set higher than in families subsisting on direct relief. Food and clothing allowances were greater and "extras" such as carfare were included in work relief budgets. The FERA ruling that work relief be paid for by cash or check doubtless raised the real relief payment somewhat. Good managers could shop around for bargains and make choices about specific expenditures. Although not insisted upon, cash payments to recipients of direct relief were also encouraged by the FERA. During 1934, after a number of large cities shifted, the proportion of direct relief extended in cash rose sharply from 9 percent in May 1934 to 25 percent early in 1935.[62]

Despite FERA emphasis on work relief, the number of direct relief cases remained proportionately greater throughout the years of the program. In 1933, prior to the introduction of CWA, work relief ran about 40 percent of the total caseload. It stood at 35 percent in June 1934, then rose steadily to 46 percent in January 1935.[63] In view of the effort made to

place all employables on work relief projects, these figures reveal the startling number of unemployables—the aged, women caretakers of dependent children, and persons physically or mentally disabled—being
supported by a program established for the relief of needy unemployed
workers and their families.

For the United States as a whole, the average amount of monthly relief
per case doubled from about $14 in July 1933 to $28 in January 1935. The
nationwide trend reflected the introduction of various work programs. Average amounts rose from July through October 1933, when they reached
more than $17, then fell during the months when CWA—the nonrelief
works program—was in operation, reaching $15.57 in February 1934.
The largest monthly increase, amounting to over $4, occurred between
March and April 1934, just after the inauguration of the new work relief
program. In April average relief payments passed $20, continuing gradu-
ally upward to the peak of $28.13 reached in January 1935.

Fewer than one-third of the states granted relief in amounts at or above
the national average. The higher-paying states were concentrated in the
Northeast and Midwest, with a scattering in the west.[64] Although the predominantly agricultural states located in the South and Southwest continued to grant relief in amounts well below the average, their payments rose
significantly. In July 1933, seven of these poor states averaged payments
of less than $5 a month. By July of the following year, no state was
averaging such a low amount, and by January 1935, payments in ten states
in this area were in the $11–$15 range.[65] Relief payments in large cities
were higher than in small towns and farming areas. In July 1933 the national monthly average for major cities was $9 more than the average for
the rest of the country. The gap had widened to $13 by July 1934, and to
$15 by January 1935.[66]

The value of these statistics is as an indicator of trends in relief payments. They tell us little or nothing about actual payments per case, let
alone the relation of such payments to standards of health and decency.
Some of the increase in relief payments merely reflected rising prices,
particularly rising food prices. Some of the increase resulted from more
widespread destitution as families hitherto partially self-sustaining ex-
hausted their resources and became fully dependent. These averages do
not represent the actual amounts received by families totally dependent on
relief. The averages are biased downward because of cases receiving only
partial support during the month, either because wages were supplemented, other resources were supplemented, or acceptance on the rolls
occurred sometime after the first of the month. Another circumstance that

helped large numbers of families survive the Depression was periodic employment in a full-time job with enough pay to take them off the rolls, if only for a time. Beginning in October 1933, distribution of "surplus commodities"—food and clothing—improved standards in relief households.[67]

Relief rolls were anything but stagnant, and were far from starting with a certain number of persons and adding others to pile up a chronic caseload. On the contrary, case turnover was extremely high. During the month of February 1934, for example, a total of 736,803 applications were accepted, but the increase in caseload was only 150,842; in July 1934, there were 665,494 applications accepted against a caseload increase of 89,773; and in January 1935, there were 638,711 applications accepted against a caseload increase of 198,171. In other words, 585,961 cases were closed in February 1934; 575,721 closed in July; and 440,540 closed in January 1935.

People from all major occupational groups—professionals as well as laborers—found themselves on relief. But unskilled and semiskilled workers accounted for over 50 percent of those on the rolls and were overrepresented in relation to their numbers in the general population. Skilled workers, who made up another large percentage of relief recipients, were also overrepresented.

By contrast, white-collar workers were greatly underrepresented relative to their numbers in the population and made up only slightly more than 11 percent of workers on the rolls.[68]

As a clearly identifiable group with little schooling, few skills, and heavily concentrated in the rural south, blacks were early comers and long stayers on the relief rolls. Nationwide, blacks composed only 10 percent of the population, but they made up about 17 percent of relief recipients. Put another way, 17.8 percent of the black population was on relief in October 1933, compared with 9.5 percent of all whites and other races. By January 1935 the percentage of blacks on relief had increased to 25.5 percent, compared with 15.5 percent of whites and others. (See Table 1.2.)

The overrepresentation of blacks on the rolls was more pronounced in urban than in rural areas—a fact that says more about racial discrimination than about need. In the South and Southwest, where racial prejudice was most marked, ways were found to circumvent the FERA regulations that forbade discrimination. Without putting anything on paper, a double standard was established—one for whites, another for blacks. Even in urban areas relief budgets for blacks were sometimes lower than for whites, while in some rural areas black families were expected to live on

TABLE 1.2. Percentage of Persons on Relief to Total Persons in Twenty-three States Having a Black Population of 100,000 or Over

	Percentage of persons on relief[a]					
	Urban			Rural		
States	White	Black	Ratio black to white	White	Black	Ratio black to white
Tennessee	6.3	11.2	1.78	7.7	3.2	0.42
West Virginia	14.6	32.5	2.23	25.8	12.5	.48
Arkansas	13.7	26.9	1.96	8.9	4.7	.53
Kentucky	8.3	16.3	1.96	22.5	12.0	.53
Mississippi	12.0	18.4	1.53	14.1	7.6	.54
Louisiana	10.7	33.0	3.08	17.3	9.6	.54
Georgia	8.7	22.4	2.58	8.7	6.1	.70
Maryland	8.4	26.5	3.15	3.8	3.0	.79
Texas	8.5	18.3	2.15	3.3	2.9	.88
Alabama	11.4	22.4	1.96	18.0	17.7	.98
Virginia	3.3	9.8	2.97	1.6	1.6	1.00
Florida	15.1	46.7	3.09	26.6	26.9	1.01
North Carolina	6.4	19.6	3.06	6.7	8.3	1.24
South Carolina	18.8	39.1	2.08	19.8	25.1	1.27
Oklahoma	12.3	27.9	2.27	20.2	26.7	1.32
Missouri	6.1	24.1	4.11	3.2	5.0	1.56
Indiana	10.3	31.0	3.01	6.2	12.1	1.95
Michigan	11.6	28.8	2.48	12.7	26.6	2.09
Pennsylvania	11.7	35.1	3.00	16.4	35.9	2.19
Ohio	10.8	39.5	3.66	8.8	27.3	3.10
New Jersey	7.9	29.8	3.77	5.7	18.8	3.30
New York	9.3	25.3	2.72	9.8	25.4	2.59
Illinois	10.7	35.6	3.33	6.7	30.9	4.61

SOURCE: "The Negro and Relief," *FERA Mo. Rpt.*, Mar. 1936, 12.
[a]Persons on relief: FERA, Unemployment Relief Census of October 1933, 14–15. Total population: 1930 Census of Population.

one-third less than white families. Discrimination was carried over into work relief through the establishment of dual wage scales that paralleled practices in private and public employment.[69]

Measures of improvement in the microcosm of relief-giving rested on choices between greater and lesser evils on a scale of value to the needy unemployed. Accordingly, those receiving relief believed that work relief was better than direct relief, grocery orders better than soup kitchens, cash payments better than grocery orders, and so on. But the macrocosm of the nation, and particularly in the marketplace, relief-giving was evaluated quite differently, in terms of fiscal policy, relative monetary costs, and access to the labor pool. This view reversed the order of evils: direct relief was better than work relief, grocery orders better than cash. The total bill for relief was a major cause of rising federal deficits. Work relief cost more than direct relief, and on some kinds of jobs emerged as a rival to private employment. Cash payments acted as a disincentive to labor at all.

Walter Lippmann summed up the divergent views in his syndicated news column:

The first point to fix in mind is that the kind of relief which is humanly the most desirable is also the most expensive. The cheapest kind of relief is the breadline and the soup kitchen. It is also the most demoralizing. The most costly relief is public work at standard wages. It is for the unemployed the most satisfactory. That is why those who are the most interested in keeping down expenditures now prefer the "dole" and why those who are most interested in keeping up the morale of the unemployed are asking for a big public works program.[70]

Toward the end of 1934, when the economy began to show definite signs of recovery, criticism of relief mounted and calls for a return to earlier methods of charity were frequently heard. The National Association of Manufacturers (NAM) was joined by other groups in demanding local administration "free from arbitrary rules imposed from the outside."[71]

In truth, no one was satisfied with the emergency relief program. Sentiment for change was universal. It was also clear that there could be no turning back, no turning away from some sort of federal commitment to help vulnerable groups manage independently, if possible, and subsist decently if compelled to rely on public assistance. When, in his annual message to Congress in January 1935, the President announced that "the Federal Government must and shall quit this business of relief," he was speaking with full knowledge of plans for just such a commitment. The emergency was over. The time had come for a permanent national program.[72]

2

From the Cradle to the Grave

EVEN AS THE President announced his administration's determination to "quit this business of relief," he disavowed any intention of abandoning the needy. The federal government, he pledged, would keep its hand in.

Committee on Economic Security

Jobs for the unemployed through a vast public works program was the immediate purpose of Roosevelt's January 4, 1935, message to Congress. But Roosevelt took this occasion to express concern for the so-called unemployables—those too old, too ill, or too disabled to work and women, usually widows, with dependent children. Unemployables made up a large group, almost one-third of the families and single persons then on relief. Responsibility for unemployables, wrote the President, belonged where it had been since time immemorial, with states, counties, cities, and private charities. Yet, however time-honored this responsibility, the administration did not plan a complete turning back. Calling attention to forthcoming proposals for economic security, Roosevelt expressed certainty that this new legislation would assist the states to carry out their duty to aid those needy who could not be expected to work.

Six months earlier, on June 8, 1934, the President had sent a message to Congress affirming his support for a federal-state program to provide for the security of the nation's men, women, and children "against the hazards and vicissitudes of life." Following Perkins, Roosevelt stated his preference for social insurance as the basic means of protection, emphasizing particularly insurance against unemployment and old age. He noted that social insurance was far from untried, various forms having been adopted in all modern industrial nations, as well as by some industries and a few states in the United States.

The President was not the first to initiate action on social insurance during the current economic crisis. The Democratic platform of 1932 had called for social insurance under state laws. Congress, moving ahead of the President, had before it, in June 1934, bills on both unemployment insurance and old age pensions. Calling attention to the interrelationship between various types of social insurance, with the consequent difficulty inherent in a piecemeal approach, Roosevelt asked for deferral of action on these bills. In the interim he promised to develop a sound, comprehensive measure to be completed in about six months. On June 29 he appointed a Cabinet-level committee to make recommendations "which in its judgment will promote greater economic security."[1]

In seeking a comprehensive measure, Roosevelt was doubtless also responding to various economic recovery schemes advanced from the right and the left of the political spectrum by neo-Fascists and Communists and by demagogues with pet ideas. Neither the groups organized by neo-Fascists nor the Communist party itself had many true adherents. The demagogues commanded much the greatest following. Among these was the Roman Catholic radio priest, Father Charles E. Coughlin, who attracted huge audiences for his broadcasts from Detroit. Coughlin's crusade for social justice centered on monetary policy. With undertones of anti-Semitism he attacked the bankers, particularly the "international" bankers. His was a Christian crusade that warred against some aspects of capitalism as well as communism. Coughlin displayed many inconsistencies, not the least among them his on-again off-again attitude toward Roosevelt and the New Deal.

Huey Long, former governor and now senator from Louisiana, aroused much greater worries, if not fears, within the Roosevelt administration. For one thing, he was a Democrat and a politician with a demonstrated capacity for winning elections. For another, he was a highly intelligent man who had pulled his state into the twentieth century and a good many of its citizens with it. Less attractive were his crude manners and the political corruption that ensured his absolute power in the state. Long preached the redistribution of wealth as the only cure for the nation and, not incidentally, for the preservation of the middle class. He would tax the

rich heavily and "share the wealth" in order to make "every man a king."
Like Coughlin, Long vacillated between support for and opposition to the
New Deal, but as time went on he talked increasingly of running for Presi-
dent as head of a third party.[2]

The choice of Secretary of Labor Perkins to chair the Committee on
Economic Security was logical by virtue of her position as well as her
comprehensive knowledge of the subject. Social insurance, "true insurance," as she insisted when Roosevelt demurred, had been on her list of
reforms when she accepted the secretaryship. Perkins knew what she
wanted in the way of economic security and went after it with intelligence
and industry. The other four members of the committee participated in
varying degree. Most faithful in attendance and interested in all aspects of
the proposed program was Harry Hopkins. Secretary of the Treasury
Henry Morgenthau, Jr., and Secretary of Agriculture Henry A. Wallace
also attended meetings quite regularly, Morgenthau showing particular
interest in the insurance aspects and Wallace in relief programs. Morgenthau often sent Josephine Roche, the assistant secretary for public health,
to sit in for him. Much less active was Attorney General Homer Cummings,
who usually sent a representative instructed to follow Perkins's lead.[3]

Presumably it was the Committee on Economic Security that would
decide policy. Certainly it was the committee's decisions that would be
laid before the President. As in all such complicated questions, however,
the views of technicians, in this case, economists, social workers, lawyers, and actuaries, entered policymaking with considerable force. The
assistance of such technicians was provided in part by a Technical Board,
authorized, along with the committee itself, by the President's Executive
Order. The Technical Board, which had general direction of fact-finding
studies and investigations, consisted of federal government employees
chosen on the basis of their knowledge of particular aspects of problems
under consideration.

The chief position, also authorized by the order, was that of executive
director, who carried day-by-day responsibility for fact-finding. With the
approval of the Technical Board, the executive director could hire special-
ists from outside the government to make such studies. The executive
director was present at all official meetings, serving as secretary of the
Committee on Economic Security, of the Technical Board, and of the
Advisory Council, a group selected in November to represent industry,
labor, and the public.

The powerful job of executive director went to Professor Edwin E.
Witte, chairman of the Department of Economics at the University of

Wisconsin. He was the candidate of Dr. Arthur J. Altmeyer, an econo-mist—also of Wisconsin—the second assistant secretary of labor, whom Perkins had asked to get things under way for the committee. Connection with the state of Wisconsin, and particularly with its university, was a high recommendation for the assignment in hand. The university had for many years been noted for its close collaboration with the state government in developing progressive legislation. Witte was not only academically qualified for his new job but had also gained practical expe-rience as chief of the Wisconsin Legislative Reference Library.[4]

When Witte reported in Washington on July 26, almost one month of the five allowed for the completion of a final report had gone by. The President had set December 1 for the report's receipt, allowing roughly a month for further study before the convening of Congress in January 1935. Early conferences with Perkins and Altmeyer and later with Roos-evelt confirmed Witte's view that his job was to develop a legislative program for action by the next Congress. The principal problems to be attacked and the general approach to them had been set by the President in his June 8 message. Witte was firm in his conviction that these commit-ments be respected. He strongly disagreed with those members of the Technical Board and his own staff who regarded the subject as wide open, offering an opportunity for research and study from every conceivable angle prior to making recommendations. He saw the job as a practical one rather than one for research.

The professional staff of the Committee on Economic Security was quite large. With research assistants it included seventy-one persons, or-ganized into six study groups: unemployment compensation, old age secu-rity, employment opportunities, unemployment relief, health insurance, and miscellaneous studies. Witte's executive staff consisted of five profes-sionals, among them Thomas H. Eliot, associate solicitor, Department of Labor, who was to draft the legislation.

Eventually this staff produced a large pile of studies—119 special re-ports plus 11 final reports and general studies. But, as Witte insisted, policy formation could not await their completion. Even by mid-Decem-ber, when the committee's formal deadline had been passed, very few of the studies were ready. Staff effort paid off nevertheless. A great deal of useful data was produced early in the process. Staff members submitted preliminary reports and, on occasion, presented their findings and recom-mendations orally at meetings of the Technical Board or the Committee on Economic Security itself. After oral briefings, lengthy questioning, and frank discussion, policymaking proceeded.

The Technical Board functioned through an executive committee and four special committees: unemployment insurance, old age security, public employment and relief, and medical care. Recommendations prepared by Witte and his staff were presented to the executive committee of the Technical Board and the pertinent special committee. Only members of the Technical Board voted on the recommendations to be sent to the Committee on Economic Security, but the committee was informed of dissents by staff members.[5]

If the President's June 8 message was to be the guide as Witte was convinced it should be, the overriding problems before the committee were unemployment and old age dependency, both assumed to be compatible with social insurance. Social insurance had been promoted by reformers ever since the early twentieth century but had gained little headway. Only workmen's compensation for industrial injuries had been successfully legislated in the states. Reformers suffered a devastating defeat in a campaign for health insurance, and thereafter retreated while New Era welfare capitalism held sway. Social insurance was thus considered new and innovative—a challenge to the old order and its traditional ways of dealing with or ignoring the economic hazards common in modern society. Regrettably, but obviously, social insurance could offer nothing to alleviate immediately the individual distress caused by the Great Depression.

Even if the numbers of able-bodied unemployed and dependent aged had been relatively small, which they were not, insurance payments to these groups could not have begun immediately. Insurance against unemployment or old age could be offered only after a considerable sum of money had been paid into a fund. The President, a former insurance man himself, insisted on a compulsory contributory system rather than reliance on general taxation to form the necessary insurance reserves.[6]

In his first tentative outline discussing possible approaches to economic security, Witte repeatedly referred to current unemployment and relief. "Either the new plans must absorb the relief load," he wrote, "or this must be regarded as an emergency situation to be met apart from the permanent program." "In either case," he concluded, "the present relief situation must clearly be brought into the program proposed for economic security." After examining several approaches to economic security, Witte saw no possibility of adopting one to the exclusion of others. Rather, he thought the committee would need to explore combinations of insurance, annuities, work guarantees, and relief.[7]

In time, "Social Security" became synonymous with old age insurance and was regarded as an essential program, distinguished sharply from "Welfare," which attained a disrepute perhaps equal to the popularity of Social Security. Indeed so sharp were the distinctions in the minds of the American people that few could have correctly identified the two programs' common origin as the Social Security Act. Nevertheless, the act was and is an artful combination of insurance and welfare. Any other conception in 1935 would have resulted in far less than the comprehensive measure signified by the Social Security Act. Perkins recalled that no reasonable person suggested "that relief should be abandoned in favor of unemployment and old age insurance, but it was thought that there could be a blend of the two."[8]

The President, always a foe of the dole, understood the necessity for a blend, at least where the aged were concerned. On the committee level, agreement upon the combination was reached early in August 1934, at the first meeting of the Technical Board: "Economic security is a much broader concept than social insurance, embracing all measures to promote recovery and to develop a more stable economic system, as well as assistance to the victims of insecurity and maladjustment"—such was the definition of the task ahead. A large part of the job lay outside the purview of the Committee on Economic Security, falling rather to the New Deal agencies created for that purpose, the National Recovery Administration to assist industry, the Agricultural Adjustment Administration to help the farmers, and the National Resources Board to coordinate the nation's efforts to make constructive use of its natural resources. Noting these tools of economic recovery in other hands, the Technical Board identified its broad field of study as "protection of the individual against dependency and distress," a more prosaic and somewhat more modest translation of the President's "security against the hazards and vicissitudes of life."

Although unemployment relief and public works were originally included as part of the committee's work, both were quickly placed outside its scope. By late summer the President had set up an informal committee of Hopkins and Morgenthau to devise a new relief policy. Nothing was put in writing, but it was soon understood that public works and relief for the unemployed lay outside the sphere of the Committee on Economic Security. The reason for their exclusion seems clear. Unlike those pessimists who viewed the Depression as proof of the inability of private enterprise to sustain a healthy economy, Roosevelt remained optimistic about the nation's basic economic condition. To be sure, reform was in order. Certain business practices were to be outlawed; others regulated. But the Roosevelt Administration was committed to *recovery,* indeed, to saving *capitalism.* To have allowed unemployment relief and relief work a place in a long-term program of economic security would have bestowed permanence upon what had previously been considered an emergency program.[9]

Old Age Assistance

In an entirely different category, and unquestionably proper to a long-term program, were relief to the needy aged and to children lacking adequate adult support. Either too old or too young to work, long-term relief to each of these groups rested on a firm historical base. Both the needy aged and needy children were from the outset included in the categories approved by the Technical Board for study and recommendation.[10]

In considering plans for assistance to the needy aged, the Committee on Economic Security was conscious of the many states with old age pension laws. Need for such laws arose from a number of factors—demographic, economic, and social—that emerged during the first two decades of the twentieth century. The aged, counted as sixty-five or over, were increasing both in numbers and as a percentage of the total population. By 1900, with 3 million, the aged accounted for 4.1 percent; by 1920, numbering almost 5 million, they constituted 4.7 percent. In 1930, the population aged sixty-five and over stood at 6.6 million, accounting for 5.4 percent. Life expectancy was increasing: at the beginning of the century it had been 47.88 years for males and 50.70 for females; by 1930 it had increased almost ten years for each, to 57.77 for males and 60.99 for females.

The modern American economy, with its large industrial base, was far less able than in an earlier agricultural time to keep the elderly at productive work. For most wage earners, savings were apt to be short-term, to be used up for normal family expenses or the demands of crises such as illness or unemployment, or invested in a home. Children, long regarded as the insurers against destitute old age, were, as wage earners themselves, less able than their farmer forebears to assume the burden of support for parents. Because the emphasis on efficiency in modern industry tended to cast out the older worker, humanity might have dictated a growth in work-related private pensions. Although the number of private pension plans—some through employers, some through unions—had indeed increased, they were concentrated in transportation and large-scale heavy industry, so much so that "industrial pension" became synonymous with "private pension." Financial management improved somewhat over the years, but many of these pension funds remained on shaky ground.

Although often called upon to contribute, workers who left an employer before retirement received only their own contribution back, with no interest. Receipt of a pension was always contingent upon long, uninterrupted service to one company. Strikes were considered an interruption. Insofar as industrial pensions put a brake on job mobility and discouraged union organization, they tended to depress wages. Most important from the viewpoint of the individual facing old age was the fact that these pension plans covered a very small portion of the labor force, at the most, 15 percent. The coverage was nominal. Of the 4–5 million employed by the railroads since the introduction of the plans, only 120,000 persons had been awarded pensions by the 1930s. In 1933 the number of industrial pensioners was estimated at 165,000, with average per capita payment of about $58 per month. Public employees had fared much better, about 75 percent having protection under systems established through joint contributions. Much the largest was that covering federal employees, but states and localities had sizable numbers under these systems. Public employment was relatively small at this time, however.

The movement for state old age pension laws to care for the destitute elderly caught on early in the 1920s. Although its roots lay in the demographic, economic, and social problems already mentioned and in the failure of private efforts to deal with them, the immediate pressure developed from humanitarian concern for those aged residing in public institutions. Often the almshouse or poor farm was the only recourse of the elderly dependent upon public funds. With few exceptions, conditions in these institutions had become scandalous. Buildings and their furnishings were run down and dirty, the food unfit to eat. Reformers and reformer groups—Abraham Epstein, the Fraternal Order of Eagles, the American Association for Labor Legislation—joined forces to prepare model old age pension legislation and to organize pressure for its passage. Their efforts were doggedly and bitterly opposed by business interests, who warned of diminished industry and thrift as well as rising taxes.

Considering the effort made by the proponents, progress in obtaining state legislation was slow. The first state law was passed in 1923, but by 1929 only eleven states had passed old age pension legislation. The governors of California, Wyoming, and Washington exercised vetoes. Courts declared the laws of Pennsylvania and Arizona unconstitutional. Greater progress was made between 1929 and 1933, when nineteen states, including California, Arizona, and Washington, enacted the legislation. By the end of 1934, twenty-eight states and two territories had old age pension laws. Included were nearly all of the industrial states and a number of predominantly rural states west of the Mississippi. The South and Southwest were almost devoid of old age pension laws; only West Virginia and Kentucky had them.

The use of the term "old age pension" to designate the state systems operating in 1934 was misleading. The proper term was "old age assistance." Common to all state laws was the requirement that the elderly recipient be needy. Most states set a property limit of $3,000 and an income limit of no more than $3,000 a year. Except for Arizona and the territory of Hawaii, all proscribed payment to persons having children or other relatives able to support them. The lower age limit was about evenly divided between sixty five (set in thirteen states and two territories) and seventy (set in fourteen states). Residence requirements were extremely lengthy. In only one state was the length of residence as low as five years; eight states required a ten-year residence; two, twenty; and the majority, sixteen states and one territory, fifteen years. If an individual could meet these eligibility requirements, he or she received a maximum payment ranging from $15 to $30 per month, the higher figure being the most common.

Receiving a grant, much less an adequate grant, during the Depression was another matter. In 1934 three of the twenty-eight "pension" states ceased payment altogether. In eighteen, the system was not operating on a statewide basis. Average monthly grants ranged from $0.69 in North Dakota to $26 in Massachusetts. In thirteen states, the average grant was less than $10 monthly. Nationwide, the average came to $15. The number of persons receiving assistance, around 236,000 in December 1934, was far below estimates of the needy eligible. Some idea of the gap between need and assistance can be seen by comparing the number of applicants with recipients in a few states. Michigan had received over 42,000 applications since October 1933, was making payments to 2,660, and had approved the applications of 6,575, leaving 27,032 persons awaiting attention. Of 26,269 applications since July 1932, New Jersey had placed 10,560 on old age assistance and had 3,080 pending applications. Ohio had received 105,000 applications since May 1934 but had only 24,000 recipients. Small wonder that so many destitute aged ended up on the rolls of the FERA.[11]

However inadequate in practice, the existence of state old age assistance laws provided something upon which the Committee on Economic Security could build. The old age security staff perceived money as the main deficiency in the states, particularly in the poor areas of the South and Southwest. Also important was the need for greater uniformity among the states and liberalization of age and residence limitations. Additional money could be made available to the states either through block or matched grants. Under a block grant system, the federal government could collect the taxes and turn over to the states amounts sufficient to cover old age assistance payments. Under a matching system, the federal government would supplement state and/or local expenditures according to some prearranged formula. Still another way to take care of old age assistance was to create a completely national system, paid for and administered by the federal government.

A national system offered the greatest promise from the viewpoint of recipients. Inequalities could be eliminated, eligibility rules made less restrictive, and grants raised to more adequate levels. Since block grants to the states utilized the broader tax base available to the federal government,this arrangement tended in the same, more liberal, direction.

Yet, adoption of a national system stood no chance whatsoever. In addition to bringing about a tremendous break with the past, federal administration of assistance would have been extremely difficult to introduce into the local units required to receive applications and investigate need. Even if it could have been carried out, no one would have liked it, least of all the local politicians who felt protective of public service jobs. Constitutional issues loomed large in the minds of the would-be law drafters in Washington. A national system would have to be justified on the basis of implied powers; the general welfare clause is general indeed. Doubtless with a good many of these considerations in mind, the President had called for a system of state-federal cooperation.

Although block grants would have ensured state administration, lack of state money suggested a weakened cooperative effort and lessened ability on the part of the federal government to influence improvements in state programs. Given the short time available for drafting a bill, seizure upon a ready model with some support in Congress is not surprising. The model existed in the Dill-Connery bill for old age assistance, which used a matching grant system as the vehicle for financing. Use of the matching grant was recommended by the old age security staff of the Committee on Economic Security with federal administration by the FERA.[12]

Aid to Dependent Children

Also ready at hand was model legislation to aid needy children. Passage of state laws termed either "mother's pensions" or "mother's aid" had, like state old age pensions, been motivated in large part by humanitarian concern to reduce the number of children being forced into institutions solely because of the financial need of the mother, often an unskilled widow. Usually these women could not earn enough money to maintain a decent standard of living and, it was claimed, frequently broke down under the triple strains of outside work, child rearing, and home management. All too often the result was placement of some or all of a woman's children in institutions.

The movement for mother's pensions got under way early in the century, a part of the growing interest in child psychology and child development, concern about juvenile delinquency, and emphasis on good citizenship. It was no accident that the first White House Conference on the Care of Dependent Children took place in 1909 during the presidency of Theodore Roosevelt. Led by members of the burgeoning profession of social work, the conferees declared home life "the highest and finest product of civilization." Children should not be deprived of home life "except for urgent and compelling reasons." Poverty alone was not one of these reasons.

Just who was to foot the bill for keeping the children in the home was another matter. Private agencies had long claimed the poor widow as part of their burden and bitterly opposed mother's pensions as unnecessary public relief. Impartial investigations showed, however, that private agencies were able to support only a small number of mothers with dependent children. Children in institutions were supported by public funds. Proponents of publicly funded mother's pensions argued that keeping children in their own homes was not only better for the children but less costly than institutional care.

Reacting to the support of a broad constituency—women's organizations, women's magazines, juvenile court judges, a good many labor unions and social insurance advocates—states were quicker to enact mother's pensions than old age pensions. Mother's pensions often became part of a reform package consisting of child labor laws, workmen's compensation, and laws regulating working conditions for women and youth. As such, mother's pensions blunted opposition to these other reforms, which in turn tended to reduce the income available to widows with dependent children. Except for the private social agencies, opposition was negligible, because costs were expected to be minimal and no threat to industry or business was foreseen.

The first mother's pension law was passed by Illinois in 1911. By the mid-1920s, forty states had joined; by December 1934, all the states except Alabama, Georgia, and South Carolina, as well as the territories of Alaska, Hawaii, and Puerto Rico, had mother's pension laws. But like old age pensions, mother's pensions cared for only a fraction of the families the laws were designed to help. State laws merely authorized counties and cities to institute a system of aid; statewide coverage was not mandatory. Even before the Depression, states showed far greater variations in assistance than could be explained by economic or social factors. In 1926 the ratios of children aided per 100,000 of the general population ranged from 1.4 to 331. Eleven states—California, Delaware, Maine, Massachusetts, Minnesota, Montana, Nevada, New Jersey, New York, North Dakota, and Wisconsin—each had ratios of more than 200 children. Most states had much lower ratios, ranging from 95 to 31. And a few—Arkansas, Indiana, Tennessee, Texas, and Virginia—aided fewer than 20 children per 100,000 of the population. By 1934 about 50 percent of the money for mother's pensions was being spent in cities of 50,000 or more population, mostly in nine of the largest—Boston, Chicago, Cleveland, Detroit, Los Angeles, Milwaukee, New York, Philadelphia, and Pittsburgh.

In urging public funding separate from the poor law, backers of mother's pensions emphasized child rearing as a service to the state for which payment was due. A corollary was the right-to-assistance angle so feared and condemned by private charities. Administration of the laws departed sharply from the pension approach. Administration followed, in fact, methods long practiced by private agencies, namely, exhaustive investigation into the mother's character before acceptance for assistance and intensive supervision of home management and child care thereafter. Opposition by private agencies subsided upon adoption of these professional social work methods.

Grants were low. Far from releasing recipients from outside employment, many pensioners worked as domestics, took in laundry, or performed other unskilled jobs to supplement their allowances. Even during the prosperous 1920s, maximum grants barely reached subsistence level. In 1934 state maximums for a mother with three children ranged from $20 to $69, but average monthly grants ranged from $9 to $60. Although mother's pension laws usually permitted assistance to divorced, separated, or deserted women, it was widows—82 percent in 1931—who were the primary beneficiaries. During the Depression, many families nominally eligible for mother's pensions were, like old age pensioners, subsisting on FERA funds. The FERA carried about three-and-a-half times as many of these families as did the mother's pension rolls.[13]

When security for children was discussed at the August 10, 1934, meeting of the Technical Board on Economic Security, the U.S. Children's Bureau was immediately suggested for preparation of the study. Itself a by-product of the White House Conference on the Care of Dependent Children, the Children's Bureau was primarily a fact-finding agency. Authorized by statute in 1912, the bureau had been administered by able women trained in the well-known settlement houses of Chicago. At first the bureau focused on child health, particularly that of infants. Later, from 1921 to 1929, the Children's Bureau administered the Sheppard-Towner Act, a small grant-in-aid program matching state funds for improved maternal and child health facilities, particularly in rural areas. Congress cut off the act's funds in 1929.

The Children's Bureau had long been located in the Department of Labor. In November 1934, its chief was Katherine F. Lenroot. The daughter of a former senator from Wisconsin, Lenroot was a Vassar graduate who had spent her working life in the bureau, joining the staff as a special agent in 1915. Martha M. Eliot, a physician trained at Harvard University Medical School, was assistant chief of the bureau. In consultation with an advisory committee on child welfare, Lenroot and Eliot prepared the final report on security for children. The report included, in addition to mother's pensions, recommendations on welfare services for neglected, abused, handicapped, and delinquent children, and on maternal and child health services, the latter a resurrection of the grant-in-aid program of the 1920s.

Witte and those around him assumed that the Children's Bureau would administer all of these programs. Although the bureau was eventually denied the mother's pension program, the assumptions made by Lenroot and Eliot in arriving at their recommendations had important immediate and long-term effects, which ranged from relatively elusive conceptions about the program's purpose and character to loosely constructed but easily grasped fiscal estimates.

Lenroot and Eliot regarded mother's pension legislation as essentially in place, including state or local policies on eligibility for assistance. As they reported to the Committee on Economic Security, "the character of the mother and her competency to give proper care to her children" constituted the core of the program. The Children's Bureau chiefs predicted an improvement in social services once the states assumed responsibility, pointing out that "if well administered, state aid will act as an effective, powerful lever in raising administrative standards of investigations, budgetary practices, and other procedures."

Historically, the burden of financing mother's pensions had fallen mostly upon local government, this circumstance being at least partly responsible for the spotty coverage everywhere apparent. Lenroot and Eliot strongly recommended state as well as federal subsidies, with state equalization funds to be available to counties. They called for a three-way division of the financial burden, one-third of the costs to be assumed by federal, one-third by state, and one-third by local government.[14]

Selection of certain vulnerable groups—the unemployed, the aged, dependent children—for major attention by the Committee on Economic Security did not go unchallenged. Other groups seemed equally at risk of dependency. Provision of protective coverage for all the needy—the generalist position—was advanced against the committee's categorical scheme. Backers of the generalist position came from social work ranks, some at the FERA, others with professional organizations such as the American Association of Social Workers (AASW). Distant from the center of power, however, the generalists could do little more than state their position.

The Social Security Act

By October 1, 1934, the Committee on Economic Security had agreed upon the essentials of the Social Security Act. On this day the committee assented to the lines laid down in a preliminary report prepared by Witte, a report entirely categorical in approach. Of those categories considered since the fact-finding studies began, some were in, some were out, and some were deferred to the future. Six categories were recommended for inclusion in legislation to be sought in the next session of Congress: (1) standby arrangements to facilitate public employment in periods of economic depression; (2) unemployment insurance; (3) old age insurance; (4) federal subsidies to states for old age pensions; (5) federal subsidies to states for mother's pensions; and (6) public health services for persons in the lowest income groups. Five were deferred: (1) health insurance for medical services; (2) insurance to cover wage loss due to illness; (3) survivor's insurance for widows of fully insured persons; (4) a more general form of survivor's insurance; and (5) invalidity insurance. Three were excluded: (1) accident insurance; (2) relief for the residual group—the needy not otherwise categorized; and (3) relief for dependent and defective classes—physically or mentally handicapped persons.

Of the categories excluded, industrial accident insurance was thought to be fairly well provided through workmen's compensation. The Department of Labor could continue to encourage the states to liberalize their programs and move toward greater uniformity. Relief for the residual group and dependent and defective classes was left with the states and localities, as was relief to the unemployed except during severe economic depression.[15]

It was very late in the game when the social workers were consulted about these recommendations. In mid-November 1934 the Department of Labor convened a conference, inviting a large number of professionals and public leaders and welcoming a score of others who attended without invitation. Perkins did not intend to alter the committee's recommendations in any significant way. No motions would be entertained, but informal suggestions were acceptable. Noting a suggestion to get into closer contact "with people on the firing line in social work," Perkins wrote Dorothy Kahn, director of the Philadelphia County Relief Board and president of the AASW, asking her to chair an Advisory Committee on Public Employment and Relief. In accepting on November 19, Kahn underlined the lateness of the hour and expressed the opinion that little more could be done than to formulate a "point of view."

The usual mix of public and private social work organizations and federations was represented on the Advisory Committee, which met once, on November 22. The committee strongly recommended a generalist approach. If the federal government confined assistance to specified categories, the committee argued, many needy persons would be thrown back upon state and local poor law administration, "the evils of which are well recognized." The committee estimated that only about half the relief families having potential wage earners would be cared for under a public works program. "Health problems, the social and personal results of long continued unemployment, [and] lack of adaptability to work available" were the limiting factors mentioned. Another large group left out of security plans consisted of chronic dependents—the physically and mentally disabled and handicapped, and children deprived of adult care due to abandonment or other social problems. Federal grants-in-aid to the states should cover not only old age and mother's pensions but also general home relief and care of homeless children and adults in a "unified welfare program." To this end, the committee advocated the establishment of a permanent fedcral agency to administer all federal public assistance systems and to develop interrelationships between public relief and other aspects of economic security. Federal grants should be made conditional upon state consolidation of welfare functions in one department with appropriate local units.[16]

The Committee on Economic Security held to its chosen course. What with the public works program and grants to the states for dependent aged and children, the federal government would be assuming a great part of the load, the committee argued in its final report. The categorical programs suggested by the committee "all seek to segregate clearly distinguishable large groups among those now on relief or on the verge of relief and to apply such differentiated treatment to each group as will give it the greatest practical degree of economic security. We believe that if these measures are adopted, the residual relief problem will have diminished to a point where it will be possible to return primary responsibility for the care of people who cannot work to the state and local governments."

The committee made one concession to its Advisory Committee on Public Employment and Relief—a recommendation that states modernize their public assistance laws, unify their administration, and emphasize efficiency. Models existed in some states. All states contained a beginning in their emergency relief agencies.

Some social workers were bitter at their failure to influence the Committee on Economic Security. Josephine Brown railed at the administration's narrow vision, which regarded unemployment as the overriding issue. Even provision for the aged—insurance and old age assistance—was simply calculated to remove older workers from the labor market. She might have added that mother's pensions fitted this pattern also. In Brown's view, the recommendations of the Committee on Economic Security "failed by a wide margin to provide that security for the men, women and children of the nation which the President in his message of June 8, 1934 had placed first among the objectives of his administration."[17]

Although the recommendations of the Committee on Economic Security failed to provide absolute security against all the "hazards and vicissitudes of life," they represented a giant step toward economic and social protection. Even some of the groups that were destined for return to the mercies of the states were in line for federal aid. Specifically, the Children's Bureau was slated to administer a revived version of the Sheppard-Towner Act in the form of maternal and child health and crippled children's services, as well as a completely new program of services to children needing care and protection outside of their natural homes. Ultimately, through congressional initiative, grants-in-aid were provided for a program to assist the needy blind. The final version of the legislation also added extra financial aid to the states for the ongoing program of vocational rehabilitation of the handicapped. The most serious omission from the committee's plans, serious also in the view of the committee itself, was health insurance. The committee bowed to the President's political decision to exclude health insurance from the proposed bill. But even in regard to health, the recommendations contained something. The Public Health Service was to be given additional money for building up its staff and for grants to states for improving their health services. It must also be recalled that Perkins and those around her thought of their efforts as a beginning, subject to change and improvement.[18]

The Report of the Committee on Economic Security was transmitted to Congress by the President on January 17, 1935, and the Economic Security Act introduced in Congress the same day. Hearings before the House Ways and Means Committee and the Senate Finance Committee began immediately. As the hearings proceeded, extensive redrafting was undertaken by Thomas Eliot under the expert guidance of the Ways and Means Committee's legislative counsel. The bill emerged as the Social Security Act. The term "social security" had been introduced by Abraham Epstein when he changed the name of his organization from the American Association for Old Age Security to the American Association for Social Security. He and others referred to "social security" during the course of committee hearings, and the term caught on.

By the time the Social Security Act came before the Congress, old age security had overtaken unemployment as the more important issue in the minds of politicians. Eliot, in a calculated response to this feeling, selected Old Age Assistance (OAA) as Title I in his draft of the legislation. There it remained, while old age insurance subsequently became Title II.[19]

The clamor for old age pensions had grown immensely since the preceding summer, due to the followers of an unemployed physician, Francis Everett Townsend, and his plan for helping the aged and the economy. Townsend's ideas had germinated in the fall of 1933 but did not become popularized until about a year later, well after the appointment of the Committee on Economic Security. Under Townsend's plan the federal government would grant all retired persons over age sixty the sum of $200 monthly, provided the entire amount was spent within the month received. Financing was to be achieved through a "transaction tax," a tax imposed each time a product changed hands. Estimates of total yearly costs ranged from those of Townsend himself, who set it at $19.2 billion annually, to the $24 billion forecast by economic analysts. At this time, $24 billion represented roughly one-half of the annual national income and amounted to twice the revenue from federal, state, and local taxes combined. Moreover, the transaction tax would have fallen heavily on the average worker, while half of the national income would be diverted to 8 percent of the population.

With few exceptions, congressmen and senators viewed the Townsend plan as a crackpot scheme. But many of them were running scared at the signs of supporters—loads of petitions, letters, and telegrams arriving daily. At their peak in 1935–1936, Townsend clubs had a total of about 2.2 million members; about 10 percent of those aged sixty and over belonged. Claims of membership ran as high as thirty million. The Townsend plan was defeated in the House in April 1935 with many congressmen absent and those present voting it down without a roll call. The Townsend movement continued to grow nevertheless. Even after passage of the Social Security Act, which was greatly assisted by the relevance of Titles I and II, the Townsendites continued their crusade.[20]

The congressional committees in charge of the Social Security bill, Ways and Means in the House, Finance in the Senate, made important changes in the content of its three public assistance titles: Old Age Assistance (OAA), Aid to Dependent Children (ADC), and Aid to the Blind (AB). Liberalization of state statutes sought by the Committee on Economic Security was sharply curtailed by these changes. The bill before Ways and Means and Finance prohibited states from denying old age assistance to aged persons not residents of public institutions who were citizens of the United States, had been residents of the state for five years or more immediately preceding application, had an income inadequate to maintain reasonable subsistence compatible with decency and health, and who possessed no real or personal property with market value in excess of $5,000. States would be permitted to set the age limit at seventy through the year 1939, after which it must be dropped to age sixty-five.

Led by Senator Harry F. Byrd of Virginia, southern members of both committees objected to the exercise of federal authority over what was in their view a prerogative of the states, namely, the decision as to who got OAA and in what amount. Witte was convinced that the bill would get nowhere unless the administration bill was changed to accommodate the South.

As finally agreed to, the federal authority relinquished a great deal. States were left free to impose whatever eligibility rules they desired, provided only that residence could not be required in excess of five years within the last nine years immediately preceding application, age could not exceed seventy, or after January 1, 1940, sixty-five years, and no citizen of the United States could be excluded from application. The standard of need based on maintenance of decency and health was eliminated. States were left free to set their own grant levels. Also rejected was the proposition that only the income of the aged applicant and spouse be counted in calculating need. The door was thus opened for states to count contributions from responsible relatives, whether made or not. The matching formula adopted was a federal contribution of 50 percent up to a maximum of $15 per month.[21]

Such matters as citizenship and residence (and even relatives' responsibility, when most recipients were expected to be widows) were far less germane to the ADC program. The age limit for a dependent child was set at sixteen years; residence for the responsible adult at one year. But adequate standards of assistance for children became less likely than those for OAA, due not only to omission of a health and decency clause but also to the manner in which the federal contribution was to be calculated. One-third federal, one-third state, one-third local with no maximum, so the formula ran in the Children's Bureau and so it was presented in the original bill. In seeking to arrive at a federal maximum to correspond with provisions in the OAA title, Ways and Means modeled the formula on pensions paid to dependents of deceased veterans. Overlooked was the fact that the veteran's system treated the widow separately, whereas grants in ADC had been figured on the children only. The upshot of this miscalculation was a federal contribution of $6 per month for the first, and $4 for each additional child, with no aid for the responsible adult.[22]

In line with efforts of Congress to ensure maximum state independence from federal control, provisions regulating administration of the public assistance titles were also toned down. The original bill granted the federal agency power to pass upon methods of administration found "necessary for the efficient operation" of the programs. The final version of the bill contained a significant exception: methods of administration "relating to selection, tenure of office, and compensation of personnel" were left to the states.

The Ways and Means Committee stressed state powers in reporting out the bill, noting that "a few standards are prescribed which the states must meet to entitle them to federal aid but these impose only reasonable conditions and leave the states free of arbitrary interference from Washington." The committee added that such standards "do not prevent the state from imposing other eligibility requirements (as to means, moral character, etc.) if they wish to do so."[23]

Nevertheless, the standards prescribed by the Social Security Act made significant in-roads on practices prevailing under the older poor laws and the newer old age and mother's pension laws. Of great importance was the departure from localism. In order to qualify for grants-in-aid within its territory, a state had to submit a plan for approval by the federal agency. This plan must show that the assistance program was in effect on a state-wide basis, ensure state financial participation, and provide for a single state agency either for direct administration or for supervision of local units. The right to assistance was substantially reinforced, guaranteeing an individual denied the money payment a fair hearing. The federal government could not match payments "in-kind"—grocery orders, second-hand clothes, or the like.

So far as the public assistance titles were concerned, all significant changes had been made before the bill was reported out of committee. The act as a whole passed with overwhelming majorities—371 to 33 by the House on April 19, and 76 to 6 by the Senate in June 1935. After the Joint Conference Committee settled the few differences, the bill sailed through to passage by both House and Senate during the week of August 5. The Social Security Act was signed into law by President Roosevelt on August 14, 1935.[24]

3

Planning Welfare Programs

AS FIRST CONCEIVED by the Committee on Economic Security, the Department of Labor was to play the leading federal role in the administration of programs authorized by the Social Security Act. Under this plan, the two insurance programs, unemployment and old age, were to be administered by a Social Insurance Board within Labor, while the Children's Bureau, also within the Labor Department, would be responsible for Aid to Dependent Children, child welfare services, and maternal and child health programs. The major exception to Labor's dominance was the administration of Old Age Assistance. The committee assigned OAA to the FERA because OAA was a relief program. Arguing that ADC was also a relief program, FERA turf protectors Aubrey Williams and Josephine Brown won their point with the committee. As presented to Congress both OAA and ADC were to be administered at the federal level by the FERA.

The Ways and Means Committee, however, was prejudiced against the Department of Labor and Secretary Perkins—in no small part due to her protection of the Civil Service against patronage—and opposed assigning the administration of permanent programs to an emergency agency. Ways and Means placed public assistance, along with the insurances, under the administration of the Social Security Board, an independent agency created by the committee with representation by the two major political parties. The decision to keep public assistance and insurance in one agency followed good administrative practice—to keep like functions together. These programs were closely related. In testifying on the bill, Witte argued that in time old age insurance (OAI) would reduce the need for

OAA. The extent of the reduction was closely tied to coverage under OAI. The Committee on Economic Security had recommended virtually complete coverage, but the act as passed limited coverage to business and industrial workers. Recommendations regarding survivor's insurance had been placed on a deferred agenda. If and when survivor's insurance became available, ADC could be expected to diminish also.[1]

Organization and Administration

Choice of a board for administration rather than an agency headed by a single individual appears less a matter of logic than of chance. Although administration by a bipartisan board or commission was usually confined to programs of semijudicial or semicorporate nature, the newness of the insurance programs probably made the bipartisan aspects of a board attractive. A recent precedent existed in the Railroad Retirement Board, which had been established to administer pensions for railroad employees.

But there was nothing new about public assistance. Even the federal role had been played under the administrator of FERA. It seems safe to assume that the public assistance titles of the Social Security Act became subject to administration by a board simply because of the decision to join OAA and ADC to the insurances.

Bipartisanship was highlighted by the President's choice for chairman and members of the three-person Social Security Board. Acting on Perkins's recommendation, Roosevelt selected John G. Winant, a progressive Republican and former governor of New Hampshire, for a six-year term as chairman. Again following Perkins, Roosevelt chose Arthur J. Altmeyer for a four-year term on the board. By the time of his appointment, Altmeyer had been thoroughly exposed to the dynamics of a social security program. Perkins, having watched this forty-three-year-old Wisconsin economist working at the NRA, the FERA, and the CWA, appointed him an assistant secretary of labor in 1934. A month later she asked him to chair the Technical Board for the Committee on Economic Security.

Altmeyer came from Wisconsin. At the university, he had been a student of John R. Commons, the foremost labor economist in the country. After earning his doctorate, Altmeyer worked for the Wisconsin Industrial Commission, first as head of statistics, later as chief of the agency. Both the workmen's compensation and unemployment compensation laws of this progressive state were administered by the Industrial Commission.

Altmeyer's position, first as a member of the Social Security Board and later as administrator, was a natural for his personality, his training, his experience, and his commitment to public service. Though he appeared a little stiff—no back-slapping with strangers—he was friendly and gracious with his staff. As one of them put it years later, he was "modest, not aloof." Altmeyer was calm and persistent when testifying, even when shouting at the top of his lungs in response to the stone-deaf chairman of Ways and Means, who kept urging Altmeyer to "speak up, young man, speak up." Members of both the House and Senate committees learned that when Altmeyer spoke, he knew what he was talking about, and they complimented him for it. In the 1950s, when Senator Robert Taft was deemed "Mr. Republican," Administrator Altmeyer was "Mr. Social Security."

Perkins submitted the names of five other available persons, all Democrats, for the third vacancy, a two-year term. She felt that of them, Margie Neal of Texas, a protégé of Vice-President Garner, was best placed elsewhere. Jane Hoey, a social worker and experienced administrator from New York City was favored by Harry Hopkins (for whom she had once worked) over Josephine Roche, best known for introducing labor-management cooperation into the Rocky Mountain Fuel Company and presently Assistant Secretary of the Treasury for Public Health. Perkins added that nothing would be gained politically in appointing Roche but that there would be in choosing Hoey.

As noted in Chapter 1, Frank Bane, a native of Virginia living in Chicago where he was director of the American Public Welfare Association, had been associated with public welfare and with the introduction of modern concepts of administration since 1920. Obviously well qualified, Bane was listed without comment. The fifth candidate, also listed without comment, was Vincent M. Miles, a lawyer and active Democrat from Arkansas who was sponsored by Senator Joseph T. Robinson, the majority leader. Miles was prominent in the Fraternal Order of Eagles, early promoters of old age pensions. The President chose Miles. However, both Bane and Hoey were subsequently chosen for important positions with the Social Security Board, Bane becoming its executive director and Hoey the director of its Bureau of Public Assistance.[2]

Although the three board members were on hand in Washington by mid-September 1935, it was only through extraordinary effort and ingenuity that the new agency began to function. Money for salaries and other administrative costs were contained in an omnibus deficiency appropriation bill that reached the Senate in August, just as that body was counting the days until adjournment. At this juncture, Huey Long, disgruntled at the administration's refusal to increase loans on wheat, began one of his filibusters. The Senate caved in, adjourning without passing the deficiency appropriation. When an ongoing agency fails to get a deficiency appropriation, it is difficult but not impossible to manage by making adjustments in funds previously appropriated. A new agency has no funds on hand, nothing to adjust. With the imminent withdrawal of federal relief money from the states, the Social Security Board had to show some purposeful activity without delay.

A sympathetic White House found some transferable money in a WPA allotment and detailed staff from the FERA, the National Youth Administration, and the rapidly liquidating National Industrial Recovery Administration. Given the enthusiasm of these New Dealers, such makeshift arrangements proved sufficient to get the Social Security programs under way. But the situation disrupted orderly procedure and slowed the board's rate of expansion. Some four-and-a-half months elapsed before approval of the appropriation for administrative expenses on February 11, 1936.[3]

Conscious of the fact that a board, even a small and harmonious one, must guard against fragmented authority and slow operations, Chairman Winant and members Altmeyer and Miles made two important decisions. They agreed that the board would act as a group, rather than divide activities among themselves. They agreed further that the major function of the board was policymaking, while administration, including the supervision of staff, would rest with the executive director. These decisions were the controlling factors in Bane's decision to accept the executive directorship, for Bane was highly sensitive to the difficulty of separating policymaking from administration.

Housekeeping functions aside, it is virtually impossible to make a clean-cut separation. Personnel seems a natural entry under administration until the question of who makes policy is raised. Professional staff in the middle ranks play powerful roles in the formulation of policy. In practice, the board clung tenaciously to the personnel function. Scarcely a meeting took place without discussion and approval of the "personnel journal." Candidates for higher positions were often interviewed by each board member as well as by the executive director. Wilbur Cohen, who came to Washington as Witte's research assistant, remembered entering Altmeyer's office in the "early days" to find Winant and Altmeyer on the floor "playing with" slips of paper. To his question "What are you *doing*?" Altmeyer replied they were fitting in names of persons they knew or knew of on an organization chart.

Given the board's consciousness of its high calling, responsibilities were taken most seriously. Because decisions were made as a unit and because Chairman Winant favored oral presentation and discussion to supplement written materials, the board met daily, often twice daily, and sometimes morning, noon, and night. Because Saturday morning was then part of the government workweek, it was not uncommon for board meetings to run on into Saturday afternoon.

During the early years, public assistance dominated board meetings. The central issue here was elucidation and development of a cooperative effort between federal and state governments for grant-in-aid programs larger in size and different in character than any undertaken previously. Bane emphasized the pioneer aspect of the effort in a talk given at the Brookings Institution in April 1937: "Federal cooperation through grants-in-aid for specific purposes—with the Federal government outlining broad general policies but with direct administration in the hands of the state—is a long familiar method of operation but never before has it been projected upon such an extensive scale, immediately affecting so many people and calling for such large expenditures."[4]

On December 4, 1935, the board formally approved the organizational pattern of the agency. Three operating bureaus, Unemployment Compensation, Federal Old Age Benefits (insurance), and Public Assistance; and five service bureaus and offices, General Counsel, Research and Statistics, Accounts and Audits, Business Management, and Information, were established. The board also planned an extensive field operation, with twelve regional offices to be staffed with a director and representatives of each of the Washington operating bureaus and services (see Organization Chart).

Social Work

The profession chosen to administer the public assistance categories was social work. Why? Why not administer public assistance with the same type of staff as would be hired to administer old age insurance and unemployment compensation? In each one of these programs, applicants would be lining up to receive money that was conditional upon specific proofs of eligibility. No one suggested that the bureaus of Old Age Benefits or Unemployment Compensation and their field offices be staffed by social workers, yet everyone assumed that the Bureau of Public Assistance

Social Security Board Organization Chart, 1936

Operating Bureaus	*Service Bureaus*
Unemployment Compensation	General Counsel
Federal Old Age Benefits	Research and Statistics
Public Assistance	Accounts and Audits
	Business Management
	Information

Field Offices (12 in Number)
Director

Operating Bureaus	*Service Bureaus*
Unemployment Compensation	General Counsel
Federal OA Benefits	Research and Statistics
Public Assistance	Accounts and Audits
	Business Management
	Information

as well as state and local agencies belonged to the dominion of social work.[5]

Doubtless the earlier plan of administration, with OAA assigned to the FERA and ADC to the Children's Bureau and subsequently to FERA, influenced this crucial choice. Unquestionably the Children's Bureau was dominated by female social workers. To a considerable extent also, social casework had penetrated the agencies that administered mother's pensions, less so those dealing with pensions for the elderly. Although social workers were a minority in the FERA, the little band led by Josephine Brown had introduced social work methods of investigation into the eligibility process. Brown had, however, drawn the line at the kind of social casework being practiced in the private family agencies.

In a statement issued in April 1935, Brown defined a new role for social workers in a public welfare agency. She declared it inappropriate for a government agency to mingle relief with social casework as was done in private agencies. As Brown saw it, "much of social casework practice is directed towards the treatment of problems inherent in individuals and families—their inadequacies, their failures, their personality difficulties," while "the administration of unemployment relief is directed at a common problem which is outside the individual and beyond his control."

Granted the unemployed might have personal problems, "it is not the function of the relief administration *per se* to inquire into these problems or to treat them," Brown continued. The social worker's job in a public assistance agency was, *exclusively*, to determine need and the extent of need—in other words, *to conduct a means test.* The applicant cooperated in this process, supplying facts and references that were then checked out "on a business-like basis, maintaining a self-respecting relationship." Nevertheless, Brown believed that public assistance workers should be trained, not only in the routines of the job, but in core elements of social work—"appreciation of human values" and "handling the human elements in the relationships." She asserted that "in the administration of unemployment relief we are creating a new type of social work and of public welfare . . . , adapting whatever is applicable from the rest of social work and adding the results of our own experience in standards, methods, training, and terminology." In reprinting Brown's statement, the *Survey* writers, Joanna Colcord and Russell Kurtz of the Russell Sage Foundation commented: "Not all social workers agree with Miss Brown's analysis which seems to delimit too sharply the case worker to the field of problems inherent in individuals. Her position with the government, however, gives her pronouncement a major significance."[6]

It was widely expected that categorical assistance under the Social Security Act—pensions as the common understanding had it—would be relatively free of social casework. Corrington Gill, Hopkins's chief statistician, commented early in 1935 that the oversight to be extended to the aged and women with dependent children receiving public assistance through the Social Security Act required study. It seemed "plain," to him, however, "that these households should not be constantly subjected to the annoyance and disturbance of casework investigation, as they did not require as constant and intimate supervision as is customarily extended to chronic incapables. They should receive pensions or insurance benefits and be permitted to arrange their lives as they see fit."[7]

As a group, social workers who dispensed relief, whether from public or private funds, had never been popular. The Depression relief experience made them even less so. Resentment and dislike were widespread. Although some of this feeling was encouraged by conservatives who regarded social workers as overgenerous humanitarians and by politicians who wanted patronage restored, at bottom lay a grass-roots revolt against the instruments of the means test. To usually independent persons reduced to dependency during the Depression, even Brown's formulation minimizing social casework could not satisfy their main objection.

The selection of social work to administer the public assistance categories seems all the more amazing after a look at the status of the profession in 1935. Although widely recognized as a group with unique interests and skills, social work differed markedly from other professions in its lack of qualifying credentials. There existed in this profession social workers and trained social workers. Trained social workers were those who had received a certificate or a master's degree in social work after attending a one- to two-year course at an institution usually affiliated with a college or university. But unlike teachers or nurses or pharmacists, let alone doctors or lawyers, many persons (probably a majority in the 1930s) who lacked formal training practiced social work. A typical social worker was a woman with four to five years experience, employed in a city of over 300,000 and earning less than $1,800 a year. She had worked in some other field before entering social work, but she had not finished college or taken a course in a school of social work.

In 1930 the American Association of Social Workers—with five thousand members the largest of several social worker organizations—laid down requirements for new admissions that stipulated some courses and fieldwork directed by a school of social work. But membership in a professional organization was not a prerequisite by law or custom to employment as a social worker.

With one exception, the schools of social work emphasized casework to the virtual exclusion of more general academic studies. The classroom emphasis on casework was carried over into fieldwork, where students engaged in a period of supervised practice in a cooperating social agency. Critics of social work education objected to its narrow concentration upon technique and specialization while ignoring the big picture with its social and economic problems. In the critics' view, the schools should be turning out leaders and administrators. The one school where casework did not overshadow all else was the University of Chicago's School of Civics and Philanthropy. At Chicago, Edith Abbott, an economist, and Sophonisba Breckinridge, a lawyer, defined the future of social work in broader terms. Abbott argued that professional schools should graduate well-rounded, knowledgeable individuals with a grounding in scientific method rather than mere technicians. Consequently the curriculum at Chicago was built around public welfare administration, social research, law, government, and economics as related to social welfare. Casework would not be sacrificed in this approach, Abbott insisted; indeed, superior caseworkers would be produced. But above all the Chicago School aimed to turn out public welfare administrators and community organizers.[8]

The most available source of social worker supply for public assistance programs was located in the liquidating state and local FERA offices. Brown considered these workers a mixed bag. Many of them, though doubtless because of pressures from the community to save money and insistence by supervisors on a rigid interpretation of rules and regulations, seemed to "bear down" on applicants, concentrating on how many could be rejected rather than on how many could be legitimately accepted. But many others reacted against these pressures and went on to assert and testify in behalf of more adequate standards, in a good many cases, successfully. Not surprisingly, Brown found the new recruits to social work more liberal and enterprising than the older experienced workers who had transferred from private agencies. As planning for categorical assistance under the Social Security Act began in the fall of 1935, the FERA under Brown's leadership advised the states on retention of staff. Social work was promoted. First preference should go to professionally trained staff, then to college graduates who expressed an interest in professional development and training.[9]

On January 7, 1936, the Social Security Board approved the appointment of Jane M. Hoey as director of the Bureau of Public Assistance (BPA).[10] Hoey was forty-four when she went on duty, having been born on January 15, 1892. The youngest of nine children of Irish immigrants, she had spent most of her life in New York City. Her family's income had originally been modest but improved as older brothers and sisters began working, so much so that Hoey was able to attend college and graduate school. After two years at Hunter College in New York, Hoey transferred to Trinity College in Washington, D.C., where she was greatly influenced by the sociologist William J. Kerby and the economist John A. Ryan, both prominent Catholic clergy and social reformers.

Continuing her education at Columbia University, Hoey earned an M.A. in political science and a diploma from the New York School of Philanthropy in 1916. At the Board of Child Welfare of New York City, where she was an assistant to Harry Hopkins, Hoey helped administer the mother's pension program. During World War I, she worked for the Home Service of the American Red Cross. She was assistant director and secretary of the Health Division of the Welfare Council of New York City when called to Washington.

Hoey acquired important political connections through her brother James, a highly successful insurance executive who had served in the New York State Assembly. Through Jim, she met such Democratic party figures as Alfred E. Smith, Robert Wagner, and Franklin and Eleanor Roosevelt. Governor Smith named her to two commissions dealing with crime and the rehabilitation of criminals.

Hoey's was a warm, generous personality, well endowed with humor and full of good stories of the "priest in the confessional" type. To her staff, Hoey was "our inspiration." In calling upon Hoey to open the first session of the quarterly meeting of regional representatives, the chairwoman so introduced her boss.

In addition, although, as Perkins had noted, some political advantage accompanied the appointment, Hoey's qualifications for directorship of the BPA were impeccable. At the time, few persons in the country could equal her professional training and experience. The Civil Service Commission did not hesitate to approve her. Hoey was to remain director of the Bureau of Public Assistance until November 1953, nearly twenty years.[11]

Attack and Defense

Hoey reported for duty on January 13, 1936, arriving in the midst of hectic activity focused on the programs for which she was responsible. Staff in the BPA consisted of three professionals who had worked under extraordinary pressure for several months. Unlike the insurances, public assistance was slated to begin payments almost immediately. States could receive grants-in-aid beginning in January 1936, provided their plans for administering public assistance programs had received board approval.

Anxious to show that the Social Security Act was truly viable, the board and Executive Director Bane pushed hard to get these programs started. Huey Long was dead, having been assassinated early in September shortly after Congress had adjourned. Otherwise, critics of the Social Security Act seemed everywhere. The Townsendites, then at peak strength, relentlessly attacked the act's old age provisions. Even those who might have been expected to be among the act's strongest supporters proved unfaithful. Outstanding among this group were the social insurance pioneers, Isaac M. Rubinow and Abraham Epstein. Epstein was particularly negative and particularly vocal. In faulting both unemployment and old age insurance for their emphasis upon principles of equity instead of stressing social considerations supporting redistribution of wealth, Epstein became an advocate for public assistance. Rubinow, critical but not extremist, chided his friend and pupil, recognizing the progress attained in making a beginning and anticipating improvements.[12] Representatives of the Social Science Research Council, an organization that had been in the forefront of planning for federal action, expressed concern about the limited coverage in old age insurance and about the high tax in relation to expected benefits for many years to come. They emphasized that OAA, which would be expected to fill in for so many for so long, did not guarantee support, much less adequate support, for all eligible persons. Protesting that too much power was left to the states in each of the public assistance titles, they argued that "some method must be devised for establishing a national minimum below which aid to those in need will not be permitted to fall."[13]

A well-known group of professional social workers remained sour about the federal government's failure to establish a comprehensive welfare agency or to provide grants for general assistance. Led by Dorothy Kahn, its president, the American Association of Social Workers assembled a conference in Washington in February 1936 to discuss "This Business of Relief."

Because the WPA could not cover "more than a large fraction" of the able-bodied unemployed, the AASW argued for a work program modeled on the CWA with intake open to all the unemployed—no means test. The "large number of other persons in need of relief" should be cared for under federal grants to states for general relief in order to prevent their exposure to "low grade pauper treatment." Such changes would lead to a "stabilized relief program" that would attract experienced staff hired under a merit system. The end result would be "a far more and increasingly selective and discriminating relief service."[14]

Three months later, in May, at the National Conference of Social Work, these criticisms and demands for a greater federal role were repeated, this time to a larger audience. Walter West, executive secretary of the AASW, claimed that the number of needy persons thrown back upon state and local general relief was "alarmingly similar" to the number on hand when the FERA came into the picture in 1933, some 2.5 million families and single persons. This gross miscalculation (the FERA caseload in May 1933 was more than twice this number) went unchallenged, but not the AASW proposals.[15]

Josephine Brown, confessing to earlier misgivings, now defended the Social Security Act. She pointed out that most states, all but eight in fact, either had or would soon have established permanent public welfare departments that would include general assistance in their programs. Three-fourths of the staffs of these departments were well qualified and experienced transfers from the emergency relief program. Regrettably, in at least twenty-one states, relief funds were inadequate, in a few states, "miserably so." Similarly, a number of states were understaffed, and some had almost no qualified workers. But she reminded her audience of the large commitments made by the federal government to the states under the

Social Security Act, which was subject to improvements in coverage and funding. While far from ideal, the present situation was one of "public welfare in the making," Brown concluded.[16]

By May, Aubrey Williams had lost all patience with the AASW. At the February AASW conference, perhaps hoping to dissuade the professionals from their obsession with relief, Williams had stressed political realities. The WPA, which had on the average doubled the relief payment in its security wage, was already under attack from those who wanted to cut expenditures. And he warned: "Even though there are people in this country who are suffering who fall between the governmental programs for work and for social security, I plead with you to believe that when you ask for a federal direct relief program, you are playing with subversive forces so powerful that the result will be first the dilution and then the demolition of the work program." At a session of the National Conference and again in a talk at the concurrent meeting of the APWA, Williams stepped up his attack. "What is that characteristic of relief as opposed to the work program and social security measures that makes it appear so desirable that your efforts are concentrated here, rather than on an expansion of the work and security programs?" he asked. In the current congressional session the issue under discussion was not whether a federal appropriation for direct relief should be made to supplement the WPA and Social Security assistance programs, but rather whether direct relief, as less costly, should not pick up the whole burden and even be returned to the states. AASW leaders had been cited as in support of this about-face. The result.

The AASW has become a power in the conservative camp; it has lent respectability to those who would reduce relief expenditures. . . . You who insist upon federal relief find yourselves in the company not only of our political opposition, but also and more serious, in the company of all who favor the form of assistance that can be stretched to the thinnest possible point, to that fine point of adjustment which costs the least to their pocketbooks and still does not endanger their loss by revolt.[17]

Not all social work leaders were of one mind. Edith Abbott and her sister, Grace, first at the Children's Bureau, then at the University of Chicago had long championed public welfare, seeking to liberalize the poor law and to transfer control of administration from political factions to the civil service. Both defended the Social Security Act from its detractors. The Social Security Act, not the WPA, was "the heart of the President's program" and "the foundation for great progress," Grace Abbott asserted. Edith, while cool to old age insurance because of the tax on low wage earners, defended categorical relief against her "eastern friends" in social work:

First, because the people themselves prefer their public assistance that way. They would rather receive an old age pension, or mothers' aid, or unemployment benefit, or a blind pension, than to go on the general poor relief lists. . . . A second reason why this method of special assistance by categories is a step in advance of the old relief pool is that the new forms of public aid have provided more adequate and more stable grants than the old relief provided, and have avoided some, at least, of the humiliations of the old system.[18]

Yet social workers covering the National Conference for *The Survey* called attention to the continuing "rift" between the "Washington crowd" and their social work colleagues, the questions bordering on "heckling" directed to Brown following her paper, and the "tensions" arising from Williams's charges against the AASW. For its part, the APWA announced its divorce from the National Conference. Explaining that welfare officials did not like "the sound" of social work, the APWA had decided to meet at another time and place in the future. Nevertheless, the APWA's director pledged support for merit appointments and promised to try "to recapture the waning prestige of social workers among elected officials."[19]

However much the critics irritated Williams—and presumably Hopkins and the Social Security Board, who had to take the political heat—certain unpleasant facts were inescapable. Although employment on WPA projects reached the goal of 3.5 million by February 1936, thousands of needy able-bodied unemployed awaited job assignments at one time or another. Although the individuals on waiting lists were constantly changing, many were subject to real distress, particularly in states that refused any emergency relief to this employable group.

State Plans

It was well known that the WPA could not provide enough jobs to reach all the needy unemployed. The FERA had closed out grants to states for assistance to unemployables. At best, the early months of 1936 would turn into a shakedown period; at worst, some persons might go hungry. The Social Security Board was eager to take the heat off federal and state legislators, to show itself capable of relieving the states of some of their fiscal burdens, and, above all, to get money into the hands of needy unemployable persons. Receipt of categorical money in the states would not only help the categorically needy but should free up additional general relief funds for the needy unemployed.[20]

Consistent with existing grant-in-aid programs, the Social Security Act weighted responsibility for the public assistance programs heavily toward the states. Indeed, states were not required to institute any of the programs, and they were free to choose one, or two, or all three of the available categories. Once an affirmative choice had been made, however, states had to assure the federal government of their compliance with the several requirements of the act. Far from burdensome, these requirements were designed to accord maximum freedom of operation consistent with guarantees of equity and integrity. Assurance of compliance was conveyed by means of a state plan that was subject to approval by the Social Security Board. Generally speaking, a state plan addressed two main topics: eligibility for assistance, and the organization and methods of administration and financing.

Although the movement for reform and modernization of state and local government had taken hold in a good many places by the mid-thirties, primitive methods persisted in most units of government. The quality of personnel was an overriding problem. With few exceptions the spoils system prevailed, having been encouraged by the scarcity of jobs during the Depression. Public assistance, until very recently completely controlled by local government, was particularly vulnerable to poor administration. State legislatures, dominated by rural interests, were typically reluctant to support programs for the needy, programs whose benefits went largely to the cities. Even with such reluctance overcome to the point of passage of legislation authorizing categorical assistance, states lacked experience in administering public assistance programs.

When the FERA was established, the APWA, with Bane in the lead, had recommended that state relief agencies be fitted into old-line state administration with its institutions and hospitals for the indigent and handicapped. In a number of states there was a foothold of good administration in these state welfare departments. Nothing much was accomplished along these lines, however. The necessity for immediate action and reluctance to place an emergency program in a permanent agency worked against the APWA's effort. To be sure, the FERA had promulgated a number of administrative standards, accepted in some quarters, still bitterly resented in others. With emergency relief a thing of the past, powerful forces reasserted themselves in favor of the status quo. In the process of state plan approval, therefore, the board often had to deal with more than met the eye.[21]

Policymaking in relation to state plan approval, development of guides and procedures to assist the states, and critical review of plans themselves had to be undertaken a number of weeks before Hoey's arrival in Washington. Many states wished to qualify for grants as of the first of the year. Under any circumstances, Bane, an expert on public welfare administration, would have devoted considerable time to this part of the board's work. In view of the pressure existing before professional staff could be hired, Bane's involvement in these activities stretched far beyond the usual demands of his position. His was the policymaking role that set the course.

Fully aware that state plans would, more often than not, prove imperfect, many of them downright poor, the board nevertheless adopted Bane's recommendations for a liberal stance. Strongly influencing this decision was the assumption that, unlike emergency relief, the categorical assistance programs were destined to be around for a long time. Get the programs started, therefore, trusting to future experience and a well-trained federal field staff to induce necessary improvements.

At the same time, Bane determined to go as far as possible in preparing a foundation for improvement in state and local administration. Here the board could exert considerable influence, justifying its stand on three of the act's mandatory provisions. The first of these provisions required the program to be operative in all parts of the state—"state wideness." The second required state financial participation. The third required the state to "provide such methods of administration (other than those relating to selection, tenure of office, and compensation of personnel) as are found by the board to be necessary for the efficient operation of the plan."[22]

Using these stipulations as guidelines, states were urged to bring together in one agency all of their welfare activities, federally aided or not. This was the ideal organization. A somewhat less comprehensive organization proved acceptable. But the board was particularly opposed to the establishment of separate agencies for each of the public assistance categories, an arrangement that seemed permissible under a literal reading of the act.

Also urged upon the states was the establishment of a county unit system as the locus for processing public assistance cases. In order to ensure state authority over local units, the board set forth a minimum of four controls to be instituted by the state agency:

1. Audit, to include the prescription and use of standard accounting forms and the auditing of local accounts;
2. Administrative rules and regulations to ensure statewide standardization of principal functions and activities;

3. Standards and specifications for employees of local units; and
4. A state supervisory force to work in the field, assisting and monitoring local units.

The board used various means to persuade the states to adopt these methods of administration. Several factors worked in its favor. Of greatest significance was the states' clamor for guidance. During December 1935 particularly, states bombarded the agency, by phone and personal visit, with inquiries about framing state legislation and state plans. Although board staff was minuscule, it was knowledgeable. Of the three persons working on public assistance, two had previously worked for Bane in the APWA and more recently in the FERA. The third, a trained social worker experienced in state administration, had transferred from the National Recovery Administration (NRA). The APWA, an invaluable ally, operated in close consultation with, and as an extended arm of, the board. The APWA pamphlet "Suggested State Legislation for Social Security," which contained drafts of bills covering administrative organization and the public assistance titles, was ready by mid-November. Not surprisingly, the suggested bills dovetailed perfectly with the administrative principles devised by Bane and adopted by the board.

Early in December 1935 the board distributed instructions and forms for use in preparing state plans. And on December 14–15, representatives of forty-two states and territories attended a conference in Washington to review and discuss the essentials for approval. At this conference Bane sought to obtain agreement on the recommended administrative organization and state agency controls. In a follow-up letter to the states, he asserted that such a consensus had been reached.

In reality, state reaction was mixed, ranging from whole-hearted enthusiasm for uniform auditing systems to mild assent on the necessity for a set of common rules and regulations to outright opposition to establishing local personnel standards. Opposition around such a tough subject as personnel was hardly unexpected. Certainly the parties had not heard the last of it. In general, however, these early federal-state negotiations got off to an encouraging start. Particularly successful was the December 1935 conference. Both levels of government learned a great deal and together faced the many unknowns that existed in the absence of precedent and experience. Most important for the long haul, federal participants believed, was the states' awareness that the Social Security Board wished to assist rather than dictate, and that federal requirements would be conceived in broad, reasonable terms.

As emphasized in the board's instructions, the purpose of a state plan was assurance of conformity with the several requirements contained in each of the public assistance titles. In general, a showing of the state's plan of organization, finance, and procedure would provide the information needed for board action. The state submittal was to include copies of laws that authorized and established the rules of eligibility for public assistance, laws that related to state and local agencies administering or supervising public assistance programs, and laws dealing with the acceptance and expenditure of federal funds and the provisions for appropriating or transferring state and local monies. Copies of rules and regulations, including court decisions and opinions, that affected the organization of the state agency and its operation of the state plan were also to be submitted. A statement citing the provisions of laws and other official documents affecting the apportionment and expenditure of funds for administration, including allocation to political subdivisions, was also required. The state must submit a chart as well as a descriptive analysis of the organization and operation of the state agency and of its subordinate units. The proposed operation of the program itself, to be presented in outline form, was to be described and documented in terms of the various requirements of the Social Security Act, for example, statewideness, state financial participation, age limitations, residence, and so on.

Although it was not until May 1936 that procedures for review of state plans were formalized, the division of labor was obvious and was followed from the beginning, with the arrival of the first plans the previous December. A plan was subjected to scrutiny by the Office of the General Counsel for legal conformity to all provisions of the Social Security Act, by the Bureau of Accounts and Audits as to financial sufficiency and controls, and by the Bureau of Public Assistance for compatibility with the requirements of the act and the soundness of proposed methods of administration. Accompanied by written comments and recommendations a plan was forwarded through the executive director for action by the board.[23]

Wisconsin was one of those states that submitted a plan for the administration of OAA in December 1935. Officials preparing the submittal followed the board's outline, filling in the blanks provided under separate headings that described the various provisions of the Social Security Act. The Wisconsin plan created a state Pension Department within an already established Industrial Commission. The Pension Department consisted of one member of the Industrial Commission, the state budget director, and the supervisor of pensions, its administrative head. Wisconsin announced its intention to appoint the person presently in charge of the existing old age pension program as supervisor of pensions. Future appointments to this position were to be made in accordance with Civil Service requirements.

Under the supervision of the Pension Department, OAA was to be administered in each county by the county judge or by a county department of public welfare—the choice a matter for county boards. Specifically, the Pension Department retained control over rules and regulations required for conformity to the act, including "efficient administration." The department pledged promulgation of its rules and regulations to county units and further to "render all possible assistance in security compliance therewith, including the preparation of all necessary blanks and reports." A fair hearing to persons denied assistance was assured and time limits for actions set. The state department held itself responsible for the submission of accurate reports required by the Social Security Board. Records would be open to inspection and audit. The costs of OAA, borne by the county in the first instance, would be reimbursed up to 80 percent from state and federal monies. Wisconsin fixed the age limit for eligibility for assistance at sixty-five and required residence in the state in five of the last nine years immediately preceding application. Eligibility was limited to citizens of the United States, either native born or naturalized.

The general counsel found the Wisconsin plan in legal conformity and the Bureau of Accounts and Audits endorsed the financial arrangements. But the Bureau of Public Assistance, while noting numerous positive aspects, could not recommend unqualified approval. The problem centered on the power of the state Pension Department over local administering units. The BPA found the provisions for local administration "weak," particularly if county courts were chosen for the job rather than county welfare departments. County courts were centers of local influence, particularly in rural areas, and the judiciary was ever reluctant to defer power to the executive. The BPA thought local staff might prove incompetent in many places. In counties with more than 500,000 population, civil service laws applied, but in less populated areas, county boards hired personnel. No provision had been made for state field supervisors or for on-the-spot consultation. Instead the Pension Department planned to rely on review of various kinds of paperwork. Counteracting these weaknesses was substantial financial leverage, evidenced by the Pension Department's power of approval to reimburse 80 percent of county expenditures as well as informal assurances that staff from the liquidating state emergency relief agency would be hired for the new jobs.

The BPA recommended approval of the Wisconsin plan conditional upon the appointment of at least eight field supervisors to be responsible for reviewing and interpreting case records. Thinking the state might offer assurances in advance of approval, Bane wired the supervisor of pensions asking what methods would be used to guarantee the employment of competent personnel by county boards and what provision, if any, had been made for the employment of traveling state field supervisors. In reply the Wisconsin supervisor of pensions announced his intention to employ "competent state field supervisors." But he hedged on local personnel standards: "State pension department has promulgated a rule and regulation requiring that each county must file with state pension department complete personnel record with information as to qualifications of each person employed, and state department will make such investigations as necessary and will insist on only such personnel as will insure efficient administration." The worth of this statement can be measured by examining the situation four years later. At the time no personnel standards for county units had been established by the state agency, and, in fact, the state expressed doubt about its power to establish such standards.[24]

The board approved the Wisconsin plan for OAA, as well as those for AB and ADC, on December 23, 1935, reserving to itself the right to another review based on more complete information. In notifying Wisconsin of board action, Chairman Winant signed one of many letters making approval contingent upon the meeting of certain conditions:

It should be pointed out that the Board is approving for the first quarter of 1936 and that its approval of the methods of administration of the plan was based on the facts before it. If, at a later date, a re-examination of the methods of administration indicates that they are not satisfactory, the Board will withdraw its approval of those methods, and, necessarily, its approval of the plan itself.

The Board will shortly request detailed information with respect to administrative procedure. In order to have a complete picture of the situation in the state, the board will request data as to personnel, methods of bookkeeping, and auditing and related matters.[25]

Conditional approval became the rule for handling these early state plans. During December 1935, only Maryland (OAA) and the District of Columbia (OAA and ADC) had plans approved unconditionally. No plans were disapproved during December. Sixteen states received conditional approvals for a total of thirty-four plans (fourteen, OAA; eleven, AB; and nine, ADC). Various conditions were imposed. To states such as Wisconsin, whose plans were relatively complete, and were believed to provide a promising basis for sound administration, conditions were made quite general, of a nature to cover the board in case of unexpected developments. Even Alabama, whose plans for OAA and ADC had been pronounced "excellent" by the BPA, received a letter identical to the one sent Wisconsin.[26]

Confronted with poor plans, the Board applied specific conditions and recommendations. Missouri's plan for old age assistance fell into the "poor" group. The state's scheme for administrative organization was primitive though perhaps forthright, offering a "Trouble Department" for handling doubtful cases and an "Examining Mill" for case review. Politics ruled staff appointments. In approving the Missouri plan, the board recommended that staff be given intensive training and supervision under the guidance of the BPA regional representative.[27]

After the turn of the year, methods of handling plan approvals changed radically. Conditional approvals were no longer used. Although most plans secured outright approval upon formal presentation to the board, a few plans were disapproved. Several factors contributed to the shift to more judicious methods of operation. Not least was easement from the extreme pressure generated by the December 31 deadline. Some of the rush turned out to have been unnecessary. Reversing an earlier opinion, the general counsel advised in January that states could claim reimbursement for the quarter in which plan approval had been granted. Even more important than additional time was additional staff. By late spring the BPA began a gradual but steady expansion, both in Washington and in the field.

Under these circumstances, extensive negotiations with the states could take place before, rather than after, formal submittal of a plan. In midsummer the board began preliminary reviews of BPA and general counsel reports on pending plans, a practice that forestalled formal action where further negotiation was indicated. With some states, the preapproval process was relatively short and simple. With others, severe problems resulted in protracted and extraordinary efforts.

Deficiencies might be ironed out with the assistance of a field representative. Plans submitted by Vermont for AB and ADC early in January were so lacking in information about methods of administration that BPA deferred judgment. Additional information received in mid-February still proved insufficient for dependable evaluation. A visit in March by the bureau's regional representative clarified questionable points, making it possible for the board to approve Vermont's plans at the end of the month.[28]

Louisiana's plan for OAA and ADC contained similar gaps in documentation needed by the general counsel and the Bureau of Accounts and Audits. In this instance the director of the state Welfare Department arrived in Washington with additional materials. Conferences brought out details requiring further explanation. Approval was granted within two weeks of the director's visit.

A favorable outcome—approval of the plan—was not always forthcoming. Massachusetts's plans for OAA and AB received approval after resolution of a few issues. Its plan for ADC ran into more serious trouble. Statewideness was doubtful and state control of local agencies tenuous. There was no real assurance that approved methods of administration would be followed. The root difficulty lay in New England tradition—the power retained by the townships. Since the welfare commissioner preferred the system set up under the state's 1913 mother's pension law, negotiations got nowhere. Even an application of Hoey's personal diplomacy failed to persuade the commissioner to make concessions. The year ended without an approved plan.[29]

Where politics mingled with inadequacies and nonconformity in plans submitted for approval, the board faced agonizing choices. The Kansas plan was a hot potato because Alf M. Landon, the state's governor, emerged as the leading contender for the 1936 Republican nomination for President. On paper the Kansas plans looked as good as many others, but their underlying validity was challenged by Senator George McGill, a Democrat, who requested a board hearing before final approval. Again the issue was state control of county administration, particularly as applied to county financial contributions and county personnel. The governor's officials, his attorney general and his welfare commissioner designate, John G. Stutz, asserted the state's power. Yet a number of county officials wired the board of their unwillingness to put up any money. Stutz, in Washington to pressure for approval, caved in after a week of conversations and questioning, admitting to Hoey and Bane the state's lack of requisite control.

The board was now in a terrible bind—approve a plan clearly out of conformity and establish dangerous precedents or risk major political repercussions including a threat to the act itself? Beginning on January 24, in at least six meetings, the board hashed and rehashed the Kansas situation, and on January 31, voted to disapprove. Thereupon Bane, Miles, and Altmeyer took turns at phrasing a letter to the state. Meanwhile Winant got on the phone with his fellow Republican, Landon, explaining that approval of the Kansas plan would violate the law. On February 11, after Bane returned from discussions with Landon, the board followed Bane's recommendation to disapprove, dispatching a letter to this effect on February 18. Although conscious of the correctness of its action, the board greatly feared distortion by political partisans. The eruption never occurred, although Landon vehemently attacked the social insurance provisions of the act during his campaign for the presidency.[30]

Republicans held no monopoly on creating problems. The Democrat Martin L. Davey, governor of Ohio, had not forgotten his humiliation by Harry Hopkins after politics was uncovered in referrals to public works jobs. As a result, social workers had become anathema throughout the state and the Eagles had moved in as the guiding administrative force in the OAA system. Business experience had become the main qualification for local staff. Reports of gross mismanagement of the state system preceded the arrival of Davey's representative, M. L. (Mat) Brown, at the board offices in February 1936. Most of these reports originated with Colonel Sherrill, a Democratic rival of Davey and former city manager of Cincinnati. Hoey, doubtless particularly sensitive to the state's attitude toward social workers, told Brown she would not recommend approval of the Ohio plan until the administration was cleaned up. Brown countered with some heat, suggesting that the board do its own investigating. Although she thought this was the last thing Brown wanted, Hoey immediately agreed and the board backed her.

The team sent to Ohio found ample evidence of sloppy administration but little outright political manipulation. Lack of periodic audits and of records of amounts paid to individuals, failure to conduct thorough investigations of applicants' need for assistance, and extremely heavy caseloads carried by inexperienced staff were the main weaknesses cited. Hoey, always more anxious to provide assistance to the needy than to play politics, recommended approval of the Ohio plan, provided Davey agreed to strengthen administration along lines suggested by the bureau. Because time was running out if Ohio was to receive a grant for the first quarter of 1936, Bane and Hoey traveled to the state to present findings and recommendations to Davey and Brown. Hoey was proud of the documents she and Bane prepared. Since business held sway in Ohio, they expressed the letter to Davey in business terms, studiously avoiding social work language:

In spite of the fact that a large sum of money, $13 million during 1935, was spent for the care of aged persons in their own homes, there is no assurance that money is not being wasted for aid to persons financially able to care for themselves, or that persons in need are receiving adequate assistance.

About three percent is spent for administration. This economy in Ohio has resulted, among other things in an inadequate number of employees, inexperienced and poorly paid, whose lowered morale has not been conducive to good work.

Davey, expressing some chagrin when faced with this assessment, agreed to sign an addendum to the plan that acceded to the board's specifications for accounting, finance, and record keeping, state supervision of counties, methods of investigating eligibility, organization of the state office, and additional personnel. Accordingly, Ohio's OAA plan was approved on March 31, 1936. In the fall of 1938, with elections coming up, a letter went out to OAA recipients asking them to vote for Governor Davey. After a hearing, the board agreed to withhold the October 1938 grant, amounting to $1,250,000. By the end of November the board was satisfied with the progress shown and paid Ohio's claim for that month, although it continued its disallowance for October.[31]

The politics of the Colorado plans arose from the intention of Governor Ed C. Johnson, a conservative Democrat, to unseat Senator Edward P. Costigan, now a New Dealer. The general counsel feared that Colorado welfare law unconstitutionally delegated state powers and objected to overlapping administration by courts and other state bodies. BPA pointed to vague language and to the inordinately large numbers of persons expected to receive OAA. The bureau also expressed concern about personnel. The state welfare agency was headed by a former street car conductor, whose assistant, though nominally qualified, was said to be amenable to any political agreements made with county administrators. The state plan, so the talk ran, was paper, simply a device to get federal money.

Meanwhile Governor Johnson began a much publicized campaign against the board, pulling out all the stops in a telegram to President Roosevelt: "Colorado's crippled children, blind, and aged still awaiting promised benefits under the Social Security Act. They have been very patient but as the weeks slip by they are losing hope." On March 13, the day after receipt of this telegram, the board disapproved the Colorado plan, emphasizing in its letter to Johnson the duplication and overlapping that only legislation could clear up. In a follow-up visit, the regional representative outlined corrective legislation. A special session of the legislature brought Colorado into legal conformity. The board took positive action early in May, though Hoey remained pessimistic about Colorado's administrative set-up.[32]

The board did not always follow the advice of its general counsel. Illinois was a case in point. Hoey considered the Illinois plan for administration totally lacking in control by the state agency, in reality simply a collection of county plans, with no provision for qualified personnel. General Counsel Eliot expressed grave doubt as to the board's authority in the matter of local personnel, but found some justification in the act's requirement for a single state agency and in the congressional committee reports charging the state agency with "final administrative responsibility." Eliot felt that a "strained" argument could be made "that a state agency could not be said to have this 'final administrative responsibility,' unless it had power to prescribe qualifications for personnel." In a state with administration entirely in the hands of the counties, the board might insist on personnel standards set by the state agency. In Illinois, however, the state agency retained power to review and investigate decisions by county boards, and even to take over the entire operation if need be. Therefore the issue of local personnel could not legitimately be raised. In recommending approval of the Illinois plan, the general counsel called attention to apparent inconsistencies on the part of the board, arguing that in at least three instances—Wisconsin among them—the board had approved plans with no greater state control. Yet the board followed the recommendations of administrators Bane and Hoey, voting two to one (Miles in the negative) to disapprove the Illinois plan for OAA. Only after prolonged negotiations followed by state legislation did the board approve a revised plan for Illinois on July 31, 1936.[33]

For all its good intentions, the board had rested its case for local personnel standards on tenuous grounds, agreeing that it had no authority when it came to state personnel, but insisting that state standards for local personnel were essential to state supervision of local units. On July 30, the board departed once and for all from its ad hoc method of dealing with this highly charged question. Altmeyer took the lead, suggesting that henceforth the board insist upon minimum objective standards to cover state and local personnel, while standing aside from control over actual qualifications. Admitting that this position was probably "stretching the law," Altmeyer expressed his belief in public support for such a stance. The Board adopted the following resolution unanimously: "The Board interprets the provisions of the Act relative to efficient operation and proper administration in Title I, III, IV, and X, as they concern personnel, to require the state agency to set up minimum objective standards of training and experience, but not to confer upon the Board power to determine any matters relating to the selection, tenure of office or compensation of individuals."[34]

The board bent over backwards to fulfill what it regarded as its primary obligation, that is, to get money into the hands of the needy. In Bane's words, "the Board . . . adopted a liberal policy in the hope and belief that more will be gained in the long pull by cooperation and definite assistance than . . . by bureaucratic edict and strict construction." This approach accomplished the board's main purpose—outright or conditional approval of a great many plans. By mid-January 1936, fifteen states had plans approved for OAA; ten, for ADC; and eleven, for AB. By the following

December, a total of forty-two plans for OAA, twenty-seven for ADC, and twenty-eight for AB had been approved. Only eight states—four of them in the South—had no categorical plans in operation.[35]

The board's actions in approving borderline plans and pushing through others conditionally are understandable, even admirable, given the political situation and the presence of acute need in some states. The path chosen was, nevertheless, fraught with danger. To deal evenhandedly with states was essential. The board had to tread very carefully through its precedent-making decisions. Faith in future negotiations to persuade states to improve programs might well prove justified. Failing success in this approach, the board had but one weapon of enforcement in its arsenal— the drastic one of cutting off grants.

The start-up of programs in so many states and the continuing submittal of plans for approval from those not yet operating one or more programs resulted in an increasingly heavy workload, both in Washington and in the field. Large sums of money had begun to flow out from the U.S. Treasury. Control and state awareness of such control, by the presence of auditors, among others, was essential. Although states held fast to their freedom to run the show, their staffs turned constantly to BPA for advice on administrative procedure, for definitions of terms in the law, and for guidance in drafting legislation. When Hoey reported for duty, Bane conveyed the board's wish that she build up her staff "as soon as possible."

To some, Hoey seemed unresponsive to the administrative challenge. Her considerable talents were strongest in policy formulation and diplomacy. Not bureaucratically inclined, she postponed the organizational task of delineating clear lines of responsibility, either verbally or on paper. In the absence of well-defined duties, staff in Washington entered into informal agreements about the division of labor. Field staff expressed impatience with the not infrequent unresponsiveness of the BPA.

Hoey's professional standards were high. Determined to hire the best persons available, she was dissatisfied with the low salaries authorized by the Civil Service Commission. Her determination to hold out and devise ways to justify higher salaries tended to slow the recruitment process.

On April 7, 1936, Chairman Winant called for more rapid recruitment, commenting that the BPA was grossly understaffed to handle the large amounts of money being granted to the states. In private discussion, Hoey expressed more disappointment than alarm at the slow pace of hiring. All in all, she felt the field staff of six professionals was responding adequately to urgent matters. Three more professionals for the field were due to report in a couple of weeks. At headquarters, the divisional-level organization had been worked out by this time. In March 1936, a director for the Regulations and Procedures Division was selected from staff within the BPA. Directors for the Division of Grants and for the Field Service Division arrived early in May. The head of the Division of Technical Training came in July. Once division chiefs had been named, other recruitment proceeded more rapidly. On June 30, 1936, bureau staff totaled a mere 27 persons. By December, the staff had almost tripled for a total of 72—66 in Washington, 6 in the field. In June 1937 the staff had grown to 98, with 83 in Washington and 15 in the field, and by June 30, 1939, the BPA was employing 177 persons, 153 in Washington and 24 working out of regional offices. The bureau relied on the "expert" clause in making these early staff appointments. Most of the new hires were social workers, a good many recruited from private agencies. These were the future negotiators, those on whom the board had pinned its faith and hope for compassionate and efficient public welfare programs in the states, in the counties, and in the cities.[36]

4

The Unsettling Question

IN ITS DETERMINED, often frenzied, efforts to approve plans and advise states on legislation and administration, the Social Security Board became a prime mover in the second stage of the nation's historic shift in social welfare. With the creation of the WPA in May 1935, the federal government made good on its pledge to stop all direct relief to the unemployed. The following month Hopkins ordered the transfer of up to 3.5 million employable persons then on direct or work relief to WPA projects, where they would earn a "security wage." Liquidation of the FERA was completed in December. The federal government had assumed administrative responsibility for future unemployed workers through unemployment compensation (Title III) and had agreed under Titles I, IV, and X of the Social Security Act to share with the states the support of the needy aged, dependent children, and the blind. Back to state and local governments went responsibility for the so-called residuals—those needy who failed to fit into a category prescribed for federal aid.

The Politics of Old Age Pensions

The shift resulting from the decisions of 1935 brought criticism, even denunciation, from many quarters, right, left, and center—too much, too little, unfair. But seldom was the criticism comprehensive, applied across the board to the entire scheme. Instead, different groups selected different targets for attack or defense. As unemployment dropped—from 24.9 percent of the labor force in 1933 to 16.9 percent in 1936 and 14.3 percent in 1937–the WPA became a prime target for attack by business and industry. Indeed, as private sector jobs became more plentiful, the unemployed receded as the group perceived as most deserving of care and attention. The unemployed were replaced at the center of concern by the aged, a large and now articulate group without hope of participating fully in the economic recovery.[1]

With two Social Security Act programs directed toward the aged—work-related insurance to begin payments in 1942 and assistance ready to go at state option—the Social Security Board found itself in the middle of extraordinary pressures to act—pressures so strong as to threaten the basic premises of the Social Security Act itself. The old age issue dominated the entire program during the early years. The primacy accorded the aged in the states had countless repercussions, affecting not only what was done for the aged themselves but what was done or not done for others equally or in greater need.

Encouraged by the actions of legislatures and governors, state and local administrators tended to operate the old age assistance (OAA) program along lines different from those of other relief. Where the BPA banked on qualified personnel—preferably social workers—to ensure efficiency and fairness, out in the countryside it was widely believed that honesty and common sense would suffice to give the aged their due. In areas lacking what the bureau believed were adequate personnel standards, political influence lurked in the wings and sometimes appeared on stage. Try mightily as it did, the Social Security Board could not hold these forces completely in check. As early as September 1937 it sought legislation in an effort to restore balance to its program and gain greater control of state-local administration.[2]

Although the Townsend movement was the only organization devoting its energies exclusively to the aged, other dissident groups were not indifferent to their cause. Huey Long's Share Our Wealth Society and Father Coughlin's Union for Social Justice offered different cures for the country's economic ills, different from each other and different from the Townsend movement. But neither Long nor Coughlin ignored the elderly. To the sympathizers in the Depression-borne groups could be added the more conservative organizations such as the Fraternal Order of Eagles, which had led the earlier struggle for old age pensions and had not departed the scene upon passage of the Social Security Act. The list of supporters fanned out to embrace the younger generation, the sons and daughters of the aged who sought relief from an economic burden.

When thoughts turned to the aged and to doing something about their obviously sad situation, did it really matter that membership in the Townsend clubs was greatly inflated? Townsend club membership reached a peak of about 2.2 million in 1936, probably including little more than 10 percent of the population aged sixty and over. Did it matter that the Townsend plan had been voted down by Congress? That Huey Long was dead? That Father Coughlin's power in Congress had eroded? None of these things mattered in 1936. What mattered was the popularity of the cause, the general agreement that the aged deserved special consideration. Such convictions were expected to be expressed in votes. Rejecting the Townsend plan as too extreme, middle-of-the-road voters and politicians looked to OAA for a way to resolve the issue upon satisfactorily reasonable terms.[3]

OAA dominated the actions of governors and legislatures in their early dealings with the Social Security Board, taking precedence over plans for grants-in-aid to the blind and for dependent children. The year 1936 ended with the map of the United States all but covered by states with OAA plans in operation. Within the first six months, all states but Virginia, South Carolina, Kansas, and Nevada had joined. Forty-four states, the District of Columbia, and the territories of Hawaii and Alaska had programs for the aged. Participation in the other public assistance programs lagged behind, with thirty-three states and the District of Columbia granting AB and thirty-four states and the District administering ADC in June 1937. In the states the number of persons eligible for OAA rose rapidly and substantially, doubling during the fiscal year ending June 1937 to reach a total of 1,293,964 recipients.[4]

Much of this increase occurred in a predictable way, as a result of applications by elderly persons already on direct relief plus those whose resources had been recently curtailed. But there was another group of elderly, smaller in number but still sizable, that appeared suddenly and unexpectedly in need of assistance. These persons, in their sixties, seventies, and eighties even, had been on FERA work relief projects and had been duly certified to the WPA for employment in the summer and fall of 1935. They were not retained on the jobs very long. The WPA, bent on creating an image of substantial projects and at least average productivity, and conscious of shrinking funds, began to cut back in March 1936. Not surprisingly, the elderly were among the first to go. An avalanche of applications for OAA descended, often landing in places unprepared to handle the load. Some states used post offices, banks, and newspaper offices as distribution points. Thousands of applications awaited action when new state and local agencies opened for business. By resorting to such unorthodox procedures, communities signaled a firm intention to help the elderly. No such gestures were made toward other needy groups. Thousands of women, in contrast, most of them with dependent children, were dropped from WPA projects at the same time as older persons. These women had to line up at the local welfare office and wait their turn to be investigated for whatever program could be found to help them.[5]

The effort to set the aged apart from other needy groups appeared in many guises. Use of the term "old age pension" persisted—whether from habit, confusion with the insurance provisions of the Social Security Act, or common agreement that help for the aged should not be considered a form of welfare. Whatever the reason, many aged assumed that they were rightfully due a monthly payment upon attainment of a fixed number of years of age. Some officials made sure that elderly applicants would not have to mingle with other needy persons. Special quarters, though not necessarily more convenient or comfortable than the regular relief office, were set up to handle their applications.[6]

Whenever the BPA heard "pension," it cried "need." To be sure, the term "relief" had been discarded. All Social Security programs, including OAA, were elevated to a higher plane than those associated with poor law administration or even the FERA. At the same time, the distinction between insurance and assistance was never forgotten. The BPA regarded need as an absolute precondition for receipt of OAA. In the bureau's view, the federal government could not match state payments to those who were not needy.[7]

The general counsel was not so sure. Thomas Eliot, drafter of the original bill, remembered the disagreements in congressional committees about defining need. He pointed out that the adjective "needy" occurred only in the preamble—the so-called hot air section—of Title I, and he thought the omission in the substantive portions of the title had been deliberate. In December 1935 he let Bane know his doubt "that we have any right to read 'needy' into the definition of old age assistance."[8]

Eliot's uncertainties were repeated when several states offered plans to pay a fixed monthly allowance—a flat grant—to all persons over age sixty-five, regardless of need. The board, believing the words of the preamble had some force and leaning somewhat upon the act's legislative history, turned down these plans. In reporting its action in the annual report, however, the words were chosen carefully: "The Social Security Board has taken the position that the law permits it to match grants only in the case of needy individuals." The board thus stopped short of asserting the primacy of need in a bold interpretation of the law. The law might be clarified when the time was ripe.[9]

The pension-at-sixty-five plans presented the board with a clear-cut proposition, one that ignored need completely. The board's neck need not be stuck very far out in making its decision. It was far more hazardous to deal with proposals that attempted to accomplish much the same thing in more circuitous ways. Having learned that need could not be ignored per se, the states set about defining need in ways designed to stretch the number of eligible persons toward the act's outer limits.

These new approaches toward OAA seemed unquestionably lawful. Everyone agreed that the Social Security Act left it to the states to define need and to set standards. Eliot elaborated his point, advising once again that a state plan must specify need as a condition for receipt of assistance. Evidence from the legislative history "justified" the board's requirement to include needs tests in state plans. However, and it was a big "however," the legislative history also made clear congressional intent that need be defined by the state, not by the federal, agency. "The Board may refuse to approve a plan only if it does not purport to contain a needs test or if it contains a purported needs test which has no basis in reason," Eliot concluded.[10] Nothing in the act specified one particular method or several alternative methods for defining need or setting standards. The BPA was free to make suggestions; the states were just as free to reject them.[11]

Defining Need

Family budgeting, the method favored by the bureau for defining need, had been developed early in the century when social work began to turn professional. This was the method currently taught in schools of social work. It had been recommended for use by the FERA. Five elements were involved: (1) a minimum community standard for maintaining health and decency, derived from costing out a list of necessities; (2) total needs of the applicant costed out with reference to the standard; (3) total income and resources of the applicant derived from statements and written documentation; (4) allowance for any specified exemptions as to income and resources; (5) ineligibility or eligibility for a given amount of assistance derived by subtracting money available to the applicant after allowable exemptions from the community standard. If the applicant was found eligible, the exact amount of assistance would be calculated by subtracting the amount of income from the amount of the community standard.[12]

Public officials with a strong bent toward pensions favored a flat-grant-minus income method over family budgeting. Under a typical flat-grant-minus-income system, the state old age assistance statute specified a minimum dollar amount as necessary to maintain health and decency. The statute also specified exemptions as to income and resources. To determine ineligibility, or eligibility and the amount of the grant, income and resources in excess of the amount of allowed exemptions were subtracted from the minimum standard.

Those favoring the flat-grant-minus-income system argued that most of the elderly would fare better under this plan than under family budgeting. But this was not the only reason they were for it; it was also simpler to administer. And, while not completely automatic, it minimized discretion on the part of the decision maker. The program would be conducted like a well-run business. Honesty and common sense would be the qualifications most valued in the program's directors and staff. No social workers need apply. Their lengthy detailed investigations would be unnecessary.[13]

In arguing against the flat-grant-minus-income system, Hoey and her staff pointed to the inequities created by it. The system seemed to be evenhanded because most individuals received about the same amount of assistance payment. In reality, those entirely without means had to get by with only the minimum standard; those who had something to start with got the minimum on top of exempted income or assets. Such inequities were compounded, the BPA pointed out, when states faced a financial crisis—a crisis not infrequently induced by unsound planning for generous assistance to the aged. When such a crisis was met by applying across-the-board percentage cuts to grants, the indigent received less than the minimum standard while those better off to start with continued with at least the minimum, some with more.

The crux of the matter lay in the degree of attention paid to the individual case. Hoey explained:

The family budget is essentially a standard which may be adapted to an individualized approach, rather than an arbitrary formula. . . . It does result in differences in the amounts paid to individuals, and for this reason it has been misunderstood by legislators and administrators who feared charges of discrimination between individuals. Individuals applying for public assistance have unequal income and resources, and individual needs differ from case to case. Granting the same amount to all individuals in effect discriminates against those whose needs are most urgent.[14]

Admittedly, family budgeting was a more complicated process than reliance on an income-conditioned formula. Family budgeting required skill
for its execution: the skill of home economists to develop and keep current
a realistic minimum standard of living applicable to a given area and, most
of all, the skill of social workers to apply the general to the particular, to
personalize, to individualize from the mass. In the absence of skill in
execution, no special advantage could be claimed for family budgeting.
States judged successful in surmounting complication to ensure fairness to
the individual typically employed one or more home economists and utilized experienced social workers to train and supervise the less-skilled
staff members who faced the daily stream of applicants. But in other
states, though family budgeting was part of the plan, it had little or no
meaning. Standards had been based on guesswork or arbitrarily set at an
unbelievably low level. These states as well as some with technically
defensible standards failed to give proper instruction and supervision to
unskilled workers. Sometimes the best efforts by state agencies met resist-
ance from local agencies. These local administrators resented the independently made list of items to be budgeted, arguing that ancient
community rights were being usurped by distant authority ignorant of the
real needs of the local applicant. Where local agencies succeeded in going
their own way with no objective standard, the BPA could only warn of
jeopardy to the mandatory single statewide plan.

One of the most desirable features of family budgeting was its allowance for differences in place and circumstance, urban and rural, for
example. Yet the existence of an erratic pattern within a state could suggest that the right of individuals to substantially equal treatment had been
violated.[15] From the BPA's own testimony, states operating under flat-
grant-minus-income standards clearly held no monopoly on problems of
administration. The BPA was convinced, however, that time and effort
would clear away deficiencies noted in states whose plans encompassed
family budgeting. The bureau was equally convinced that states with income-conditioned standards were or would become hopelessly out of control. The general counsel and ultimately the board did not see it that way.

In the spring of 1937, the West Coast regional office notified the BPA
of proposed amendments to California's OAA and AB laws. California,
with its large proportion of elderly residents, the birthplace and continuing
stronghold of the Townsend movement, was bursting with pension sentiment. Since Republicans held the governorship and a majority in the legislature, proposed changes in the assistance laws were a conservative
response to insistent demands that more, preferably a great deal more, be

done for the elderly. The decision was for a flat-grant-minus-income system with generous exemptions. For OAA, the monthly grant was to be $35 minus income. Exempted from consideration as income were the rental value of premises owned and occupied by the applicant as well as other income up to a total of $15. The AB grant was set at $50 minus income and allowed exemptions of income up to $33.33.

On May 4, with these amendments pending in the California legislature, the board debated the recommendations from the BPA—disapproval—and the general counsel—approval—should the state submit a plan based on such legislation. Board member Miles reminded the meeting of his often-stated conviction of a state's right to determine need. Did it follow, Hoey countered, that a state had a right to determine the method of measuring need? Altmeyer reviewed past policy:

We have taken the position that these grants-in-aid shall be only in connection with a plan that provides aid to needy persons. The legislative record is clear that the Federal authorities shall have no right to pass upon the question of the degree of need in the individual cases. . . . Thus far we have said we shall require funds to be paid only to needy individuals; we have said they shall be paid only to needy individuals in accordance with their need. We have not yet taken the third step which you [Hoey] suggest and said whether the state or the federal authority shall establish the basis for determining the degree of need.

Altmeyer saw no way to disapprove the expected California plan. The basis for assistance was within the bounds of reason. It was not a flat grant, because the individual's need was to be determined after consideration of exemptions.

Far from prepared to take action regarding methods of determining need, yet clearly worried about the dangers of escalating OAA grants, the board instructed Hoey to try her powers of persuasion. She was going to California in a few days. Let her tell the state government what the board's thinking was, that the pending legislation was contrary to good social policy. She could also warn the state that if it persisted and later ran out of money to cover an entire eligible group, the board would be forced to withdraw the federal grant. Hoey's efforts came to nothing. The legislation passed, and on September 9 the board approved, over BPA objections, California's flat-grant-minus-income plans for OAA and AB.[16]

Though in a decided minority, the number of states choosing a flat-grant-minus-income method for the adult categories was increasing in 1937. Massachusetts, Nevada, and Washington adopted a $30 minus income standard, while Colorado pushed the scale up to $45 by constitutional amendment, even though the federal government was limited to a $30 matching ceiling.[17]

On the whole, the political leadership in these states could claim relative success in responding to pressures from old age pension advocates. Flat-grant-minus-income states made much higher payments to their elderly than states operating a budgetary deficiency system. To be sure, payments were greatly below the $200 a month demanded by the Townsendites. But payments in the so-called pension states were at or above the federal matching level in a large percentage of cases. Only a few other states made grants of this size to approximately the same portion of the caseload.

During the fiscal year 1937, both California and Colorado awarded grants of $35 or more to over 50 percent of those accepted for OAA. In California, 66.4 percent of the grants were for $30 and over; in Colorado, 82.3 percent reached that amount. Although Nevada and Washington awarded none above $30, and Massachusetts very few, all of these states had a high proportion of grants around $30. Among the family budgeting states, only New York and Kansas and the District of Columbia made any grants exceeding $35, New York having the highest percentage, but still under 10 percent. In only three states (Connecticut, New Hampshire, and Arizona) and the District of Columbia did payments of around $30 reach more than 20 percent. Nationally, only 8.4 percent of those receiving OAA got the federal maximum or a few dollars more.

For the country as a whole, the average payment per recipient in June 1938 was $19.48. The median payment, a more representative figure, was $18. In all of the flat grant states the median was higher than elsewhere, ranging from $23 in Washington to $38 in Colorado. In the fourteen family budgeting states where the median payment exceeded $18, the range was from $19 in Illinois and Minnesota to $26 in Connecticut and Arizona. In seventeen states, median payments fell below $15. In Mississippi, Arkansas, Georgia, and North Carolina the median was less than $10.[18]

Although the flat grant states pulled ahead, comparable wealthy states with a family budgeting system proved only slightly less generous in granting exemptions that would ensure higher grant awards. The day had passed—at least in dealing with the elderly—when hunger and rags were preconditions for aid. Accordingly, exemptions on income and resources were common to both systems. Most states exempted a home used as a residence, though some placed a limitation on the value of such property. A great many states exempted the value of personal property and savings

or investments of modest amounts. Some states required children to contribute to the support of parents if able to do so. Others exempted contributions from children, particularly if small or irregular. The trend seemed to
be away from strict adherence to relatives' responsibility. Many states
sought to recover something upon the death of a recipient, some by establishing a first lien on real property or a claim on the estate. States on the
flat grant system often exempted small amounts of earnings from work.
Exemption for earnings was not usually specified in states on the family
budgeting system, but allowance was made for extra food and clothing for
those who went out to work.[19]

With all these similarities among states, no matter what the system, and
with pressures for liberalization mounting everywhere, how long would it
take before all distinctions disappeared in substance if not in form? True,
the family budgeting states more often administered the program through
rule and regulation than states on the flat grant system, where standards
were prescribed by law. Seemingly, the state welfare department that operated under general legislative authorization was a comparatively free
agent. In reality, the area for discretion was only as wide as could be
tolerated in a democratic system confronted by a dynamic issue.

At the risk of seeming illiberal, Hoey and her social workers stood firm
in opposition to blanket exemptions, particularly if prescribed by law.
During the discussion of the pending California legislation, Hoey bore
down especially hard on the $15 earnings exemption, and then went on to
advocate a new policy. The board should insist that all resources available
to an individual be considered in investigating the need of each applicant
and allow no exclusions of regular income, Hoey maintained.[20]

At a meeting in December 1938, Chairman Altmeyer and board member George Bigge encouraged a free exchange with regional office staff.
Foremost in the minds of everyone was the movement toward flat grants.
In making the federal match conditional on deduction of income, the
board had applied the only brake, keeping the grants somewhat below
$30. Larger amounts were being discussed by the public—amounts such
as $40, $50, $60 were thought reasonable. The country could not support
such a fiscal burden, declared Altmeyer. A $40 monthly grant to everyone
aged sixty and over would mean collection through taxes from all persons
with incomes over $5,000, with other government costs borne from in-
comes below $5,000.

Rank-and-file social workers attending the meeting saw the solution the
same way that Hoey did—tighten up the means test. "We can't say we are
giving assistance strictly on a needs basis if we don't take the total picture

into consideration in figuring each grant," a regional representative insisted. This meant income and resources in one column, need in the other, calculated individual by individual. If the individual owned a home, no rent allowance as such, but taxes and upkeep should be entered in the needs column. The value of food produced and consumed at home should be entered in the resources column, not exempted from consideration as in some states.

But Altmeyer and Bigge saw the folly of slamming the door on all strategies of the pension movement. Too rigid a stance might drive the moderates to support more extreme measures. Equity was one thing; fairness another. Altmeyer thought the states sought fairness in exempting modest accumulations:

It may be wise public policy to exclude certain things in determining need. There is no hard and fast rule that can be laid down. You have to say that within reason certain things may be exempted. And why should they be exempted? Perhaps to encourage that old-fashioned virtue of individual initiative and thrift, because if a person can benefit to some extent, then you have encouraged him to make some provision. That is true whether he is able to take advantage of it or not; at least, you have extended the encouragement to him.

Similarly, Bigge favored a modest exemption for earnings. Suppose the budget did allow a little more—if the recipient worker needed more clothing, the extra clothing allowance wasn't helping him at all if his earnings were subtracted from his grant.

Altmeyer probed to get at the differences he and Bigge had with the social workers. Suppose there were two households, one neat and clean with obviously self-respecting people, the other a rundown shack on the wrong side of the tracks with slovenly people. Wouldn't the good social worker decide that the first family had been thrifty and should be allowed more to maintain a higher standard of living than the second that had been shiftless? The social workers agreed that they would gear the assistance payment toward the family's previous standard of living. There was but one explanation for the seeming inconsistency, Altmeyer concluded—social workers feared that state legislatures would rob them of their professional skill.

Altmeyer could agree that professional skill was a very fine thing—"an idealistic thing. Individual case work, recognizing the family as a unit, taking into consideration its whole past history and making grants accordingly is the best way, but. . . . " There simply weren't enough social workers to handle each case on such a refined basis. In any event, wouldn't the establishment of a standard budget limit the extent of discretion applied to the individual case?

As a practical matter, Altmeyer lectured the social workers, the board had to allow state legislatures some leeway: "If we don't, they will go the whole way and we will get flat grants," perhaps even flat grants paid from federal funds, at which point, "we will sink." For the present, Altmeyer urged the regional representatives to work hard to convince the states to keep exemptions within reason. For the future, he mused, some help might be found through amendments to the Social Security Act.[21]

The 1939 Amendments

Hoey had seen what was coming as early as October 1936. Old age assistance and old age insurance were on a collision course, she told Bane. And, barring some drastic change, contributory old age insurance would suffer total demolition. She pointed to the statistics. Forty-two states already had OAA programs. The 1937 legislative sessions were sure to bring in several more. Look at the average grant level—more than $18 a month. Consider the pressures to abolish the means test. Flat grants to the aged were far from untried. Most European countries adhered to a flat grant system, though many in addition required contributions from employer and employee. Hoey noted also that European governments had found it necessary to supplement employer-employee contributions to ensure the solvency of their old age pension funds.

Bane had asked Hoey for suggestions on possible amendments to the Social Security Act. She warned:

If there is a lapse of five years before the contributory scheme goes into effect and the average grant after five years of contribution is less than that which can be secured under the non-contributory scheme it would seem to me to be practically impossible to put into effect the contributory plan. . . . We have made a great point of the fact that persons could receive the pension as a right on the contributory basis. If, however, in a five-year period, the means test is lessened and the right of the individual is established for the non-contributory scheme, then the distinction between the two systems is eliminated.

Hoey concluded that payments under old age insurance must begin "much sooner than 1942," even if initial contributions had to be raised and a federal supplement made.

Regardless of what steps were taken to make the two old age pension systems more compatible, some way should be found to get more federal money to the poor southern and southwestern states. Under the uniform 50 percent match, Hoey pointed out, states with the most limited resources received less from the federal government than the wealthy ones, simply because the poor states could not afford to set a decent standard for their needy aged. Again referring to European practices, Hoey noted that these countries collected more comprehensive information about local financial resources than was true in the United States.[22]

Landon's defeat in November 1936 and the Supreme Court's 7–2 decision affirming the constitutionality of Title II the following May boosted the morale of all those who greatly preferred old age insurance to old age assistance. But neither the election nor the Supreme Court decision changed the facts as delineated in Hoey's October 1936 memo. If anything, subsequent developments were proving her argument more and more correct.

During 1937 and 1938, the insurance concept came under attack from yet another angle. At this time, various economists (including at least two at the Treasury Department), private insurance experts, and business and labor leaders began to object to both the payroll tax and the trust fund. The payroll tax and the trust fund were, of course, what the planners had deemed essential to an insurance system. This was the way private insurance companies operated—premiums paid in, money invested. With this difference: money in the Social Security trust fund was invested in government bonds. Though not voicing identical objections, these critics believed the tax and the trust fund threatened the still shaky economy by curtailing consumer spending and investment, and saw the trust fund as an invitation to liberalization of benefits. M. Albert Linton, president of Provident Mutual Life Insurance Company of Philadelphia, led the opposition to the trust fund. The danger, as he saw it, was political, not actuarial, and would originate with Congress, not the Social Security Board. He summed up his frankly cynical view of politicians: "Enough experience has been gained in the field of pensions to make it clear that the politician has but scant appreciation of the significance of a reserve fund and of the necessity of foregoing the expenditure of current revenue in favor of investing it to benefit voters of the more or less distant future."[23] By 1980, when the old age insurance program would mature, the trust fund would have accumulated $47 billion. Under the tutelage of Linton, Senator Arthur H. Vandenberg, the Michigan Republican who sat on the Finance Committee and led the opposition forces in Congress, found it "scarcely conceivable that rational men should propose such an unmanagcablc accumulation of funds in one place in a democracy." Vandenberg pressed hard in committee and on the floor, introducing a concurrent resolution calling on the Social Security Board to offer a plan for abandonment of the huge reserve. Finding himself outmaneuvered, Altmeyer reluctantly agreed to the appointment of an advisory council made up of the usual mix of business, labor, and the public.

But he put off calling the council together for as long as he could. If forced to arrange a meeting, he wanted to have something new to offer for consideration. He used the spring and summer as a time to analyze, consult, and plan, and by mid-September 1937 he was sufficiently optimistic to engage the President. He thought it "possible," he informed Roosevelt, "not only to offset these attacks on the Social Security Act, but really to utilize them to advance a socially desirable program, fully in accord with present fundamental principles . . . and within our financial capacity."[24]

To Altmeyer a "socially desirable program" would build on the "fundamental principles" of social insurance. Attacks on the insurance principle, specifically on the trust fund, would be utilized by going off a "full reserve." How? By "increasing and extending both the size and character of the benefits." Dipping back into Witte's original list of possible insurable conditions, he suggested an additional allowance for wives of old age insurance beneficiaries and also that survivors—widows and dependent children—of deceased workers who had paid into the system be entitled to benefits. Echoing Hoey, he argued that old age insurance payments should bcgin carlicr than planned and that payments to those retiring during the early years of the system's operation be liberalized. These immediate and increased expenditures would reduce and slow the growth of the trust fund.

This was not all. Beginning insurance payments sooner and assuring beneficiaries of larger amounts could be expected to take the steam out of the Townsend movement and discourage flat grants in OAA. As Altmeyer told FDR, changes along these lines would supplement Hopkins's program for the unemployed and, "as time went on take care of a larger and larger segment of the problem without affecting the federal budget during the next fifteen years and without the necessity of increasing the present total payroll taxes more than 1% (figured on the payroll) during that period of time."[25]

Ingenious, if not inspired, the reforms outlined by Altmeyer were well calculated to disarm conservative critics and fortify liberal advocates of social insurance. Perkins and Hopkins were supportive, as was the President. On April 29, 1938, Roosevelt told reporters about the administration's intentions, adding that he would expect a detailed study with recommendations before Congress convened the following January.[26]

The Advisory Council, appointed in May 1937, proved more than willing to underscore the insurance principle. Its recommendations, submitted on December 10, 1938, endorsed the essentials of the Altmeyer package. In strongly advocating social insurance over old age assistance, the council pleaded for equity. Other claimants—dependent children, the sick and disabled, the unemployed, the low wage tax-paying wage earner—should not be shortchanged as they would be if the elderly received too large a share of scarce funds. By virtue of its contributory method of financing, social insurance for the aged would tend to reduce pressures to bring about a greater and greater portion of public funds into "free" old age pensions.[27]

The most important elements of the administration's recommendations for amending the Social Security Act—essentially those presented in the Altmeyer memorandum—emerged intact from Congress. The huge reserve being built up to cover old age insurance, inviting raids on the Treasury for all manner of pet projects, was halted in favor of a pay-as-you-go system. As signed into law by the President on August 10, 1939, the date for beginning monthly old age insurance payments was advanced to January 1, 1940—less than six months away. A supplementary allowance for elderly wives of insurance beneficiaries was provided. Survivor benefits, to be paid monthly rather than in a lump sum, were authorized for widows aged sixty-five and over and for all widows with dependent children. The level of benefits was increased by changing the method of calculation to employ an average of past earnings rather than total accumulated wages as the base. The program, known thereafter as Old Age and Survivors Insurance (OASI), had moved in just four years from individual to family protection.

To be sure, the administration did not get everything it requested. A somewhat tentative recommendation to insure against permanent and total · disability was not picked up. A greater disappointment was Congress's refusal to expand coverage to include agricultural workers, domestic servants, and employees of nonprofit organizations. The Ways and Means Committee reported itself unanimously opposed to expansion to these groups. The administration accepted without enthusiasm congressional action to freeze payroll contributions through the year 1942, forestalling a scheduled rise to $1\frac{1}{2}$ percent on January 1, 1940, and further conceding to conservative critics. All in all, however, the administration won an impressive vote of confidence in the insurance principle. In the House, the count was 364–2 in favor; in the Senate, 57–8.[28]

The strong affirmation of social insurance became evident as well in the handling of amendments on public assistance. Congress balked at granting what the board considered the most important and liberalizing public assistance amendments, but willingly agreed to tighten up rules on eligibility. The tightening manifested itself around the old question of "need" and how to define it. Up to this time, the board had sought to protect itself from challenge by reliance on the preambles to the public assistance titles, and by persuading the congressional committees to include "needy" in the language of the appropriation act. Now that the Social Security Act was up for major amendment, the board moved to make its position unassailable by a change in the language of the act itself. In order to remove the last trace of ambiguity, the board sought yet another change—to require that any income and resources be considered in determining the need of an individual. Wary of alerting the Townsendites to loopholes in the present law, the board made no written recommendations on the subject. Nor did Altmeyer raise the question in his public testimony. Rather he waited until the doors were closed in the executive session of Ways and Means to present the problem and suggest new words to solve it. In reporting out the bill, the committee explained:

The purpose of all three assistance programs is further clarified by inserting the word "needy" in the definitions of those who may receive old age assistance, aid to dependent children, and aid to the blind. A closely related clarifying amendment is applied to all three assistance titles and provides that the states, in determining need, must consider any other income and resources of individuals claiming assistance.

As agreed to by Congress the income and resources amendment was to become effective July 1, 1942.

But Ways and Means could not resist showing its goodwill toward the aged. On its own initiative, the committee raised the OAA maximum from $30 to $40 monthly, $20 to be matched by federal funds. The committee's action placed in jeopardy the entire strategy to hold the line on OAA while OASI caught up. J. Douglas Brown, the most knowledgeable and most vocal pro-insurance member of the Advisory Council, opposed the increase. In his testimony before the Senate Finance Committee, he expressed doubt that it would be of much help to particular individuals. It seemed more of "a gesture" than a significant move toward solving overall problems. Brown, an economist at Princeton, expected the additional funds to be picked up by the wealthier states, while the poor states would continue as before, unable to afford even the lower $30 maximum. Echoing the words of the Advisory Council, which he may well have drafted, Brown summed up his concern:

Now the problem does arise as to what proportion of a state's income it cares to put into old age assistance over against the public school system, over against dependent children, and many other things. I do think there is a danger if the Federal government offers very attractive ratios to a state for the old age assistance group that it will tempt the state to expand old age assistance at the expense of other necessary social services.[29]

Need, Ability, Willingness to Pay

Since the early months of the program the Social Security Board had deplored the low public assistance payments that prevailed in the poor states of the South and Southwest. All but three of the seventeen states with median old age assistance payments under $15 monthly were located in these areas. Though making no secret of his preference for insurance, Altmeyer possessed a keen sense of loyalty and duty to the program as a whole, and was consequently not inclined to countenance low standards in any part of the board's work. He raised the issue early, arguing that federal funds allotted to the states for public assistance—"our money"— should not be "spread so thin" as to fall to the emergency relief level. If state funds were short, he preferred giving fewer persons an adequate amount to live on, even though others might get nothing from Social Security programs. The board did not—probably could not—agree to Altmeyer's suggestion that such a policy be adopted, Chairman Winant remarking that Altmeyer was making a false distinction between "relief" and public assistance programs that were misnamed "pensions."[30]

In the BPA low standards were regarded as a disgrace to the social work profession, which held firmly that once need was established, payments must be adequate to ensure a decent level of living. The BPA also frowned upon other actions that states resorted to when chronically or temporarily short of money. States experienced in public welfare tended to limit the number of recipients, while preserving the established standard of assistance (Altmeyer's preference). The welfare agencies in these states either stopped taking applications or, more usually, stopped putting eligibles on the rolls. The effect was to create waiting lists certain to consist of a significant number of needy persons. Frequently the inaction appeared downright cynical, as when waiting lists occurred in the very states that had enacted generous old age assistance laws. In the fall of 1938, Los

Angeles County had a waiting list of 12,000 persons. Ohio had more than 20,000 on its waiting list, with investigations running six months to four years behind. In Delaware, investigations of applications took place only upon the death or withdrawal of a recipient. Nationwide, in June 1939, an average of 13 applications per 100 old age assistance recipients was pending, with a range from 0.9 applications per 100 recipients in Utah to 204.2 applications per 100 recipients in Georgia.

When state welfare agencies chose the spread-thin method of conserving funds they most often chose an across-the-board percentage cut in the amount of individual assistance payments. This was less complicated than figuring out some graduated system that favored the most needy, but worked the most hardship upon that group. The percentage cut was popular with administrators wishing to avoid pressure on the agency. An observer from the Social Science Research Council explained:

A recipient of a small amount is less apt to complain, appeal, or rally political or other support to his aid than is an applicant whose claim has been denied or a recipient whose grant has been discontinued. Recipients may all receive a mere pittance, and thus no single eligible person really attains security from want; and though the program may be, in reference to its objective, a total failure, yet, so long as each eligible person receives something, most of them will not complain lest they lose that; and since all receive little, few can complain that others are more favored.

Altmeyer and the other members of the board agreed with the BPA that waiting lists were the lesser of the two evils. This position was taken despite the fact that waiting lists raised a question of conformity that percentage cuts did not. According to the general counsel waiting lists violated the act in three ways: uniform operation; efficient administration; and right to a fair hearing. Percentage cuts could be made without fear of legal challenge under the appropriation section of the act that enabled each state to furnish financial assistance to aged needy individuals, "as far as practicable under the conditions in such State," and to the silence of the act regarding standards of assistance payments.

The board preferred waiting lists to percentage cuts because lists offered a greater opportunity to develop a statewide system of adequate assistance in the future. Thousands of applicants waiting to present their case or to receive a promised check were bound to arouse public sympathy if not stir up trouble. Regional representatives could needle the state agency about noncompliance, even though no action was seriously intended by the board. In the more prosperous states, such pressures could be expected to induce governors to call for, and legislatures to pass, appropriations and

increases in taxes in amounts sufficient to meet the requirements of persons eligible for assistance.

In the board's view, the resort to percentage cuts meant lasting program
deficiencies. With little complaint from recipients, little was likely to be
publicized, and community leaders, particularly political leaders, remained ignorant of the true situation. Consequently the spread-thin policy
would fail to create a climate of opinion that would force action to channel
sufficient funds into the program. Regional representatives tried, usually
unsuccessfully, to discourage state agencies from taking this seemingly
easy way out of fiscal crisis.[31]

Pressures from without, needling from within, and other persuasive
techniques might well bring about desired change in states with average or
above-average resources—the states with highly developed industrial and
commercial facilities or rich agricultural production. These states could
afford to take care of their needy at a decent level. It was pointless to make
such representations in the poorer states, however, where resources were
limited to low-priced crops or extractive industries. The poor states were
doing all they could. Studies showed that their fiscal effort exceeded that
of many wealthier states.[32]

State per capita income ranged from $923 in Delaware to $207 in Mississippi. Fourteen states, located in New England, and the middle Atlantic, east north central, mountain, and Pacific regions of the country, had
per capita income levels of over $600. In eight states located in the south
Atlantic, east south central, and west south central regions, per capita
income fell below $300. Delaware, with its waiting list and median OAA
payments of $10 a month, was a state worth talking to about adequate
assistance. Mississippi, though its median grant was only $5, was not.
States like Delaware were rare. The expected correspondence between
high per capita income and high assistance payments usually held true.
The eight states with lowest per capita income each had very low median
payments.[33]

The poor states obviously needed additional federal money if assistance
payments were to be increased. In her October 1936 memo to Bane, Hoey
referred to studies then under way in the Bureau of Research and Statistics
that were examining alternative ways of helping the poor states by some
sort of an "equalization" scheme. Altmeyer pushed the studies and actively supported the equalization idea. He pushed for two reasons now. As
a matter of principle, he wanted decent assistance standards in all the
states. He had also come to fear that the poor states would drive for full
federal assumption of old age assistance if they continued to face no in-

crease at all. Yet Altmeyer opposed an increase in the total cost of public assistance. To avoid an increase he instructed the researchers in December 1936 "to reduce the amount going to the richer states in order to grade up the poorer states, but I would hope not to any considerable degree."[34]

For their part, the researchers were entering a new field of inquiry. Very little data about the comparative wealth of states had been collected at the national level. Significant progress in measurement of the national income—forerunners of the GNP—lay but a few years behind. The first study, Simon Kuznets's *National Income, 1929–1932*, was published as a Senate Document in 1934, a year after Kuznets had joined the Commerce Department's Bureau of Foreign and Domestic Commerce. No studies of state income were published until April 1940. In fact a concerted effort to measure state income did not begin at Commerce until December 1938, two years after Social Security Board research began.[35] Nevertheless, assurance was received from the experts at Commerce that state per capita income would suffice to measure economic capacity. The board's research was narrowed accordingly.

Flying in the face of numerous uncertainties, the board recommended, and the President endorsed, a change in the federal matching formula to a percentage calculated to vary inversely with the economic capacity of a particular state. The President's message to Congress, written by Altmeyer, ventured beyond the immediate purpose, opening up the possibility that the new method of matching might, in the future, be applicable to other federal grants-in-aid. The board considered the federal matching change the most important of its proposed public assistance amendments.

Like the proposal on consideration of income and resources in establishing eligibility for public assistance, discussion of the matching change was confined to the executive session of Ways and Means. There it fared badly. At some point during the course of the preparatory work at the board, the phrase "variable grant" was substituted for the more positive sounding "equalization grant." The substitution was unfortunate, because the term "variable grant" reinforced the suspicions of committee members that the scheme was laid on shifting sands. At the root of their distrust was the method used to apply the formula. Comparing state economic capacity by statistical analysis of various data was so new and mysterious as to render the method questionable as a basis for parceling out federal money. Some committee members also feared increased pressure for a complete federal takeover if the time-honored 50–50 pattern of matching were broken. Altmeyer, it will be recalled, feared the opposite—irresistible pressure from the poor states for a federal takeover if nothing were done to help them. Ways and Means voted against inclusion of the amendment in the House bill.

Similarly, the Finance Committee voted down the variable grant amendment in the form proposed, but there was more sympathy here for helping the poor states. Tom Connally, a member from Texas, proposed a formula that would allow two-thirds federal matching for the first $15 of the average monthly old age assistance payment in a state plus one-half federal matching of the balance, up to a total state average payment of $40. Under the Connally formula, the federal government would assume a larger proportion of the cost in all states, but a larger proportion still in the poorer states. Although favored by Chairman Joe Robinson of Arkansas, the committee rejected it. When Connally took his amendment to the floor, however, it passed after further amendment by Senator Ed Johnson of Colorado requiring the states to contribute no less than $10 monthly per recipient.

When the House and Senate bills went to conference, the Connally amendment caused a prolonged deadlock. Altmeyer then drafted an amendment to continue 50–50 matching but set a minimum monthly federal grant of $7.50 per recipient. Under this compromise, which was agreeable to the senators, about $10 million additional federal money annually would have benefited fourteen states, mostly those with low per capita income. The Altmeyer proposal was much less costly than the Connally amendment, which was estimated to run about $120 million. Still the House conferees refused to go along. When the entire bill appeared in jeopardy as the adjournment of Congress drew near, Altmeyer approached the President for assistance in support of the compromise. To Altmeyer's surprise, Roosevelt came down on the side of those in Congress who thought a change would open the floodgates. Ignoring his own message, Roosevelt went on to denounce variable grants as "lopsided grants" and to refuse to support any change in the 50–50 match. Whereupon the Senate conferees retreated from the Connally amendment and the deadlock was broken.

Thirty years later Altmeyer remained puzzled about Roosevelt's about-face. Had the President not absorbed the content of the message? Or the reminder that Altmeyer had sent at another stage of the fiasco? It is at least arguable that Roosevelt changed his mind when he heard about the position of the Ways and Means Committee. As Altmeyer concluded shortly after the struggle was over, varying the matching formula was not a question for decision by experts. It was instead, he told BPA staff, "a large political question," and he predicted a long wait before Congress moved to resolve the issue.[36]

If the matching formula seemed a lost cause for the foreseeable future, the board could take satisfaction in the passage of two other amendments. Each tended to remove partisan politics from public assistance administration. One answered a long-felt need for greater control over the qualifications of state and local personnel; the other ensured the confidentiality of recipient case records. The unwanted negative phrase contained in the original act that excluded the board from participating in state actions "relating to selection, tenure of office, and compensation of personnel" was dropped. Added, effective January 1, 1940, was a positive provision mandating personnel standards on a merit basis. In his testimony, Altmeyer was at pains to assure Ways and Means that a merit system did not mean a requirement for "trained social workers . . . throughout the operation of state agencies." On the contrary, in those states having merit systems, the percentage of trained social workers was less than 5 percent. Altmeyer was responding to complaints from representatives of both parties: complaints about lengthy social investigations of the elderly, with checking into medicines and other personal matters; overemphasis on property ownership and on support from relatives; and attempts by federal regional representatives to influence state legislation. As the Democrat John McCormack of Massachusetts put it: "Congress has not, let us say, an antifeeling, but they have a feeling of hesitancy, if not opposition—and I am one of them—toward those fine people who are the social workers of the country, operating out of Washington on a matter which we feel could be best administered locally." But Altmeyer insisted that "instead of encouraging Federal domination, a merit system does the reverse." He recalled the painful recent past, when after reports of irregularities board staff had to go into the states and make special investigations, hold hearings, even withhold grants with resulting "worry and hardship" for the needy. He recalled the "bad situation" that resulted from the use of recipients' names for political campaign literature rife with "promises, counter promises and warnings and counter warnings." Confidentiality of records and above all a merit system would promote mutual trust, producing stable and impersonal federal-state relations, he concluded.[37]

Passage of the 1939 amendments marked a powerful bipartisan endorsement—first and foremost, of the social insurance principle; second, but not inconsequential, of the comprehensive protective concept of the Social Security Act itself. Certainly Altmeyer saw it this way, sharing his pride and pleasure with central and field staff of the bureaus of Public Assistance and Employment Security:

There never was, either on the floor of Congress or before the committees, in open session or executive session, the slightest trace of a partisan approach to any of these recommendations of the Board. . . .

They didn't follow all our suggestions, but nevertheless they were thoroughly considered, and even when they didn't follow them it wasn't a flat rejection, but a feeling that at the present time under the present circumstances probably it wasn't as expedient to follow through entirely all of the recommendations of the Board. So I think we have a right to be encouraged and very happy not only because of the very great accomplishments achieved through legislative action this year, but the fact that our recommendations did receive such a sympathetic consideration and unquestionably paved the way for consideration in the future, not only of these suggestions that have not been followed in whole, but also of any additional suggestions we may develop as a result of increased experience and thinking.[38]

Yet the final form which old age security would take remained an unsettled, if not quite so unsettling, a question in 1940 as it had been throughout the previous five years of the dual system. During the debate in the House the low projected payments from social insurance ($35 a month after 40 years of work at $100) were compared with public assistance in the flat grant state of California, where payments were already at $30. The poor states lined up to support the amendment of Mississippi representative William M. Colmer, which provided a $4-to-$1 federal match up to a $20 maximum. The defeat of the Colmer amendment—174 to 97—while far from close, was nevertheless a reminder that in a good many quarters the state old age "pension" system was believed worth shoring up. The increase in the maximum to $40 was yet another.[39]

5

An Orphan Program

LITTLE NOTICED during the framing of the Social Security Act, more or less slipped in to round things out, then funded on a less comprehensive basis than Old Age Assistance or Aid to the Blind, the program for Aid to Dependent Children continued in relative obscurity during the shakedown years when support for the elderly emerged as the dominant issue. The Social Security Board agreed with the BPA that excessive attention to the needs of the aged led to disregard of the needs of children. The observation was true as far as it went. If most of the available money went to the aged, funds to care for the many needy children would be insufficient. But the root of the matter lay elsewhere. Unlike the aged, children did not vote, held no property, and made but trifling purchases. Children could not, on their own, form a powerful competing constituency.

In the overwhelming number of cases, a child had one or two adults responsible for his or her support, adults who, if unemployed, were eligible for unemployment compensation or public works jobs. ADC was designed to cover the unusual cases—according to the act, children "deprived of parental support or care by reason of the death, continued absence from the home, or physical or mental incapacity of a parent." To be sure, this special group of children had some adult backing—women's organizations, child welfare agencies, and on the federal level, the Children's Bureau. But compared with the old folks lobby, this was minuscule.[1]

Only the Nice Families?

Even the Children's Bureau, whose chiefs had drafted Title IV in full expectation that they would administer it, thought in terms of a small, select program. In making cost estimates, the bureau assumed that only about 50 percent of the FERA caseload in this category would be eligible for the new program. "Not all fatherless families can possibly qualify for mothers' pensions—probably not more than half of them," so the bureau informed the Committee on Economic Security. Taking half of the 358,000 female-headed families currently on FERA rolls meant 179,000 "qualifying" families. When this total was added to the 109,000 families currently receiving state mother's pensions, roughly 300,000 families with about 700,000 children would seem to qualify for ADC. Using a monthly average payment of $40 for cities and $20 elsewhere (admittedly an inadequate standard but higher than currently prevailing payments) the Children's Bureau estimated a total annual outlay of $120 million, about $125 million less than what was then being spent to support these families. Because a gradual transition from FERA to ADC was expected, federal contributions of $25 million per year for the first couple of years, increasing ultimately to not more than $50 million, were calculated. The Committee on Economic Security went along with these estimates in its report to the President.[2]

The number of children receiving ADC quickly reached and surpassed Children's Bureau figures. In June 1938, 243,000 families with over 600,000 children were receiving ADC. By the following year families numbered 298,000, children 718,000, at a total cost of $103 million and a federal share of $34 million. Even so, the board's Bureau of Research and Statistics thought the program was failing to reach a large number of needy children. Research and Statistics admittedly lacked comprehensive hard data to prove its assertion. Its "tentative estimates" were based on scattered reports. No reliable statistical series existed. Yet Research and Statistics believed it had enough data to indicate that no fewer than one million children were potentially eligible for ADC, with a likelihood that almost two million needy were in the pool of eligibles.[3]

In an article written for the 1939 *Social Work Year Book*, Hoey suggested several reasons for the estimated gap between assistance needed and assistance received. Most obvious was incomplete coverage. Eight states—Connecticut, Illinois, Iowa, Kentucky, Mississippi, Nevada, South Dakota, Texas—and the territory of Alaska had no ADC program, although these states continued to grant some assistance under their mother's aid laws. Reports from the states with ADC programs raised puzzling questions. On the whole, state plans followed the liberal lines of the Social Security Act. Why, then, were more than 50 percent of the families being aided because of the death of the father? The numbers of women aged fourteen to thirty-four years who were widowed were slightly fewer than those divorced. Yet only 28 percent of ADC families were headed by a woman whose spouse was absent from the home due to divorce, separation, or desertion. Parental disability accounted for 22 percent of ADC cases. Was disability being defined too narrowly? Were illegitimate children—90 births per 1,000 nationwide—getting more than token consideration? Only 2 percent of children living with unmarried mothers were represented in the caseload. In five states no illegitimate children were accepted; eleven other states assisted fewer than fifty cases.[4]

The great variance among states in the proportion of children aided could be explained only in part by state fiscal capability. The number of children receiving assistance, compared with the total population under sixteen years, averaged 24 per 1,000, ranging from more than 40 per 1,000 in seven states to 16 or less per 1,000 in eight others.

Drawing on reports from her field representatives, Hoey attributed the puzzling characteristics of the program to "opinion and attitude." Although restrictive qualifications regarding the mother's character—pervasive in mother's aid—were no longer so obtrusive in state ADC law and regulation, the viewpoint that inspired the administration of earlier programs remained potent, subtly but surely affecting ADC administration. Hoey spoke for the board in announcing her stand to her peers in social work, unmistakably putting miles between the Bureau of Public Assistance and the Children's Bureau: "Denying children this form of aid because their parent's behavior does not conform to a certain pattern is coming to be recognized as no solution of such problems. Yet transfer from general relief to aid to dependent children is still frequently made on a basis of promoting the nice families." In her reference to "nice" families, Hoey took a swipe at Edith Abbott, who had used this phrase in testifying in behalf of ADC at the 1935 hearings on the Social Security Act. A simple addition of the 350,000 children disqualified by the Children's Bureau brought the number of needy children to the figure of one million, the lower estimate made by Research and Statistics.[5]

Hoey knew full well that many of these needy families were far from perfect. But she maintained that "in many border-line cases the family— which may have genuine values for the child in spite of its inadequacies

—can be kept together if the parent can be offered practical and constructive guidance." Hoey insisted that state and local practice reflect objective standards laid down in federal and state law, so that equitable provision could be made for all families with eligible dependent children. This meant more than determination of eligibility and a cash grant, basic as these were. Equally important were services to help the family deal with problems of housing and health and, if necessary, to provide counseling for the well-being of the children in the family setting. Overall, the goal was "adequate and appropriate assistance and service for each child and each family in accordance with its particular needs."

Such conditions could not be fulfilled through state or local general assistance. General assistance was poorly funded. No federal, and often little or no state money, was invested in the program. In all but the most liberal urban areas, general assistance was a throwback to pre-Depression days, with grocery orders and warehouse clothing rather than a money payment. Even where a money payment was made, it was usually less than that available through ADC.[6]

Concern about the lagging ADC program took hold early in the BPA and was conveyed to Executive Director Bane and the board. Top administration encouraged staff to explore ways to bring about improvement. Could Title IV be interpreted so as to strengthen the board's hand in liberalizing state and local administration? What amendments to the Social Security Act might be feasible? With what expected effect? Or, given the federal-state relationship in public assistance, would desirable change come about only after a sustained effort of education, interpretation, and negotiation—state by state, county by county?

A review of the legislative history of Title IV confirmed what everyone already knew—the fixed bond to mother's aid. The President's 1935 Message to Congress called for federal grants to states in support of "existing mother's pension systems." During the congressional debate, the chairman of Ways and Means justified federal aid in order to "permit the mothers' pension type of care to become nationally operative." Federal restrictions on state action were minimal. In emphasizing state freedom of choice and action, the chairman of Finance dismissed the idea that states would be required to help every needy child—a burden too great for many states. "The provisions are not for general relief of poor children but are designed to hold broken families together," he said. States could shape the contours of their programs according to their own lights. One state might "limit aid to children living with their widowed mother," another might include "children without parents living with near relatives." In reporting out the bill, Ways and Means noted that states could impose additional eligibility requirements—for example, those having to do with financial resources or moral character.[7]

Amending Title IV

Legislative history revealed nothing to strengthen the board's hand in liberalizing state practice. Perhaps an entirely new departure should be tried, one that would make a clean break with mother's aid. This could be achieved through amendment to Title IV, specifically to change the definition of what constituted a dependent child, to get rid of all the qualifications about death, absence, and incapacity of parents. A dependent child would be simply a child "deprived of parental support or care."

The board quickly backed away from this drastic approach. Such an amendment could bring the federal government back into "this business of relief" through the back door, because unemployment certainly caused loss of parental support. Persons laid off or awaiting assignment to WPA would fall into this group. Families with children under a specified age who were receiving general relief for whatever reason would be eligible under the shortened definition. In sum, only single adults without children or families lacking required residence without minor children would be ineligible for assistance under Title IV.

There was little reason to believe that such a proposal would get anywhere. A small but influential number of social workers were sure to protest change. This group, headed by the Abbott sisters and their colleagues at the University of Chicago, was strongly in favor of retaining special categories, because, they argued, their special needs attracted public support which in turn encouraged higher standards of administration and levels of assistance. It was also recalled that the social work leadership based in New York had received little attention for its proposal for federal general relief at the hearings on the Social Security bill.

Helen Jeter, chief of the Division of Public Assistance Statistics, Bureau of Research and Statistics, felt that the board should firmly oppose an amendment that purported to change only the definition of a dependent child but would in reality change the character of public assistance. "If the Federal government is to re-enter the field of general relief," Jeter concluded, "the problem should be faced squarely and discussed openly and should not be dealt with by an amendment slipped into the Social Security Act under a title which has a quite different connotation." Neither Jeter nor the Abbotts, for that matter, opposed the extension of federal aid to help states carry the burden of general relief. But they insisted on an additional category, a separate title. This the board agreed with. A new title covering general relief was very much open to future consideration and was, in fact, recommended as early as 1940.[8]

The decision to leave the definition of dependent child intact left the federal government with only one major route toward liberalization within Title IV, the usual inducement offered in a federal/state program: more money. As the law then stood, the federal share in ADC was one-third, with a maximum of $18 for the first child and $12 for each additional child. The mother or other caretaker received no specific allowance. On the average, ADC families had 2.5 children.

In the participating states, the monthly payment per family averaged $31.29. Payments ranged from a high of $57.50 to a low of $10.65. Except in the higher-payment states, most families could not get along without supplementation from another source—work outside the home or assistance from general relief. ADC looked particularly inequitable when compared with OAA, where payments, usually for only one person, averaged $19.48 a month. The average ADC family of 3.5 persons was receiving less than half the amount of money granted to a sole recipient of OAA. With such facts on the line, there was every reason to expect favorable action to increase the amount of federal financial participation (FFP).[9]

In 1937, those planning the 1939 amendments hoped an increase in the FFP would cause ADC grants to rise to more adequate levels and, at the same time, encourage the addition of more liberal standards of eligibility. Not a clean break with mother's aid, to be sure, but better care and extended coverage of needy children.

Most obvious in any discussion about financial incentives was the unequal treatment of the programs in regard to the federal match. States could receive only one-third of their administrative expenditures for ADC. Reimbursement was at the rate of one-half for OAA and AB. There was no logic behind the ADC arrangement. The explanation lay in the lack of attention paid to Title IV during the initial passage of the Social Security Act. The Children's Bureau looked to past practice—a fifty-fifty state-local financial share, added a federal share, and divided by three. The same reasoning could have been applied to OAA, for the same division of state-local financing obtained in the administration of old age pension laws prior to 1936. No one doubted that Congress would act to bring ADC on a par with the adult programs by authorizing a 50 percent federal match. The Social Security Board put the 50 percent match for ADC on its agenda of legislative recommendations as early as 1937.[10]

Also obviously in need of an increase was the maximum amount—$18 for the first child, $12 for each additional child—subject to the federal match. Arrival at a recommendation for revision of the maximum was not nearly so clear-cut as was equalization of the federal match, although here, too, Title IV had been little scrutinized for inherent logic and fairness. The maximums had purportedly been set to parallel aid to dependent children of veterans, but unlike the veteran's program, the mother had been omitted from the ADC calculation.

Discussion about possible ways to liberalize the maximum took on a freewheeling character during the planning days at the board. Because ADC—unlike OAA and AB—was a family program and was remote from political pressure, it might be desirable and feasible to get rid of the maximum altogether. Family budgeting could then be applied in a realistic way to arrive at family need and a rational assistance payment. An alternative was to retain a maximum but raise its level.[11]

Although OAA was different, ADC could not be isolated from the pressures around pensions for the elderly. A decision to recommend elimination of the maximum in ADC might encourage abandonment of maximums in OAA and AB as well. As a legislative specialist told a field conference, BPA chiefs feared "possible dangers to the other two titles if we opened up the top limit by providing no maximum whatever [in ADC]." The bureau expected considerable congressional agitation to raise OAA grants. "It is possible," the legislative liaison continued, "if we remove the level on aid to dependent children, we are going to have something happen to old age assistance we may not like, and there will be no provision to safeguard grants on the basis of individual need."[12]

After the decision was made to recommend retention of a maximum in ADC, discussion shifted to possible dollar amounts. Some thought it possible to go as high as $60—a figure that seemed reasonable enough, since twenty-three states were already granting this and more to families who demonstrated that amount of need, regardless of the amount of FFP. The larger family tended to fare better under the present matching rules. The one-child family, with only an $18 matchable grant, almost inevitably needed some sort of supplementary income. Couching the matching conditions in terms of a family rather than simply children would introduce more flexibility and more realism into the budgeting-grant process.

But here again Hoey and her chiefs foresaw difficulty. They were uncertain how caretaker relatives could be handled. Often such relatives were able to support themselves, but needed additional money for the dependent child. Perhaps aid for the first child should be raised substantially, to $36 with $18 for the second, or to $30 and $12 respectively, or not all that much, say, $24 and $18. The presence of so many dollar amounts in the hopper and the absence of hard data as to the probable effect of adopting one or the other led the Social Security Board to a very soft position on the Title IV maximum. The board offered no dollar amount for congressional consideration, settling instead for a simple recommendation that the maximum be increased.[13] In its final form the administration's recommendations for the 1939 amendments included three proposals directed exclusively to Title IV: (1) grants to states to be authorized on a 50 percent matching basis; (2) maximum payments to individual children to be increased; and (3) the age limit to be raised from sixteen to eighteen years for children regularly attending school.

However, several other proposed amendments would, if adopted, affect ADC significantly. On the public assistance side was the radical scheme for variable grants to states, the restriction of assistance to needy individuals, and the requirement that all income and resources be considered in establishing need. On the insurance side was the very important addition of survivor's insurance to Title II, the old age insurance program. The administration asked that coverage be extended to children of insured workers who died before reaching retirement age and to their widows if caring for these children.

The hullabaloo over variable grants excepted, these recommendations were completely overshadowed by those related to old age insurance and old age assistance. In congressional committee and on the floor, action on the other matters was taken with a minimum of discussion, let alone debate. As enacted into law the 1939 amendments extended social insurance coverage to widows caring for minor children of insured workers, authorized 50 percent matching for ADC, and increased the age limit from sixteen to eighteen years with the school attendance proviso. Eligibility under each of the public assistance programs must be based upon establishment of need after consideration of income and resources available to the applicant. Rejected were the variable grants scheme and the increase in the ADC maximum.[14]

For public assistance programs taken as a whole, the most serious disappointment was the rejection of variable grants. For ADC taken separately, the most serious disappointment was the failure to increase the maximum. Members of Congress clung to their belief that ADC children should not be entitled to more than needy veterans' children, again ignoring the benefit received by veterans' widows. In their view, to increase the $18 maximum would push ADC grants higher than the $20 allowed the children of veterans. Surely this sort of opposition could be broken down in due course, particularly if the board offered a more definite recommendation based upon a comprehensive analysis.

The greatest gain for ADC was, of course, the 50 percent match. It should be emphasized that the 50 percent match offered a great deal more standing alone than a raise in the maximum standing alone. A mere raise in the maximum would have had no effect in the poor states. With increased matching, it was thought that even the poor states could do somewhat better. Yet cautionary words were in order. Thus the ranking Republican member of Ways and Means followed his party's "enthusiastic" endorsement by expressing the "hope" that the additional money would be spent on "those now being denied rather than to relieve States of any part of their present expenditures for such assistance." Altmeyer expressed even greater pessimism. In some states, he feared increased matching would "just mean the release of funds for old age assistance rather than the use of more funds in the field of dependent children."[15]

In the long run the shift of responsibility for widows and dependent children of insured workers from ADC to OASI was expected to reduce ADC rolls—some thought drastically. In submitting the amendments, the Social Security Board noted that 43 percent of ADC recipients were children of a deceased father. Those now on the ADC rolls would stay on, however, unless their economic circumstances changed. Also, social insurance coverage was still limited to business and industrial workers, leaving large numbers—agricultural laborers, domestics, government employees, and employees of nonprofit organizations—outside the system of insured protection. But extension of coverage was only a matter of time. In the board's view, congressional inaction in 1939 was just a temporary setback. Meanwhile Altmeyer predicted that about 20 percent of potential ADC children would collect insurance beginning in the next decade, and that the numbers would increase as coverage was extended. If this turned out to be so, many of the "nice families" would never appear at the door of the welfare office.[16]

Hard Facts

Hoey considered the increased match in ADC a valuable tool in bringing the lagging program into step with OAA and AB. Yet she knew that financial incentives must be accompanied by grass-roots support. She knew too that, unlike OAA, grass-roots support for ADC was not self-generating. Support for ADC would have to be aggressively cultivated, community by community. "After all," she exhorted her staff, "most of the people in America are interested in their own children. Can't we stretch that out to this other group that needs their interest, too?"

Well, maybe. But it wouldn't be easy. Hoey herself noted the "deep prejudices towards minority groups that you find in every community, the intolerance towards the different points of view about the essentials of living that you find in every community." Her staff was with her all the way—all of the hopes, all of the fears. Peter Kasius, Hoey's deputy, contrasted the old days with the present scene, when "these nice private agency setups . . . . had a certain kind of prestige and a certain kind of protection that I think was very unreal. . . . The old supporters are gone and the new supporters haven't really been cultivated and haven't been mobilized." What new supporters might be mobilized? Up to now, Hoey ventured, perhaps support had been sought only from old friends such as the League of Women Voters, "when we know how limited their area is." Not that she was "belittling" the league, Hoey assured her staff. The league was "excellent" so far as it went, "but after all they don't get over to the man on the street often." She wondered how the bureau might reach out to labor groups "and the other groups that are effective in making public opinion." The American Legion had a long history of interest in child welfare, she mused. The private child welfare agencies must be reclaimed.

It was going to be difficult, however, to shake the convictions of those who were running state and local ADC programs. Many were holdovers from mother's aid, with ten to twenty years' experience. A regional representative expressed her frustration: "Their ideas are well defined about what their program is to be, and, as I see it, it is not in line with the philosophy of the Social Security Act which, it seems to me, has as its first basic an acceptance of responsibility for the total ADC group."

In truth, the BPA was in no position to take its message directly to local communities. By law, the bureau was restricted to working at the state level. By custom, the bureau could offer advice only when asked to do so, as congressional questioning of Altmeyer showed, and the days when states were lining up for advice were long gone. Going over the heads of the states by mounting a nationwide appeal to organizations such as the American Legion was out of the question.

One legitimate and potentially influential route lay open to the bureau—publication of research and statistical studies of program operations. Hoey advocated the use of research and statistics as an excellent way to "make the states see themselves as others see them, . . . which shows them what is happening and the variations between counties as to number and type of cases," adding that "sometimes very simple material does bring them up short and they begin to question also."[17]

With Hoey's purposes in mind, the BPA began a series, soon referred to as the "characteristics studies" because of their descriptive and analytic data on ADC and its recipients. The first characteristics study, undertaken in 1941, was conducted by the Division of Administrative Surveys. The second, in 1942, and those that followed, approximately every two years through 1979, were under the direction of a research and statistics unit. Methodology and tone changed over the years. For the 1941 study, BPA staff went into six states, supplementing their review of legislation and administrative regulations with interviews of state and local staff and examination of a sample of case records to test actual practice. Subsequent studies, wherein state coverage was enlarged to sixteen states in 1942 and included fifty thereafter, depended upon state staff for collection of data, which was analyzed in Washington. The early studies, particularly that conducted by the Division of Administrative Surveys, were frankly didactic. In later years, the characteristics of programs and families on ADC were set forth with little comment, the facts allowed to speak for themselves.

Thus the bureau made no bones about the design and purpose of the 1941 study. Four problem areas were singled out for particular attention. Random observations showed that three of these—parental incapacity, continued absence from the home, and suitability of the home—were often defined so restrictively that needy children were deprived of ADC. In each of these areas more liberal definitions in law, regulation, and practice would tend to open up and increase the ADC caseload. The fourth problem area—determination of budgetary need and payment—bore directly on active caseloads, addressing the question of the adequacy of support once a family had been accepted for assistance. The bureau hoped, even "anticipated," that conclusions drawn from examining these problem areas would "point the way" toward "more comprehensive measures" to assist needy children.[18]

The 1941 and 1942 characteristics studies confirmed in a systematic way what was already known through scattered reports. State and local welfare officials had failed to extend ADC to the full extent possible and to the extent the bureau believed desirable under the broad criteria established by Title IV. The studies went further, however, in elaborating on the details of restrictive practices, providing at the same time an opportunity for comment by the BPA.

Nationwide data about cases accepted because of parental incapacity showed that 99 percent centered on the father and 98 percent centered on his physical incapacity. Cases in the study samples were only slightly less skewed. ADC had been granted in a few cases where the father was mentally incapacitated, and in a few cases where the mother was either physically or mentally afflicted. States shared no uniform definitions of incapacity beyond an attribution to loss of earnings. Some followed earlier mother's aid practices, insisting on total disability; others allowed for partial incapacity. The required duration of incapacity also varied—from no limitation, to six months or one year, to evidence of permanent disability. All the states relied on physicians, in some cases panels of physicians, to assess the condition of the person claiming disability. In the few accepted cases where the parent suffered from mental illness, nearly all were hospitalized.

The bureau recognized the practical difficulties presented in defining disability, even where the will existed to move away from the mother's aid tradition. Because the principal wage earner was usually the father, it was natural to find paternal incapacity in the great majority of accepted cases. In many parts of the country, diagnostic services for mental illness were inadequate or nonexistent. Hence the reliance on hospitalization to prove mental disability. The Bureau believed agencies could do a better job in assessing the adverse effects of partial disability on the wage earner, however, so more of such cases would be found eligible and none dismissed out of hand. Most arbitrary in the bureau's opinion were lengthy elapsed time requirements, ranging from three months to a full year. Since case records showed periods of unemployment stretching over several years prior to acceptance for assistance, it seemed reasonable to assume that disability and consequent need usually threatened family stability long before assistance became available.[19]

Evidence of hoped-for liberalization could be found in statistics that indicated a relative increase of ADC families where the father was absent from the home. During the fiscal year ending June 30, 1940, families accepted for this reason made up 38 percent of the caseload, a sizable growth of 10 percent since 1938. Although only a small number of widows with dependent children had been covered under OASI by this time, their numbers on ADC had declined relative to mothers who were divorced or separated. Death of the father and continued absence of the father accounted for about the same numbers of ADC families in the early 1940s.[20]

The studies showed, nevertheless, that welfare agencies went to great lengths "to protect the program" against encouraging fathers to leave their families. Investigation of eligibility followed lines designed to make certain that the father was truly absent from the home and likely to remain so. This being the case, attempts were made to locate him as the first step in getting him to contribute to the support of his family. Welfare agencies tried to define a clean break in family ties. Divorce constituted a legal break, but some county agencies required further evidence from the investigation. Abandonment—either through refusal to support or failure to locate the absent parent—had to be proved as well in these localities. Agencies were even more circumspect in dealing with cases involving separation. Unless legally formalized, separation sometimes had to be accompanied by proof of desertion. And, as in cases claiming disability, agencies usually required anywhere from three months to one year to elapse before accepting the finality of the broken relationship.

Once continued absence of the father had been established to the agency's satisfaction, attention turned to locating him and getting him to contribute support. Although state laws fixed responsibility for child support on the father, at least insofar as legal unions were concerned, legal processes were seldom invoked. This phase of the investigation was also undertaken by the social worker. In some counties, location of the father meant automatic denial of ADC, the welfare agency reasoning that support was his responsibility, not the public's. Whether he was employed and earning how much or how little, or unemployed, did not enter into the decision. The mother was free, of course, to pursue such legal channels as were open to her. She might also be helped through general assistance if no support from the father was actually forthcoming. The point was that those welfare agencies that followed such a policy were not willing to "pension" families while an adult responsible for their support remained in the picture. Noting that support received from an absent parent was rarely a significant factor either in closing cases or in refusal of assistance, the BPA dismissed as impractical the elaborate efforts to locate and collect, while creating, unnecessarily, undue hardship for needy families.[21]

Although some rules and regulations affecting eligibility due to incapacity or parental absence struck the BPA as unduly arbitrary and others a waste of time and effort, all had a demonstrable direct connection to stipulations contained in Title IV. No such connection could be shown in regard to "suitability of the home," a condition of eligibility present in the laws or regulations of thirty-one of the forty-three states with ADC programs. States usually defined a suitable home under the vague minimum standard of "health and decency." Judgments of suitability of the home followed local attitudes and standards and varied accordingly. Some local agencies, clinging to mother's aid standards, applied strict criteria. Here the mother's character or reputation, housekeeping, ability to manage money, and quality of child care were minutely scrutinized. But in more places than not the ways of the past had seemingly been replaced by more permissive attitudes. Here the governing element was a positive finding in favor of home and mother, provided there was no doubt that the children could remain in her custody or, to put it another way, provided there was no indication of neglect, mistreatment, or physical harm.

As a result of this liberal definition, less than 3 percent of families sampled in the 1941 study had been denied ADC because the home had been found unsuitable. BPA staff hailed this finding as evidence of a shift in focus from a model parent requirement to children's needs, concluding that "these modifications appear to be rooted in greater understanding of the importance to children of the intangible values of family life as against physical or mental considerations and to an increasing willingness on the part of communities to attempt to bring about changes in home situations by means of financial assistance." In other words, the battle against the "nice family" partisans was being won.[22]

Unfortunately statistics gathered through characteristics studies, no more than statistics collected on a routine basis, contained neither a complete count of families potentially eligible for ADC nor the reasons why they were not on the rolls. Included among those potentially eligible were needy families receiving general assistance rather than ADC because the agency deemed them "unsuitable for the long time care and security" envisioned under the federal program, or because of agency backlogs. Their numbers were not inconsiderable. One agency reported only twenty-five ADC applications pending while, at the same time, eight hundred potential ADC families were being carried on general assistance.

The number of families deemed "obviously ineligible" could not even be guessed. Families so tagged were simply turned away without being allowed to make a formal application. The reasons for such tagging could often be traced to requirements for lengthy time periods to elapse before acceptance of parental incapacity cases or cases involving separation and desertion. Doubtless also informal judgments labeled the home "unsuitable."

Not all refusals worked to the detriment of the applicant family. The known tendency to deny ADC to one-child families (50 percent of families refused aid in the 1941 study sample) arose, in part at least, from the small

ADC assistance payment available to such families. Mothers with one child might be placed on general assistance while encouraged to find work. After the mother found work, ADC was often granted to supplement earnings, bringing her standard of living up to a level of decency.

Handling applications from unmarried mothers raised particularly troubling questions. Clearly Title IV did not exclude them from consideration, but just as clearly some local agencies did just that. However, the trend toward fair treatment seemed, on the surface at least, to be moving in the right direction. Unmarried mothers were represented in the caseloads of each and every state. Overall these families made up almost 10 percent of the caseload in the 1942 study. Yet the study states showed marked differences. The percentage of unmarried mother cases ranged from 16.3 in the District of Columbia to 2.6 in Utah. Four states in addition to the District were carrying 10 percent or more unmarried mother cases. In six states, including Utah, the unmarried mother caseload was under 6 percent. It was impossible to determine precisely what these state differences meant because the incidence of illegitimacy by state had not yet been compiled. The BPA expressed confidence, however, that state differences were not great enough to account for the exceptionally wide range. Because illegitimacy ran highest among socially or economically disadvantaged persons, states with large concentrations of the poor and downtrodden could be expected to have more illegitimate births. In many states, the bureau concluded, "moral attitudes make it more difficult for needy illegitimate children to get assistance than for children dependent for other reasons."[23]

Moral attitudes or racial attitudes or both? The bureau stopped short of making a direct connection. But in discussing racial patterns in ADC a similar linkage was made. Poverty, mortality, morbidity, and desertion were highest among nonwhites. It stood to reason that relatively more nonwhite than white children would be on the rolls. This was clearly the case in some states and just as clearly not the case in others. Taken together the sixteen states studied in 1942 contained a black child population about the same as the nation as a whole (11 percent), but in three of these states—Arkansas, Louisiana, North Carolina—and the District of Columbia blacks made up more than 20 percent. The remaining twelve states each had less than 13 percent blacks.

Of the states with high concentrations of blacks, only the District of Columbia showed the expected high ratio of ADC recipients—54 blacks to 5 whites per 1,000 aided. North Carolina aided only 14 blacks and 17 whites per 1,000. In the ten study states having more than 5,000 black children receiving ADC, the recipient per 1,000 rate is shown in

TABLE 5.1.   Black-White Recipient Rate in ADC, 1942 (per 1,000 population)

State	Black	White
Illinois	173	17
Oklahoma	148	44
Kansas	125	24
Missouri	84	26
Massachusetts	76	21
District of Columbia	54	5
West Virginia	50	45
Louisiana	46	39
Arkansas	22	22
North Carolina	14	17

SOURCE: BPA, *Families Receiving Aid to Dependent Children,* Oct. 1942, pt. I, 3–4.

Table 5.1. The BPA expressed certainty that at least in West Virginia, Louisiana, Arkansas, and North Carolina, needy black children were suffering from discrimination.[24]

Low Standards—Low Grants

Once found eligible, what could a family expect in the way of assistance? Sufficient to maintain the standard of health and decency set by most states in drawing up their guides for family budgeting? Hardly. The best the BPA could do in evaluating the results of the study was make the weak statement that "cash payments were being received without interruption and represented something regular for the family to count on." The worst was damning: "In general, assistance was not sufficient to meet the requirements of the family as estimated by the agency." The full amount of a family's budgeted case deficit was met in only one of the six states studied in 1941. The others specified dollar amounts—maximums—that could not be exceeded regardless of need. The maximum did not necessarily become the minimum. Further cuts in the maximum might be made down to the level of the family's previous income, the local WPA wage scale, or by the amount of an anticipated contribution, such as child support, whether or not such a contribution was made.

The result:

Neither the families who had some form of income in addition to public assistance nor those whose only means of support was public assistance received aid in an amount equal to the agencies' estimates of their need. Even when the aid to dependent children payment . . . was supplemented by another form of public assistance, by income from employment, contribution from relatives, and miscellaneous income or resources, about four of every ten families had combined resources that were less than the agencies' estimate of their financial need.[25]

After five years' operation, the ADC program was a long way from its proclaimed ideals and purpose: an assistance payment sufficient to support families in decency, this payment to enable the mother to devote substantial time to her own home and children. Not only were assistance payments insufficient, employment outside the home ran high. Three-fourths of ADC mothers worked, most in part-time low-paying jobs. The higher paid were clerks, pieceworkers in factories, waitresses. But over half of the employed mothers were doing other people's housework or taking in other people's laundry. They could do little else. Low educational attainment restricted these women's earnings to a far greater extent than men's. Construction, heavy industry, railroading, trucking, automotive assembly—none required much education, but particularly if the shop had been unionized, workers took home a decent wage. Because men were employed exclusively on the well-paid jobs, women who stopped school at the sixth grade, as was usual for these mothers, found nothing but drudge work at low pay open to them.

This situation obtained in 1941 even though the nation was in the midst of the huge military buildup that preceded its entry into World War II. Opportunities for employment—better jobs at better pay—did become available for women soon thereafter, and by 1943, as the wartime manpower crunch became acute, even hitherto all-male preserves—shipyards, ordnance plants, airplane factories—opened their gates. Under the wartime demand for labor many ADC mothers got jobs paying enough to support themselves and their children. The number of families receiving ADC dropped from 372,000 in 1940 to 274,000 in 1945, a decline of nearly 25 percent.

Even if earnings proved insufficient to take mothers and teenagers completely off the ADC rolls, work outside home and school attracted them for the simple reason that they ended up with more money in pocket. In states having maximum payments, welfare agencies allowed families to supplement the ADC grant with earnings until combined income equaled the full standard of need. By the fall of 1942, three-fifths of all ADC families in the 1942 sample had earnings that represented about 40 percent of their total income.[26] (See Table 5.2.)

The BPA was less than enthusiastic about these developments, charging

TABLE 5.2. Average Monthly Cash Income per Family on ADC Rolls and Percentage of Such Income from Specified Source, October 1942

State	Average total cash income	All sources (%)	ADC (%)	Other public aid (%)	Sources other than public aid including earnings (%)
Total 8 states	$62.88	100.00	50.7	3.3	46.0
Arkansas	29.71	100.0	52.6	.1	47.3
District of Columbia	63.42	100.0	61.2	1.8	37.0
Massachusetts	100.92	100.0	62.0	2.1	35.9
Missouri	65.27	100.0	48.1	3.9	48.0
Montana	60.07	100.0	52.7	8.3	39.0
North Carolina	44.20	100.0	38.9	1.9	59.2
Oklahoma	46.85	100.0	48.1	4.8	47.1
Wisconsin	86.84	100.0	46.4	3.6	50.0

SOURCE: BPA, *Families Receiving ADC,* Oct. 1942, pt. II, 10.

in 1942 that mothers and teenage children had been "forced" to go to work because assistance payments had not kept up with the rise in cost of living. The wartime labor shortage was temporary, the social workers pointed out. Trouble lay ahead. "Values" ensured by ADC were "sacrificed" in order to gain a little money. Children were left at home unsupervised for lack of adult caretakers. Boys and girls who quit school for work might well turn up on welfare when a more competitive labor market returned at war's end. The bureau defended a mother's "right to choose aid" whenever going to work led to neglect or inadequate care of children, emphasizing that this right had been endorsed by the War Manpower Commission, the agency in charge of dealing with the labor shortage. The bureau also criticized local welfare agencies for encouraging mothers of young children to look for jobs and called for higher assistance payments so they could stay at home where they were needed.[27]

In sum, the wartime economy, with full employment for the first time in twenty years, did not cause the BPA to deviate from its determination to defend and extend the ADC program in its pure form. After a sharp decline in recipients and expenditures beginning in 1941, federal emergency agencies—the WPA, the Farm Security Administration, the National Youth Administration's out-of-school program—were all gone by June

1943. Without suggesting an exact parallel between these "emergency" programs and the "permanent" programs established under the Social Security Act, it must be emphasized that the BPA's stance was unduly obdurate. During the war years, day care for the children of working mothers became increasingly common, and much of it was free. Women in all walks of life, many with young children, seized the opportunity to work outside the home. To take a position against work for ADC mothers was simply to segregate them further from the mainstream. School dropouts were another matter, but the sad fact was that ADC children tended to leave school for work as soon as they could anyway. Wartime employment may have offered a good many dropouts job training at a higher level of skill than they would have received otherwise, and consequently better prepared them to compete in the postwar labor market.

Advice from Consultants

Not content with its own studies and analyses and far from content with ADC's failure to fulfill its promise, BPA engaged Grace M. Marcus, a distinguished social worker, as a full-time consultant for one year ending in the fall of 1944. Marcus had been a supervisor of casework method for the National Committee for Mental Hygiene. Later she had worked for, and been a consultant in casework to, the Community Service Society of New York City, the country's most prestigious private family agency. She was aligned with the functional Rankian rather than the diagnostic Freudian school of social work theory.

Consultants are usually brought into public agencies to put a stamp of approval on what is already being done or to bring outside authority down on the side of changes that public administrators want to bring about. Consultants usually do just that, telling their employers what they want to hear.

Marcus was no ordinary consultant. She had been called upon to help improve the program, to suggest ways and means to get the states in agreement with the BPA's thinking, and to formulate arguments for putting the children's case before the public. But Marcus found no way to reach the mutually desired end—assistance to all needy children—through the instrument of ADC. It was not that she disagreed with the bureau's findings. She too thought the mother's aid tradition constituted a drag, that maximums on FFP led to undesirable restrictions and inadequate assistance payments, and that general assistance funds were insufficient to meet need not covered by ADC. Yet Marcus felt strongly that improvements along these lines would not necessarily lead to a good program for needy children.

ADC "as a category" was "fundamentally defective," she argued. To work well, an assistance category must be easily defined in objective terms, as was the case with OAA and AB. Categories such as these called attention to characteristics of the group that were easily accepted by the public as "innocent and justifiable reasons for dependency." Not so with ADC: "Children eligible for aid to dependent children must be sorted out of the mass of dependent needy children according to combinations of parental circumstances, and of these circumstances only death is easily determined and accepted as an objective cause of need. In actuality, the characteristics of parental absence and incapacity undermine the appeal that a category for children might otherwise carry, and they divert, rather than strengthen, the concern with need." Far from being accepted at face value, desertion, separation, and divorce aroused emotional responses— blame, prejudice, social stigma. Incapacity was similarly suspect unless the debilitating condition was self-evident and devoid of personal or anti-social origins such as alcoholism or venereal disease.[28]

The more Marcus commented, the more she echoed state and local public welfare agencies. No wonder the public assistance worker tended to play it safe. In actual practice it was very hard to draw the line between absence, unemployment, and nonsupport. Even more difficult to determine was incapacity.

So long as public mental health facilities remained inadequate to their task of sound diagnosis she felt it preferable to confine assistance to those with "extreme and incurable conditions." The alternative would invite "all sorts of complaints and behavior" to justify eligibility. Good social worker that she was, Marcus also expressed concern about the program's underlying tendency to encourage family breakup. This undesirable outcome was not, she thought, nearly so much that fathers left home to put the family on ADC as it was to stand in the way of reconciliation once the family was on the rolls.

As published with only minor editing in the February 1945 *Social Security Bulletin*, Marcus's report fell short of an outright recommendation for drastic or immediate changes in Title IV. The bureau was encouraged, though, to seek aggressively the general assistance category endorsed by the board in 1940 or, as an alternative, to promote a system of children's allowances. Such legislation would be very hard to get. General assistance, the expressed preference of the social worker advisory group to the Committee on Economic Security, had been rejected in favor of categories because general assistance would have put the federal government back into the "business of relief." Children's allowances had seldom been discussed in the United States. The system had a "foreign" connotation and had been used to encourage population growth in Europe after the devastation of World War I. Children's allowances had never seemed applicable in the United States since population growth had been more than sufficient in the twentieth century. The BPA decided to promote an amendment to authorize FFP in general assistance when a favorable opportunity developed.

Meanwhile, a careful reading of Marcus's report opened up another possibility for rescuing ADC. Although no specific recommendation had been made, the report contained several pointed references to requisite qualifications and abilities of welfare agency staff. For example, if a more liberal interpretation of absence from the home were adopted, public welfare agencies would have to command "a high degree of skill and judgment in their staffs." Similarly, "highly specialized" medical and psychiatric social work skills were called for in determining psychological and social factors often accompanying physical as well as mental illness.[29]

To build up, almost from scratch, a corps of social workers possessed of such qualifications and to confront as well the prevailing disfavor in which all social workers were held at the time would have daunted most ordinary men and women. But to Hoey and her staff the possibility of even partially meeting this challenge justified the effort they determined to make. The time seemed ripe for such an effort, because the 1939 amendments allowed a greater say in personnel matters. As of January 1, 1940, state plans were required to provide for the "establishment and maintenance of personnel standards on a merit basis."[30]

6

The Main Stem

THE LANDMARK AMENDMENTS of 1939 occurred within four years of the enactment of the Social Security Act itself. Eleven years were to elapse before amendments of similar significance were added. The 1950 amendments would be passed after Harry Truman became President in his own right. During World War II and for five years after, the Social Security Board had to work with what it had. Because what it had was considerable, this period of legislative barrenness offered an opportunity to look inward, specifically to focus on administration, perhaps even to achieve, through creative interpretation in rule and regulation, a liberalization of policy and practice, an advance toward the goal of protection against the hazards and vicissitudes of life.

Administrative Reorganization

During the war years the social workers extended and consolidated their influence over the administration of public assistance programs. A good part of their success resulted from the 1939 amendments, specifically the increase in federal authority in regard to state personnel and the requirement for consideration of income and resources in establishing need. The transfer of a large share of the board's auditing function from the Bureau of Accounts and Audits to the Bureau of Public Assistance in 1940 further enhanced the bureau's direct influence on state administration. Finally, the bureau gradually shifted from reliance on ad hoc decisions for policy development to written and more formalized summaries.

The board entered this phase of its activity with a change in status. The Roosevelt administration was notorious for creation of independent "alphabetical" agencies, often short-lived. Partly on this account FDR had a reputation as a poor administrator. Contrary to reputation, however, Roosevelt was not wedded to administrative disorder. As early as 1936 he appointed a Committee on Administrative Management to tidy up the executive branch. The committee's recommendations were embodied in a reorganization bill that passed Congress in 1938.

Reorganization Plan no. 1 established the Federal Security Agency (FSA), which grouped together one very old, one middle-aged, and three New Deal agencies: the Public Health Service (1798), the Office of Education (1867), the Civilian Conservation Corps (1933), the National Youth Administration (1935), and the Social Security Board. Appointed to head the FSA was Paul V. McNutt, a former governor of Indiana and, given FDR's silence about the 1940 election, a presidential hopeful. According to Altmeyer, FDR called him to the White House and told him there would be no change in his own position as chairman, nor in his direct access to the President. The Social Security Board was transferred to the FSA on July 1, 1939.[1]

By this time the board itself and its executive director had changed. Upon Winant's resignation in 1937, Altmeyer was elevated to the chairmanship. George E. Bigge, a labor economist, a Republican, and a strong advocate of social insurance, was confirmed by the Senate as a board member in August 1937. Bigge had taught at Brown University, had served on Rhode Island commissions on labor and industrial relations, and on the state's commission to establish an unemployment compensation agency under the Social Security Act. Ellen S. Woodward of Mississippi, formerly in charge of women's projects for the WPA, joined the board in January 1939. Altmeyer, Bigge, and Woodward were to serve together until the board was abolished as such in 1946. In November 1938, Frank Bane resigned to become director of the Council of State Governments, a position in which he would continue to share in Social Security's interests, particularly in welfare. The new executive director, Oscar M. Powell of Texas, transferred to Washington from his position as director of Region X.[2]

An early major incident challenging the board's authority pivoted on the perennially unsettling question of flat grant old age pensions versus social insurance. On March 27, 1940, Altmeyer received a courtesy copy of a speech McNutt was to deliver to the National Industrial Conference Board in New York City the following evening. According to the text McNutt wanted to abolish both social insurance and OAA in favor of a single universal old age pension, financed by personal income taxes. The pension was to be "modest," far removed from the extremist demands of the Townsendites. It would render unnecessary the "vast bureaucracy" engaged in record keeping for the social insurance program. It would encourage redistribution of wealth.

Altmeyer swung into action with a memorandum to the White House press secretary, reminding him of the President's earlier rejection of a similar scheme as a "baby Townsend plan that was sure to grow up." The same could be said for the "modest" sum McNutt was advocating. "Needless to say," Altmeyer concluded, "we in the Social Security Board are shocked at the casual way seven years of planning and progress are brushed aside."

The President backed Altmeyer, agreeing he did not want McNutt to deliver the speech as written, and above all, did not want him to argue for flat old age pensions regardless of need. Thereupon McNutt's speech was recast in orthodox terms by the board's speech writers. The FSA administrator traveled to New York by train; the board's messenger took a plane. The "official" speech was handed over and dutifully delivered.[3] Yet a few months later, when Roosevelt formally launched his campaign for a third term, he himself seemed to waver in his loyalty to the Social Security Act as gospel. In a speech to the Teamsters Union in September 1940, he expressed his "hope" for a universal flat old age pension as a floor under old age insurance, a so-called double-decker scheme. Any basic change in the Social Security Act had become most unlikely by this time, however. A large national defense program had been launched in the spring of 1940. In the months preceding Pearl Harbor and the formal entry of the United States into World War II, the country was preoccupied with the defense buildup. As military service absorbed young man and woman power, war production reached out to employ large numbers of older workers who might otherwise have been clamoring for pensions.[4]

It is significant, nevertheless, that all of these proposed changes for old age pensions would have done away with OAA. The old folks and their supporters remained convinced that a pension was their due. They felt they had earned it whether they had worked in a factory or on a farm, or whether or not they had something saved up. They were unable to fathom the logic of the means test or to welcome the social worker who carried it out.

Expansion of Federal Social Work Power

When, in 1938, the Bureau of Public Assistance began to draft an administrative manual, a metaphor of life was chosen to suggest a plan of operations for a state welfare agency. In this plan the Division of Social Work formed "the main stem" of the entire organization, the principal operating division. Field representatives from the state agency's Division of Social Work were to provide the link with county welfare agencies where applications for assistance were made and the means test applied. "The rudiments of a welfare program may be instituted by the state agency," BPA cautioned, "but in the local unit they will take root and grow."

Knowledge of general social work concepts and skill in applying social casework in its several variants—family casework, child welfare, group work, and work with the blind—were deemed essential for staff in order to ensure "individualization of services" as well as financial assistance for the recipient. To this end, the BPA recommended employment of "trained and experienced investigators" and "trained and experienced supervisors" from "the field of social case work."[5]

The call for trained social caseworkers, and particularly the emphasis on services, went far beyond the individualization represented in the eligibility and budgetary processes. The BPA seemed to be edging toward the position occupied by the private family service agencies in the years before the crash. It was not at all the position that had been asserted by Harry Hopkins and Aubrey Williams and articulated by Josephine Brown. To the FERA leaders, economic need did not equate with pathology; financial aid was not a tool in treatment; it *was* the tool. In all fairness, neither Hoey nor her staff were thinking about a return to the 1920s or applying psychoanalytic concepts to the public assistance caseload. But Hoey never lost an opportunity to mention services and to emphasize their importance. As she put it in a 1938 radio address:

Those who are old or blind, and families with dependent children have many problems, not all of which can be met by a cash allowance, necessary as it is. A mother with several children may, for example, need help on all sorts of problems—the physical health of one child; the vocational training of another; the spiritual and social development of a third. So also, those who are old or blind have a variety of problems, with the need for medical advice and care standing out as most frequent and most serious.

. . . . More and more, States are coming to realize that public welfare is on a par with, let us say, public health and public education, and that, like these other public services, its administration requires persons equipped with special training and experience.[6]

Altmeyer had been willing to stick his neck out in insisting on personnel standards under the "efficient administration" clause in the Social Security Act. He was more than willing, and had succeeded, in getting the act amended to give the board more specific power over such standards. But he was far from convinced that trained, experienced social workers were required—certainly not in any large numbers. On the contrary, he assured Congress when testifying on the 1939 merit system amendment that states employed only a few social workers and he expected the situation to remain this way. Altmeyer's interest, in which Bigge enthusiastically joined, was to rid both the state public assistance and the unemployment compensation programs of the spoils system and thus ensure staff stability regardless of the fortunes of political parties.

In pushing for state and local merit systems, the board sought to capitalize on a wave of interest. The 1930s saw a resurgence of pressure for civil service reform. The decade began with fewer than ten states operating under civil service or merit systems. By 1940 the number had about doubled. On the local level, the picture was mixed. While fewer than 200 out of more than 3,000 counties were covered, some 750 cities had their employees under civil service by 1939.[7]

Hoey, who was certainly familiar with social work's historic stand against politics in public welfare and who came from New York, the pioneer civil service state as well as the locale of Tammany Hall, was ready to affirm her support of state and local merit systems in principle. Yet she feared that the advance of civil service might retard the growth of social work professionalism. Her differences with Altmeyer and Bigge became apparent as soon as generalities began to be translated into specifics some two years before the 1939 amendments went into effect.

In carrying out the board's policy of July 1936 that required the state agency to set up minimum standards of training and experience for personnel, the BPA practiced a piecemeal approach that attempted to individualize states like welfare recipients, allowing for low salary scales and/or low educational requirements to be explained away by legislative indifference.[8]

By late 1937 the board began to insist upon definitive action, particularly when states requested guidance in establishing merit systems. At a meeting on December 17, Hoey defended the state-by-state advisory process because she did not want to "crystallize the low standards" now existing in some states. To which Altmeyer and Bigge replied that Hoey was blind to reality; standards had already been crystallized.[9]

But the BPA continued to hold off. One year later, on December 2, 1938, the board was covering the same ground, Altmeyer wanting to push the states to give open competitive examinations, the BPA expressing fears of crystallizing low standards. "We must meet this difference of opinion between the Bureau and the Board and settle it once and for all," declared Altmeyer.[10] Moving quickly now, the board received and approved two policy statements before Christmas. The first, covering both unemployment compensation and public assistance, set forth a state's obligation to establish a merit system and submit a description of its plan of operation. The second contained more specific guidelines regarding classification and compensation plans, the development and conduct of examinations, recruitment, promotions, and so on. Included were recommendations for a continuing merit examination committee having one or more members "familiar with the public welfare field." Again, persons "technically familiar with the field" (presumably social workers) should participate in preparing examinations. The three-part examination consisted of an education-experience rating based on prescribed minimum qualifications, a written and/or performance test, and an oral interview "designed to evaluate the personal qualifications and traits of the competitor in terms of the specific requirements of the positions." The oral interview was to be conducted by a board of at least two persons familiar with the "character" of the work, "at least one of whom is technically qualified in the field" (presumably a social worker). Inclusion of an oral interview was a victory for Hoey, who had insisted that reliance on written questions would fail to get at the true ability of an individual.[11]

What, if anything, could be expected to result from these statements? They were advisory only. Moreover, they were not sent from the board to the states as an official communication. Rather, following its usual procedure in policy matters not contained in the law, the board turned the statements back to the BPA for use through its regional representatives in negotiating with the states. Unquestionably, having something concrete in writing would strengthen the bureau's regional representatives in those states that were committed to a merit system or that needed a slight push toward commitment. But in states indifferent or hostile to the merit system concept, whose political leaders were determined to hire and fire along party lines, the new personnel standards could have little or no effect.

At the time the standards were adopted only eleven states had merit systems covering public assistance employees. In a number of very populous and wealthy states, moreover, the spoils system persisted despite a legally adopted merit system. In a report to Altmeyer in April, Hoey counted twelve such states, among them California, Illinois, Massachusetts, Michigan, and Pennsylvania.[12] Most of these twelve were under a merit system, but politicians had used one tactic or another to evade it. Since Colorado law exempted clerical personnel from coverage, a number of counties classified executive and professional positions as "clerical." Massachusetts confined its merit examination for new positions to persons already employed by the welfare agency. Pennsylvania counties continued to make provisional appointments of individuals not on the list of eligibles. Michigan seemed headed away from its merit system under a new law that removed over 60 percent of previously classified positions. The bureau reported outright political manipulation—forced campaign contributions and improper electioneering—in California, Ohio, Illinois, Indiana, and Kentucky.[13] The decision to seek the personnel amendment in 1939 signaled the board's determination to mandate a spoils-free merit system.

Once the amendment had passed in August 1939, the question became, as Altmeyer said in a staff meeting, "what to do now that we have the bear by the tail." Gone were the days when excuses about "selection, tenure of office, and compensation of personnel" had provided an alibi for poor administration. "Beginning January 1st," he went on blandly, ". . . we really have to let go the tail of the bear and just take our chances." On the whole, though, Altmeyer expressed optimism. The effect of the amendment on administration might well be "revolutionary," he thought. The ninety thousand employees working in public assistance and unemployment compensation offices constituted a significant proportion of state and local personnel. Their conversion to merit status could spread to other public employees.

Still, the undertaking facing the board was difficult. What about those thousands already employed? Blanket them in? Make them compete with everyone else in the state? Those extremes seemed both unwise and impractical. Something in between was called for. Everyone agreed that standards issued by the board would have to be drafted along generally broad lines in order to open up a number of alternatives for adoption in state regulations. It would fall to the regional representatives to negotiate with state welfare departments on acceptable components of their merit systems.[14]

The Standards for a Merit System of Personnel Administration, approved by the Board on October 20, 1939, applied to both public assistance and unemployment compensation programs. Except for the usual policymaking positions, all state and local personnel were covered. As applied to welfare agencies, the positions that could be exempted included members of the state board, the executive head of the state agency and one confidential secretary, attorneys serving as legal counsel, members of local welfare boards, and certain state and local officials serving ex officio. Political or religious partisanship and political activities beyond the expression of views and voting were prohibited. In addition to the written test, applicants for the more responsible positions would be rated on their training and experience, and applicants for positions requiring frequent contact with the public or that involved important supervisory or administrative duties would be given an oral examination. Social workers with training and/or experience would seem to have a competitive advantage, and the oral interview, long used by social work professionals to size up personal attitudes, was yet another mark of Hoey's successful leadership. Those already on the job were also given an edge over outside applicants. A person employed by an agency already under a merit system need not take another examination. Where a new merit system was being installed, persons already employed could be retained contingent upon a passing grade.[15]

Once the amendment was a fact of life, the troublesome patronage issue disappeared rapidly. In a little over a year all state and local public assistance personnel were under a merit system, and all but five of these systems had been approved by the board. The systems were specific, including job classification and compensation plans. The effect had been salutary. Joint examinations of unemployment compensation and public assistance applicants had called attention to the lower salary scales in public assistance and had encouraged upward adjustments with resulting attraction of better-qualified individuals. Hoey was pleased. "We believe," she wrote the regional offices in April 1941, "that on the whole there is a reason to be gratified at the progress that has been made during the past 15 months."[16]

The Shortage of Social Workers

Public welfare agencies employed more than fifty thousand persons, most of them in county or city offices, at this time. The number of employees declined by about seven thousand during the war years but rose steadily in the late 1940s to reach more than fifty-six thousand in June 1949. Somewhat more than half of the staff were in executive or social casework positions, with clericals accounting for most of the others.

Within social casework jobs the largest single group—two-fifths of all staff—were rank-and-file caseworkers.[17]

On the whole, public assistance caseworkers were well educated. Two-thirds of them had a bachelor's degree or better, and another one-quarter of the group had some college education. The individuals having the lowest average level of education were directors of local offices who were political appointees, almost one-fifth of whom had only a high school diploma. At the other end of the scale, over three-fourths of the supervisors and field representatives had college degrees or better. It was in this group also that formal social work training was most likely to be found. More than 10 percent of supervisors and 20 percent of field representatives had a full two years of graduate social work education. Although fewer than 2 percent of caseworkers had graduate degrees in social work, over 16 percent had some formal training. Furthermore, the caseworker group contained a very large number of individuals—almost 50 percent—who were eligible for graduate social work education because they already had an undergraduate degree. Hoey might well have been gratified on this score also. Her position against "low standards" had always contained the warning argument that lack of a college degree would bar the individual from a graduate social work degree.[18]

Even so, the gap between supply and demand was formidable. The total number of social workers with any graduate training at all—about thirty thousand—was less than the total number of social workers employed in public and private agencies combined. It was, in fact, about equal to the total number of social workers employed in public welfare agencies. The more refined the analysis, the less favorable the outlook. Private agencies already employed by far the greater number of trained social workers. More than half the social workers on private agency staffs had some graduate social work training, compared with less than one-fourth of the social workers in public welfare. One of the first of Hoey's actions, begun in 1937, was to obtain the board's authorization to use federal administrative funds to pay the salaries of state and local staff while on educational leave in approved schools of social work.[19]

By approved schools of social work Hoey meant schools that were members of the American Association of Schools of Social Work (AASSW). This organization, founded in 1919, had gradually assumed leadership in curriculum planning and standardization, and during the 1930s was seeking an official role in accreditation. The emergency relief program had posed no real threat to these goals. Josephine Brown, though she later voiced misgivings, chose only member schools for the training given FERA workers. But once the categorical programs were in place and the demand for social workers by public welfare agencies was recognized as more or less constant, AASSW dominance, both real and aspiring, was seriously challenged.

AASSW member schools were few in number—about thirty, poorly financed (under $2 million annually), and concentrated in urban areas in the Northeast and Midwest. Rural America had been largely ignored. Schools of social work preferred locations near modern welfare establishments staffed by trained social workers so that fieldwork would be a "truly educational experience" for the student. The medical model was much in evidence, the doctor, not the nurse, being the professional in mind.[20] Clearly, if "approved schools" were to respond to the massive potential demand created by public welfare programs, a dramatic increase in social work training capacity, including a more balanced geographical coverage, was imperative. Moreover, the traditional tendency to downgrade relief-giving, particularly that dispensed by public agencies, had led most approved schools to omit public welfare from the curriculum and practicum. Although some of the schools—notably the University of Chicago—expressed interest in training public welfare administrators, all shied away from preparing the rank-and-file social worker for public agency service.[21]

Hoey was hopeful, even insistent, that the AASSW broaden its scope of curriculum and fieldwork opportunities in public welfare and was eager to do what she could to foster the desired shift. To this end she acted as a go-between for AASSW and the Rockefeller Foundation while a study grant was prepared. She told the staff at Rockefeller "how much we, as a public agency, need the schools of social work," assuring them "that the schools were openminded about changes in curriculum or new emphasis which might be needed in terms of producing people for the public field." At the same time she cautioned Elizabeth Wisner, a faculty member at the Tulane University School of Social Work who was working on the grant proposal, to refrain from asking for the "impossible amount of money" that would be necessary to undertake a full-scale study of social work education. The Rockefeller people had made it "quite clear" that "their concern was with public administration and not with professional education for any given field." Hoey urged that the proposal be narrowed and focused directly on education for public welfare—evaluating the schools in terms of what they were already doing, making concrete suggestions for raising standards, and devising ways the AASSW could serve as a channel of information from public welfare to the schools.[22]

The proposal was narrowed and the study funded. It took forever to complete. A draft began to circulate in October 1940, but the final report, *Education for the Public Social Services*, was not published until 1942.[23] Even so, the report was demonstrably short on plans for concrete action and long on recommendations for further study. Rather than zero in on specific courses to be added to the curriculum, the report called for "exploration and development." Rather than suggest ways to open up welfare agencies for field work, the report settled on a call for "joint effort" toward this goal. Given these deficiencies, it is hardly surprising that *Education for the Public Social Services* passed over the desks of a small audience and was quietly shelved.[24]

AASSW-approved schools were not, however, the sole source of social work education. Although AASSW would have it otherwise, training for social work, particularly public social work, was offered in many land grant colleges and state universities, mainly, to be sure, on the undergraduate level, and usually located in departments of sociology. State universities had long fulfilled a felt obligation to supply state agencies with qualified persons in many different fields. Land grant colleges were especially attuned to rural needs. After the passage of the Social Security Act, both types of institutions lost no time in offering to expand their course offerings. Soon, too, using these institutions as a base, a movement to challenge the AASSW began.

The anti-AASSW movement was instigated in 1938 by W. B. Bizzell, president of the University of Oklahoma and then president of the National Association of State Universities. He was egged on by the head of the university's Sociology Department, who had repeatedly failed to gain AASSW approval for his one-year graduate social work program. These educators at Oklahoma compiled a list of reasons for establishing an independent "accrediting" organization, circulating it to the forty state universities that were not affiliated with AASSW. Only large educational institutions (such as state universities) could absorb a free-standing school of social work, they argued. In contrast, AASSW goals and structure were aimed at private colleges and universities where little attention was paid to the needs of rural areas. Public funds could and should be available to public assistance workers. The lack of higher degrees in AASSW school faculties was notable, and the curriculum "too rigid." Finally, the AASSW was described as "an autocratic organization dominated by the thinking of two or three schools" concerned with "maintaining its own positions at the expense of the needs of the field."[25]

Some active and potentially powerful support for the public educator group existed in Washington, though not at the Bureau of Public Assistance. Its locale was the WPA in the person of Josephine Brown, who was still working as head social worker to Harry Hopkins, and in the Children's Bureau by Katherine Lenroot. The two were close friends. Brown had called attention to the need for social work in rural areas as early as 1922. Just as she had distinguished mass unemployment relief from the pathology of personal and family problems associated with dependency by private family agencies, so she saw rural poverty as calling for different casework solutions than those in urban settings. Naturally she looked to the land grant colleges as likely sources for training social workers to practice in those settings.

In the summer of 1937, Lenroot circulated a memo containing Brown's thoughts on training social workers in public colleges and universities. It was pounced upon and denounced by Wisner at Tulane, Edith Abbott at Chicago, and Agnes Van Driel at the BPA, Van Driel dismissing Brown's recommendation as "normal school training." Wisner and Abbott labeled Brown's plan "dangerous, unsound, unfortunate," Abbott adding, incorrectly, that Brown's "only experience is with an emergency program and both she and Katharine Lenroot think you can start a new school overnight in every state university and turn out social workers wholesale."

In 1943, after rejecting unread an article Brown had submitted to the *Social Service Review* and, in the ultimate putdown, suggesting it might be worth mimeographing, Abbott reflected with satisfaction on her success in "preventing 'many of the very foolish things that Harry Hopkins and Miss Brown were planning to do.'" Although Brown was then teaching public welfare at Catholic University's School of Social Services, she was clearly off the social work professional's network.[26]

In spite of negative attitudes, the state university–land grant college revolt blossomed for over a dozen years. Upon publication of *Education for the Public Social Services*, which affirmed AASSW opposition to undergraduate education for social work and a strong preference for two-year graduate study, a sizable group of public educators organized the National Association of Schools of Social Administration (NASSA). By December 1943 two accrediting organizations were in the field. There ensued a series of conferences, joint committees, heated exchanges, backbiting, and, in 1951, the publication of yet another study, *Social Work Education in the United States*. The following year saw the merger of the AASSW with NASSA to form the Council on Social Work Education. Both the study and the new accrediting organization held fast to two years of graduate education leading to a Master of Social Work degree as the distinguishing mark of the trained social worker. State universities could fit into this scheme but not the undergraduate programs, in either colleges or universities.[27]

Leslie Leighninger, author of a comprehensive study of the development of professional social work, concludes:

The broader field of social work, caught in a debate between standards and public service, lost the chance for meaningful involvement in the development of the new public programs. Although representatives of the American Association of Social Workers and the Chicago School were concerned about staffing the public social services, they recommended a selective, high standards approach which was impossible to implement. . . . Public welfare gradually resumed its role as a peripheral concern of professional social work.[28]

At this juncture, in 1950, fifteen years after the launching of the federal public assistance programs, a contemporary observer might well have asked, "So what?" Nothing ground to a halt during the years of debate among social work educators. To be sure, as the 1949 study by BPA showed, public welfare agencies had fewer "professionally" trained social workers than private agencies, particularly among rank-and-file employees. But public welfare had a good many professionals, particularly among its administrators and supervisors. And undergraduate social work programs, though not counted in elite professional circles, supplied a substantial number of recruits for state and local welfare agencies.

Nor were newly hired employees simply given a desk and told to get to work. In-service training or "staff development," as it was officially referred to, eventually became an integral function of every state and local agency. The Social Security Board approved guidelines on staff development prepared by the Division of Technical Training in March 1941. During the orientation period new hires were given a general understanding of the agency's purpose, its legal base, administrative organization, rules and regulations, and office procedures. Orientation also included a historical sketch—the background of the agency and its relationship to other services in the community, past and present. Orientation paved the way for on-the-job training. The "supervision of the day-by-day work of the individual" was viewed as "a continuing process" in order to ensure "growth on the job." Supervision could also be exercised through staff meetings. Group conferences fostered "creative leadership." But the most important mode of supervision was a regularly scheduled individual conference between the caseworker and her supervisor, which in the official statement was described as "a cooperative undertaking with positive educational value based upon the day-by-day work."[29]

Individualized supervision was not unique to the public assistance agency and had little or nothing to do with the skills acquired through education or experience. Supervision occupied the same exalted position in the advanced private welfare agencies, the agencies whose staffs were composed largely of professionals. Social work would seem to be the only profession, or semiprofession, where the practitioner, once trained, cannot be let go. All professions have some controls, some provision for consultation and continuing study, but teachers and nurses, let alone doctors, are not subjected to the case by case, individualized, weekly going-over that is par for the course in social work from student days until the practitioner leaves her caseload for a supervisory position or administrative duties.[30]

The content of supervision could be expected to vary according to the type of caseload carried by the agency. Supervisor and worker discussed different matters in a private family agency, where financial assistance was incidental to the treatment of personal problems and social functioning, and in a public welfare agency, where financial assistance was paramount. Yet the staff development program recommended by the bureau's Division of Technical Training and promulgated to the states by its regional representatives adhered to the system prescribed by private family welfare agencies and the all-important fieldwork segment of social work education. Adherence to traditional training methods signaled the BPA's determination to be one with the rest of the profession. There was to be no breaking away.

During 1943 and 1944, the bureau employed two leading social workers as consultants to prepare publications for use in training public welfare workers. One of them was Grace Marcus who, in addition to studying and making recommendations on the ADC program, produced a report—*The Nature of Service in Public Assistance Administration*. The other was Charlotte Towle, who wrote *Common Human Needs*. Neither had any experience in public welfare. Both had been greatly influenced by psychoanalysis. By the time of her work at the bureau, Marcus, the originator of the "relief as a tool in treatment" concept, had become a proponent of the so-called "functional" school, which focused casework on the specific service offered by the agency. Towle, who taught at the University of Chicago's School of Social Service Administration and refused to be labeled, was, nevertheless, rooted firmly in the "diagnostic" school, which focused casework on the individual's need as elicited by the social worker.[31]

The invitation to Marcus resulted from concern that establishment of

eligibility for assistance—regarded as a cut-and-dried operation suscep-
tible to routine formulas—had been separated from service—regarded as
undue interference in a family's private life. The invitation to Towle grew
out of requests from trainers for help in better understanding people. In
theory, greater understanding of people would round out other essentials
in the social worker's repertoire, such as information about economic and
social conditions.[32]

Although both consultants received guidance from Van Driel's Technical Training Service, neither of their publications provided the kind of text
that could be readily applied to the social workers and their work situation.
Consequently these publications were eyed with reservations in BPA and
handled with extreme caution.

The Marcus report contained an enthusiastic affirmation of the "right to
assistance." But to the disappointment of BPA staff, service in the public
welfare agency started and stopped with establishment of eligibility:
"Since the agency is an agency of government, its workers should not
employ the powers and resources of government for purposes that are
individually determined by them. Service that is directed to changing the
individual's behavior or relationships or to supervising or regulating his
management of his affairs is therefore at odds with fulfillment of the
agency's primary duty, the provision of assistance as a right." Provided
they were needed and desired, the caseworker was free to refer the welfare
recipient to other agencies for medical care, vocational guidance and training, or counseling on personal problems.[33] Here was Josephine Brown
reincarnated.

Finally, after a delay of two years, *The Nature of Service in Public
Assistance Administration* was issued. In her foreward, Hoey pointed out
that discussions within and without the bureau made clear "that no single
point of view exists . . . with regard to the character of service in the
administration of public assistance." She noted that the Marcus report had
not been submitted to the administrator of Social Security for approval and
was not "an official publication."[34]

Common Human Needs, the Towle report, had much easier going
through the review process, and was published without any disclaimer in
1945. Towle, like Marcus, recognized the establishment of eligibility as
the core service, applauded the statutory right to assistance as a significant
breakthrough, and emphasized the importance of money in the well-being
of the individual and society. But unlike Marcus, she did not stop there.
For Towle, services in addition to assistance could and should be "prof-
fered as a right to which recipients are entitled but which they are not

obligated to use by reason of the fact that they have utilized their right to financial assistance." Towle's overriding purpose was to interpret normal human behavior, which she held was largely governed by emotional forces. Knowledge of basic human behavior patterns was essential to public assistance workers, Towle asserted, despite the fact that their function precluded the treatment of behavior difficulties "in and of themselves."[35]

Common Human Needs began with a summary of expected emotional responses from infancy and adolescence through maturity and old age, and continued through case histories of individuals and families. In and around these cases various attitudes and reactions—toward receiving assistance itself, toward work, toward illness and disability, toward spouses and children—were related to previous life experiences. The caseworker's responses were critiqued and outcomes evaluated.

Although each of these case histories was identified as receiving one or another of the categorical types of assistance, taken together they were not representative of the caseload of the mid-1940s. At this time Old Age Assistance accounted for more than twice as many recipients as Aid to Dependent Children—2.0 million adults on OAA, 862,000 recipients, including children, on ADC. Yet in Towle's report only one case—that of an elderly unmarried woman who was recalcitrant about entering an institution—dealt with OAA.

Most of the cases discussed were receiving ADC. Here again Towle made no attempt to cover the various significant reasons for childhood deprivation. All the examples were drawn from cases of widowhood or the incapacity of the father in a two-parent household. To be sure, death of the father accounted for close to 40 percent of the cases currently aided, while his incapacity accounted for more than 20 percent. However, estrangement due to divorce, separation, desertion, or illegitimacy accounted for 37 percent of the caseload. These latter, the "problem" cases for the current as well as the future caseload, went unnoticed in *Common Human Needs*.[36]

When *Common Human Needs* was circulated to the regional representatives in September 1945, the bureau expressed no concern about its imbalanced case selection, but went to great lengths to caution that this book must be interpreted by agency trainers down to the last detail. The text was complex, "sometimes disturbing." Training staff would have to relate its content to the agency's "day-to-day work" and to "current problems and needs" to enable novices to grasp its import.[37] In less than three years, in the wake of determined opposition to further advances toward the welfare state, both of these publications became a major embarrassment, if not a major disaster. At the time of publication, however, they were simply written off as a somewhat disappointing attempt to introduce advanced social work theory into the training of public welfare workers.

The impracticality of applying psychoanalytic theory to the establishment of eligibility or of adding much more than the most obvious referrals to the public welfare worker's duties was further underscored by an assessment of the personnel situation in the late 1940s. By this time, the acute staff shortages of wartime had eased considerably. In June 1949, the 56,000 state and local employees in public assistance represented a 30 percent increase over those employed in December 1945. Although this same period was marked by a 40 percent rise in public assistance cases, vacancy and turnover rates had dropped.

Perhaps size of caseload was the best measure of what a welfare worker could reasonably be expected to handle. Nationwide, the median average caseload in OAA was 224; in ADC, 113; and AB, 228. In most agencies, however, a worker carried a mix of the less complicated OAA and AB cases and the more complicated ADC cases. Caseloads ranged between 100 and 250. By contrast, caseworkers employed by private agencies were expected to carry only 20–30 cases. A standard caseload for the public assistance worker had not been determined. The bottom line was simply the amount of money available to the welfare agency for administration.[38]

After a decade of fostering social work professionalism in state and local welfare agencies, the BPA had managed to do little more than hold its own. Social work educators had not only chosen the two-year Master of Social Work as the qualifying degree but had insisted on generic training and refused to permit any sort of specialization in public welfare. Social work theorists continued to relegate financial assistance to the lower-class status of those receiving it. Establishment of eligibility remained the core service in public assistance and, in the vast majority of welfare agencies, the only direct social service offered. Yet the professionals in the BPA never lost faith in their vision summed up a bit wistfully in the *Social Security Bulletin* of February 1952: "There are differences of opinion as to the minimum amount and kind of education needed to do an adequate job of administering public assistance, but many persons would agree that it would be highly desirable for all employees to have at least some education directly related to their jobs. Many would agree further that the type of education best fitted to equip workers to administer public assistance is graduate social work training." In view of the shortage of trained social workers, it was conceded, staffing public welfare agencies with the professionally trained remained "a long-range goal," but it remained nevertheless.[39]

Audit and Administrative Review

Unlike old age insurance, where the law allowed several years' lead time to design a system for collection and disbursement of funds, federal public assistance grants to the states were payable beginning with the first quarter of 1936. True, federal grants-in-aid were not as new to the government's experience as was social insurance. Nevertheless, the board's quarterly obligation to certify to the Treasury Department the amount of payment to be made to each participating state presented an unprecedented problem in accountability. Although accountability suggested some sort of audit, it was difficult to identify what elements should be included. A public assistance audit would differ sharply from, say, the audit of state highway grants-in-aid. The propriety of expenditures by welfare agencies was contingent on judgments about eligibility for assistance and the amount to be paid an eligible recipient in relation to the state standard of need. Individualization of each case and application of family budgeting to compute the payment, which had been the choice of most states rather than flat grants, and, after 1940, the requirement to consider income and resources, made the task even more complicated.

Because the public assistance caseload was large and growing—1.3 million in 1936, 3.2 million by 1940, 5.0 million by 1950—the total bill commanded attention. Expenditures rose from $172.9 million in 1936, to $631.3 million in 1940, and reached $2.0 billion in 1950.[40]

Having begun in 1936 with an elaborate and exhaustive review of case records by the Bureau of Accounts and Audits, the board later took a hard look at these lengthy procedures. Impressed with Audit's complaint that it was unduly involved in making decisions about proper administration, the board, in the summer of 1939, decided to subsume the so-called audit of eligibility under a continuing review of state and local administrative procedures and operations. This review, effective January 1, 1940, was to be carried out by the BPA.[41]

Recruitment began in order to increase total regional staff to ninety professionals, one to two persons for each state, at a medium grade level. To develop and direct the "administrative review" from the central office, Hoey selected her deputy, Kathryn D. Goodwin. The administrative review was conceived as a major activity. For the first time, the BPA had the power to evaluate local administration—a power that had to be used with utmost discretion if the state agency were to be held to its own responsibility for supervision of its local units.[42]

Flat Grants versus Family Budgeting

The strong preference for family budgeting over a flat grant method of determining eligibility and calculating the amount of the grant had been expressed by the BPA from the earliest days of the program. But only after the 1939 income and resources amendment which provided that "the State agency shall, in determining need for . . . assistance, take into consideration any other income and resources" was it possible to put a brake on exemptions such as home ownership or work expenses. With the income and resources amendment due to become mandatory on July 1, 1941, the bureau began, in the summer of 1940, to work up guidelines for regional representatives to use in consultation with state welfare officials and drafts of possible formal issuances to state agencies.

The bureau pointed out that family budgeting was more complicated when applied to categorical assistance than to the assistance given by private charitable agencies on which this system was based. Absent the categories there was one general fund. Heads of households and their dependents were budgeted as a unit, basic total requirements balanced against total income and resources. Categorical assistance for the aged, the blind, and dependent children was directed more or less exclusively toward the individual, just as were private pensions. Titles I, IV, and X were silent on spouses or dependents in the adult categories and on the caretaker relative in the children's category. In the case of an adult living alone, the family budgeting method, though an anomaly, was easy to apply. Complications arose in the more usual situation where two or more persons lived together as a family. How far did the individual applicant's requirements reach within the family household? According to Hoey, state welfare agencies had made various "adaptations" during the previous four years and were "eager to experiment further" with improvements provided they could be assured of continued FFP.[43]

Previous "adaptations" of family budgeting techniques to categorical programs had been guided by an important policy decision made by the board in October 1936. At that time, Executive Director Bane, in reply to an inquiry, advised the state of Louisiana that common household expenses—food, rent, utilities—could be budgeted as part of the applicant's requirements and matched by federal funds:

In our opinion the proper measure is individual need, but in determining individual need, the circumstances under which the individual lives must be considered and reasonable discretion used by the administrative officers. . . . Federal funds may not be used for the purpose of matching payments made with respect to specific needs of persons not eligible for assistance under the Federal Social Security Act. It is impossible, however, to indicate an arbitrary point at which there might be a separation of common expenditures in maintaining a family home. At the discretion of the State agency, payments made on the basis of such common expenditures may be matched from Federal funds up to the maximum specified in the Social Security Act.

Under this interpretation, a sixty-five-year-old man could receive an assistance payment that would cover food and shelter for his sixty-year-old wife but not for her clothing or other personal expenses. When the wife attained age sixty-five, she could, of course, apply for OAA on her own, in which event her personal expenses would be included in budgeting the total requirements of both in the family household. This was a liberal policy. All board staff who dealt with public assistance—the executive director, the general counsel, and the Bureau of Public Assistance itself—considered the 1936 policy decision a broad interpretation of the Social Security Act—an interpretation in line with the board's inclination to lean toward socially desirable decisions.[44]

In seeking further interpretation in light of the income and resources amendment, Hoey sought a decision to mark the outer limits of the allowable FFP, or, as a BPA staff member expressed it, "the Bureau was recommending that the categorical system ought to be used and ought to be strained as far as it possibly could to meet . . . general relief needs."[45] The ensuing effort to define the liberal limit occurred in a very different economic environment than that of 1936. Industrial mobilization for war generated a huge job market, and during the last years of the war, even a labor shortage. By no means all the elderly or all mothers with dependent children could work, but thousands could and did. The general assistance caseload, which included many persons considered too disabled for work in normal times, dropped from 5.1 million in 1938 to less than 0.5 million in 1944. Not to push the point too far, it seems fair to assume that pressures for liberal interpretations of the public assistance titles of the act had lessened even as the bureau pushed for further liberalization.[46]

Discussion of the family budgeting–flat grant issue stretched over forty-seven months, from June 1940 to May 1944. During this period, about thirty formal memoranda were generated. A two-to-one split in the three-member board was apparent from the very earliest discussions, with Altmeyer leaning toward the liberal BPA recommendations and Bigge and Dewson/Woodward insisting on a more literal interpretation of the act. Implicit, and on occasion expressed, were dissatisfactions with the categorical approach, with the casework approach, with family budgeting itself.

The possibility of amending the law came up frequently—sometimes in the context of establishing another category for general relief, sometimes as a specific amendment to authorize the inclusion of other needy family members in the categorical grant.

To Hoey the question was whether the board had authority to interpret need. At a board meeting on June 29, 1940, she elaborated the problems faced by the BPA in the absence of more specific rules and regulations. Out in the states, money was being added onto the individual categorical assistance grant willy-nilly. Caseworkers found it impossible to figure out a budget for an individual without counting his or her family. Yet leaving the states free to continue making ad hoc decisions led to "unworkable and unrealistic" programs. She hoped the board would agree to the legality of a broadened concept of individual need, or, that failing, would favor an amendment to legitimize the concept.

Bigge voiced strong objections. Counting the recipient's income and resources as assets as the law required was one thing. Granting additional money from the categorical program for the recipient's dependents was another and an altogether separate action. In Bigge's view, shifting around "to carve out a section of . . . unmet need and bring it under the categorical program" would not only flout the law but would introduce a means test in many families "where we haven't any business doing it." Because most dependents were spouses under sixty-five, Bigge also expressed concern about altering the balance with OASI since the 1939 amendments had limited benefits to wives and widows over sixty.

Although Altmeyer agreed with Bigge from a strictly legal viewpoint, and he himself also expressed his opposition to family "snooping," he believed state welfare agencies could and would "interpret need within reasonable bounds." As usual, Altmeyer grasped for the political settlement, arguing that the board "would be cheered and not criticized" by the public, which would pronounce the BPA course "reasonable and realistic."[47]

By late spring 1941 the bureau had approved a short statement drafted by Bigge to guide the states in making adaptations on the requirements side of the family budgeting equation when the applicant lived in a needy family. The Bigge statement affirmed the 1936 policy allowing consideration of common household expenses and legitimized a limited extension of federal matching for the personal needs of other family members:

Under the public assistance provisions of the Social Security Act, the condition of need must be found to exist with respect to the individual applicant and determination should be made to insure the well-being of the applicant. However, under certain circumstances, individual need may comprehend requirements that also serve the welfare of other individuals in the household.

The Board has not, for example, questioned payments which covered common household expenses if the maintenance of such household was necessary to the welfare of the recipient. The Board expects to continue this policy. Such payments, however, should not be extended to cover the additional needs of other members of the household unless the presence of such members is essential to the well-being of the recipient in question.[48]

Bureau staff was satisfied that Bigge's definition of essentiality could be extended without strain to those persons the bureau had earlier given as examples—spouses, caretakers, mothers—but would hold the line taut when it came to brothers, sisters, cousins, and aunts.[49] Within the year, the policy statement was made more explicit. On March 24, 1942, after a long wrangle stemming from the payment of a wife's burial expense, the board approved, with Bigge's enthusiastic agreement, a rewording of the Bigge statement. Payments for common household expenses would continue to be allowed but "such payments should not be extended to cover the additional expenses incurred because of the presence of other members of the household unless the presence of such members is essential to the well-being of the recipient in question."[50]

In Bigge's view, however, these policy statements failed to constrain an extreme liberal trend in some states. Several plans awaiting approval in the spring of 1943 covered persons he felt the board had intended to exclude. Kansas, for example, proposed to cover the additional expenses of older children who had a physical or mental handicap. Bigge concluded that bureau staff, particularly its regional representatives, had gone overboard in "promoting" family budgeting. He felt they should be instructed to stop this activity.[51]

Accordingly, on October 15, 1943, the possibility of including an admonition to prevent this effect was considered in a board meeting, but, after a long discussion, this step was not taken.[52] Instead, the board directed the bureau to work on yet another policy statement. On December 3, 1943, the matter was closed so far as policy statements were concerned in the form of a "clarification" for guidance to the states:

Whether the presence of other members of the household is essential to the well-being of the recipient, is a question to be determined by the State agency in accordance with the State law and general instructions issued by the State agency thereunder. However, with respect to Federal matching the determination of whose presence is essential to the well-being of the recipient should be made on the basis of a finding as regards the need of the individual, and may not go beyond the inclusion of spouses in the instance

of the aged and blind; parents, or relatives acting in the place of parents, in the instance
of dependent children; and persons who render specific services of a kind which, if the
applicant were living alone, would have to be provided for him."[53]

This statement spelled out for the first time precisely which persons other
than the individual eligible recipient could be included in the categorical
grant so far as their additional personal expenses were concerned. It was
issued in a Regional and Field Letter and in State Letter no. 35 in 1944.

Some states had never used the concept of a person deemed essential to
the well-being of the recipient. Others developed procedures that would
hold under the new instructions. Still others developed procedures that
would currently be held out of conformity. Indeed when a count was made
for the board in the spring of 1944, most state plans were out of conformity—in OAA, 32 out of 51 jurisdictions; in AB, 34 out of 46; and in ADC,
40 out of 49. Moreover, only six states were completely in conformity in
the sense that all three categories showed an acceptable method for computing assistance payments. Sixteen states that were out of conformity
used a household deficit method, computing the payment by figuring the
difference between the requirements of all members of the household and
the income available to them. Another twenty-two states included requirements of persons other than the spouse in OAA or AB and of the parents of
relative caretakers in ADC without a justification for their essentiality to
the recipient.

What the plans said proved nothing about the extent of nonconforming
activity on a case-by-case basis, however. The BPA made this point as
part of its state plan study. Although about one-third of the families receiving ADC contained persons who should be excluded from the budget,
the extent to which the needs of these ineligible persons were included in
actual payments could not be readily determined. In a further effort to play
down the adverse fiscal effect of liberalized family budgeting, the BPA
pointed to numerous errors in underbudgeting, to failure to meet full budgetary need, and to irregularities among counties in the same state. Attention was also called to the "very low" payments in eleven southern states,
where more than half of the needy aged received payments under $20
monthly and more than half the needy children less than $30. In nine of
the eleven states the percentage receiving less than $20 ranged from 75 to
98 percent; and less than $30 from 55 to 84 percent.[54]

The board instructed the bureau to have the plans cleaned up—many
required only the inclusion of specific words—by September 1, 1944.
New cases would be subject to the conditions specified in the revised

plans; old cases would be subjected to the new conditions upon rein-vestigation under penalty of fiscal exceptions.[55]

Many state welfare directors expressed dissatisfaction with the limita-tions imposed by State Letter no. 35. But only in the South was there widespread concern that low assistance payments might become lower still. These were the states that had no general assistance programs. These were the states, too, whose large agricultural populations lacked coverage under old age and survivor's insurance. These were the states that had adopted restrictive practices—such as paying only a certain percentage of need or arbitrarily omitting certain items from the budget. Reconsideration of affected cases, however, showed that reductions in actual payments could be avoided by realistic computation of the need of the recipient. Further, as Hoey reminded the director of the American Public Welfare Association, the allowance of common household expenses, which re-mained in effect, constituted a significantly broad interpretation of the act.[56]

Although more or less content with the 1944 policy, Bigge had come to question both the utility and the propriety of family budgeting as a method for establishing eligibility and determining the amount of the welfare pay-ment. Bigge preferred a flat grant. He presented his case in a long lead article—"Looking Ahead in Public Assistance"—in the September 1944 issue of the *Social Security Bulletin*. While acknowledging that categori-cal assistance under the Social Security Act marked a great improvement over poor law practices, he decried the persistence of grave deficiencies, particularly in the application of the means test. To most persons, from taxpayers to recipients, the means test was "quite abhorrent."

Rather than determine need individual by individual, Bigge proposed a blanket determination based upon the need of the average individual. "If the assured minimum—including . . . the individual's own resources—is reasonably adequate," he argued, "then it is clear that the large majority of recipients will be able to meet their needs in their own way without having to discuss the purpose for which the aid was given or the way in which their income was spent." Adequate funding, which was a must, would doubtless result in a costlier program. But that was the price for "real security" and "freedom from want."[57]

Bigge's plea for flat grants to replace the social worker–preferred indi-vidualization inherent in family budgeting simply came too late. Not only had previous board decisions tended to validate family budgeting, but amendments to the public assistance titles, most notably the inclusion of "need" as the overarching criterion in establishing eligibility and the obli-gation to consider "income and resources," represented negative responses to the earlier movement for flat grants. Even the amendment to guarantee merit appointments was at least in part recognition of the wisdom to place discretion in the hands of qualified persons. Moreover, the politics of the 1940s raised questions of equity. Heretofore all state action involving flat grants had focused on OAA, leaving ADC out of consideration, although Bigge did include ADC in his scheme.

The technicalities of legislation aside, once the states had programs in place, Hoey and her staff moved aggressively to install social work at the center of administration. Trained social work staff was viewed as most desirable, but that being out of reach, welfare agencies were urged to "develop" staff along the lines of private family agencies. In a less successful venture, the bureau sought to break out of the assistance framework to provide counseling and other social services through validation of social work consultants and educators.

By World War II's end, state welfare administration showed considerable improvement. Gone were the days of fumbled state plans and political interference. The BPA, using its regional representatives as if they were caseworkers, encouraged officials to modernize their organizations and procedures.[58] The tone of these relationships carried over into State Letters and the Handbook of Public Assistance. Although the purpose of these submittals was to notify the states of federal mandates, their contents were often far from clear-cut, cluttered up with goals and suggestions rather than spelling out precise requirements. As early as 1935 many federal agencies began to issue federal regulations to guide the states. For whatever reason—perhaps the existence of the state plan and the administrative review—BPA passed up this opportunity to forge tighter control over state administration. State Letters remained the guide until 1967.[59]

7

The Safety Net

WITH AN UNEMPLOYMENT rate of less than 2 percent, the World War II
economy was notably artificial. Profits, wages and prices, labor mobility,
strikes, and production and distribution of civilian goods were all successfully controlled. Yet, with the Depression in such recent memory,
only the heedless would have dismissed the possibility of a postwar bust.
The thoughtful were also reminded of the role the worldwide depression
had played in the rise of fascist dictatorships in Italy and Germany and the
territorial expansionism of Japan. Poverty also fostered that other enemy
of democracy and capitalism—Marxist communism.

The Welfare State

The New Deal legacy of economic and social legislation was expected
to have a stabilizing effect in case of a postwar recession. The uncontrolled wheeling and dealing of the 1920s would be impossible. Regulatory laws now governed the operation of banks and securities exchanges.
Bank deposits were insured; home mortgages could be refinanced; credits
and loans were available to farmers. The National Labor Relations Act
guaranteed the right of employees to join labor unions and to engage in
collective bargaining through representatives of their own choosing. The
Fair Labor Standards Act established a minimum wage and maximum (40-
hour) workweek, and outlawed child labor under the age of sixteen. The

New Deal had also sponsored vast economic development projects, particularly in electric power and transportation in rural areas.

During the war years themselves, the labor movement built on gains made during the late 1930s when the newly formed Congress of Industrial Organizations (CIO) signed collective bargaining contracts with giant companies in steel, automobiles, and electric appliances. In 1939, union membership—AFL, CIO, and Independents—totaled 6.5 million, about double the AFL and Independent union membership in 1935. Ten years later at war's end, union membership had doubled again, covering 12.5 million workers.

The make-up of the industrial labor force changed during the war. There was a huge migration from farms to munitions factories and shipyards. Many of these migrants were black and poor. Government contracts forbade racial and sex discrimination, enabling blacks to move into plants and jobs hitherto closed to them. The federal government put some teeth in its policy through the Fair Employment Practices Committee, which established formal guidelines and appeals procedures. Although progress was uneven, some gains were made. Discriminatory practices by unions also tended to break down during the war.[1]

Having announced that "Mr. New Deal" had become "Mr. Win-the-War," President Roosevelt refrained from pushing further social reforms. However, he soon introduced and repeatedly emphasized social and economic goals in his war aims and plans for peace. Freedom from want, one of the Four Freedoms, was first mentioned at a press conference in the summer of 1940. It was formalized six months later in the January 1941 State of the Union message and, along with the other three—freedom of speech and expression, freedom of worship, freedom from fear—was included in the Atlantic Charter signed with Winston Churchill and also in the first proclamation of the United Nations.[2]

Expanding on the broad freedom-from-want theme, FDR, in his 1944 State of the Union message, announced an economic "bill of rights" for the American people, "a new basis of security and prosperity for all—regardless of station, race, or creed." Included were the right to a job with earnings sufficient for a decent living; access to good education; the opportunity to enjoy good health and adequate medical care; and, in a strong endorsement of the Social Security Act, the right "to adequate protection from the economic fears of old age, sickness, accident, and unemployment."[3]

The economic bill of rights was to be President Roosevelt's last significant statement on postwar social policy. He died suddenly on April 12,

1945, having served only fifteen months of his fourth term. Still on file at the time of his death were recommendations for legislation made by the Social Security Board in 1941. Although Roosevelt had promised Altmeyer the administration's active support on these amendments, he backed off in a few months, as the war occupied his attention, thus ending the possibility of amendments for the duration.

Harry S. Truman, who succeeded to the presidency, was a liberal Democrat who had been nominated for Vice-President when the conservative wing of the Democratic Party objected to the more radical incumbent, Henry Wallace. Truman had come up through Kansas City, Missouri's machine politics, and was elected to the Senate in 1934. He became nationally known and wielded considerable power as chairman of the Senate Special Committee that investigated war production—management, labor, profits. The committee's reports pulled no punches, yet were generally conceded to be honest and constructive. "Give 'em Hell, Harry" exemplified his scrappy nature. Yet Truman was a serious servant of the people, devoted to his country and its democratic institutions, with a down-to-earth approach typical of America's heartland.

Truman assumed the leadership of a country that was satisfied with its social and political structure. The public was proud of the war effort, its success as the "arsenal of democracy" no less than its victories on land and sea. A huge market of consumers stood ready to buy as soon as cars, radios, electric irons, and nylon stockings began rolling off the assembly lines once more. With all that demand for goods, jobs were bound to be plentiful. During the Truman presidency, the unemployment rate averaged less than 4 percent. Differences among Democrats and Republicans were minuscule. Both parties held strong commitments to private enterprise. Both believed in public education. Both believed American citizens should be protected from exploitation. The Socialist and Communist parties, whose goals were to substitute government ownership of production for capitalism, had very small followings.

The United States stood almost alone in its total support of the capitalist system, however. In less than a year after victory over Germany and Italy, the Soviet Union, with its commitment to revolutionary Marxism, had expanded its borders into central Europe, lowering an "iron curtain" across the Continent. The fall of China to the Communists was only a matter of time. And this was not all. Communist and Socialist parties had long existed in varying degrees of strength in western European countries. They reemerged after the war to claim considerable political power, particularly in France and Italy.

But the real shocker occurred in Great Britain, where the Labour Party, Britain's socialist party, won a smashing victory over Winston Churchill's Conservatives in July 1945. The Labour Party, convinced of its mandate to convert the country to a socialist state, accomplished much of its aim within the next few years. The private Bank of England became public. Railroads, the coal industry, iron and steel, all were nationalized. Although the owners were compensated, profits were gone forever.

Existing social insurance protection was consolidated and coverage made virtually universal under the National Insurance Bill. For good measure, the government added the National Health Service Bill, which effectively socialized medicine. All health services were free: hospitals, doctors, nurses, and druggists would be paid by the government, not through social insurance but out of general revenues. Labour's majority was reduced in 1950, but the party retained control of the government until 1951.

The sum total of these postwar events created an atmosphere of apprehension in the United States that resulted in such actions as the Marshall Plan for the economic rebuilding of Europe, swift military response to Communist aggression in Korea, the Truman Doctrine to protect Greece and Turkey, and, finally, the beginning of the long-running Cold War with the Soviet Union.

At times Truman's political leadership seemed quite shaky; at other times, the country rallied firmly behind him. The Democrats lost both houses of Congress in the 1946 mid-term elections, but Truman won re-election in 1948, bringing his party back with him. In Congress the bipartisan agreement continued in foreign affairs, but bitter battles occurred over domestic issues, with special interest groups entering the fray with unprecedented force. The Communist issue, now domestic as well as foreign, became particularly ugly. After a few cases of infiltration and spying by American Communists were exposed, the area of suspicion widened, leading to blacklisting, loyalty oaths, and similar measures usually deemed unacceptable in a democratic society. Certain words—"socialist," "socialized," even "welfare" as in "welfare state"—acquired a Communist aura and were frequently used as proofs of disloyalty. In this emotion-laden context social reform lost much of its former prestige. Truman was no radical. But he did, like Lyndon Johnson in a later decade, hope to carry the New Deal forward, to apply his own stamp of social reform in his "Fair Deal."[4]

Truman based his Fair Deal on Roosevelt's economic bill of rights. From it he and his domestic policy advisors selected for highest priority two guarantees requiring entirely new legislation: the right to a job and the right to medical care.

Picking up a phrase used in the 1944 Democratic platform, Truman called for legislation guaranteeing "full employment." Liberal Democrats wanted a statute requiring the federal government to underwrite new investment and jobs as needed to prevent cyclical downturns as prescribed by the British economist John Maynard Keynes. But because conservative Democrats had joined Republicans to make this approach unworkable, Truman did not propose it.

The Employment Act of 1946 authorized the federal government to do what it does best—collect and analyze information. The act created the Council of Economic Advisors, directed the President to supplement the State of the Union message with an Economic Report, and created a congressional Joint Committee on the Economic Report to study and propose legislation. The Employment Act of 1946 laid the groundwork for the heyday of the economists, many of them Keynesians, which began in earnest with President John Kennedy and continued under Lyndon Johnson and Richard Nixon.[5]

Truman's proposals for improved health care were prepared by a staff of experts from the Public Health Service and the Social Security Administration working under the direction of Judge Samuel Rosenman, a holdover White House advisor and speechwriter. The health proposal consisted of four parts. Three of these were certain to be popular, because they would disburse federal money for hospital construction, public health, maternal and child health services, and for medical education and research.

The fourth, a federal health insurance system, was highly controversial. Although the President insisted from his very first message that federal health insurance was not "socialized medicine," the American Medical Association (AMA) insisted that it was precisely that. The AMA hired a public relations firm that mounted a costly and, for its time, extremely sophisticated campaign to defeat "government-controlled medicine." Both before and after the 1948 election, bills were introduced and hearings held on the health care package only to have them die in committee. The Republicans would not budge on national health insurance, but with their support the rest of the administration's health care measures were approved.[6]

Truman, who was much interested in orderly administrative processes, instituted an extensive reorganization of the executive branch. Much of this streamlining resulted from the work of a special commission headed by former President Hoover which made its report in 1949. Important changes affecting the administration of the Social Security Act, however, were made earlier.

In July 1946 the Social Security Board was replaced by the Social Security Administration (SSA). At the same time the Children's Bureau was transferred from the Department of Labor to the SSA. On the surface, the changes seemed innocuous enough. Altmeyer was named commissioner of Social Security, which ensured continuity in the existing bureaus as well as the Commissioner's Office itself. Yet the abolition of the board wiped out all semblance of bipartisanship at a time when a vigorous Republican party was calling for cutbacks in federal spending and voicing vehement opposition to further advance of the welfare state. Altmeyer's access to the President was completely cut off. He could only try, with some success, to go around the administrator of the Federal Security Agency through informal contacts with friends and neighbors who had direct channels to Truman.

Altmeyer's power was stripped, not only within the FSA, but also within his own agency. His immediate office, formerly the central office of the board itself, and now the Office of the Commissioner, had a staff that performed such functions as coordination and supervision of the bureaus; overall planning and research; and public information services. When the board lost its independent status in 1938, a large number of transfers had been made to the Office of the Administrator, FSA. Over the years such transfers continued, a good many to the BPA and other SSA bureaus. In 1947 and 1948 the Republican-controlled House Appropriations Committee began to cut SSA staff sharply and deeply. Beginning July 1, 1948, the Office of the Commissioner was authorized a total of only fifty-nine professional and clerical staff, a reduction of over three hundred positions from the previous fiscal year. Even allowing for transfers, the total loss within SSA from 1938 to 1948 was sizable. Almost nine hundred positions had been dropped from policymaking and the administration of social programs.

The "streamlining" continued with the loss of one of Social Security's three key programs. Acting on a Hoover Commission recommendation in 1949, Truman transferred the Bureau of Employment Security, which administered unemployment compensation, to the Department of Labor. It was clear, to no one more than to Altmeyer, that the SSA was losing control of what had been conceived as a necessarily integrated program.

The future looked even less bright when viewed in light of the bitter lost battle over health insurance. In 1947 Truman had appointed Oscar R.

Ewing administrator of FSA. Ewing was an Indiana lawyer of some prominence, long active in the liberal wing of the Democratic party. Truman told him to prepare for Cabinet status and handed him the foundering medical care bill for a starter. The result was disaster all around. The Department of Welfare that was duly recommended by the Hoover Commission to replace the FSA was duly killed after the AMA swung into action again. The AMA simply would not have Ewing, who had spearheaded national health insurance and who now carried the dubious honorary title of "Mr. Welfare State Himself."[7]

The Social Security Amendments of 1950

The furor over socialized medicine and the advent of the welfare state, the Republican control of Congress in 1947–1948, agency reorganization and budget cuts, as well as a healthy economy helped divert attention from the SSA's recommendations for amendments to the Social Security Act. Not until May 24, 1948, did President Truman send a special message to Congress on Social Security. Except for failure to go along with a recommendation for federalizing the unemployment insurance system, the President accepted the SSA legislative agenda, an agenda basically the same as that sent to Roosevelt just before Pearl Harbor. Meanwhile, one study had been completed for the Ways and Means Committee and the Senate had its own study under way.

Shortly after the 81st Congress convened, work on the Social Security amendments began in earnest. At Altmeyer's insistence, two draft bills were sent to Ways and Means. To avoid controversy, neither contained anything on health or unemployment insurance. In this sense, one bill concerned social insurance; the other, public assistance and the child welfare program of the Children's Bureau. The big items in the social insurance bill were the extension of coverage to all workers including the self-employed, provision of higher benefits, and protection for persons forced out of the work force because of disability.

The big items in the public assistance bill were the addition of a new category for general assistance, revision in the federal matching formula to reflect state fiscal capacity, an increase in the federal maximum for matching in each category, inclusion of the caretaker relative in ADC, authorization for federal matching for direct payments to doctors and other medical care suppliers and for payments to public medical institutions in the adult categories, and authorization for federal matching for the cost of social services.[8]

In presenting testimony on its legislative agenda, the SSA had a strong ally in the American Public Welfare Association. During the 1940s the APWA greatly enlarged its interests, activities, and influence. Its original purpose in promoting and facilitating modern public welfare administration and helping with drafts of state welfare laws was by now largely fulfilled. Its leadership could turn its attention to extending and otherwise improving overall social protection in ways that would appeal to its state constituencies. It was natural and mutually beneficial for the APWA and the SSA to form a close working relationship. In practice, it was the SSA that proposed and the APWA that analyzed state feedback, negotiating state by state, through its Welfare Policy Committee, to arrive at consensus.

Beginning in these years and extending through the Johnson administration, two persons, one from the SSA, one from the APWA, formed the necessary human alliance that makes things happen. The SSA representative was Wilbur Cohen, Altmeyer's key assistant for legislation. Cohen had come to Washington straight out of the University of Wisconsin in 1934 as a research assistant to Witte, whose promising economics student he had been. Cohen listened and learned while reporting the congressional hearings on the Social Security Act, had a hand in drafting the 1939 amendments, and, by 1950, at age thirty-seven, had mastered the technical material. Perhaps more important, Cohen was respected and liked by staff both in the SSA bureaus and on the Hill. He met his wife, a Texan with some graduate social work training, at the SSB water cooler. Married in 1938, the couple had three sons. At their suburban home in Maryland, the Cohens were hosts to long-remembered cookouts where warmth, informality, and talk of social reform charmed visiting students and government interns. As the *Washington Post* summed it up after his death in 1987, Cohen was "admired for his expertise and renowned for his amiable nature."

The Washington representative of the Chicago-based APWA was Elizabeth Wickenden. Like Cohen, she had come to Washington soon after graduating from college, in her case, Vassar, where she had majored in economics, though she aspired to be a writer. Wickenden got a job with the FERA and was soon de facto head of the Transient Bureau. While an assistant to Aubrey Williams at the National Youth Administration, she became a friend of Lyndon Johnson, who was then with the NYA in Texas. Married to Arthur (Tex) Goldschmidt, Wickenden had three children and followed her international expert husband whither he went. Whether in Washington or New York, she continued to use her outstanding organizational and writing talents in numerous social welfare causes all of her life.[9]

When congressional hearings on the 1950 amendments were convened, Wickenden presented the APWA's twelve-point welfare policy platform, explaining that it had been first developed in 1945, revised in 1947, and affirmed in January 1949. The platform, she went on, "represents the general common denominator of thinking in the field of public welfare even though, as in all broad-based organizations, there may be occasional disagreement on some of its specific points."

Asked if the APWA had written the administration bill, Altmeyer replied in the negative, but added that the great majority of state welfare directors, bearing in mind the position of their governors and legislators, favored the APWA platform. Moreover, the APWA platform supported the administration bill, including federal financial participation for general assistance; FFP for direct medical payments to providers; and variable grants to states.[10]

Extension of coverage and increases in the level of payments were common denominators in the social insurance and public assistance recommendations. With their preference for social insurance always openly advanced, SSA policymakers developed strategies to make public assistance a less necessary resource. The amendments were intended to move the total program forward toward fulfillment of the original promise to protect American citizens from common social hazards, such protection to be predictable, dignified, and decent, regardless of the source of funds.

Even a cursory review of program operations showed the great distance between reality and promise. Most glaring was the large gap between Old Age and Survivors Insurance (OASI) and OAA. In the number of persons receiving monthly payments and in the payments themselves, OAA was the larger program. In 1940, the first year of payments, OASI carried 131,000 beneficiaries, while the four-year-old OAA system cared for 2.07 million. By 1949 the gap had been closed somewhat, but OASI beneficiaries were still one-third fewer than OAA recipients—1.67 million to 2.49 million. Comparisons between monthly payments were even more worrisome. By 1949 the OASI average monthly benefit had reached $25.30, an increase of only $3.30 in nine years. Average monthly OAA payments had more than doubled during this time and at $44.75 were almost twice as much as OASI benefits.

To top it off, millions of workers remained locked out of the social insurance system because their occupations were not covered. The large migration from farm to industry during the war might have been expected to increase the percentage of coverage, but this was counterbalanced by a growth in the total civilian labor force. The result was a net decrease from 57 to 45 percent from 1939 to 1949.[11]

Altmeyer believed that contributory social insurance stood at the crossroads in 1949. Failure to reverse the inferior position of OASI in relation to OAA would, he feared, discredit efforts to insure against other economic risks. The APWA pushed the point a significant step further, arguing that "a really satisfactory welfare program cannot be achieved except as a corollary to a social insurance program which is adequate as to coverage, benefit level, and scope of risks covered." In sum, a weak kingpin threatened to bring down the whole structure of interlocking protections.[12]

In 1949 total annual expenditures for OAA exceeded $1 billion, all general revenue dollars, half of them state money. The old rationale still seemed valid. If a substantial portion of this money were freed up through reliance on payroll taxes for OASI, the states would be in a better position to care for needy children and persons on general relief. As it was, annual expenditures for about the same number of ADC recipients were less than $500 million. Monthly payments per ADC recipient averaged $21.70, again just about half that received by an elderly individual.[13]

The 1950 amendments to the Social Security Act provided sufficient expansion of coverage and benefit increases in OASI to bring about the desired turn-around in relation to OAA. Coverage was extended beyond industrial workers to encompass important groups of agricultural workers as well as the self-employed. This addition of 8 million persons under compulsory coverage and another 2.5 million eligible on an optional basis moved coverage to 75 percent of the labor force.

Left to another day were agricultural operatives and some professional self-employed. Benefits rose a hefty 80 percent, somewhat more than the increase in prices and about one-third less than the increase in wages since 1937. In perhaps the most disappointing setback to policymakers, the 1950 amendments confined all extension of coverage within the old age and survivor categories. The much-desired protection for disabled workers was passed by the House but rejected by the Senate, whereupon the House receded from its earlier approval in conference.[14]

The real, but still limited, progress in social insurance brought its own measure of satisfaction and disappointment to welfare professionals. The social worker took no offense when Altmeyer referred to public assistance as a "residual load" that would shrink appreciably in the wake of "a comprehensive contributory social insurance system." Altmeyer's statement, made during the House hearings, was exactly the way welfare professionals themselves referred to public assistance. Speaking for the APWA, Wickenden emphasized the "unanimity among public welfare people in believing that public assistance should not become the primary reliance of any substantial group in our population, including the aged." Public assistance "should rather be a diminishing but comprehensive underpinning to all other measures to assure freedom from want."

But this was hardly construed as the beginning of the end of public welfare. Welfare professionals were dedicated to the notion that even as public assistance shrank, public welfare would grow.[15] The statement of the APWA Policy Committee explained that the platform "reflected the growing conviction of those carrying out the public-welfare functions that needed changes could no longer be approached piecemeal but must be formulated and presented in the context of a comprehensive program." The platform reflected a definite shift of thinking away from the concept of public welfare as a series of independent programs grouped together fortuitously for administrative convenience and toward acceptance of its role as one of the basic areas of government service in which the parts were at once interdependent, complementary, and bound together by common underlying philosophy, professional content, and purpose.[16]

Take general assistance. APWA Platform no. 1 strongly endorsed expansion of the categories by authorizing federal matching for aid to "all needy persons." According to Wickenden, "our position is . . . you take assistance as the *safety net,* the court of last resort, for those people who fall through the insurances, who do not fit in any single category, and that you make this program a catch-all, a last resort for any needy person who finally has to come to the assistance agency."[17]

The number of general assistance recipients was currently running between 800,000 and 1 million. It had been as high as 5 million in 1938 and as low as 500,000 in 1944 and 1945. In response to questioning, Altmeyer admitted that the number receiving assistance under state and local laws might increase "somewhat" under a federally aided category. Playing down the possible effects of additional aid and paraphrasing Harry Hopkins in 1933, he offered assurances that "a vast new system of home relief" was not contemplated. Most of those in need of general assistance were elderly—wives of OAA recipients lacking a year or two of qualifying on their own, or persons too disabled to work, he argued.

But skeptical members of Congress feared that opening the door to all the needy would, indeed, in case of high unemployment, create "a vast system of relief," whether a new one or one modeled on the FERA. Uncertainties about the strength of the unemployment insurance system contributed to their anxieties. SSA's dissatisfaction with state management of unemployment insurance was on record. Coverage was limited, benefit levels low, and duration of insurance protection unduly short. Yet neither Roosevelt or Truman had picked up a recommendation for federalization. Truman had, instead, asked for and failed to get a temporary emergency supplementary system, financed solely with federal money, but state administered.[18]

Altmeyer's portrayal of general assistance as a modest, easily contained categorical program was not helped by the public statements of his boss, Oscar Ewing, that general assistance might indeed provide "the framework for plans to cope with a depression." In such a worst-case scenario, funding would be vastly different than under FERA, where Congress made yearly appropriations. The estimate on the table was $230 million additional per year, a little more than current state expenditures, but the obligatory federal matching for a program that included an uncertain number of unemployed scared Democrats and Republicans alike. Wilbur Mills of Arkansas, now in his seventh year on Ways and Means, assumed a lecturing tone:

I think it is wise for us to know ahead of time what these programs are going to cost, and not to wake up with an Appropriation Bill under our nose some morning proposing an expenditure of half a billion or a billion dollars, and with the Appropriations Committee advising us that the reason they have to call upon us to pass such an appropriation is because we authorized the expenditure. I know from my own experience here in a very limited time that you do not reduce these items of cost for Social Security, so far as the funds available to the States are concerned. We are not going to reduce those amounts in the Congress. We have not done it, and the Appropriations Committee tells us that there is no way we can reduce them, because we obligate ourselves ahead of time to pay so much of the cost incurred by the State.[19]

When the worst-case scenario was shunted aside, worries about work disincentives arose. Wartime experience showed that large numbers of so-called unemployables could and did work. With this in mind, the Advisory Council to the Senate Finance Committee had made adoption of general assistance conditional upon a lower percentage of matching than the existing categories. Under no circumstances could general assistance be considered a pension, the committee insisted.

Altmeyer, always the watchdog when it came to maintaining high standards, could not swallow this. Faced with the necessity for some sort of compromise, he made his choice when John Byrnes of Wisconsin commented: "You do not really know what you are getting into for sure." Altmeyer, uncharacteristically stumbling over his words, replied: "My feeling is that, if there is fear that this fourth category is too ill-defined— and I do not share that fear, because I believe, with the techniques that have been developed for determining individual need, this category can be kept within bounds—it would be perhaps better to restrict that fourth category to the handicapped than to introduce a lower ratio of matching." The 1950 amendments added Title XIV, Aid to the Permanently and Totally Disabled (APTD), to the Social Security Act, the program to become effective October 1, 1950. The new program was expected to pick up some 200,000 needy disabled, about one-fourth of current general assistance rolls.[20]

The drive to raise assistance payments through a combination of variable grants to states, increases in federal maximums, and inclusion of the caretaker relative in ADC had not only been studied and discussed but had received some concrete action during the immediate postwar period. This flurry of activity revealed continuing deep-seated controversy in these touchy areas where so much money was at stake for so many. The Advisory Council to the Senate Finance Committee expressed the fear that variable grants would tempt poor states to raise assistance payments to an unreasonably high level.

In the Ways and Means Committee, however, all had moved forward in line with SSA recommendations. A bill that substituted variable grants for the uniform 50 percent matching ratio was reported out in 1946. The proposed new formula employed a range from 50 to 66⅔ percent in inverse proportion to state per capita income. House Republican opposition to this formula was so strong that the entire bill was held hostage by the Rules Committee. After the House passed a watered-down substitute bill, the Finance Committee, with Republican support, restored the variable grants formula.

The Finance Committee report dismissed arguments that the great disparities in public assistance payments were due to differences in the cost of living and argued that raising federal maximums without special federal aid to low income states would only foster further inequities. Under the compromise that emerged from conference, the federal government would pay 66⅔ percent up to a specified maximum ($15 in OAA), and 50 percent above that amount up to the full maximum allowed by the statute. This formula favored the low income states to some extent. Because of their substandard assistance payments these states would receive reimbursement for a higher proportion of their expenditures. But the wealthy states got a raise, too. Pennsylvania Congressman Herman P. Eberharter of Pennsylvania was outraged. The new formula would not help states like Georgia and Kentucky reach adequate standards, Eberharter protested. Yet the ten wealthiest states would collect 86 percent of the additional federal money. "It is a soak-the-poor plan," he concluded helplessly.[21]

Federal maximums for matching purposes were increased in the 1946 bill and were increased again by the Republican-controlled Congress in 1948. In OAA and AB, the adult categories, maximums rose from $40 to $45 and then to $50; in ADC, maximums rose from $18 to $24 and then to $27 for the first child, and from $12 to $15, and then to $18 for other children in the family. In yet another affirmation of old age insurance, Congress did not raise the adult maximums further in 1950.[22]

ADC payments were liberalized considerably. The caretaker relative was finally included as an individual whose needs could be met and matched up to $27 a month, while the maximum for the first child remained at $27. The net increase was not as large as it looked. In most cases, the common household needs of the caretaker were already budgeted. Under the new formula, personal needs could be covered, making a difference, of course, but not all that much difference. The rational arguments that would have tied increases in maximums and variable grants in the same package failed to convince the Congress in 1950 just as they had earlier. As Altmeyer had said in 1939, variable grants were a political question. Such questions do not yield easily to logical reasoning. Neither Democrats nor Republicans could find political profit from helping the solid South.

Two important amendments encouraged welfare agencies to increase provision for health care. Far from approving any system that smacked of socialized medicine, both the national government and the states heartily supported efforts to improve the nation's health. It was at this time that the National Institutes of Health and the National Institute of Mental Health were created. World War II had increased the nation's health consciousness by revealing on the one hand the inordinate number of draftees rejected for physical and mental deficiencies, and on the other hand the "miracle cures" brought about by antibiotic drugs.

The ban on assistance to individuals residing in public medical institutions—written into the Social Security Act to bring down the infamous almshouse—was lifted. In an acknowledgment of the modern retirement/nursing home, assistance could be made to persons living there, provided state standards were set and met. An allowance for medical care payable to the recipient only had always been included in the "needs" column of the family budget. In low payment states, however, it was often dropped, throwing the sick on charity medicine. The 1950 amendment removed the medical allowance from the family budget, authorizing instead federal matching for direct (vendor) payments to physicians, hospitals, and other health care providers. There was a catch, however. Medical vendor payments must be held within the payment maximum. In 1956, reimbursement to the states was greatly expanded, however, facilitating their ability to make medical care a reality to the welfare recipient. Under the 1956 amendment, states were encouraged to average their medical costs (in the adult categories at $6 per case) to receive a federal match on a 50 percent basis, within a specified maximum.

These medical amendments were seen as an opportunity to work with doctors, hospitals, public health officers, and others to improve the quality and quantity of medical care for welfare recipients. Medical vendor payments tended to be approved even by critics of welfare—a direct payment might buy booze and cigarettes. Nevertheless medical vendor payments, inasmuch as they were payments in kind, can be viewed as a step backward from the pension idea toward poor law philosophy.[23]

The federal role in administrative procedures was strengthened somewhat when the local welfare agency was required to act upon applications for assistance "with reasonable promptness." The tactic of establishing waiting lists to meet a shortage of funds would not be tolerated after July 1, 1951. In the event of a fiscal crisis, the funds available must be divided up among those eligible for assistance, even if this meant across-the-board reductions for all. The BPA interpreted "reasonable promptness" as thirty days.[24]

But congressional committees remained stout defenders of states' rights on matters deemed central to establishing eligibility. When faced with the recommendation to abolish all residence and citizenship requirements as obsolete in a highly mobile society, Congress refused. When it was argued that states should follow the federal act, which was silent on relatives' responsibility to contribute to the support of needy kin, Congress refused again.[25]

Relatives' responsibility in ADC was another matter entirely, no less a matter than the basic social duty of parents to support their children. In 1948, nonsupport by absent fathers accounted for 44.5 percent of the caseload, an increase of almost one-third since 1942. Yet the BPA did not believe that the federal government should inject itself in child support enforcement actions. Indeed, bureau staff felt that state laws placed undue burdens on caseworkers and tended to delay prompt assistance to needy children. The child support amendment that came in 1950 was unsolicited, purely a creature of Congress. The amendment itself, Section 402(a) of Title IV, was mild. All that was required of state welfare agencies was transfer of information. As of July 1, 1952, the state plan for ADC must "provide for prompt notice to appropriate law-enforcement officials of the furnishing of aid to dependent children in respect of a child who has been deserted or abandoned by a parent" (NOLEO). The NOLEO requirement marked the first statutory signal of growing disfavor with ADC.[26]

The second statutory signal, the so-called Jenner amendment, was attached as a rider to the Revenue Act of 1951. For all practical purposes the Jenner amendment revoked the "confidentiality" amendment of 1939. It was a response to demands that the names of welfare recipients be opened to public scrutiny so that fraud and abuse could be more readily exposed. Specifically, it was a response to a finding that the state of Indiana, which had passed such a law, was no longer in conformity with the Social Security Act and would consequently lose its federal match. Once it became clear that Senator William E. Jenner of Indiana had solid support for his amendment across a broad spectrum of governors—Democratic and Republican, conservative and liberal—who took their stand on the platform of states' rights, objections from welfare professionals carried little weight. As signed into law by Truman in October 1951, the amendment circumscribed the power to withhold federal funds when welfare rolls were opened to the public, provided the law prohibited the use of such information for commercial or political purposes.[27]

Social Services

In this context, social services might emerge as a suitable way to help people get off welfare and into the mainstream. Or social services might be dismissed as part of the personal meddling and do-goodism that tended to sap independence and perpetuate dependency. Elizabeth Wickenden, representing the APWA, had this pro-con thinking very much in mind as she made the case for a social services amendment in 1949. Everyone could understand the need for food and shelter. It was more difficult to imagine the need for "advice, information, or a temporary helping hand in solving some problem," she argued. Yet the more social insurance with its "properly impersonal machinery" assumed burdens now carried by assistance, the more essential the existence of an agency to offer "more personalized service when it is needed."

Presumably some social insurance beneficiaries might seek services from the welfare agency even though financially independent. Others could be helped to fend off debilitating illness, delinquency, and dependency through preventive services. The APWA Policy Committee further identified "services" as "personal services rendered by professional workers," presumably trained social workers. "Assistance" meant "financial aid to those who need it." No sharp distinction was implied in practice because "a maximum degree of administrative flexibility" would encourage "service and financial aid to supplement, underpin, and implement each other."

No *sharp* distinction, but still a distinction. Most desired was a freestanding social service system. To achieve this, "social service must be recognized as a welfare function in its own right, serving needs not necessarily economic in character, and should therefore not be subordinated to assistance or treated as a part of the cost of its administration." Instead, "federal financial aid should be available to both [assistance and social services] on a comparable basis as part of a comprehensive welfare plan."[28]

Hoey, to whom Altmeyer deferred for discussion of this subject at the hearings, was a moderate when it came to social services. She assured an audience at the National Conference of Social Work in 1937 that the bureau "deemed inadequate" any state plan that failed to include services, but did not claim that such "inadequate" plans went unapproved. She confided to her staff her strong feeling that "if the majority of the people in the United States had a minimum for subsistence, much of the casework we try to do would be wholly unnecessary." She considered "intensive casework" for all ADC families both unnecessary and unaffordable. Many ADC mothers had managed quite well before misfortune struck. A caseworker guiding their every action would sap their independence and leave them incapable of carrying on after their children were grown.

Hoey was impatient also with the failure of professional social work to research and make generalizations from the "wealth of information" contained in case records, to "bring together the accumulation of that experience" as a basis for recommendations about economic and social action. In 1945 she confessed to the National Conference that "the development of services has thus far been disappointingly slow," a fact she attributed partly to the silence of the Social Security Act and its resulting "limitations" as to matching, but also to the preoccupation of caseworkers with eligibility factors. "The greater the number of eligibility factors to be considered, the less the opportunity for rendering constructive service," she concluded.[29]

Hoey's testimony in 1949 mirrored her convictions. Refusing to be pinned down as to exactly what services would be offered, she simply noted that different states would want to do different things. She went on to emphasize the importance of financial assistance in keeping young families together and the elderly living in their own homes. Homemakers sent in to manage when a mother was ill had kept many children out of institutions. Severely handicapped persons had been instructed in self-care and introduced to community activities. Counseling had enabled families on the verge of breaking up to "find their way through their emotional confusions to a sound basis of mutual understanding and relationship." She cautioned that expansion of services, particularly family counseling, depended on the availability of trained social workers. In cities and towns, private agencies could provide family counseling, but such was not the case in rural areas. Yet Congress should support the social services amendment, she concluded, because "any effective steps to prevent family disintegration are worth taking, for nothing is more socially wasteful, both in terms of human values and expense, than a broken home."[30]

Wrapping a desired expansion of Children's Bureau child welfare services into the same package with public assistance services, as was done, did not prove mutually helpful. By law, the Children's Bureau program focused on problem children and children with problems, children who were homeless, neglected, or predelinquent. The vast majority of cases handled involved the placement of children in institutions or, preferably, foster homes. Title V of the Social Security Act restricted these services to rural areas because some churches, particularly the Catholic Church, had objected to their extension into urban areas where, it was argued, Catholic and other private agencies were firmly in control of the situation.

At the hearings on the 1950 amendments, Father John O'Grady, secretary of the National Conference of Catholic Charities, blasted the Children's Bureau and all of its works. After describing his travels about the countryside in a vain search for effective child welfare services, O'Grady suggested "that the Federal Government concentrate on the areas that it has already taken over." Somewhat indirectly, however, O'Grady supported services for ADC families. Recalling the expectation that ADC would obviate much if not most of the demand for placement of children, O'Grady faulted public welfare agencies for failure to provide services to children and families obviously in need of them.

But O'Grady was silent on separate funding for preventive services as presented in the administration bill. The Children's Bureau did receive additional authorization for expansion, with the proviso that voluntary agencies be utilized as had been customary in state and local communities.[31]

The short list of preventive and rehabilitative welfare services, the even shorter evidence of successful results, and the familiar cry for more social workers, hardly justified the global assertions contained in the APWA platform and testimony. Viewed in this light, the Ways and Means Committee's decision seems appropriately circumspect. The committee decided to make no change. Welfare services would continue to be lumped in with state administration and their costs matched, like the salaries of caseworkers, at the 50 percent rate. Recipients of, and applicants for, public assistance could receive any welfare services offered, presumably even services that might prevent applicants from actually getting on the rolls. But the prestige of a free-standing service function was disallowed, and along with it the desired open door to all comers with problems regardless of financial need.[32]

Withering Away

References to public assistance as a "residual program" during the course of the 1949 hearings were so frequent that the phrase became a kind of theme song. Assurances that public assistance would "wither away"— to use Gilbert Steiner's phrase—had been made before. In 1939, Altmeyer told the Senate Finance Committee that passage of survivor's insurance "ought to remove a large proportion of these dependent children from state mother's pension rolls." In 1947, he told a House Appropriations subcommittee that OAA and ADC would "decline rapidly" with universal social insurance coverage. In 1949, however, Altmeyer became more venturesome and more specific, predicting a repeal of the public assistance provisions of the Social Security Act: "If we have a comprehensive contributory social-insurance system covering all of these economic hazards to which the people are exposed, I believe that in time the residual load of public assistance would become so small in this country that the States and the localities could reasonably be expected to assume that load without Federal financial participation." But he could not say when. "The major element is this aged, the load of the aged, and that takes time," he admitted. Following along, Ways and Means saw a substantial place for public assistance for the next five to ten years. After that the "current load will be gradually diminished as aged recipients die and dependent children grow up." Apparently the Ways and Means Committee had forgotten that ADC had long outgrown the widow's pension characteristic. Altmeyer knew otherwise. But Altmeyer may have been thinking about costs.[33]

The total cost of ADC in 1949 was less than half that of OAA. States were paying roughly $686,000 as their share of OAA, while the ADC state share was only $236,000. In terms of cost, the argument that states could pick up ADC once the burden of OAA was lifted, is defensible, given a reasonably stable ADC caseload. Again, to give Altmeyer the benefit of the doubt, he may have reasoned from past state performance. So far his own BPA had pleaded in vain for more liberal eligibility standards in ADC.[34]

If the party line on public assistance was "wither away," Hoey was not constrained to follow it. Testifying after Altmeyer, she sought to put public assistance in its "proper perspective," to register the limitations of social insurance:

There will always remain a group of people who cannot qualify for benefits or for whom the benefits are inadequate. The objectives of our Social Security system cannot be fully attained unless we make adequate provision for this group of the needy. It is important to emphasize that employment should be maintained and protection through the social insurances should be effective so that the number of people who find themselves in need should be at a minimum, but I should also like to emphasize just as strongly that to the extent that other provisions are not adequate to attain our objectives of freedom from want, the public assistance program should be available to provide for unmet need.[35]

The truth or fallacy of the "wither away" prophecy, much less the justice of casting aspersions at its prophets, are of less consequence than evidence of a virtually universal wish that the prophecy come true. Walter George of Georgia, chairman of the Finance Committee, put the matter succinctly: the primary purpose of the 1950 amendments was to replace public assistance with social insurance. That purpose had not been attained. Rather, to the dismay of both Altmeyer and Hoey, the 1950 amendments and the debate preceding their passage contained the necessary elements for shattering the "original comprehensive concept of Social Security" and erecting in its place the dichotomy of Social Security and Welfare.[36]

Republican Surprise

The 1950 amendments having set the course, social insurance moved rapidly ahead to a commanding position by the end of the decade. In 1952

General Dwight D. Eisenhower, the choice of moderate Republican politicians, was elected by a personal landslide that failed to carry working majorities into Congress. The Senate was controlled by just one; the House by only eight. In two short years, the Democrats had the chairmanships back in the House and the Senate and increased their majorities both in 1956, when Eisenhower was reelected, and in 1958. Political realities thus dictated a bipartisan stance in social policy.

Conservative Republicans, the fraction of the party that preferred public assistance to social insurance, had minimal status during the Eisenhower years. Moderate and progressive Republicans who remembered the reasons why Herbert Hoover served only one term had no intention of repealing the New Deal, much less the Social Security Act. Rather, as Martha Derthick has pointed out, policymaking for Social Security became the private preserve of progressive Republicans. When Altmeyer, gracefully responding to political pressures, applied for Civil Service retirement, he was replaced for a brief time by John W. Tramburg, a nominal Republican and trained social worker, then director of the Wisconsin Department of Public Welfare. In 1954 the Social Security commissioner's position was given to another social worker, Charles I. Schottland, a nominal Democrat, who had been the Republican governor Earl Warren's director of public welfare in California.

Eisenhower was happy to stamp approval on the Hoover-Truman plan to create a Department of Health, Education, and Welfare (HEW), and with Oscar Ewing gone, Congress was glad to approve. As its first secretary, the President appointed Oveta Culp Hobby, a Texas Democrat-for-Ike, who had commanded the Women's Army Corps in World War II. Hobby was succeeded by Marion B. Folsom (1955–1958) and Arthur S. Flemming (1958–1961). Folsom, a leading welfare capitalist on leave from Eastman Kodak, was an old hand at Social Security. His experience reached back to the Committee on Economic Security, and he had served subsequent Advisory Councils as well as key committees of the National Association of Manufacturers. Although Flemming was president of Ohio Wesleyan University at the time of his appointment, he had worked repeatedly for the federal government—as-a member of the Civil Service Commission and the War Manpower Commission during World War II, and as director of the Office of Defense Mobilization during and after the Korean War. HEW's second echelon shared the same positive attitudes toward social insurance—Nelson A. Rockefeller as undersecretary (1953–1955), Roswell B. Perkins (1954–1957) and Elliot L. Richardson (1957–1959) as assistant secretaries for legislation.[37]

To say this is not to suggest that the atmosphere bore even a passing resemblance to the "good old days" when Altmeyer could work it all out directly with FDR. Progressive Republicans were not liberal Democrats. Among the more important differences, progressive Republicans were more fiscally cautious, more protective of states' rights and responsibilities, and more insistent about the work ethic than were liberal Democrats. Consequently, Republican brakes were applied at strategic points of the SSA legislative agenda. Sometimes the brakes held. More often a compromise was reached. But there was no turning back or grinding to a halt. By 1960 a record number of major amendments had established universal coverage for wage loss due to old age, death of the breadwinner, and disability. Old Age and Survivors Insurance had become Old Age, Survivors, and Disability Insurance (OASDI). At the same time benefits were increased an average of 110 percent, while access to the system was facilitated.[38]

As intended, the pro-insurance amendments of the 1950s had a decisive withering away effect upon old age assistance. A less marked but still significant movement occurred or was anticipated over the entire public assistance caseload, including general assistance. In September 1950 OAA recipients outnumbered OASI beneficiaries by about 700,000. OAA was making payments to 2.8 million persons, 226 persons per 1,000 aged sixty-five and over. By 1960 the figures had been impressively reversed: 10.1 million elderly—646 of every 1,000—were receiving insurance benefits, while the number of OAA recipients had decreased to 2.4 million at a rate of 151 per 1,000.

But collection of Social Security benefits did not ensure independent living. For millions of elderly retirees, savings and other assets supplemented Social Security benefits to allow them to continue their customary standards of living. For hundreds of thousands of others who lacked personal means, Social Security benefits were insufficient to sustain even a poverty-level existence. For these poor retirees, OAA substituted for savings. Concurrent receipt of Social Security and OAA rose steadily from 276,200 to 675,600 throughout the decade, by 1960 making up 28 percent of the OAA caseload. Insofar as the needy blind had worked sufficiently long in covered employment to accumulate the necessary wage credits, they were able, at age sixty-five, to transfer from AB to OASDI, here again with benefits subject to supplementation.

Extension of coverage to additional occupational groups meant the transfer of more and more widows from ADC to OASDI. Dependency due to death of the father declined from 17.1 to 10.0 percent during the 1950s. Although some widows with children were unable to manage without supplementation, most of these young women had life insurance and other inheritance or could obtain full or part-time work. The number of families receiving OASDI and ADC concurrently never exceeded 50,000 and remained a low 5 percent of the ADC caseload.[39]

Disability insurance could be expected to affect the size and cost of public assistance, but just how and how much was difficult to predict. One major question was the amount of prior work force connection among the disabled. Many disabled persons would not have worked in covered employment at all, and many would not have worked the required twenty quarters. A second major question revolved around the all-important matter of defining disability. The language of the law sounded ironclad: disability must be expected to result in death or to be of long and indefinite duration. But human beings had to make a judgment that could not in the very nature of things be altogether clear-cut, let alone consistent. As enacted in 1956, disability insurance was collectible only from age fifty to sixty-four. In 1958 coverage was extended to dependents of beneficiaries in this age group. Two years later the SSA got what it had always wanted—disability insurance without an age limitation.[40]

Although the very title of the more inclusive Aid to the Permanently and Totally Disabled conjured up visions of helplessness, the BPA promoted a more liberal definition. The key to eligibility was the ability to work. State welfare agencies were instructed to define "permanently and totally disabled" as "an individual [who] has some physical or mental impairment, disease, or loss that substantially precludes him from engaging in useful occupations within his competence, such as holding a job or homemaking." Permanency of the disability would be evaluated by medical doctors and was indicated when the individual's condition was not likely to respond to known treatment or to disappear spontaneously and would therefore continue for life. With the medical report in hand, the social worker would evaluate the totality of the disability, using information about the individual's age, education and training, skills, work history, activities required at home or on the job, and various personal characteristics, all directed toward arriving at the individual's competency to perform.

Many needy disabled persons were already assisted by three of the four federal categorical programs, and, as Altmeyer had testified, by state and local general assistance. Each of these programs had its singular definition of disability. For example, states defined the eligibility standard in AB as corrected vision of 20/200 or less in the better eye.

"Physical or mental incapacity," the words used to describe a parental condition leading to a child's deprivation in ADC, had been interpreted

TABLE 7.1. Number of Recipients or Beneficiaries in Selected Social Programs, 1950–1970 (in thousands)

Year	OAA	AFDC	AB	APTD	GA	OASI	DI
1950	2,786	2,233	97	69	866	3,477	—
1951	2,701	2,041	97	124	664	4,379	—
1952	2,635	1,991	98	161	587	5,025	—
1953	2,582	1,941	100	192	618	5,981	—
1954	2,553	2,173	102	222	880	6,886	—
1955	2,538	2,192	104	241	743	7,960	—
1956	2,499	2,270	107	266	731	9,128	—
1957	2,480	2,497	108	290	907	10,950	150
1958	2,438	2,486	110	325	1,246	12,133	268
1959	2,370	2,946	108	346	1,107	13,244	495
1960	2,305	3,073	107	369	1,244	14,157	687
1961	2,229	3,566	103	389	1,069	15,468	1,027
1962	2,183	3,789	99	428	900	16,778	1,275
1963	2,152	3,930	97	464	872	17,583	1,452
1964	2,120	4,219	95	509	779	18,236	1,563
1965	2,087	4,396	85	557	677	19,128	1,739
1966	2,073	4,666	84	588	663	20,797	1,970
1967	2,073	5,309	83	646	782	21,565	2,140
1968	2,027	6,086	81	702	826	22,225	2,335
1969	2,074	7,313	81	803	860	22,827	2,488
1970	2,082	9,659	81	935	1,056	23,564	2,665

SOURCES: U.S. Department of Commerce, Bureau of the Census, *Historical Statistics of the United States: Colonial Times to 1970. Part 1*; U.S. Department of Health and Human Services, Social Security Administration, *Social Security Bulletin: Annual Statistical Supplement 1987*; U.S. Department of Health, Education and Welfare, Social Security Administration, *Social Security Bulletin: Annual Statistical Supplement 1956, 1957, 1958,* and *1959.*
Prepared by Howard Iams, Social Security Administration, Bureau of Research and Statistics.

KEY: OAA = Old Age Assistance
    AFDC = Aid to Families with Dependent Children
    AB = Aid to the Blind
    APTD = Aid to the Permanently and Totally Disabled
    GA = General Assistance
    SSA, OASI = Old Age and Survivors Insurance
    SSA, DI = Disability Insurance

more broadly than in any other of the categorical programs. The BPA defined "incapacity" as "loss of earning power" that arose from individual rather than external or social causes. Disability was almost always present in a case of incapacity, but disability was but one side of the equation. The other side was social adjustment. Incapacity was said to result from the interaction of a physical or mental disability with other factors in the parent's social setting that determined an inability to provide for the children. The disabled, who appeared in such large numbers on state and local general assistance rolls in 1950, included just about anyone who was needy, was under age sixty-five, and who was not blind by medical definition.[41]

Aid to the Blind reached somewhat under 100,000 persons annually during the 1950s. Disability insurance could be expected to lower this caseload, at first affecting the group aged fifty to sixty-four, and, during the 1960s, all blind persons who had sufficient prior attachment to the work force. In its first full year of operation, APTD helped 124,000 persons. By July 1957, when age fifty to sixty-four disability insurance payments began, APTD cases had increased to about 200,000. In 1960, when the disability age limit was dropped, recipients of APTD totaled 369,000. Analysts in the BPA believed that the rate of growth would have been faster absent the disability insurance program. They noted that in March 1960 insurance beneficiaries outnumbered assistance recipients for the first time. Insurance beneficiaries were growing at a rate of about 8,000 monthly compared with an assistance recipient growth of 2,000.[42]

APTD offered an opportunity to transfer some of the burden of ADC to the new category. Deprivation due to the incapacity of a parent—always a large segment of ADC—accounted for about 25 percent of the caseload in 1950. Prior to the 1950 amendments, these two-parent households had been held pretty much to the common-household expense allowance so far as one adult, usually the father, was concerned. Often general assistance was necessary as a supplement.[43]

Now the caretaker relative, usually the mother, was to receive a specific personal allowance. State welfare administrators attending a briefing conference in Washington in September 1950 expressed eagerness to transfer as many recipients as possible to the federally funded category for the disabled. The BPA was equally eager to smooth the way, ruling that transfers of individuals in the active caseload could be made either from ADC or general assistance, provided "sufficient medical evidence exists in the case record to support a diagnosis which falls within the classification of specific conditions believed to result in complete helplessness." Cases could be reviewed later in reference to state plan submittal.

With specific reference to ADC, the BPA ruled that each of the adults in a family with an incapacitated parent could receive a separate personal allowance. Under this policy the mother could receive the caretaker allowance up to the current maximum of $27, while the incapacitated father could receive his own payment from Aid to the Disabled irrespective of the $27 maximum. Should this turn out to be applicable in a large number of ADC cases, the total cost of welfare programs would rise substantially.[44]

Given the broad interpretation of "incapacity" in ADC and the even less exact measures applied in general assistance, about all that could be ventured in the absence of experience was that there were a lot of people out there whose extreme poverty could be traced to some sort of disabling condition. Although BPA staff welcomed APTD as a way to extend federal help to another group of needy persons, the new program was regarded as a half-measure—"no substitute" for federally aided general assistance. Nevertheless, BPA staff echoed Altmeyer and the leadership of the APWA in their assessment of the overall situation after passage of the 1950 amendments. Social insurance was expected to move steadily toward assumption "of its proper role as the major defense against loss of income resulting from retirement and death" (and, it was hoped, disability). Then, the argument ran, if economic conditions remained favorable while social insurance took over these major burdens, public assistance should stabilize and the rising caseloads and growing costs of the immediate postwar years could become a thing of the past. Whereupon welfare agencies could direct expanded social services to the smaller group that remained dependent, helping many of them, in turn, to make their own way.[45]

The prosperous, low inflation 1950s, beginning with a Democratic president but for eight years thereafter headed by a Republican, marked a watershed in the growth of America's welfare state. In signing the 1950 amendments on August 28, Truman echoed Altmeyer and the Congress in predicting that social insurance protection would "ultimately reduce dependence on public charity."[46] Yet the 1950 amendments tended to encourage the growth of public assistance, however temporary its detractors hoped that would be.

Although general assistance was again denied, the compromise was still an additional whole new category—Aid to the Permanently and Totally Disabled. Social services were denied separate status, but no one perceived that as a lost cause. The separate actions on medical care added federal money for in- and out-patient care to needy individuals. Maximums had been raised both in 1946 and 1948, and the adult caretaker given a separate allowance in 1950.

But, negative actions were there. Confidentiality of records was breached with passage of the Jenner amendment, and dissatisfaction with failure to collect child support from deserting fathers was expressed through NOLEO. Moreover, the strong emphasis on the "withering away" concept and the unprecedented decision to allow public assistance separate testimony at the hearings signaled a decided weakening of the commitment to "the original, comprehensive concept of Social Security."

8

The Welfare Mess

SANGUINE PREDICTIONS OF declining caseloads and costs ignored actual rising caseloads and costs, not to speak of strident warning signals of public disapproval of welfare programs, particularly ADC and general assistance. Not since WPA days had there been so much sensational welfare news.

Back on Page One

The first wave of criticism began in 1947 and lasted five years. Welfare not only returned to page 1 of the newspapers but was featured in popular magazines, on radio, even on that new powerful media instrument, television. "Welfare boom" stories zeroed in on chiselers and cheats, runaway husbands, live-in boyfriends, unmarried baby breeders, loafers, and drunks. But these articles also contained numbers, big numbers—$2.3 billion yearly going to 5.7 million persons "in the midst of record prosperity," noted *U.S. News and World Report.*

The taxpayers, many of whom had become liable for federal income taxes for the first time during World War II, now saw state and local taxes climbing also, with sales taxes on necessities one of the newer ways to raise revenue.[1] For married couples the federal income tax filing requirement dropped from $5,000 in 1939 to $1,200 in 1942, where it remained. The first tax bracket, which stood at 4 percent in 1939, reached 22.2 percent in 1952, dropped slightly to 20 percent in 1954, and remained at that level until the tax cut of 1964. State individual income taxes accounted for $343,000 of state and local revenue in 1944; $1,065 million in 1953; $2,463 million in 1960. Revenue from sales taxes rose from $2,289 million in 1944, to $6,927 million in 1953, to $11,849 million in 1960.[2]

Many, if not most, of the lurid exposés of life on welfare emerged from local investigations, sometimes sparked by the newspapers, sometimes by city auditors, sometimes by politicians, sometimes by private citizens' "watchdog" associations. These official and unofficial representatives of the public worked together as the assaulting force against incumbents at city hall and welfare professionals on the state and local payroll. Typically the first round of an investigation charged that there were thousands of chiselers—30 to 60 percent—on the rolls. Explanations and reinvestigations would whittle this down into the hundreds—10 to 15 percent. Often, too, illustrative cases would turn out to be overblown. The $4,000 speedboat reportedly used by a welfare recipient to cruise on the Detroit River had actually been purchased for $800 during the owner's better times, had a leaky bottom, and no takers at $50.[3]

The end of the first wave of welfare criticism was signaled by the *Saturday Evening Post*, the popular magazine that had commissioned the longer articles. In July 1952, the *Post* published an article presenting the SSA viewpoint. Retracting nothing, the magazine explained its position in a foreword. The editors stood by their previous stories, which they insisted had been "justified." They were not opposed to welfare, only the "shoddy, and at times scandalous, administration of it." Yet because so much money and so many persons were involved, they had agreed that "the other side" deserved a hearing. The photos showed white children dressed for church and school in simple, neat clothing.[4]

By this time the *Post* editors had doubtless concluded they could afford to publish a rebuttal, the antiwelfare campaign having made its point in several important practical ways. On the federal level, the Jenner amendment opened the rolls for public inspection, and the NOLEO requirement affirmed parental responsibility for the support of children. On the state level, the Council of State Governments (whose executive director was Frank Bane) developed model legislation for collecting support obligations across county and state lines. By the summer of 1951, thirty-seven states and two territories had enacted reciprocal legislation to compel support for dependent wives and children. On the local level, large city welfare departments were beginning to hire special investigators to look into cases suspected of fraud and abuse.[5]

One other event that occurred before the Eisenhower presidency indicated an unmistakable challenge to federal power over state and local welfare administration. In the two years since its publication in 1945, *Common Human Needs*, the training pamphlet written by Charlotte Towle, had been reprinted twice and had sold almost thirteen thousand copies. Probably somewhat more than half of these had been distributed to public welfare agencies. Given that there were about twenty-five thousand public welfare workers at any one time and a high rate of turnover, it is clear that central office guidance suggesting selective use of Towle's book had been followed at least to some extent. Sales had been helped by the book's adoption on reading lists in schools of social work. Doubtless, also, *Common Human Needs* had wide distribution and considerable use in large city welfare departments in the Northeast, Midwest, and California, where professional social workers had been in charge since FERA days. The Baltimore Department of Public Welfare fits this description.

In Baltimore, in December 1947, the Committee on Governmental Efficiency and Economy, a group of business leaders that regularly monitored city hall, released a report on welfare. The major conclusion—that social work practices fostered continued dependency—was bolstered by quotations from *Common Human Needs*, leading off with this: "Social security and public assistance programs are a basic essential for attainment of the socialized state envisaged in a democratic ideology, a way of life which so far has been realized only in slight measure."[6] As the Baltimore report made the front pages nationwide, the BPA/FSA struggled to deny that *Common Human Needs* expressed "official policy" but instead was intended to provide general orientation for nonprofessional workers; to suggest that the Baltimore investigation, like many others conducted recently, was mostly about general assistance, which was not a federal program; and, most of all, to plead for a reading "in context," an understanding that the word "socialize" was a technical term used here to mean "render social, especially to train for a social environment." Hoey hoped that the 1947–48 criticism would die down. It did, only to be revived in the midst of the battle over national health insurance.

This time, in 1950–51, *Common Human Needs* was linked directly to Oscar Ewing, to socialized medicine, and to the welfare state by the American Medical Association. In April 1951, after nine months of hearing *Common Human Needs* used against him, Ewing disclaimed all responsibility for the publication. Arguing that it had been written before he came to FSA (right) and that it was not being currently distributed (wrong), he called on the editors of the *Journal of the American Medical Association* for a retraction and an apology, which he did not get. With his back to the wall, Ewing ordered the remaining copies of Towle's pamphlet withdrawn from sale and the plates destroyed. Whereupon the BPA sent word to the regions that *Common Human Needs* was no longer to be included in staff training. The "book burning," as the social workers regarded it, was defended by Ewing on the ground that he had "more important things to do" than argue the fine points of language. In a letter to Towle, Hoey seemed to agree. She had not followed up Towle's earlier offer to revise the fateful sentence because "the frequent use of the word socialized and the possibility of its further misinterpretation" had led her "to feel that if the publication were to be revised, more than one change would be advisable to forestall further misunderstanding."[7]

Although welfare programs did not emerge completely unscathed, neither did they suffer irreparable damage from the first wave of public criticism. When it came to what really mattered—money, that is—welfare programs were not abolished, were not cut back, were not even brought to a standstill. Successively, beginning in 1952, Democratic or Republican administrations and Democratic or Republican Congresses authorized more money to the states for welfare. Both the federal maximum and the federal share of the grant were increased in ADC as well as in the adult categories. Under the 1952 amendments the federal share in OAA, AB, and APTD was computed as four-fifths of the first $25 of a state's average monthly payment per recipient plus half of the remainder, and individual maximums were raised from $50 to $55. For ADC the federal share became four-fifths of the first $15 of a state's average monthly payment per recipient plus half the balance, within individual maximums of $30 for the caretaker adult, $30 for the first child, and $21 for each additional child. In 1956 the adult maximums went up another $5 and ADC another $2. The ADC matching formula was raised to fourteen-seventeenths of $17 plus half the balance.

A huge liberalization came in 1956, when separate matching was introduced for medical vendor payments, freeing them from ties to individual matching. In the adult categories, the medical maximum was established at $6 times the number of recipients, while for ADC, the maximum was $6 times the number of adult caretakers and $3 times the number of children. In 1958, maximums for individual recipients and medical vendor payments were combined into one—$65 for the adult categories and $30 for ADC. Also in 1958, the long-sought variable grant formula was finally adopted. Henceforth federal financial participation would be fixed at 50 percent for those states where per capita income was equal to or above the national average and would range upward to 65 percent for states where income fell below that.[8]

TABLE 8.1. Public Assistance Payments Compared to Wages, 1930–1970 (Average monthly amounts in then-current dollars)

Year	Public Assistance[a]					Wages[b]		
	OAA	AFDC	AB	APTD	GA	Manufacturing	Retail trade (clerks)	Farms
1930	—	—	—	—	—	100	—	38
1936	19	9	26	—	24	93	—	24
1940	20	10	25	—	24	108	92	28
1945	31	15	34	—	33	191	124	79
1950	43	21	46	44	47	253	172	99
1955	50	24	56	49	55	328	211	123
1960	59	28	67	56	72	388	250	149
1965	63	33	81	67	69	466	288	170
1970	78	50	104	98	112	579	357	251

SOURCES: DHEW Pub. No. (SRS) 73-03101, NCSS Report A4(71), *Trend Report—Graphic Presentation of Public Assistance and Related Data*, etc. (10-6-72), 7. Gives monthly data for June and December. December data (slightly higher) presented here. For retail and manufacturing weekly wages: DOL BLS, reprinted in *Economic Report of the President* (1975) Table B-30, p. 230; and for farm wages, *Historical Statistics of the United States*, Part I, p. 468.

KEY: OAA = Old Age Assistance
    AFDC = Aid to Families with Dependent Children
    AB = Aid to the Blind
    APTD = Aid to the Permanently and Totally Disabled
    GA = General Assistance

[a]*Money* payments per *recipient, except* GA, which is per case. AFDC likely more than one recipient per household or case.

[b]Manufacturing and retail trade monthly wages are derived from "average gross weekly earnings in private non-agricultural industries" multiplied by 4.33. Farm wages are "per month" "with board and room."

While the most important aspect of the liberalizing amendments was the life-sustaining vote of confidence represented by the money itself, it is also notable that these amendments were initiated in the House or Senate rather than offered as part of an administration bill. They were often suggested by "consultants" such as Wilbur Cohen or Elizabeth Wickenden, and were the amendments usually tacked on to the Social Security bill itself.

Liberal Republicans in the Eisenhower administration had been won over—some would say "taken in"—by social insurance. At the same time they were committed to preventing the budget deficits that would result from continuing increases in the federal share of public assistance costs. The Eisenhower administration wanted the states to assume more financial responsibility, not simply to realize savings in the federal budget but, more important, to lodge policymaking and administration more firmly at the state-local level. But as long as social insurance (the Republican baby) and welfare (the Democratic baby) were locked together in the same bill and voted under a closed rule, Republicans could not prevail, not even under threat of a veto. On the one occasion, in 1958, when a veto was threatened and a pocket veto was possible, a compromise was arranged to reduce the amount of the increase in the maximums and the formula for the federal share. Whereupon, the following year, the higher figures were restored by amendment to a tax bill. As Russell Long of Louisiana, chairman of the Finance Committee and sponsor of the amendment explained: "Justice delayed is not always justice denied."[9]

The liberalizing amendments passed in the 1950s helped states raise their standards of assistance and, in doing so, contributed significantly to the rise in caseloads and welfare costs. With a raise in standards, thousands of persons became newly eligible for assistance. The effect was greatest in Long's area of the country. But as he argued in June 1959:

my amendment would benefit almost every person on public welfare by an average of about $3 a month per person. . . . It would benefit the dependent children, the needy, the blind, the disabled, and the aged. It would benefit the high income states and the low income states. . . . More than half the states in the Union are doing more for their aged than the federal program envisions. . . . This is simply a matter of getting the federal government to move in stride with the states and to keep up with the states in their efforts to provide adequately for the needs of the aged.[10]

The liberalizing amendments found their greatest justification in the group of needy adults who could not work because they were old or disabled, the group that would be cared for eventually by OASDI. Long would just as soon have left the ADC program off his list of increases, and he certainly wasn't alone. The children's program had some friends, though, enough of them to make it understood that ADC was always to remain part of the package when maximums and federal sharing were under consideration. For its part the Eisenhower administration never suggested that it be otherwise.[11] The only justification for ADC rolls and costs to go down, the friends of the program argued, was to reduce the need for the program. Most of its critics conceded that, too. The critics were calling for child support from absent fathers, for putting more mothers to work, for fewer cases of illegitimacy, and for purging the rolls of chiselers and cheats.

Child Support Enforcement

Because the amendment requiring notification to law enforcement officials in absent father cases (NOLEO) did not become effective until July 1, 1952, the BPA had about eighteen months to prepare regulations and recommendations to the states. Although the BPA was quick to endorse the father's duty to support his children, it was no secret that the bureau was uncomfortable, if not downright opposed, to becoming involved with law enforcement. The ADC program had moved a long way from the discredited Societies for the Prevention of Cruelty to Children—known as "The Cruelty" to poor people—which had often removed children from parental custody for no other reason than failure to support because of unemployment.[12] Faced with having to do something to comply with the NOLEO amendment, the BPA was at pains to maintain a sharp distinction between welfare and law enforcement.

Far from attempting to do it alone, the bureau established an advisory group with representatives of state and local welfare agencies. It held its first meeting in conjunction with representatives of APWA, the National Legal Aid Association, the Children's Bureau, and the FSA general counsel's office in November 1950. A second meeting was held in June 1951. At the third and final meeting, held on March 31 and April 1, 1952, those attending included an assistant attorney general, a juvenile court judge, and representatives from private family and child welfare agencies.

The draft recommendations for policy and practice presented to the advisory group's final meeting contained key sections about identifying the types of cases subject to notification as well as the content and method of informing the applicant or recipient about the amendment. Its main thrust was the exclusion of identified groups from the legal requirements. Workers would not be called upon to send notices in all cases where the father was absent from the home. Even after involuntary absences (incarceration, longtime hospitalization) were excluded, a large number of cases, depending on state law, would not automatically fall into the category of "desertion" or "abandonment" specified in the statement. Divorced or legally separated absent fathers would usually be exempt, as would fathers of illegitimate children either where paternity had not been established or where a support obligation was not required.

The importance of personal counseling as the applicant/recipient was told about the new requirement was deemed paramount. She might be helped to understand the impending legal procedures, given suggestions on how to locate the absent parent, or referred to legal aid or another community service. Compulsion was to be avoided and reconciliation or "voluntary adjustment" preferred to court action. Eligibility for assistance should not be dependent upon cooperation of the mother beyond the agreed-to notification. Although the BPA understood that "cooperation of a child's mother in any action against the deserting father will be indispensable in most instances," it insisted that cooperation would "generally be more effective if enlisted rather than compelled by the withdrawal of assistance."[13]

The BPA's draft drew severe criticism from the APWA Policy Committee and the California Department of Social Welfare. The director of the APWA, Loula Dunn, wrote to Altmeyer, "the materials so far issued . . . are not sufficiently clearcut and positive," and should be revised to render them "more definitely related to the language contained in the amendment." Policies and procedures developed at both federal and state levels should "leave no doubt that the legal intent of the amendment will be fulfilled." Dunn went on to point out that the interrelationship between NOLEO and the Uniform Reciprocal Enforcement of Support Act (URESA— draft legislation issued by the Council of State Governments), cried out for close cooperation between the Council of State Governments, SSA, and APWA "in order to secure the most fruitful results under these two laws."[14]

Charles Schottland, the director of California's Department of Social Welfare, said much the same thing, but more bluntly. The "general tone" of the material disturbed him, for "it appeared to accept the expressed policy of the law so reluctantly that it gives the impression of wanting to avoid the law." Noting that California law now required the mother to give "reasonable assistance" to law enforcement officers under pain of forfeiting ADC, he pronounced "unsound" the recommendation to deny a link between a mother's active cooperation with eligibility. As to the definition of cases to be reported, Schottland, taking his cue from his department's legal advisor, recommended a broad net to include referral of all cases of nonsupport unless clearly inappropriate. It simply would not do to excuse divorced or legally separated fathers automatically. Clearly, Schottland argued, "the Legislature of California was concerned with those situations in which parents were not supporting." Since divorced and separated fathers remained legally responsible for child support, technical desertion in nonsupport cases was implied. He concluded that failure to obtain support from this group would only invite serious criticism.[15]

Final federal recommendations, issued June 26, 1952, were all but completely unresponsive to these important critics. The BPA rested with its earlier brief description of the amendment and the minimum requirements related to the working of the state plan. Like earlier drafts, the new recommendations emphasized the negative, leading off with the following: "Basic to planning is the recognition that the amendment . . . applies only to certain areas of the total question of nonsupport—that of desertion and abandonment." It was then strongly suggested that the amendment was but a small part of the very large area of nonsupport activities that state agencies were already carrying out. A clear understanding of the distinctive functions and responsibilities of the welfare agency, law enforcement agency, and families themselves was also basic to planning. "Constructive use" of law enforcement services in relation to the individual needs of families lay with the welfare agency, while "what action, if any" was indicated in a given case lay with law enforcement. Emphasis continued to be placed upon preselection of cases by the welfare agency, with the divorced, the legally separated, and fathers of illegitimate children singled out as likely exclusions.

Here and there a new sentence or two added a positive note, such as the statement, "It is important that the parent or other relative be brought into early discussions with the law-enforcement official to present personally all pertinent information needed to assist the law enforcement official in making a decision on action to be taken and in carrying out such action." But the bureau "advised against legislation that makes the actual commencement of action on the part of a parent to obtain support . . . a condition of eligibility." The bureau used the recommendations as yet another platform from which to point out the value of casework service, not just for understanding procedures, but in deciding what action should be taken whether to "undertake a plan of reconciliation; work out a voluntary agreement for care and support; initiate a civil suit or criminal prosecution; withdraw the claim for assistance and try to find some other solution; or, if no other course seems practical, to utilize the assistance grant and the family's remaining resources." Since runaway father's legislation was a matter of state law, the bureau was not compelled to mention URESA and did not do so.[16]

Shortly after the inauguration of President Eisenhower, while Altmeyer was still commissioner of Social Security and Hoey still director of the Bureau of Public Assistance, state public welfare agencies were told they could obtain addresses of deserting fathers from the Bureau of Old Age and Survivors Insurance (BOASI) upon formal request. Some precedent for breaching the confidentiality of OASI records existed in that welfare agencies had earlier been granted permission to check for possible duplication of payments under OASI and OAA. This precedent was followed precisely; the information to be provided was "within the family." It was not available to law enforcement agencies directly. Altmeyer's order was issued as an exception to SSA Regulation no. 1, and states were expected to call upon the BOASI only as a last resort.[17]

When Charles I. Schottland became commissioner of Social Security in 1954, he predictably asked questions about the ADC nonsupport problem. The result was a bureau study.[18] Conducted three years after NOLEO became effective, the study showed far less than the spectacular results predicted by some of the sponsors of the new federal requirement. In ADC families broken by divorce, separation, or desertion, only 18.3 percent received support contributions; in cases of illegitimacy, only 10.2 percent. Yet the study also failed to confirm the predictions of those in BPA who believed that there wasn't much potential support money out there and little hope of collecting even that. Of those cases in which a support order or agreement was in effect, 41.8 percent of fathers who had married the mother contributed. The trouble was that in 57.6 percent of absent father cases, no support order or agreement had been obtained. And a large part of the failure to issue support orders was due to the fact that in 54.5 percent of the cases, the whereabouts of the father was unknown. Thus while it was true, as the study pointed out, that collections from the many fathers that quickly established second families would be difficult, and that the incomes of estranged men tended to be lower than those living in intact families, there was substantial indication that stepping up the effort would yield better results. In terms of dollars, the savings so far were a drop in the bucket. For the twenty-seven states with available data, only

$9.2 million had been contributed on a $350 million program expenditure. Still, it was something. In states with maximums on assistance payments a few families actually had more money to live on because these states allowed contributions from the father to be retained.[19]

BOASI records turned out to be a valuable source of information in locating absent fathers. During the twelve months beginning in April 1958 BOASI handled 58,407 requests from welfare agencies. A spot check made in April 1959 showed that information from social insurance records led to the location of 40 percent of the missing fathers. More than half of this number were placed under orders to contribute, and most paid. At this time Congressman Charles A. Vanik of Ohio and William Beck Widnall of New Jersey pressed for opening the records to law enforcement officials also—a procedure that stood to benefit women not on welfare and was in line with the preferences of many local welfare workers. But SSA Commissioner William L. Mitchell, Altmeyer's former deputy, stood firm. He recommended that the procedure be opened routinely to public welfare agencies but continue to be restricted to them. After Secretary of HEW Arthur S. Flemming agreed, the new policy became effective on June 9, 1960.[20]

Suitable Homes

As ADC came to be equated with immorality, particularly immorality as identified with the presence of so many illegitimate children in the caseload, many states adopted various restrictive rules under the rubric known as a "suitable home." The suitable home requirement was deeply rooted in the tradition of mother's aid to nice families. Although Title IV did not mention home conditions or morality, congressional intent sanctioned consideration of "moral character" in defining the terms of eligibility.[21] This, together with the general freedom of the states to establish rules and regulations for eligibility, nearly ensured a suitable home clause in state plans. Accordingly, the APWA included the following statement in its model act: "Assistance shall be given . . . to any dependent child . . . who is living in a suitable family home meeting the standards of care and health, fixed by the laws of this state and the rules and regulations of the State Department thereunder."[22]

Only after a number of states began to use the suitable home clause to restrict eligibility in arbitrary ways did the BPA step in with formal recommendations. Some states had attempted simply to cut off families that had more than one illegitimate child. In most states governors vetoed these bills. Georgia enacted such a law but quickly removed it when the SSA expressed the opinion that it was illegal and that federal funds would likely be cut off. But the states had lawyers, too. Using regulation rather than law, South Carolina devised a "substitute parent" policy. The man who lived in a common-law relationship became a "substitute parent" who was responsible for the care and support of all children within the household, whether fathered by him or not.[23]

A State Letter issued in March 1945 stressed the impossibility of precise definition of a suitable home. Cutting off benefits to the mother was not an immediate and direct help to the children. If the home presented a danger such as neglect or abuse of the child, protective services through child welfare agencies and the courts should be utilized. On this basis, the bureau recommended deletion of suitable home provisions from public assistance laws. In the interim, welfare agencies were urged to reexamine their policies with a view to separating the protective from the eligibility function.[24] Fifteen states did repeal their suitable home provisions, but five others passed new suitable home laws. By 1960 almost half the states had such laws. All regions of the country except the Far West were represented.[25]

Many of these state laws adhered closely to the protective function as defined by the BPA. In others, the protective function was extended to include moral aspects. Still other states, using Georgia as a model, omitted suitable home restrictions per se but substituted restrictive policies less likely to arouse federal opposition.

In 1952 Georgia formalized a "policy package" consisting of three propositions that wrapped together suitable home and substitute father restrictions:

1. A family is not eligible unless the home is suitable.
2. Children are not deprived of support if they have an able-bodied father or stepfather living in or in-and-out of the home.
3. Birth of an illegitimate child raises a question in regard to both the suitability of the home and the presence of a substitute father.

State guidelines told the caseworker what to look for:

1. Conduct of adults is "obviously" a threat to welfare of the child.
2. Continuous presence of men for "brawling or prostitution."

3. Adult caretakers have been repeatedly convicted or repeatedly charged with disorderly conduct, and forfeited bonds, or repeatedly arrested because of behavior.
4. Repeated illegitimate births.

The SSA, acting on BPA recommendations, approved this revision to the Georgia plan.[26]

A series of steps begun by Mississippi in 1954 was accompanied by a good deal of wrangling between state and federal lawyers. The end result in 1958 was denial of ADC to all children whose parents were not legally married. Because the state had abolished common law marriage the year before, many children whose legitimacy had gone unquestioned for years were now and in the future automatically denied access to ADC. New laws in Virginia, Arkansas, and Tennessee also focused on illegitimacy.

Florida was another state where the protective function was extended to include moral considerations. Six out of seven of the Florida law's conditions defining unsuitability named commonly recognized neglect factors, such as abuse, failure to provide acceptable physical needs, lack of parental supervision, or repeated convictions of the parent for disorderly conduct, alcoholism, or prostitution. The seventh was similar to other state laws: "Failure of the parent or relative to provide a stable moral environment for the child, by engaging in promiscuous conduct either in or outside the home, or by having an illegitimate child after receiving an assistance payment . . . , or by otherwise failing to demonstrate the intent to establish a stable home."[27] What made the Florida statute different was its method of enforcement. Unlike the usual procedure accorded neglect cases, Florida welfare recipients who failed one of these tests would not (except in the most flagrant cases) be brought into court for disposition of charges. Instead, welfare recipients were offered an option to give up their children voluntarily. If the choice were made to keep the children and the recipient failed to correct the neglect or immoral condition, the family would simply be cut off ADC. The welfare department had further defined promiscuity to include "sexual relations with any person other than the legal spouse." Common-law marriages were no longer recognized in Florida either. Illegitimacy was newly defined as any birth resulting from sex with a man other than a legal husband. When faced with the choice of changing their life-style or giving up their children, a great many (about 40 percent of the first cases judged unsuitable) withdrew from ADC. As the new policies became known among poor families, applications dropped. The result was a precipitous decline in Florida's ADC cases, from 27,828 families in August 1959 to 23,871 a year later, computed to result in a savings to federal and state governments of over $5 million.[28]

Although the Florida law, its execution, and its resulting decline in ADC caseload and cost were the most spectacular of the many state efforts to exploit the suitable home issue, other states experienced some degree of caseload decline and savings also. It should be emphasized, however, that even in Florida the savings were not net savings. The poor law, in the form of general assistance, was often the resort of needy families cut off ADC. Either sympathetic caseworkers referred those "unworthy" of ADC to general assistance or needy families themselves found the way to this resource. And general assistance programs, though not providing the universal geographical coverage of ADC, were reasonably pervasive. Even in the South and Southwest, where general assistance programs were fewer than elsewhere, all cities and towns of any size and major counties offered this help. That program was, nevertheless, a harkening back to poor law practices in many ways. It was possible under general assistance to avoid the money payment, to issue grocery orders and pay rent directly to the landlord, a practice that appeared a good fit for families with a history of failure to manage money. General assistance, with its avoidance of merit system requirements for administration and caseworkers, also opened the door to those local politicians who were eager to help their supporters with jobs that assisted the poor. The practice of paying "in kind" or relying on political patronage to fill jobs in general assistance was by no means universal. Modern public welfare agencies in industrial areas of the country had long since adopted the money payment as well as merit systems in the administration of general assistance. But grants were lower than in ADC.

Working Mothers

Work, work for wages, preferably outside the home, seemed to present a viable alternative to welfare for many mothers. Friends as well as critics of the ADC program were likely to agree that welfare mothers should act like other women who worked, not just for pin money, but because their earnings were needed even when husbands were present and earning themselves. In 1955 women made up 30.2 percent of the labor force, with white women accounting for 34.5 percent and black women 46.1 percent of all employed women. Of working women, 46.4 percent were single,

29.4 percent were married (27.7 percent with husband present), and 36.0 percent widowed or divorced.[29] About one-third (32.7 percent) of married working women with husbands in the home had no children under eighteen years. But slightly more (34.7 percent) had children under eighteen. Most significant for its implications in regard to ADC was the evidence of labor force participation among women with children under six. In 1955, 16.2 percent of these women were working, an increase of over 5 percent since 1948. By 1960, married women with children under eighteen made up 39.0 percent of the female labor force; those with children under six made up 18.6 percent.[30]

ADC rolls were known to go down in periods of high employment. In this respect the experience of World War II had been repeated during the Korean War. In 1950, ADC recipients numbered 2.2 million. Each year for the next three, the number of recipients decreased, reaching 1.9 million in 1953, the year of the armistice.[31]

Just how far eligibility should be conditioned upon a mother's working or seeking work was up to the states. Federal guidance on work or welfare policy placed the mother at the center of the decision. According to the Handbook of Public Assistance, the ADC program should "make it possible for a mother to choose between staying at home to care for her children and taking a job." The caseworker should "help the mother exercise some degree of choice" as to what action she should take in seeking or continuing employment and to base her decision on her own circumstances, "especially the extent to which the age or condition of her children may make her continuous presence at home desirable or necessary."[32]

But as in child support enforcement policy, many state practices were at sharp variance with federal recommendations. More than two-thirds of the states required work so long as child care was available. In other jurisdictions, less formal pressures to work might be applied. Again, as with child support payments, the greatest monetary incentive to work was in states with maximum assistance payments where earnings could be retained up to the amount of the standard budget. Elsewhere, earnings reduced the welfare payment dollar for dollar, although allowable work expenses might include a new outfit and perhaps more flexibility when it came to fixing up the living quarters. Getting out to work also meant meeting new people, including, perhaps, a potential husband employed full-time, a far from insignificant bonus.[33]

During the 1950s and early 1960s studies of closed cases showed that about one-third of the mothers did some outside work, either full-time, part-time, or seasonal, during the period they were on ADC. ADC mothers thus worked about as much as women in the general population who were married and had children. Examination of work status on a one-month-only basis showed a far lower degree of participation. On a national basis, only 4.6 percent of ADC mothers were working full-time, with another 8.3 percent having part-time work. The choice of month, November–December, not being favorable to agricultural work, some undercounting of participation must be assumed. What is most striking about this particular analysis are the state–regional differences. Thus Florida, with 24.9 percent full-time working mothers, ranked highest, while the District of Columbia, with 0.4 percent, ranked lowest. Looking at part-time work, high-ranking South Carolina had 28.4 percent engaged as compared with low-ranking West Virginia with only 1.3 percent. The mid-Atlantic region ranked lowest with an average full-time and part-time work participation of only 1.1 and 2.6 percent, respectively. The west-south central region ranked highest with 9.5 percent full-time workers, while the east-south central region was highest (17.5 percent) when it came to part-time work. Eighteen states, all predominantly agricultural and all with maximums on the public assistance grant, reported more than 10 percent working mothers. California and New York, the states with the largest ADC caseloads, made very poor showings. California had only 5.2 percent part-time workers; New York, only 2.4 percent.[34]

Such wide variations suggested that work participation could be increased. If it were unthinkable (which it was) to goad mothers to work by imposing maximums on a universal basis, some further departure might be made from the 100 percent tax on earnings. Day care facilities might be expanded. But would such changes result in any real payoff? Could these women, in numbers that would make a real difference, work their way off welfare? The analysts thought not. After studying the work potential of more than five thousand mothers, the University of North Carolina sociologists M. Elaine Burgess and Daniel O. Price concluded: "The fact that the majority of homemakers and/or ADC parents had less than high school education, were concentrated in unskilled and service type occupations, had few special skills, plus the fact that approximately 29 percent had partial or total limitations on the kind of activity they could perform, suggests that the potential for employment and self-support is poor unless real emphasis on vocational education and rehabilitation should become a reality."[35] The vast majority of ADC mothers, those on the current rolls and those who had a past history of dependency, were at best marginal workers. In two-parent households, with husbands working, women with no better education or skills were often secondary wage earners, their low earnings helping to keep the family off welfare or, in some cases, lifting its standard of living to middle-class status. It was a different story for the welfare mother who had to go it alone.[36]

Chiselers and Cheats

Keeping the ADC program "honest" by making sure that assistance was going only to families that had no other resources: this was the sine qua non, far more important than making fathers pay or mothers work. An occasional chiseler or cheat on the rolls might be tolerated, but not for long. Determination of eligibility in the modern public welfare agency was a shared responsibility between caseworker and applicant, the caseworker listing what "proofs" of need were initially required and explaining to the applicant the continuing responsibility for reporting any change in circumstances, such as earnings or child support payments. In the early days of the program, home visits were routine, but as welfare work became more "professional," caseloads became larger, and in many cities, poor neighborhoods became crime-ridden, office interviews or telephoned inquiries became standard procedure. Put simply, a great deal depended on good faith. Policies and administration were grounded on the conviction that persons on welfare had the same basic human characteristics as the rest of the population and, further, that those on welfare were "essentially honest in their dealings" with the caseworker in the local agency.[37]

In the wake of the first wave of welfare scandals, the home visit was reinstituted with a vengeance. Special investigators used law enforcement techniques and usually worked at night, intending to discover the "absent father" or some other man returning home. Outraged at this violation of social work practice, the BPA insisted that such tactics were unnecessary. Welfare agencies could solve the doubtless greatly exaggerated "man-in-the-house" problem by beefing up standard practice—clarifying policies, improving training, and paying more attention to the possibility of evasion and concealment.

In an opposing yet mollifying stance, George Bigge, speaking from his position in charge of interstate relations for the SSA, agreed with the states that investigating procedures had a legitimate place in coping with man-in-the-house problems. Such investigators need not be agents of harassment, he argued. If integrated into the overall organization with clearly defined authority and responsibility and properly trained and supervised, they might well do a constructive job.[38]

"Midnight raids" implied the use of force, called up visions of vice squads breaking down doors, and, in this case, letting the bloodhounds loose under the bed. But such images were exaggerated. According to regional representatives who conducted an inquiry in late 1953, most of the special investigatory activity was located in large cities—Denver, Detroit, St. Louis, Cleveland, Chicago, Baltimore—and was focused upon the man in the house, unreported employment, and hidden resources. Some units also attempted to locate missing fathers. At this time at least, caseworkers were responsible for making referrals, and, in many of the special units, caseworkers were employed as investigators. Some agencies informed the recipient of an impending investigation, but the "surprise visit" was more often the technique of choice. Recipients were not told about collateral contacts either. Agencies were convinced that they had implicit authorizations through the initial agreement with the applicant to investigate his or her circumstances. Although extremely wary at first, social work staff came to recognize a number of benefits resulting from special investigations: the units had helped restore public faith in the welfare agency; questionable cases had been cleared up; fraud and abuse had been reduced; some money had been saved. Reservations remained, nevertheless, mainly among social workers who felt that some of their duties had been taken away. All were aware, however, that their very large caseloads—ranging from 63 cases per worker in New York to 359 in Texas—made it impossible for them to devote sufficient time to validate eligibility in problem cases.[39]

The Division of Administrative and Fiscal Standards struggled throughout the postwar years to develop a statement of "principles" regarding special investigative units. The aim was to keep the social worker and the social work method in the foreground and, as in the NOLEO guidance, to maintain as complete a separation as possible from law enforcement. Some members of Congress thought the audit should be restored. Bigge was dead set against it. Special investigating units were preferable. The audit could no more ferret out the man in the house than the administrative review that had replaced it.[40]

From the outset in January 1940, there had been considerable tension about use of the administrative review as a vehicle for the liberalization of state administration or for ensuring conformity with federal law and the state plan. An exchange during a meeting in 1945 illustrates this point. When Kathryn Goodwin, the staff member most responsible for the design and execution of the review, stated that eligibility determination and amount of payment were its primary objects, someone challenged the concept as "too narrow." Hoey jumped in immediately—the concept was "essential" to the entire program. Goodwin also stood firm, pointing out that the General Accounting Office "would certainly expect . . . a continuing determination that payments to recipients are proper." She conceded that eligibility and need had been defined more broadly than the simple determination of eligibility, but she cautioned that ensuring the integrity of the program was "an aspect of the administrative review . . . which we can probably not afford to neglect."⁴¹

By the end of 1942 the administrative review had ended its trial period and was under way in all the states. For the next six years the review was carried out, as intended, with comprehensive coverage of state and local administration. Reports were unsparingly critical and voluminous. Although not officially classified as confidential, they were treated as privileged material to be shared with the state agency for purposes of negotiation. Ineligible or payment-in-error cases that emerged from the small sample of cases read by reviewers were reported to the state agency and even back to Washington. Jules Berman, chief of the Division of Program Standards and Development, remembered "some charade gone through about taking exceptions" in which "the papers toward taking a deduction from the state share" would be started, only to be stopped as the bureau "got talked out of it." The administrative review was considered an "educational tool," not an "auditing tool," he recalled. "These reviews were always used as a device for helping the states, encouraging the states, advising the states how to improve their programs. The result was that the failures of the states to do what they were supposed to do were never really emphasized enough." Even with an emphasis on the positive, however, states did not necessarily change. An administrative review in Massachusetts in 1960 repeated in much the same detail the very same deficiencies found ten years earlier.

Viewed as an educational tool, the administrative review tended to become specific to individual states and thus to lose a basis for regional or national comparability. Early on, the review began to lose its specific identity. As staff shortages developed during the 1940s, information from the review proper was supplemented and presumably contaminated by information from other sources. Coverage by the review itself dropped from 284 local agencies and 36,720 assistance cases in 1943 to 172 local agencies and 17,167 cases in 1950. In 1949 the review was shifted from an annual to a biennial basis. With passage of the 1950 amendments, the bureau became swamped. Work on the review practically ground to a halt, with its focus almost exclusively directed to the new APTD category authorized by the amendments.

The acute crisis over, but with staff shortages persisting in a program under attack, the bureau announced a renewed emphasis on eligibility and payment factors and special emphasis on problem areas such as disability, incapacity, and absence from the home. The stated goal was "securing information needed to assure that necessary corrective action will be taken by State agencies with respect to problems identified." The prospect for success seemed dim. Evaluation of the effectiveness of methods used in reviewing problem areas had yet to be made; the regions would have to prepare some of the materials on their own. The decade was played out and the second wave of welfare criticism begun before any real attempt was made to restore the administrative review as a tool, educational or otherwise.[42]

With the arrival of Charles Schottland as commissioner of Social Security in 1954, the Bureau of Public Assistance had a true friend of social work at the top. Although an advocate of child support enforcement, of work for welfare mothers, and of strict accountability in eligibility determination, Schottland also believed that social services had a rightful place in the public welfare agency. He was eager to get a positive statement about social services into the law but recognized the futility of attempting a broad authorization with separate funding, like the one defeated in 1950. Instead he reached into California law and pulled out wording that was easily sold to Ways and Means and Finance in 1956.

Title IV of the 1935 act began: "For the purpose of enabling each State to furnish financial assistance so far as practicable under the conditions in such state, to needy dependent children." The 1956 preamble read: "For the purpose of encouraging the care of dependent children in their own homes or in the homes of relatives by enabling each State to furnish financial assistance and rehabilitation and other services as far as practicable under the conditions in such State, to needy dependent children and the parents or relatives with whom they are living to help maintain and strengthen family life and to help such parents or relatives to attain or retain capability for the maximum self-support and personal independence consistent with the maintenance of continuing parental care and protection."

Further encouragement to the states to provide services was entered by way of the state plan, which was to "provide a description of the services which the State agency makes available." For the first time, services were specified as reimbursable costs under the 50 percent match for administration. Since the shortage of trained social workers continued to stand in the way of providing the desired social services, an authorization to appropriate funds for training was included. Also encouraged through an authorization to appropriate funds were research and demonstration projects.

Beginning with the stated purposes in the "hot air" section, this was a well-meaning but feeble attempt to repackage the ADC program. There was no carrot and no stick. No carrot was possible without the active encouragement of the House Appropriations Committee, and such encouragement was not forthcoming. The 50 percent match continued to be available for services payable from funds for state and local administration. States were not required to provide social services, only, as was made clear in the State Letter on the amendments, "to outline the services, if any." The result was brief euphoria in social worker ranks, but no appreciable change in state and local practice.[43]

Schottland was succeeded as commissioner of Social Security in 1959 by his deputy, William L. Mitchell, a Republican who had also served under Altmeyer. Concerned about the continuing attacks on ADC, Mitchell sought someone qualified to study and report on family policy. He selected Alvin L. Schorr, a trained social worker who had received his degree from the George Warren Brown School, Washington University, St. Louis. Schorr had worked in both public and private agencies in the Midwest and Northeast and had directed at least one large demonstration project on families and published its results.[44]

After extensive library research and much informal consultation with middle-level BPA staff, Schorr produced a draft article titled "Problems in the ADC Program." He proposed four interlocking ways in which ADC operated to "damage" needy families:

Work: The idea that the ADC mother had a real choice about work had been canceled by changes in society as whole and by welfare agency pressures to reduce costs. The high tax on the low earnings that most of these women could expect was a powerful work disincentive.

Maternal families: The program placed a premium on the father's absence—real or asserted. Illegitimacy, nonlegal but stable unions, casual sexual contacts all impinged on the decision to grant or withhold assistance, drawing the welfare agency into moral judgments not enforceable in the courts. ADC appeared to reinforce the maternal family tradition present in black culture.

Instability of families: Children lived in an unsettled, unpredictable environment known to be a bar to healthful development. Changes in family structure, irregular work patterns, irregular child support were intensified by the program itself.

Scapegoating: The typical ADC family, uneducated, unskilled, often in poor health, with children of unstable unions, invited public disapproval, which was expressed in recurrent attacks and a refusal to fund the program adequately. Conversely, other needy children with fathers present, those of the working poor, for example, were excluded by definition.

Schorr concluded that "it was time to design a more constructive way to meet the needs of children."[45]

Initial comments from BPA were made by Jules Berman, one of the middle-level bureau staff whom Schorr had consulted. Berman was a veteran of seventeen years' service and an old hand at legislative negotiation, having worked side by side with Cohen as the welfare expert on the 1950 amendments. The tone of Berman's comments was gentle—general agreement with the points made—but firm—it must be made clear that this was not an evaluation of ADC—and critical—what about practical problems in dealing with alternatives?

Once the paper passed from the informal comment stage to Mitchell's announcement on March 20 of his intention to publish it in "an early issue of the *Social Security Bulletin*," Berman, writing for the bureau chief's signature, attempted to shoot down the idea forthwith. Schorr's paper should not be published in the *Bulletin* "because we feel that . . . what is essentially a critical statement . . . would give an official status to such criticism." To this end, the bureau would welcome the distribution of Schorr's paper to individuals "who are constructively interested in meeting the needs of young children."[46]

Forthcoming comments from social work professionals, including public welfare administrators, were generally favorable. Nearly all encouraged wide circulation or publication of Schorr's paper. Many suggested administrative or legislative changes. From the Welfare Council of Greater Chicago:

The temptation to deny the presence of problem families by countering criticism through the recital of success stories has left some impression either that there is a "cover-up campaign" or that ADC does not know the facts of its own caseload. . . .

I never expect to see any relief program free of criticism and it would be unfortunate if that day ever came. I do believe . . . the majority of the public would respond with understanding to a frank admission of the nature and characteristics of the problems of the ADC caseload, an honest appraisal of the potentialities for change, and a forthright program which gave promise of bringing about constructive change.

From Wilbur Cohen, then professor of public welfare administration, University of Michigan: "I think it would be best if the Federal agency had something in print which recognized the existence of the problems ADC faces. This might help to achieve the kind of legislative and administrative changes that are necessary to improve the program and to prevent dependency and family breakdown." Cohen listed ten possible legislative or administrative changes and sent a copy of his letter to Berman. The National Social Welfare Assembly, where Elizabeth Wickenden was then working, presented an exception to the general line of responses, one more in accord with the BPA: "We are convinced that Mr. Schorr has put his finger on many of the basic problems and weaknesses in the program and its administration. . . . But our real concern is what we can do about it without throwing out the baby with the bath."[47]

After a six-month pause for more discussion and revision, Mitchell announced himself ready to publish. As a concession to the BPA he planned to include a personal introduction indicating the "family life" context of the article and "making it clear" that "no radical departure in policy" was implied. A "digest" of various outside comments would also be included. Kathryn Goodwin, now director of the BPA, prepared her own answer to Mitchell. It was still negative:

We would like it to be clear that we are not recommending against publication because of any desire to stifle criticism, but because when that criticism comes from the Commissioner's office and is published in the *Social Security Bulletin*, it is given a prestige and official status which we do not believe the paper in its present form should have. We believe that no matter what is said in an introductory statement, it cannot be interpreted otherwise than as criticism by the Commissioner's office of the Bureau program and its administration.

Mitchell backed down, but not meekly:

I, of course, would not want to press the matter of publication . . . when the Bureau has taken so strong a stand in opposition. . . . However, I am not willing any longer to maintain the status quo regarding ADC. I have never seen a factual defense against the charges repeatedly directed at ADC. We have about worn out the use of defensive assertions to off-set critical assertions. If we are to preserve the essential values in ADC, we have got to propose constructive measures to meet public criticism. I am convinced that if we do not move to meet this problem, we will be relieved of the initiative.[48]

The BPA, while bureaucratically correct throughout this episode, was not innocent of the defensive attitude that Mitchell found so frustrating. It was not so much its failure to come up with a factual defense of the criticism. Perhaps the nature of the program made such a defense impossible. The bureau's deep fault was its failure to come to grips with what the states were already doing in an effort to validate their caseload. When it came to child support enforcement, to welfare mothers working, to special efforts to control fraud and abuse, bureau staff assumed a negative stance. Convinced that such efforts were punitive and that they would fail to save money or reduce the caseload, the BPA issued regulations and recommendations inappropriate to the real world of welfare and consequently useless to state agencies. Many of these guidelines took months, even years, to get to the field. Instead of dealing practically with the points of criticism, the bureau reiterated demands for a program to cover all needy children or a program for general assistance. With even more intensity they held that social casework was the only answer to any problems in the ADC program—social casework, that is, in the hands of professionally trained social workers.

Schorr's paper was published in the April 1960 issue of *Social Work*, the journal of the National Association of Social Workers. It was picked up by a good many newspapers and magazines, doubtless more than would have scanned the *Social Security Bulletin*. Since Schorr's thoughtful paper was miles away from the sensational exposés of welfare that dominated the early 1950s, it provided a foundation for subsequent efforts (including research and publication) to reform ADC.

Summing Up the 1950s

Studies of the characteristics of families receiving ADC, conducted every two to three years by the BPA's Division of Program Statistics and Analysis, indicated the directions of the program in some detail: place of residence, race, reason for dependency. In February 1956 the ADC caseload consisted of 609,000 families, totaling 2,221,000 recipients— 1,682,000 children and 539,000 adults. These numbers marked an increase of 303,000 recipients in two years. About half the recipients lived in metropolitan areas, the rest in smaller towns or rural areas. Sixty percent of the caseload was white; 40 percent nonwhite, with blacks accounting for 94 percent of nonwhite recipients. The recipient rate for blacks was very high—87 per 1,000 as compared with 19 per 1,000 for whites.

In 61 percent of the families, the father's absence from the home was the cause of dependency. Absence due to divorce or separation accounted for 18 percent of the total. Desertions were almost as high—15.5 percent—while illegitimacy was even higher—22.7 percent. In 22.1 percent of families, the father was incapacitated and usually living in the home. The father was dead in only 13 percent of the cases. Estrangement was

substantially higher among blacks—72.4 percent—than among whites—
45.7 percent. Incapacity was higher among whites—29.8 percent—than
among blacks—10.5 percent.

The "characteristics studies" also contained a brief analysis in terms of
national and program dynamics. The 1956 study attributed the increase in
caseload "primarily" to (1) unfavorable economic conditions following the
truce in Korea; (2) substantial increase in the total number of families in
the population; (3) rapid growth in the child population; (4) high rates of
estrangement and illegitimacy; (5) a high rate of increase in the number of
families headed by women; and (6) the low average income of families
headed by women as compared with families headed by men. Other than
to note the effect of survivor's coverage under OASI in reducing the fre-
quency of dependency due to death of the father, the 1956 study was silent
on program dynamics.

These dynamics, factors such as increases in federal financial participation, changes in state standards of assistance or in eligibility requirements,
had, for the most part, occurred earlier as a result of the 1950 and 1952
amendments. That such changes could have a considerable impact was
shown by an analysis of the 292 percent increase in ADC costs in the
1940–1950 decade. Amendments increasing the federal share in 1946 and
1948 helped to increase the proportion of the population aided. Together
these program factors accounted for 79 percent of the 292 percent
increase.

The nationwide recipient rate rose 36 percent from 1940 to 1950, with
by far the largest growth occurring in the South, where federal matching
had the greatest effect. In an affirmation of the program's values, the ten-
year analysis concluded that complex social and economic factors "beyond the control of legislators and administrators" explained the greater
part of expanding need for welfare in an expanding economy. ADC had
experienced "real growth" in coverage and "true" upward movement in
the standard of living provided to its recipients.[49] The limitations of such
analyses in answering critics are all too obvious. The statistical count assumed a valid caseload and payments geared to honestly reported deficiencies in meeting basic necessities. In the end, it would be necessary to take
a dispassionate look at the rate of ineligibility and incorrect payments in
the caseload.

Meanwhile, led by its Committee on Public Welfare Policy, the APWA
undertook an evaluation of the ADC program in terms of its effect on the
children it was designed to serve. For the title of its study APWA harked
back to the Report of the Committee on Economic Security, using a phrase

that emphasized the mother's duty to rear her children to become "citizens capable of contributing to society." *Future Citizens All* was written by Gordon Blackwell and Raymond Gould, sociologists at the University of North Carolina's Institute for Research in Social Science. Their work was funded by the (Marshall) Field Foundation of Chicago. A small (6,521) national sample of case records closed during the fall of 1950 and January 1951 was selected.

Blackwell and Gould found ADC children existing in a sea of troubles. If capable citizens were assumed to get their start from healthful living conditions, adequate medical care, and normal progress through school, ADC children were being poorly prepared. A very low level of income dictated a very low level of living. Only a third of these families received even a minimum standard. It followed that food, clothing, shelter, and furnishings were at or below subsistence level. Preventive health measures—smallpox vaccinations, dental care, routine physicals—all were received far less often by ADC children than by those in the population as a whole. Progress in school was slower and dropouts before high school graduation were greater than in the general population. One-fourth of the boys aged eight to seventeen years were one year, and slightly more were two years, behind in school. Girls made somewhat better progress. For both sexes, though, failure to graduate from high school was an alarming two-thirds of those eighteen and over.

There were signs, however, that ADC should not be written off as a complete failure. The overwhelming number of ADC children under eighteen years of age were living in their own home under the guardianship of their mother, mother and father if incapacitated, or caretaker relative. Cases of child neglect as measured by court hearings were few. A good number of preteens and teenagers were participants in community youth organizations. And one in ten ADC children had received an award or special recognition either in school or elsewhere.

Because living on welfare was such a debilitating experience, the length of time families remained dependent was regarded as a powerful indicator. Reaching back for an old-fashioned word, Blackwell and Gould noted with satisfaction "strong evidence that ADC is not pauperizing families or children." The median length of time in receipt of ADC was two years and one month. Only 11 percent were on the rolls for seven or more years; only 3 percent for eleven years or more. This was not, however, a real measure of chronic dependency. The Blackwell-Gould analysis failed to count prior episodes on ADC.

Although far from a whitewash, the study, unlike Schorr's article, leaned heavily toward affirmation of the program as it stood. ADC children had made "remarkably good adjustments" in their progress toward "full citizenship." Antisocial behavior was "slight indeed." "Real accomplishment in the face of great handicaps" was evident. Most ADC families functioned "relatively well under a heavy weight of hardship." Progress in school and work training seemed "remarkable in some instances." Juvenile delinquency, crime, child neglect, and illegitimate births "occur less frequently than one would expect in such a stress-ridden group." Failure to attain program goals more completely was attributed largely to low family income, although casework services were called for to help mothers guide their children and to prevent abuses.[50]

In 1960 the APWA commissioned a similar study of ADC, again funded by the Field Foundation and again carried out at North Carolina's Institute for Research in Social Science. The new researchers, M. Elaine Burgess and Daniel O. Price, announced a change of focus from dependent children to dependent families. The change was made in recognition of the fact that "the weaknesses of ADC, real and imagined, are, according to the critics, centered in ADC as a *family* program not as a child welfare program." In an effort to face up to controversial issues more directly, the 1950 questionnaire was modified, new questions added, and additional variables stressed. The sample—5,517 cases—was drawn from those closed in January, February, and March 1961. The title of the study, *An American Dependency Challenge*, suggested that ADC was a program in such serious trouble that old answers to new problems could no longer be tolerated.[51]

The worst sign of trouble was the fact that ADC was a large and costly program that had experienced real growth. In December 1950, the program served 34 children under age eighteen per 1,000 population. By June 1961, it was assisting 39 per 1,000. Overall the total number of families on ADC had increased 26 percent, outdistancing the increase of families in the general population by more than 10 percent. Nationwide costs had passed the $1 billion mark by 1960, up from $556 million in 1950.[52]

Burgess and Price did not attempt the all but impossible task of measuring the exact causes of ADC growth. That ADC families shared with many others the effects of the postwar baby boom, family breakdown, erosion of skills, rising costs of living, and other nationwide socioeconomic trends was certainly true and certainly influential. Just how influential could not be said. The other potent influence on program growth was change in law and policy—change "designed to provide more extensive and adequate coverage to those in need." The decade had been notable for the passage of liberalizing amendments.

Very high rates of dependency were revealed by a probe into family history. Information could not be obtained about all the parents of current ADC mothers but was available on well over two-thirds of them. More than 40 percent of the 4,156 reporting families had received some form of welfare during the time the mother was growing up. This record of itself was not surprising, because the Depression was less than thirty years past. Far more worrisome was the chronicity indicated by length of time on ADC. The median length of time on ADC appeared to have shortened somewhat from 1950. The lower figure of 17.5 months included six-month episodes. When such short periods were excluded, the 1960 median was 27.1 months as compared with 25 in 1950. Moreover, when the time spent during previous ADC episodes was taken into account, the median increased markedly. Thirty-six percent of the sample cases had been closed more than once. For white families with two prior closings, the median number of months on ADC was 29.0; for blacks it was 38.9. The median for white families with five or more closings was 39.7 months; for blacks, 46.3 months. Some cases (less than 10 percent of the sample), though never previously closed, had been running for nine years or more.

Most of these mothers were in their working years, aged twenty-five to fifty-four, but they were poorly educated and lacked special skills. Over three-fourths had not finished high school and almost half had eight or fewer years of schooling. Though only about 16 percent had some skills, almost two-thirds had worked, at some time or other, usually at unskilled or service jobs. As in 1950, ADC children continued in an educational pattern similar to that of their mothers—large numbers dropping out before finishing high school. Some 15 percent dropped out because they got jobs or married.

For the rest, most indicators had not changed much in the past ten years. Families continued on the average to be small, having from three to five persons, with a median of 2.8 children. Although actual family income had improved somewhat, the vast majority continued to live in "dire poverty." Dependency resulting from family breakdown was up significantly. Among whites, it rose from 27.0 percent to 35.6 percent; among blacks, from 30.0 to 40.3 percent in the decade. Illegitimacy also rose more than 4 percentage points to 19 percent of the total caseload. The black–white rate differential was striking: 34 percent of black children were illegitimate as compared with 10.9 percent of white children. For both races the proportion of illegitimate births was considerably higher than in the nation as a whole.

In their overall conclusion, Burgess and Price did not find ADC "as bad as its harshest critics have maintained nor as good as its strongest supporters have claimed."[53] Unmentioned as well as unmeasured was the paradoxical success of ADC. No longer an "orphan program," it extended far beyond the "nice families." Although ADC families remained desperately poor, their incomes were in fact not far below the incomes of many intact families with wages as their sole support.

As the decade ended, so too the prosperous Eisenhower years. In September 1957 the economy went into an eight-month recession, recovered somewhat, and then receded again beginning in May 1960. By election time in November, unemployment had risen contraseasonally to four million and by Inauguration Day was up to five million persons.

The winner of the very close race with Richard M. Nixon was John F. Kennedy. He came to office with very specific proposals for change in ADC. These proposals had been developed by a preelection task force headed by Wilbur Cohen, who, in 1960, returned to the Department of Health, Education, and Welfare as assistant secretary for legislation.

9

More Than a Salvage Operation

THE SHARP RISE in unemployment during the months immediately preceding the inauguration of President Kennedy was paralleled by a rise in welfare dependency. Even OAA went up, though only slightly. A BPA staff member noted "startling increases in APTD," increases that ranged from 20 to 40 percent in a total caseload of more than 300,000 in this newest of categorical programs. She speculated that the recession was pushing states to more liberal eligibility criteria. ADC rolls passed the 3 billion mark and general assistance the 1 billion mark during the Eisenhower recession.[1]

In dollars, expenditures for welfare in 1960 totaled $3.8 billion, an increase of more than $1 billion in the last ten years. The welfare state had been much discussed throughout the previous decade, often with more heat than light. Statistically defined, a welfare state exists when government expenditures for all types of goods and services targeted on the needy reaches 8–10 percent of GNP. By 1960, with expenditures at 10.6 percent of GNP, the welfare state had officially arrived.[2]

The Liberal Agenda

The arrival of the welfare state caused no particular uproar during the campaign of 1960. Both parties pledged to promote civil rights for blacks, and this time, unlike four years earlier, southern Democrats remained in their seats at their national convention. Both parties also pledged support for some form of health insurance for the aged, the Democrats proposing to achieve this through amendments to the Social Security Act. However, although Kennedy spoke often about "getting the country moving again," foreign, rather than domestic, policy dominated the campaign.

The Kennedy administration had two sets of welfare recommendations in hand when it took over on January 20, 1961. The first, a report of the Advisory Council on Public Assistance, was technically an Eisenhower leftover. This council had been established by Congress in 1958 to soothe the incumbent administration about state welfare responsibilities. In signing the 1958 amendments, Eisenhower warned that increases in the proportion of the public assistance programs financed by the federal government could lead to weakened responsibility by states and communities. This was the first advisory council devoted exclusively to public assistance, signaling once again the change from previous practice when advisory councils viewed Social Security programs as an interlocking whole to be considered in relation to each other.

Council members consisted of such regulars as Loula Dunn, director of the APWA; Katherine Ellickson, assistant director of the AFL-CIO's Department of Social Security; C. Arild Olsen, executive director of the Division of Christian Life and Work, National Council of Churches; and Wilbur Cohen. Others included state and local officials, one or two representatives of business, and a sociologist who was affiliated with the New York State Catholic Welfare Commission. For most of these persons Eisenhower's warning about state responsibilities was not a real issue.

To a large extent the council's recommendations followed previous liberal lines laid down by the APWA's policy committee in the 1940s and 1950s. The council would eliminate residence requirements; establish a federal category for general assistance, include an unemployed parent and a less seriously disabled parent in the ADC grant; work toward a single state assistance standard; and provide adequate medical care. Endorsing the Social Security amendments of 1956, the council promoted training for social workers to staff welfare programs and research and demonstration projects to strengthen family life. The council viewed criticisms of ADC, "where valid," as just another indication of widespread family breakdown. It saw no need to back away from federal support of welfare programs, although it felt that state governments should contribute more toward local financing.[3]

The second set of welfare recommendations was developed, at the request of President-elect Kennedy, by a Task Force on Health and Social Security chaired by Cohen. Signaling the interest in health insurance, three of its members were medical doctors, a fourth a geneticist. The other two members were Herman M. Somers, a professor of political science at Haverford College, and Elizabeth Wickenden. The Cohen task force quickly seized on the current high unemployment rate by suggesting that "the unemployment of a parent" be added as a temporary provision to the list of reasons why children could be deprived of support or care under ADC eligibility guidelines. Calculating along trendy Keynesian lines, the task force estimated that $1.4 billion would be put "into the buying stream of families in the nine months beginning April 1," if unemployment were included in ADC. If federal funding of general assistance, which the task force also recommended, proved acceptable to Congress, the impact on the economy would be even more beneficial.[4]

The task force also called for a major reexamination of welfare grant-in-aid programs, particularly ADC. For a start it suggested a closer linking of financial assistance and social services to ADC families and child welfare services under Title V of the Social Security Act. To further this goal, certain organizational changes should be considered. If elevated to the Secretary's Office, the Children's Bureau, together with a new Office of Aging, could be charged with studying emerging problems among chil dren and the elderly that were common to all social classes, and devising programs to address them. At the same time, grant programs for Maternal and Child Health and Crippled Children should be transferred from the Children's Bureau to the Public Health Service, which had claimed them as integral to its mission from time immemorial. The part of the Children's Bureau that administered grants for child welfare services would be transferred to whatever new organization emerged under a plan for linkage of financial assistance and social services.[5]

These two reports seem to exist in a world apart from the welfare mess that had become the accepted term for ADC. The Cohen task force did not mention criticism of the program. The advisory council simply shifted the blame elsewhere, expressing the opinion that "rather than the aid to dependent children program's being a major cause of social evils, we regard it as a reflection of their existence."[6]

For his secretary of HEW, Kennedy selected Abraham Ribicoff, former governor of Connecticut. Ivan Nestingen, mayor of Madison, who had headed the Kennedy for President campaign in Wisconsin, was named undersecretary. Cohen was appointed assistant secretary for legislation. Nestingen found himself handling administrative and patronage matters for the department, while Cohen picked up immediately on the legislation recommended by the preelection task force he had headed.[7]

But, as it turned out, the first order of business was a leftover. Appointed, but not yet confirmed, Cohen was asked by Ribicoff to help pacify several states—Mississippi, Florida, Louisiana, and Michigan—by figuring out how to get rid of a midnight ruling by just-departed HEW Secretary Flemming. The ruling covered the suitable home issue. Cohen's reply to Ribicoff was, "Not me. I happen to agree with it 100 percent."[8]

In July 1960, the state of Louisiana, using newly passed suitable home legislation, had suddenly dropped from the ADC rolls almost six thousand families with over twenty-two thousand children. By the end of September, after additional investigations had been made, a total reduction of over six thousand families with over twenty-three thousand children had been attained. The Louisiana legislation declared that a woman who gave birth to an illegitimate child after receipt of her first welfare check or who was cohabiting with a man without benefit of formal marriage was, ipso facto, providing an unsuitable home for her children and consequently was ineligible for ADC. Ninety percent of the cases were dropped because of postwelfare illegitimacy; 9 percent because the children sprang from a common-law relationship; and only 1 percent because of promiscuity or neglect. The new law fell almost exclusively on black welfare recipients. Only 5 percent of the families affected were white.

Families were given an opportunity to reapply to local lay boards of welfare rather than to the welfare agency itself, and about two-thirds did so. A little over one-half of the reapplications brought reinstatement. The net reduction in the ADC caseload was 3,029 families.

Louisiana's dramatic action attracted nationwide attention, and no wonder. Welfare now had a large readership. Civil rights issues, brought into the forefront by the 1954 Supreme Court decision, *Brown* v. *Board of Education*, ensured interest in news stories involving blacks and their treatment in American society. Moreover the Louisiana numbers were large—particularly when the children's figure was used. As the idea of starving black children took hold, donations of money and clothing poured in. These gifts, some from as far away as England, were collected by the Urban League and distributed by black churches in Louisiana.

Louisiana had modeled its actions on the approved Mississippi suitable home law. Moreover, Louisiana's ADC program compared favorably with those of other states: its standard of assistance was the highest in the South; a large proportion of state and local funds went into ADC; and it was above the national average in the proportion of children supported by the program. The state was therefore not prepared to cave in when Mitchell called a conformity hearing.

The Louisiana commissioner of public welfare accused the Feds of springing a technical trap. It was "inconceivable" that "the federal agency which has been in the business of approving suitable home provisions in State Plans for many years . . . has not developed guides or criteria for states which wish to adopt such procedures." The state's counsel protested that the department "has never issued a bulletin, has never issued a regulation, has never published a rule, has never ordered us, or any of the States by a directive to the effect that a suitable home provision was not valid." The state prevailed. On January 16, 1961, Mitchell, pointing out that recent improvements in administration had been made, ruled "with reluctance" that Louisiana's plan was in conformity.

But to Secretary Flemming the use of "suitable home" as an excuse to deny assistance constituted a violation of the spirit of the law. He all but ordered the department's general counsel to write the words that would get rid of the practice and would at the same time be legally defensible. On January 17, three days before the Kennedy inauguration, Flemming issued a ruling. As of July 1, a state plan was obliged to continue assistance so long as the child continued to live in the home. If the home was indeed unsuitable, efforts should be made to improve the offending conditions and, failing that, to arrange for placement of the child elsewhere.[9]

With Ribicoff's blessing Cohen approached Mills of Ways and Means and Senator Robert Kerr of Finance. "The last thing the new Administration needs is a conflict [over] the blacks and the whites and states rights and federal rights," Cohen argued. The three put together a provision for inclusion in the Cohen task force package. The Flemming ruling was thus given the force of law.[10]

The Cohen task force proposals were presented to Congress as "emergency" legislation, in much the same way as the bill that created Harry Hopkins's FERA. To be sure, the "Eisenhower recession" was not to be compared with the "Hoover depression." Still, the 1958–1960 recession was the most serious economic downturn since World War II. As such it could be argued that lengthy congressional hearings should be avoided. In the absence of thorough study, however, the administration conceded a time limit on the new legislation. On May 8, 1961, Kennedy signed two amendments to Title IV that were to run for fourteen months. They included, at state option, assistance for the support of a child whose parent was unemployed and living in the home and assistance for children in foster homes. General assistance was refused by Mills and Kerr.

But coverage of the unemployed parent absorbed yet another large group for FFP, a group comparable to the disabled who came in under the 1950 amendments. If the emergency legislation were made permanent, as Cohen expected, only nondisabled persons with no current family attachment would remain in the general assistance pool. The foster care amendment was devised to make the legalized Flemming ruling stick when homes were found unsuitable. It also tended to strengthen the argument for the integration of public family and child welfare services and the organizational merger of this segment of the Children's Bureau with the BPA.[11]

Newburgh

Within a month all hope of restoring and reinforcing public trust in the welfare system through liberalizing reform had been shattered. On Sunday, June 24, 1961, the front page of the *New York Times* carried an article headlined "NEWBURGH FACING CRISIS OVER RELIEF." Newburgh was a town of thirty thousand perched in the hilly Hudson River country with its spectacular views and abundance of Dutch names. The town had long been summer host to migratory workers who picked the fruit and berry crops and then turned back southward. The one small local industry—women's pocketbooks—tended to slump with downturns in the business cycle.

It was generally agreed that the relief crisis had been brought on by migration both into and out of the town. The migratory workers were mostly unskilled blacks who had been born in the South—part of that group of cotton pickers and field hands who had been jolted off their native soil by agricultural mechanization. During the hard winter of 1960–61 more migrants than usual settled down in Newburgh, where a good number of relatives joined them. Meanwhile the town itself had lost population as its more prosperous tax-paying citizens moved over the Orange County line into the pleasant countryside.

A summary of welfare expenditures showed clearly enough that the "relief crisis" was not just talk. Welfare payments—about $500,000 per year—absorbed one-sixth of the city budget, amounting to more than was spent on police protection, almost as much as for fire protection, and four times as much as on parks and recreation. Although the aged and disabled accounted for some of the welfare cost, ADC and general assistance were the real issue. The cost of ADC had risen to twice the original estimate and general assistance by one-third. In describing the "moral tone" of the black ghetto, the *Times* reporter noted that high illegitimacy rates reflected crowded living conditions, and the schools reported that pregnancies among girls twelve to fifteen years old were not uncommon.

The general response to the crisis from the taxpayers left in town was growing "sounds of rebellion." More specifically, the city council had voted to have Orange County take over the welfare program. A Citizens Committee of three found that "the inability of Planned Parenthood to advise unwed mothers is a factor," but argued that "promiscuity cannot be condoned and that the answer lies elsewhere." Some random sampling of passersby suggested that migrants be sent back where they came from, but wiser heads pointed out that the law forbade this except in the case of aliens.[12]

Formal action was taken when the Newburgh city council approved thirteen welfare rules developed by its city manager, Joseph McD. Mitchell, who had been hired with the welfare problem in mind just nine months previously. Born in Chevy Chase, Maryland, Mitchell had spent most of his adult life in military service, having enlisted and reenlisted after serving in World War II. He had earned a college degree and a graduate degree in public administration while in the service.[13]

Each one of the thirteen Newburgh welfare rules had a familiar ring. Either they had been resurrected from past practices or were a stricter reading of current ones. The first rule harked back to the poor law:

1.   All cash payment which can be converted to food, clothing, and rent vouchers . . . without basic harm to the intent of the aid, shall be issued in voucher form henceforth.

The thirteenth rule was as recent as the Flemming ruling:

13.   Prior to certifying or continuing any more Aid to Dependent Children cases, a determination shall be made as to the home environment. If the home environment is not satisfactory, the children in that home shall be placed in foster care in lieu of welfare aid to the family adults.

The rules can be broken down into four categories: work, fraud and abuse, fiscal control, and morality. Rules 2, 3, 5, and 6 centered on work:

2.   All ablebodied adult males on relief of any kind who are capable of working are to be assigned to the chief of building maintenance for work assignment on a forty hour week.

3.   All recipients physically capable of and available for private employment who are offered a job and refuse it, regardless of the type of employment involved, are to be denied relief.
5.   All applicants for relief who have left a job voluntarily, *i.e.,* who have not been fired or laid off, shall be denied relief.
6.   The allotment for any one family unit shall not exceed the take-home pay of the lowest paid city employee with a family of comparable size. Also, no relief shall be granted to any family whose income is in excess of the latter figure.

Rules 1 (above), 7, 9, and 10 were attempts to control fraud and abuse:

7.   All files of Aid to Dependent Children cases are to be brought to the office of the corporation counsel for review monthly. All new cases of any kind will be referred to the corporation counsel for review monthly. All new cases of any kind will be referred to the corporation counsel before certification for payment.
9.   Aid to persons aged, blind, and disabled shall be limited to three months in any one year—this is a feature similar to the present policies in unemployment benefits.
10.   All recipients who are not disabled, blind, ambulatory, or otherwise incapacitated shall report to the Department of Public Welfare monthly for a conference regarding the status of their case.

The objective in Rules 8, 11, and 12 was fiscal control:

8.   All applicants for relief who are new to the city must show evidence that their plans in coming to the city involved a concrete offer of employment, similar to that required of foreign immigrants. All such persons shall be limited to two weeks of relief. Those who cannot show evidence shall be limited to one week of relief.
11.   Once the budget for the fiscal year is approved, by the council, it shall not be exceeded by the Welfare Department unless approved by counsel for supplemental appropriation.
12.   There shall be a monthly expenditure limit on all categories of welfare aid. This monthly expenditure limit shall be established by the Department of Public Welfare at the time of presenting the budget, and shall take into account seasonal variations.

Rules 4 and 13 (above) addressed morality:

4.   All mothers of illegitimate children are to be advised that should they have any more children out of wedlock they shall be denied relief.[14]

Omission of child support enforcement and the absence of any reference to the substitute father or stepfather may have been simple oversight in this otherwise exhaustive list. A more likely explanation is the fact that the target group consisted of migratory workers, or migratory *families* as they were referred to by the press, and hence desertion was not seen as a major cause of dependency. It may be also that the perception that there was nothing in the Newburgh ghetto to collect was quite evident in the confines of such a small town.

Welfare professionals saw immediately that the Newburgh reform package was riddled with illegalities, particularly with regard to the categories of needy covered by the Social Security Act. While it might be permissible to assist those on general assistance with vouchers for food, clothing, and shelter, the money payment was a pillar of the public assistance titles. To subject elderly, blind, and disabled persons to the same limitations on aid as able-bodied workers receiving unemployment compensation was patently illegal and defied all human experience.

Many states had shown there were legal ways to restrict assistance to girls and women who had repeated illegitimate pregnancies, but an absolute denial of assistance, including general assistance, to the one-time repeater would never survive a conformity hearing in New York State much less in Washington. Such a rigid restriction appeared mean-spirited or, to use the social workers' term, punitive. Unlike many other states, New York had no residence requirements. Additionally, citizens had certain civil rights; they could not be treated in a way "similar" to aliens, even though the "commonsense" solution to the Newburgh crisis might be to force the migrants to move on.

Welfare professionals also knew that many of the rules would be impossible to administer. Back in the days when a rural county had a few ne'er-do-wells on its rolls, it was feasible to bring them in to the courthouse from time to time for a hard look at their current situation. But thousands of case files to be reviewed each month by the corporation counsel? Had the impoverished widow remarried? Who was that man then? Hadn't that old man died? This was a system guaranteed to break down as soon as it began.

Yet as Steiner has pointed out, a good many Newburgh welfare rules were but a shade different from those operating legally elsewhere. California had a fairly strict regulation for dealing with ADC mothers who refused offers of work. New York State itself had recently enacted legislation that addressed the migrant issue. Applicants that caseworkers suspected had migrated with welfare in mind were to be directed to the State Employment Service. Oregon's new ADC-Unemployed Parent (ADC-U) law denied assistance to persons who had quit a job without good cause.

In fact, it was the federal interpretation of the new ADC-U amendment that was preventing the start of work relief projects in other parts of New York State and even calling into question a number already under way.

The state was free of federal constraints in cases where general assistance was the source of aid. But the Social Security Board's 1936 ruling that grants for categorical assistance could not be worked off, precluded work relief for ADC, OAA, and AB recipients. Work relief was always subject to the criticism—particularly in times of recession—that it tended to reduce the number of job openings across the board. Using this argument, organized labor had successfully outlawed work relief in New York City. Since ADC-U was conceived as emergency legislation to help fight the recession, HEW's general counsel followed economic theory. New York State, anxious to shift families from general assistance to ADC-U in order to collect matching federal funds, was not prepared to let a few work relief projects get in its way. The state was said, however, to be protesting the federal ruling on ADC-U.[15]

Early action by the state was clearly necessary, and the New York Social Welfare Board appointed a special five-member panel to investigate. On July 7, the verdict was in. The panel, which was assisted by board counsel, found the Newburgh plan in violation of both state and federal laws. Warning of the possible loss of $200 million in federal aid, the panel recommended that Newburgh be forbidden to enforce the new rules. Within a week the Department of Social Welfare had ordered city manager Mitchell to withdraw the plan.[16]

By this time, however, Mitchell's plan had triggered a resounding positive response. Letters of approval piled into Newburgh itself, into Albany, into Washington, and into newspaper offices all over the country. Although their letter went unsigned, a dozen employees of New York City's Department of Public Welfare endorsed "every item" of the code, because, they wrote, Newburgh's difficulties "reflect in a small way the tremendous problem loaded on the city of New York." With few exceptions, the rest of the country, from large city to small town, seemed to agree that Newburgh's "welfare mess" was a copy of its own experience. One exception was Newburgh's own mayor, also chairman of the New York State Conference of Mayors, who viewed the crisis as a "moral issue" and its proposed remedy as lacking a sound economic approach. The powerless mayor declared himself against policies that would "deny needed relief to innocent children, slam the door against those who came here in search of jobs, and cut off needy families from assistance nine months of the year." The *New York Times,* from all reports the sole dissenting newspaper of note, condemned not just Newburgh but its entire company of supporters. Echoing the state board, the *Times* accused Newburgh of "following an outlaw course." But the *Times* added to the board's purely legal stance a condemnation of Newburgh as "a city where mercy took a beating." Acknowledging that "the voice of man's inhumanity to man is loud in the land applauding Newburgh," the paper called upon "Albany [presumably Governor Nelson Rockefeller]" to assert leadership in "the cause of decency."

In dissent, the *Wall Street Journal* expressed outrage at the official response:

It's a fine commentary on public morality in this country when a local community's effort to correct flagrant welfare abuses is declared illegal under both state and local law. That is exactly where the matter rests in the case of Newburgh. The small New York city has announced a 13-point program to reduce the burden caused by its bums, cheats and loafers, many of whom came to the town and remained for the deliberate purpose of living on relief—which is to say, on the hard-earned money of honest residents.

Some magazines, however, the *Nation* for one, were closer to the *Times*. While Carey McWilliams, the *Nation*'s editor, saw no merit in the Mitchell crusade, he argued that the protest, with its nationwide support, should arouse sober thought: "We have not sought to rehabilitate the destitute; it has been much too easy to send them a welfare check and forget about them. Local communities have, in consequence, neglected to establish training programs or language classes; nor have they sought to find new industries or to challenge the need of surrounding farms for migrant labor (which usually ends up on the relief rolls)."[17]

Inevitably Newburgh was injected into national politics. Barry Goldwater, the conservative senator from Arizona, a rival of Rockefeller for the Republican presidential nomination three years hence, met with Mitchell in Washington and endorsed the code as good for all cities in what he declared was an "unpolitical comment." The *Times* came down hard on this one, too.

With such evidence of widespread popular support, including a profile in the *Times* headed "Famous Overnight," Mitchell understandably insisted that his code would be instituted as planned. Equally understandably, his defiance led, by way of the New York Department of Social Welfare, to court action. On August 19, the New York State Supreme Court issued a temporary injunction against twelve of the thirteen points. The game was over, at least so far as Mitchell and his particular code was concerned.[18] Yet if Mitchell had been a person sincerely dedicated to welfare reform rather than the gadfly that he was, he could have rested satisfied that his actions had a lasting impact on public welfare. To be sure, the

1960 advisory council report and the Cohen task force report were in hand and several other studies of welfare problems and their possible resolution were under way when the Newburgh crisis erupted. But Newburgh all but ensured that big changes would be forthcoming forthwith.

Services, Services

Fresh from six years as governor of Connecticut, where welfare costs had presented him with one of his most "bothersome and frustrating" problems, Secretary of HEW Ribicoff was convinced that federal action was called for. He had been on the job just four weeks when he told the Ways and Means Committee that the "entire [welfare] problem" required "a very good and thorough new look." He promised that HEW would examine "all of these programs to see if we can make some new sense out of the programs that have been in existence a long time. If we do," he continued, "we will come to Congress and tell you so."[19]

Although he found a great deal of merit in the Cohen task force recommendations, Ribicoff was reluctant to stop there. He thought more might be done to help the states on the issues that seemed uppermost to them and had seemed uppermost to him as governor. They were the issues that Newburgh confirmed as uppermost in the minds of the concerned American public. Ribicoff also wanted to make sure that all the angles had been considered and that there was maximum consensus—among the welfare professionals at least—before making further recommendations to the White House.

To this end Ribicoff enlisted the interest of the NASW leadership, which soon joined forces with other private social work federations and the APWA to form an Ad Hoc Committee on Public Welfare. Sanford Solender of the National Jewish Welfare Board chaired the committee, consisting of twenty-two individuals who were affiliated with, but not representing, a broad spectrum of public, private, religious, family, children's, and character building agencies as well as schools of social work. In addition to Loula Dunn, director of the APWA, directors of the welfare departments of Pennsylvania, New Jersey, and North Carolina were members, as were the directors of the New York City and Richmond, Virginia, departments. The ad hoc committee was formally appointed in May and delivered its report in September 1961.

Ribicoff also called on George Wyman, who had recently left his position as assistant commissioner of social security, to elaborate on and make specific recommendations for administrative and program changes, with particular attention to bringing about a closer working relationship between the BPA and the Children's Bureau as recommended by the Cohen task force. Wyman had spent most of his social work career in California, having been director of the Los Angeles Regional Welfare Council and of the State Welfare Department. He became director of the New York State Department of Welfare shortly after submitting his report to Secretary Ribicoff in August 1961.[20]

A third report, *Public Welfare: Time for a Change*, resulted from a Project on Public Services for Families and Children sponsored by the New York School of Social Work, Columbia University. Elizabeth Wickenden, then working out of New York City as a social welfare consultant, designed the project and wrote the main body of the report. Winifred Bell, a doctoral candidate at the New York School, designed and evaluated the research. This, as well as the two other reports, was funded by the Field Foundation of Chicago.[21]

These three reports clearly contained the desired consensus on major recommendations from social welfare professionals. It could hardly have been otherwise, because many of the same persons from the same social welfare organizations and schools of social work were represented in one way or another in the preparation of all three. To be sure, this personnel duplication was more pronounced in the case of the Ad Hoc Committee and Wickenden-Bell reports, neither of which had any representation from currently employed federal staff. Wyman's consultants were largely drawn from the federal bureaucracy—HEW's Office of the Secretary, the SSA Commissioner's Office, the BPA, and the Children's Bureau. Wyman also called upon Wickenden, Solender, and other members of the ad hoc committee, however, for comment and recommendations. Nevertheless, Wyman's report, both in tone and in some of its specific recommendations, was more responsive to public criticism of welfare.[22]

Although change was certainly proposed, the entire scheme had a familiar ring. Most notably, the APWA Statement of Principles and Wickenden's testimony on the 1950 amendments contained the rationale and the specifics for Ribicoff's "new look." And why not? If old ideas represented good social policy, shouldn't they be reintroduced? The 1956 amendments had offered lip service to an old goal—rehabilitation and services to strengthen family life and help individuals attain self-support. But the goal had yet to be encouraged by appropriations. The welfare professionals seized upon the Louisiana and Newburgh crises in a last-ditch effort to convince the new Democratic administration to give their old ideas a serious try.

Wyman expressed this in his report:

Public indignation over program abuses calls for Federal leadership in directing States to concentrate intensive casework and other services on cases involving serious socioeconomic and behavioral problems. Federal plan requirements could call for specific provision of rehabilitative, preventive, and protective services in those case situations warranting them.

The kinds of cases which call for action are those of illegitimacy; fraud; misuse of assistance payments; neglect and abuse of children; child misbehavior such as persistent stealing, truancy and conflict with the law; and adult and child idleness.

It did "no good" to shift responsibility by asserting that public welfare did not "cause" the social problems presented by certain families in the caseload. Purely and simply, declared Wyman, "the public wants to know what will be done about them!"[23]

"Rehabilitative, preventive, and protective services" targeted on problem cases by trained social workers—this was the basic, agreed-upon change in answer to public demand. The Ad Hoc Committee emphasized an indispensable connection between required social services and trained caseworkers:

Information is already available, and has been tested, on measures of treatment for families in which the incidence of multiple problems has created a pattern of dependency. With enough trained workers available, these patterns could be broken by application of this knowledge. . . .

Special Federal support to States on the basis of 100 percent of cost is suggested to permit smaller caseloads, with skilled workers to give intensive treatment to [unmarried] mothers and children, including counselling; use of psychological services; and other specialized services, as indicated by the individual nature of a problem.[24]

None of the reformers asserted that the entire caseload consisted of problem families, however. Wickenden suggested that "perhaps the majority" needed only some form of "practical assistance" such as money, medical care, or special living arrangements. Wyman believed the number of problem cases was "small." The Ad Hoc Committee, perhaps reflecting the larger representation of private agencies whose raison d'être was non-monetary service, conceded only that "some individuals and families" required *only* financial assistance. It was also the Ad Hoc Committee that pressed hardest for professional training. Deploring the fact that almost 90 percent of public assistance caseworkers "dealing directly with troubled individuals" had no graduate social work education, the committee called for 33 percent MSWs in ten years. Attainment of this goal would put public assistance workers on a par with child welfare workers, 30 percent of whom were professionally trained.

Wyman, who predicted a lapse of "many years" before shortages could be overcome, emphasized improvements in agency staff training and the introduction of modern methods of management. Problem cases should be assigned to workers with proven skills. To undergird the services strategy, research and demonstration projects were to be generously funded and the ADC program evaluated in terms of its purposes and objectives. And in order to make sure that state and local welfare agencies became seriously engaged, social services of direct benefit to recipients must be separately accounted for, not lumped together with overhead administrative costs. The matching rate could then be equalized with that of the assistance payment, resulting in reimbursement as high as 75 percent in some states.[25]

Beginning with the Cohen task force, integration of child welfare services under the Children's Bureau with family social services under the BPA became a key element to those planning change. Child welfare services were invoked in cases where children required care by adults other than parents. Although organized separately, cooperation between private family agencies and child welfare agencies had always been close. In an important aspect of such cooperation, family welfare agencies would refer cases involving parental neglect or abuse for temporary or permanent care in foster homes or institutions. After placement through the courts, the child welfare agency would follow the child until maturity. After the Depression, when family agencies were no longer heavily involved in relief-giving, a good many merged with child welfare agencies for administrative purposes. At the practice level, however, separate spheres were maintained. This pattern persisted in public welfare. At the federal level, the Children's Bureau and the BPA reported directly to the commissioner of Social Security, occasionally preparing joint reports at his request. In all but two states, public assistance and child welfare services were located in the same agency. In some local agencies, staff might be integrated, but in areas of any size, staffs remained separate.

If contrary to the course of events, the Children's Bureau, rather than the Social Security Board, had been chosen to administer ADC, there is no reason to suppose that the Title IV program would have been integrated with Child Welfare Services administered by the Children's Bureau under Title V. For one thing, Title V followed the traditional mission of private child welfare agencies. Like them, Title V made no distinction regarding the material status of the child. Grants to the states for child welfare services were intended for "the protection and care of homeless, dependent, and neglected children, and children in danger of becoming delinquent"— conditions that could be found among the financially independent as well as families on welfare—the Children's Bureau was at pains to point out.

For another, financing of the two programs was vastly different. Grants for child welfare services were made on the basis of a closed-end appropriation, the total sum allotted among the states by the Children's Bureau. The Flemming ruling, followed by the temporary authorization to provide Title IV support for needy children in foster homes, created a wedge to bring about greater cooperation, if not total integration, of family and child welfare services. Congress had recently lifted the ban restricting child welfare services to rural areas, and indications of increased funding, including the possibility of an open-end appropriation, implied solid support ·for a national program. Moreover, there was some intimation that child welfare workers could be involved on the practice level in welfare cases, particularly with the predelinquent minor in an ADC family.

Wyman, who was particularly charged with making recommendations in this regard, called for submission of a single State Plan for Child Welfare and Family Services. At the federal level, he recommended, the bureaus should accelerate joint planning and reporting and adopt uniform personnel standards. Noting that the full authorization of $25 million for child welfare services had never yet been appropriated, both Wyman and the Ad Hoc Committee asked that at least this much be made available.[26]

The Children's Bureau and its supporters in the various national children's federations and agencies could rally around the call for more services and money to pay for them. But they dug in their heels in opposing integration into the "welfare mess." They could see the skills of their better trained staffs dissipated if they moved into public family service as envisioned by the new look in public welfare. Commenting from retirement on the most drastic proposal in the Wickenden report, Katherine Lenroot pronounced:

The proposal to lift the welfare functions and grants from the Children's Bureau and place them in an office of Public Welfare which would also be responsible for public assistance would destroy the Children's Bureau, which was founded on the assumption, increasingly verified by scientific understanding and professional experience, that the needs of children cut across all professional lines and boundaries, and must be considered from all aspects of child life.[27]

Beyond the cover of benign helping services, upon which there was eager agreement, lay two coercive measures the reformers accepted with some reluctance. One of these was the suspension of money payments to families where welfare payments were habitually spent for purposes other than the intended purchase of food, clothing, and shelter. To grant assistance to families through protective payments, that is, by vouchers or to a party other than the adult recipient, would require an amendment to the Social Security Act. It was not with tongue in cheek that the Ad Hoc Committee viewed its favorable action on this point as "safeguarding the principle of cash payment through limited use of vouchers." Rather, reasonable heads had concluded that to hold out any longer in defense of the money payment might result in a rather complete turn-about in the direction of Rule 1 of the Newburgh code.[28]

The second coercive measure was work relief. Depending on the degree of federal involvement, work relief projects might or might not require federal legislation. In any case, however, a relaxation of the 1936 board ruling prohibiting recipients of OAA, AB, or ADC from working out their relief payments would be required. The complication introduced by the unemployed parent amendment would also have to be overcome. In Wyman's opinion, the 1936 ruling, instituted at a time when the WPA was in full swing, was now outdated. In his view, the new unemployed parent amendment made action all the more necessary to stem criticism of idle, able-bodied men collecting welfare. Wyman recommended that the secretary revise the 1936 ruling to permit "work-for-relief" projects, subject to federal standards, including a forty-hour week with pay at the minimum wage, or relief at this rate to be worked out at fewer hours.[29]

The Ad Hoc Committee put a different cast upon proposed work projects, tending to separate them from the work-for-relief concept by calling them "community work programs." The committee urged that such programs should contain a strong element of training and retraining, a service element. Recipients should be paid "not less than prevailing wages [usually higher than the established minimum] for comparable work." Public assistance funds, including federal funds, would be used to reimburse the local agency in charge of these projects. The Ad Hoc Committee cautioned against over-optimism in expecting work to reduce much of the welfare burden, reminding enthusiasts that "approximately 90 percent of the persons receiving assistance are too young to work, too old to work, disabled, or are caring for young children and should remain at home."[30]

It was agreed, nevertheless, that work in the private sector was a good route off welfare, and not just for able-bodied males. Everyone knew that choice was no longer an option for ADC mothers. "Young children" had yet to be precisely defined. The new strategy was to call for a sizable increase in day care services (a natural for the Children's Bureau), though Wyman thought some less formal sharing of child care by recipients would lead to speedier results. With work requirements should come tangible work incentives. To this end, the Income and Resources Amendment of 1939 should be relaxed in order to allow the adult recipient or older child to retain some earnings beyond clothing and carfare. This would bring welfare programs into line with OASDI, where a certain amount of earnings were allowed over and above the insurance payment.[31]

Conspicuous by its absence was any recommendation to focus on child support enforcement as a way to reduce welfare costs. Certainly the omission could not be attributed to increased contributions since the passage of NOLEO and interstate collection laws. Failure to collect from absent fathers became a self-fulfilling prophecy, a "hopeless task" in Wickenden's words. Wyman, in discussing illegitimacy, suggested that support from the putative father be sought. But he offered no special steps that might be taken in this most difficult of child support areas, an area where some state statutes forbade any legal action on the child's behalf. And he had nothing at all to say about the obligations of the absent fathers of legitimate children. The Ad Hoc Committee did not mention the issue.[32]

The omission of child support enforcement was partly redressed on December 11, 1961, when Ribicoff announced a series of actions to improve welfare administration in order to show some movement prior to submission of the promised reform legislation. "More effective location of deserting parents" led the actions list. Henceforth states would be required to establish a special unit, "separately identified and adequately staffed" to help law enforcement officers locate and obtain support from absent parents. Child support enforcement was one of two actions directed toward abuse of ADC. The other pointed at fraud—estimated at less than 1.5 percent of caseload—asking the states to improve their procedures by spelling them out more explicitly and by assurances of follow-up and reporting.

The remaining eight specified actions, identified as "constructive approaches to get people off assistance," picked up the main recommendations in hand, urging the states to make a substantial commitment to providing "a variety of helpful *services*" to the "entire *family*" with a staff "adequate in number and appropriately trained." For emphasis, the Bureau of Public Assistance was designated the Bureau of Family Services (BFS).[33]

President Kennedy's message transmitting the administration's welfare reform bill to Congress lifted a few key words from the Ad Hoc Committee report to sound the call for change. "Public welfare," he wrote, "must be more than a salvage operation, picking up the debris from the wreckage of human lives."[34] On July 25 he signed the public welfare amendments of 1962 into law. The high purpose of the legislation was plain:

This measure embodies a new approach—stressing services in addition to support, rehabilitation instead of relief, and training for useful work instead of prolonged dependency. This important legislation will assist our States and local public welfare agencies to redirect the incentives and services they offer to needy families and children and to aged and disabled people. Our objective is to prevent or reduce dependency and to encourage self-care and self-support—to maintain family life where it is adequate and to restore it where it is deficient.[35]

This time, as compared with 1956, the services strategy was backed up with money. The federal share for social services and for in-service training to enhance caseworker skills was increased to 75 percent. Money for training grants to educational institutions was also authorized.

Child welfare services themselves were somewhat broadened to include "preventing or remedying, or assisting in the solution of problems which may result in the neglect, abuse, exploitation, or delinquency of children." But the joint planning by the BFS and the Children's Bureau favored by Wyman was not presented in the administration bill. The 1962 legislation simply required the child welfare services plan to provide for coordination with ADC. Although slated for more money, grants for child welfare services were continued in the closed-end appropriation form. In view of the predominance of foster care in child welfare services, matching grants were deemed too great an invitation to remove children from their own homes. Yearly authorizations for grants were due to rise from $30 million in fiscal year 1962 to $50 million in fiscal 1969. Ten million of this money was earmarked for day care.[36]

Although the 75 percent match marked a clear intention to greatly expand and extend the services offered by the public welfare agencies themselves, provision of services by other public agencies could be arranged by agreement if necessary. In this connection, special requirements were made to accommodate vocational rehabilitation. Recurring references to "rehabilitation" in justifying the amendments had aroused some concern in the Office of Vocational Rehabilitation (OVR), HEW. The program of grants to the states to restore disabled persons to employability dated back to 1920 and had been slipped in for funding under Title V of the Social Security Act in 1935. More recently, state programs under OVR had been singled out to accommodate referrals from OASDI under the disability amendments. Vocational Rehabilitation agencies were also considered a resource in the administration of APTD. In order to protect OVR's turf, the 1962 amendments stipulated that rehabilitation services, in the sense of restoration of work capacity, were reserved to the Vocational Rehabilitation agency.[37]

Services were also encouraged by demonstration projects. States wishing to try out innovative ideas either in direct services or through administrative changes could obtain a waiver to deviate from the state plan, again with the support of federal funds.

Coercive provisions directed toward a recipient's failure to spend grant money properly and to prevent idleness among the able-bodied were included in the amendments, but in forms so mild as to appear to be yet other benign services. Protective payments were authorized as a last resort in cases of money mismanagement, but not through the use of vouchers. The authorized remedy was to continue the money payment to another interested person or legal representative, with invocation of civil or criminal penalties authorized by state law a last resort. Protective payments were limited to 5 percent of the monthly caseload. Work projects were *not* to be carried out on the work-for-relief model as endorsed by Wyman.

The amendments followed the Ad Hoc Committee in authorizing community work and training projects to conserve existing skills and develop new ones, payment to be made at the state minimum and local prevailing rate. Reasonable work expenses were to be included in determining need. Arrangements for child care must be assured.

But the 1962 amendments weren't all services. They contained important and costly provisions that liberalized eligibility in ADC and raised federal sharing in the adult categorical programs. The temporary unemployed parent provision was extended for five years. The two-parent needy family was further undergirded by federal matching for the needs of the unemployed or disabled father living in the home. Matching for the care of children in foster care was made permanent. Noting the matter of equity, Chairman Mills of Ways and Means saw to it that recipients of OAA, AB, and APTD received a $4.00-a-month increase, bringing their maximum to $70.00.[38]

The public welfare amendments of 1962, which contained no significant departures from the administration bill, passed the House 357 to 34 and were approved in the Senate by voice vote. Hearings by Ways and Means had run for only three days and by Finance only four. Both the number of witnesses and the questions put to them were few. Such an overwhelming endorsement could mean one of two things—either indifference to the welfare problem (including a disregard of public opinion as displayed during the Newburgh crisis) or a conviction that this legislation would result in a real decline in the program now renamed Aid to Families with Dependent Children (AFDC).[39]

If conviction rather than indifference explained the legislation's easy passage, conviction was rooted in faith. A few success stories had been recounted: a former nurse, overburdened with children from an unhappy broken marriage, was restored to proper household management and parental care and planned to return to part-time work; a semiliterate man, with a weak wife and children running wild, was steered into a welding course and found a job; a young woman on ADC was valedictorian of her high school class and went on to college. Demonstration projects—the tests of social services cited by the ad hoc committee—were also used to witness success. Wickenden inserted in the record a report on some of these demonstrations by her assistant, Winifred Bell.

Somewhat cautious, though highly supportive of the amendments, was Ellen Winston, representing the APWA:

The basic purpose of public assistance categories from their beginning has been to provide assistance to needy individuals and families. This will obviously continue to be true. . . . It is not possible to predict how many public welfare recipients will be enabled to leave the assistance rolls through increased services, and it may be that the results can never be precisely measured. . . . However much or little preventive and rehabilitative services result in a net cash saving in assistance costs, they can be justified by their accomplishments in strengthening the fabric of family life, and in helping children to become productive and responsible citizens.[40]

A disappointed White House staffer summed up the negative conclusions of the nation's governors:

The feeling was that the proposed changes were social work changes and while good, were not practical to the point of meeting our immediate need, that the practical changes recommended . . . were ignored, that the proposed changes did not represent the changes Administrators and the public have been led to believe would be made, that Plan requirements make the changes ineffective and that the proposed changes did not give the State Administrators a program they could sell to their respective Legislatures.[41]

Unquestionably, however, the public welfare amendments of 1962 had been sold and had been bought on the premise that AFDC rolls would come down—in fairly short order. At his first opportunity, Cohen cautioned state welfare directors "not to oversell what public welfare can do in the way of rehabilitation as it may not be possible to achieve the success

. . . that may be expected by the Congress and the public." But by then it was too late to tone down the rhetoric.[42]

The Man in the House

No sooner had the Commissioner's Office and the BFS begun to attack the mountain of organizational and regulatory tasks than Senator Robert C. Byrd of West Virginia, chairman of the Subcommittee on Appropriations for the District of Columbia, abruptly changed the subject from social services back to eligibility. The senator, having become concerned about a growing welfare load, asked the General Accounting Office (GAO) to assist the District Public Aid Department (PAD) in an investigation of families receiving AFDC and general assistance. The results were almost too bad to be true. Of 236 AFDC cases studied (about 5 percent of the caseload) 141, or 58.7 percent, were found ineligible. Yet the results of the investigation were not challenged. Neither the GAO nor the PAD had any quarrel about methodology or conclusions. Fewer than a dozen families appealed the decision to close their cases. Although some of the discontinuances may have been based on technicalities, the vast majority were not.

Sixty-one of the families were ineligible because a man was in the house, not absent as claimed. In about half of these families the mother was living with her husband and/or the father of her children. In about one-third, the mother was living with a man other than the children's father. In the rest of the cases, a man was living in the home but his exact relationship to the mother and children, or the amount of money he was contributing, was undetermined. Only a few cases—13 of the total of 133 ineligibles—would have been eligible if the District of Columbia had adopted the AFDC unemployed parent provision. Two-thirds of these men were working. In other families, ineligibility rested on other grounds in addition to the man-in-the-house rule, such as higher-than-usual living standards unexplained by declared income, unreported work or ability to work in the face of claimed incapacity, and refusal to cooperate in the investigation.

The general assistance program showed much the same level of ineligibility as AFDC. Persons receiving general assistance were supposed to be unemployable because of a physical or mental disability that precluded full-time work in competitive industry. Recipients were to be medically reevaluated every six months, and were bound to accept offered medical treatment or rehabilitation services to restore them to productive work, if possible. Persons eligible for APTD were to be referred to that federally supported program. Under these terms, the GAO found only 20 percent of the sixty-eight (5 percent of caseload) cases eligible for general assistance. Another 20 percent belonged on the APTD rolls. The remaining 60 percent were ineligible for any public welfare, mostly because of employment or unreported resources.

Pulling no punches, the GAO included in its report some twenty of the "more flagrant cases" uncovered by its investigation:

A 24-year-old mother of four children, fathered by three different men, none of whom were her husband, successfully withheld from the social workers the knowledge of the birth of her youngest child. . . . The father of this child and of one of the other children was found hiding in the bathroom of the ADC mother's home at 6:10 a.m. on a Sunday morning. He admitted spending the night with the ADC mother. He admitted also that he was employed. . . .

A 26-year-old mother of six illegitimate children, fathered by three different men, was again pregnant by a man whom she did not identify. . . . The April 1962 assistance payment was suspended pending further inquiry into the matters disclosed by the investigation including (a) birth of a child in February 1962, (b) relationship with a man who, she admitted, spent nights with her "too often to mention" and who provided her with money in excess of $100 a month, (c) presence of another man, his wife, and three children in an apartment in the dwelling, (d) an unidentified sick child in the home, and (e) squalid, overcrowded, and rat-infested premises.

A 34-year-old mother of seven children fathered by three different men had concealed the birth of the seventh child from the PAD for three years through fear of being removed from the ADC program. The father of the seventh child had been living with the ADC mother until the time of the investigators' first visit to the home, although the ADC mother had professed to have terminated the relationship in September 1961 when he got into trouble with the police.

The methods of investigation—visits made at night or early on Saturday or Sunday morning by two teams, one to conduct the interview and the other to guard against a quick getaway by a man-in-the-house—flew directly in the face of the social work tenets that permeated the 1962 amendments. Unlike the Newburgh code, the Byrd report, as it came to be called, presented no challenges to law or regulation. What it called into question was the ability of social workers to ensure adherence to law and regulation as they stood. The head of the District's Division of Public Assistance agreed that the "social service staff is not equipped to do the job it is expected to do with today's caseload." He explained to Byrd and the District Appropriations Committee:

We tried to do the old type of social work which is a helping relationship. We tried to create a public image that the social worker is not a snoop who looks under the bed and in the closet, but is, as one well-known training film put it, a friend at the door. . . . This may all have been true at the time when the program started, when we had the so called "nice" people on relief. . . . What we are having now is the bottom of the barrel. . . . Most of them . . . are problem cases. . . . They are . . . people with problems of alcoholism, drug addiction, with criminal records, and are not the type of people whom social workers are trained to deal with.[43]

Possibly Washington was a special case. The nation's capital, an urban area with a population of 764,000, was atypical. Persons living within its borders and having no legal residence elsewhere had no franchise. The city was governed by a three-person Commission of Army Corps of Engineers officers and one civilian appointed by Congress. Although many federal employees resided in the District, young middle-class families were apt to buy their homes in the suburbia of surrounding Maryland or Virginia. Washington had an unusually large number of middle-class blacks in its large black population. In 1960, the city was 54 percent black. As in other cities outside the agricultural South, the number of black in-migrants was increasing as field labor was driven off the land by machinery. This poorly educated, unskilled group had a hard time fitting into available jobs in any city, let alone Washington, where the only industry was the federal government itself. Blacks made up a huge 92.9 percent of the District's AFDC caseload.[44]

In this sense, then, the District's welfare mess as described in the Byrd report might turn out to be as atypical as the city itself. But the argument could be pushed too far. Nationwide, over 50 percent of AFDC families lived in highly urban areas and another 18 percent lived in somewhat less concentrated urban locales. And what of the assertion that problem cases were but a small blemish on the general picture? That ineligibility was present in only 1.5 percent of this small blot? And that fraud, willful misrepresentation, that is, was just a speck, a fraction of the 1.5 percent of ineligibles?[45] In the wake of the special investigation, it might have been expected that District of Columbia court dockets would be crowded with persons found to have collected welfare payments illegally. But dockets were not so besieged. This failure to cry "fraud" or to count as fraud this type of case in any official report resulted from the necessity to offer verifiable proof of an illegal act. When did the man move into the house? Did he work steadily? The family was going to call the worker to report before the next check was received? The man left again two weeks ago? Prosecuting attorneys could not be expected to take such cases.

For this very good reason cheating on welfare was defined as "abuse," an act that could be redressed within the welfare system itself without reference to proofs beyond a reasonable doubt. To the public, however, and to its representatives in Congress, the fine line between fraud and abuse was a fuzzy one. The Byrd report won praise from liberal and conservative senators in both parties as well as favorable attention from the news media. It was regarded as a scientific study that raised serious questions about the validity of the entire AFDC caseload. However much too high that 58.7 percent of ineligibles might be, the distance between 1.5 percent was so great as to render the smaller figure equally unbelievable. In six months, after a nationwide review, it was determined that the rate of ineligibility in the District of Columbia was atypical by a very large margin. It was also determined that the rate of ineligibility was a great deal closer to 1.5 than to 58.7 percent. But almost everywhere ineligible cases were found to be higher than 1.5 and in some states were a significant 10 percent or more.

The study, carried out by the states under close direction by the BFS, had been requested by the Senate Appropriations Committee at the instigation of Senator Byrd. Both state and local staff and, in ten states, the GAO participated in reading records and making home visits. Unlike the District of Columbia, however, most of those delegated to the review of eligibility were drawn from the regular staff of caseworkers and supervisors rather than relying solely on special investigators. This method tended to mirror actual practice, where it was up to caseworkers to determine eligibility and up to them to refer doubtful cases to special investigators. Yet the review was very different from day-to-day operations. Reviewers were handpicked from the more highly trained and experienced, assigned a small number of cases, instructed to exhaust all possible avenues of inquiry, and given time commensurate to the task.

The results of the review, which were generally accepted as valid, indicated room for improvement rather than a hopelessly unacceptable program. Ten states had ineligibility rates above 10 percent, but only two above 15 percent.[46] Six of these high percentage states were in the South. States with some of the highest caseloads had some of the lowest ineligibility rates—California only 1.2 percent and New York only 3.7 percent. Overall, the conclusion could be drawn that good state and local performance followed low caseloads per caseworker, more frequent reinvestigation of eligibility, and more adequate assistance payments. There was nothing here to contradict the claims that had been made for social services. On the contrary, lower caseloads per worker and frequent family contact were part and parcel of the 1962 amendments.[47]

The Welfare Administration

Implementation of the 1962 amendments had presupposed some sort of administrative reorganization at the federal level. Reorganization was discussed in the Cohen task force report and the Wyman report and was very much a part of Wickenden's thinking. Basically, reorganization was believed necessary in order to provide sufficient time and attention to welfare, which no one now believed would wither away.

The Commissioner's Office of the Social Security Administration had never recovered from the loss of positions suffered upon its transfer to the Federal Security Agency. Meanwhile the social insurance programs themselves had burgeoned. Robert M. Ball, the newly appointed commissioner, had spent his life in the insurances, first in the New York field office, then as director, Division of Program Analysis, BOASDI. Ball, a gifted administrator, was credited with "selling" social insurance, particularly disability coverage, to the Eisenhower administration. Now his immediate future was seen as the indispensable right hand of Cohen in the push for medical insurance for the elderly. A possible remedy for easing the work burden at the top echelon was the appointment of an additional deputy commissioner for welfare programs with appropriate staff assistance. What emerged from conversations among Cohen, Ball, and Wickenden was a much more radical plan.

Ball viewed a reorganization primarily in managerial terms. Except at the policy level he regarded social insurance and welfare as on two different tracks. Mid-level employees of the BOASDI and the BFS could not communicate in any meaningful way because they had nothing in common. Coming into the commissioner's job at the time of the Byrd report crisis, Ball became immediately enmeshed in welfare and quickly became convinced that rather than deputize anything, each major program should have a commissioner of its own, that Social Security should be separated from Welfare.

Wickenden was extremely receptive to this idea. She saw the 1962 amendments as an unprecedented opportunity for public welfare to emerge as a vital entity in its own right. She reflected with satisfaction upon the fact that social services could now be offered to anyone requesting them regardless of financial need. Though not a social worker herself, she regarded the social work profession as the unifying force in public welfare—the dispenser of money and of social services. And she thought that functions, not special groups—such as children or the aged—should drive the organizational pattern.

Cohen, recognizing the size and complexity of both programs and the weakened overlapping in aging and disability, could agree that the days when one person like Altmeyer could handle both were gone forever. Cohen also had his eye very much on Medicare, which would make huge demands on Ball both before and after passage.[48]

From the sidelines, Altmeyer, who lived until 1972, stood firm behind social security spelled with a lowercase "s." He believed that only the closest possible integration of programs both at the administrative and policy level could ensure continuing protection against the hazards of life. But the rank and file as well as the leadership, in the states as well as in Washington, favored separation. Cohen and Ball had no difficulty selling the reorganization to Anthony V. Celebreeze, who succeeded Ribicoff as secretary of HEW in July 1962.

The Welfare Administration was formally established by departmental administrative order on January 28, 1963. In addition to the Bureau of Family Services and the Children's Bureau, the Welfare Administration provided an umbrella for the Office of Aging, the Office of Juvenile Delinquency and Youth Development, and the Cuban Refugee Program.

Lenroot and her Children's Bureau supporters having won their point, the bureau was transferred to the Welfare Administration intact. Control over the grants program for child welfare services was retained. Joint planning with BFS, such as combined state plans for family and child welfare services, were not to be undertaken. Thus the Children's Bureau stood in precisely the same position in relation to the commissioner of Welfare as it had to the commissioner of Social Security.

The Welfare Administration was, in fact, a very loose federation. The two major organizations therein, the BFS and the Children's Bureau, had their own separate personnel offices, while personnel functions for the Office of the Commissioner of Welfare, the Office of Aging, and the Office of Juvenile Delinquency were handled by the Office of Personnel in the Secretary's Office. Each of these components, large and small, issued its own publications, although *Welfare in Review*, published by the Commissioner's Office, carried articles about the various constituent offices from time to time.

A Division of Research, also located in the Commissioner's Office, was staffed with persons from various disciplines—sociology, economics, psychology, history, social work—signaling the intention to study poverty and dependency in some depth. Grants for research contracts, monitored by Research, could also be made with scholars outside the government. Demonstration grants, funded separately, were administered by the BFS.[49]

The choice for commissioner of welfare was made by agreement of the three persons responsible for the reorganization. Cohen, Ball, and Wickenden were very positively in favor of Ellen Winston, who had served for eighteen years as commissioner of the North Carolina State Board of Public Welfare. During these years she had emerged as a leader in national public welfare, serving as chairperson of the important APWA Committee on Public Welfare Policy and later as its president. It was during her tenure as head of the policy committee that the APWA platform on welfare was developed. She had also chaired the advisory committees that guided the Blackwell and Gould and Burgess and Price studies of AFDC. She had testified before congressional committees on many occasions, representing the APWA as well as her own state.

Winston's father was a lawyer, and both he and her mother were leaders in the small mountain town of Bryson City, North Carolina, where Ellen was born in 1903. After graduation from Converse College, Winston taught school in Raleigh for a few years, but with the encouragement of her husband, who was in the Sociology Department at North Carolina State University, she entered the University of Chicago, where she took a doctorate in sociology in 1930. She taught again, this time at Meredith College. In between she worked on a number of studies for the WPA, the Farm Security Administration, and the U.S. Office of Education. Overall, Winston conveyed a businesslike professionalism, expecting from others the high standards and long work days she exacted of herself.

Winston's deputy was Joseph H. Meyers, a specialist in welfare law. Winston leaned heavily on Meyers, who was greatly respected by BFS staff. "Sometimes," Winston recalled, "if it was really a tough thing, I would ask Joe to do it because sometimes he was a little more patient, a little more deliberative than I might have been." To head the BFS Winston selected Fred H. Steininger, who had made a favorable impression as director of the Welfare Department in Indianapolis. But by and large, the old hands stayed, working in the same jobs they had held previously. This reorganization was no shake-up. Years later Winston described it as "an ongoing operation that could almost run itself."

For all her trust in the old-line staff, Winston found it hard to delegate work to any significant extent. She read everything, overtiring herself in an effort to make a memo or article just a little better. She praised her secretary for being willing "to work the kind of hours I did . . . staying late and coming in on Saturday."

According to Wickenden, Winston antagonized the state administrators because of a demanding stance on standards such as limiting the size of worker caseloads to sixty—practices they were unable to exact from their governors or legislatures. It was deeply disappointing to Wickenden that the family and children's services remained as divided as ever. But if these were faults in Winston's management or management style, the Welfare Administration was nonetheless headed by a person of high intelligence who could articulate her ideas to all kinds of audiences in a truly impressive way. Cohen praised her for prompt delivery on her commitments. Indeed, given other times and circumstances, many of the high hopes for improvements in welfare administration might well have been achieved. And these would have been Winston's achievements. As it was, Winston's considerable talents were consumed in trying to accomplish the impossible.[50]

State Letter no. 606, covering policies and procedures on the social services, was released to the states on November 30, 1962, almost two months before the Welfare Administration was established. Its text, after going through thirty-eight drafts, ran for sixty-eight single-spaced typed pages.[51] Despite its length, the letter did not define social services specifically. It contained no listing that could be neatly checked off to claim the 75 percent match. Instead, matchable social services were defined in terms of problems, such as "aged and disabled individuals in need of protection," followed by suggested actions, such as "enlistment of relatives, friends, and other resources for needed planning and protection; security and maintaining safe living conditions; personal, home and money management; security and using needed medical services." Or, in AFDC cases, "unmarried parents and their children with specified problems, i.e., children whose status under State law is not clarified, legal questions affecting rights of mother and child, support from the absent parent not explored, unmarried mothers with first child, repeated out-of-wedlock children, out-of-wedlock pregnancies, and conditions that foster illegitimacy." And for this group, "services to help such families and their children in respect to: the need for prenatal, confinement, and post-natal medical care for the mother and child; planning for the future of the mother and child; child care and training if child remains with the mother or planning in respect to placement elsewhere" were among those listed. So exhaustive was the problems-services listing of State Letter no. 606 that the 75 percent match was all but guaranteed when the family caseworker engaged in any word or deed that was not exclusively eligibility determination.

In moves that would help control eligibility as well as allow sufficient time for service delivery, the maximum caseload for workers was set at sixty (less than half the median caseload for the nation), with home visits at least twice a year. For "multiproblem" families, worker caseloads were to be even lower, twenty-five to thirty-five cases, and, regardless of higher caseloads, home visits should be as frequent as necessary, and at least every three months.

This important State Letter, ready for insertion in the Handbook of Public Assistance Administration, explained in equally great detail the various ways services would be made available. The basic method was counseling, although homemakers, foster family care for adults, social group work, or child welfare services were also available.[52] Although questions had been raised regarding the propriety of tying the money payment to needy persons so closely to social services as to add a condition of eligibility without legal sanction, State Letter no. 606 made only one brief reference to the recipient's opinion and role as a recipient of services: "Services aimed at helping the individual and family are based upon the client's interest and desire for help with his problems and upon respect for his right to freedom of choice in accepting or rejecting agency proffers of service."[53]

Although social services were considered the heart of the matter so far as reforms in the AFDC program were concerned, the Welfare Administration gave due attention to the "administrative" regulations issued by Secretary Ribicoff on December 11, 1961. Child support enforcement was encouraged by forming special enforcement groups both in the central office and in the regions, with lawyers represented in Washington and in some of the regions. Speaking to the first meeting of these groups, Winston emphasized the importance of the enforcement effort, giving her audience the benefit of her experience in North Carolina. There she had found it essential to have a full-time lawyer on her staff. The lawyer had made all the difference in North Carolina, where collections rose from $300,000 to $1 million annually over a three-year period.[54]

Similarly, fraud and abuse received special attention through follow-up of the nationwide study of eligibility in AFDC families. As early as February 1963, state agencies were alerted to the imminence of a new system for administrative determination—a system to be known as "quality control" (QC). By August, the sampling plan for QC was submitted to the states. September brought schedules and instructions for judging case actions in AFDC; October brought instructions for handling the adult categories.

When errors in regard to the amount of the money payment were taken into account, statisticians in the Welfare Administration judged that nearly all the states had error rates exceeding 10 percent. This meant that nearly all the states must do better. Ten percent, a very high rate of error, was designated the ceiling of tolerance. States with an error rate above this level were advised to take preventive or corrective action.[55]

Most states moved quickly to forward plans for prescribed social services to the BFS. The initial surge, evident in the earliest days of the Welfare Administration, showed fifty-three of fifty-four jurisdictions claiming a 75 percent match for services in one or more of the categorical programs, usually AFDC.[56] By the summer of 1964, all but Arizona had AFDC services plans approved. Thirty-six states had approved plans in OAA, AB, and APTD as well as AFDC. Many of these states were unable to provide the full scope of services in such short order, however, and therefore took advantage of permissible actions during the progression period. Thus by June 30, 1965—two years short of the deadline—only nineteen of the fifty-three states offered the full range of prescribed services in AFDC on a statewide basis. The remaining thirty-four states had selected areas they considered most urgent or those in line with staff capabilities, some states offering less than the full scope of services in some areas, while providing it fully in others. Much the same pattern was followed in services for the adult categorical programs. Almost a year later there had been little change: fifty-three jurisdictions had approved service plans for AFDC and thirty-nine had approved plans in all four categories.[57]

States showed less eagerness to act where changes would result in additional expenses with no compensating additional match from the federal government. As late as June 1966, only eleven jurisdictions had established community work and training programs, only seven had made provision for protective payments, and only twenty-one had added the unemployed parent in the intact AFDC family as a cause of deprivation.[58]

The Advisory Council on Public Welfare, appointed in July 1964 under the 1962 amendments and reporting to Secretary of HEW John W. Gardner in June 1966, was accordingly reserved: "Sober, objective analysis of the progress to date leads to the inescapable conclusion that the goals of the 1962 amendments have not been reached. . . . For many recipients of public assistance, for the even larger group within the poverty sector not receiving public assistance, and for many children, and young people, and families, and aged in need of aid, social services remain more theoretical than real."[59]

The shortage of trained social workers was deemed as crucial in 1966 as it had been earlier. Estimates in 1966 indicated a requirement for ninety-five thousand social workers to staff state and local public welfare agencies—about twice the number presently on the job. Both the council and an HEW departmental task force on social work manpower repeated the calls for more schools of social work, for higher salaries, for better working conditions. They also conceded that the undergraduate social work major was acceptable for many social work positions and encouraged additional emphasis along these lines.[60]

The Advisory Council on Public Welfare was strongly supportive of social services, recommending that "social services through public welfare programs be strengthened and extended and be readily accessible as a matter of right at all times to all who need them." The council thought it undesirable, as some had suggested, to separate money-granting functions from services, arguing that "poverty and dependence are usually the ultimate results of a variety of social or emotional causes." The council did not take issue with those critics who saw a danger of "forcing" acceptance of services because of the recipient's fear that the money payment be withdrawn. And the council emphasized once again the value of services to the "financially self-sufficient who have social problems."[61]

But, in addition to services, the advisory council introduced and emphasized a subject that had been all but ignored by the rhetoric preceding the 1962 amendments: the money payment. The council had, at the time, the pioneer measurement of poverty—the poverty index—developed by Mollie Orshansky of the Social Security Administration's Bureau of Research and Statistics. Orshansky's work fitted in with the interests of President Kennedy's Council of Economic Advisors, which adopted $3,000 yearly as the "poverty line" for a family of four in its January 1964 *Economic Report of the President*. Taking off from this concept, the Advisory Council on Public Welfare criticized with additional certainty and authority the "grossly inadequate and widely variable" public welfare payments.[62]

Its first recommendation was for "a minimum standard for public assistance payments below which no State may fall." If this were agreed to, a reversal of federal and state roles in devising assistance standards would be instituted. Under the proposed scheme, the federal government would specify standards for financial assistance, social services, and program administration for each state. The state share of financing the cost of meeting these standards would be based upon a percentage of total personal income payments in the state, and would vary to ensure reasonable and equitable fiscal effort. The federal government would assume full financial responsibility for the difference between the established standard and the state share.

Who would be eligible for assistance payments (now referred to by

Elizabeth Wickenden on the advice of lawyers as "entitlements")? Under the advisory council's plan there would be but one criterion—need:

All persons with available income falling below this established budget level would be entitled to receive aid to the extent of that deficiency. Need would be the sole measure of entitlement and irrelevant exclusions such as those based on age, family composition or situation, degree of disability, presumption of income not actually available to the applicant, low earning capacity, filial responsibility, or alleged employability would not conform with requirements of this program.

Moreover, eligibility would be established by the applicant's personal statements, usually on a declaration form. Regularized sample reviews would replace lengthy investigations and reinvestigations of each family. Simplification at intake and minimum reinvestigation would free caseworkers to carry out social services in timely fashion.[63]

In the usual course of events, the secretary of HEW would have issued a press release calling attention to the major recommendations of the advisory council report and indicating the next planned steps. In this case, Secretary John H. Gardner took no action. Finally, six months after completion, the 148-page "'Having the Power, We Have the Duty,'" was accorded a four-page summary in *Welfare in Review*. The summary, which was not signed, blandly predicted that the report's recommendations would be subjected to extensive discussion and debate. Nothing short of a miracle could have brought about such a result. As it was, Gardner, who had succeeded Celebreeze in 1965, had his own ideas about welfare changes, but he was not prepared to air them until after the retirement of Winston, now close to sixty-five.

Winston did, in fact, resign in April 1967, giving as the compelling reason her husband's retirement and their desire to retain their residence in Raleigh. Others thought her disappointment at Gardner's negative reception of the advisory council's report a major factor in her decision. Some believed she chose to devote herself to the many activities of interest to her in a setting more conducive to successful outcomes.[64]

Admittedly, the Welfare Administration had been given a very short time in which to show that social services could turn public welfare into "more than a salvage operation." Winston certainly thought of building for the future. "I think that everyone who has carefully studied the 1962 amendments, in terms of their overall impact, has recognized that if there were to be relatively substantial changes, as a result of them, it would be sometime in the future, as we increase services; improve services; and as we try to do more about children and young people. Those are the things which will ultimately reflect results," she told Congressman John Fogarty in 1965.[65] But research studies in the 1960s raised serious questions about the effect of social services upon people with socioeconomic problems. In at least two carefully designed and evaluated studies, cases handled by highly trained workers turned out no differently than those handled on a routine basis by untrained workers.[66]

As to the salvage operation itself, that is, the number of recipients and the cost of their care, the 1960s were later singled out as the years of the "welfare explosion." Total costs rose from $4.4 billion in 1962 to $11.5 billion in 1969. In AFDC, 1962 costs totaled $1.4 billion; in 1969 they had more than doubled at $3.5 billion, as did the caseload from 3.7 million to 7.3 million AFDC recipients.[67]

By no means could these increases be attributed to economic recession. The period 1961–1968 was marked by growing prosperity and high employment. In October 1968, the seasonally adjusted unemployment rate was 3.3 percent, the lowest since the Korean War. At the same time, the 1960s were noted for an unusual amount of attention to the existence and persistence of poverty. In such an affluent society, the American public could be persuaded that those on the bottom should be given a lift, an opportunity to share in the abundance. Attempts to eradicate poverty, however, did not necessarily imply indifference to the "welfare mess." In fact, attacking the welfare mess head-on through intensified efforts to combat fraud and abuse, collect child support from absent parents, and put all the able-bodied to work preceded the large-scale war on poverty.

10

Workfare

THE WELFARE EXPLOSION was but one recurrent shock that characterized the 1960s. The decade saw years of protest, years when heretofore unobtrusive groups rose up against what they judged to be endemic injustice in a capitalist democracy. They sought major reform across the entire social spectrum. Youth, women, blacks—usually separately, though at times together—demanded an end to racial and gender discrimination in politics, education, housing, and jobs. Above all, they demanded an end to the Vietnam War. No longer was it sufficient to write letters or telegraph Congress. Such long-tried means to reform changed as if overnight to mass demonstrations, some peaceful, others erupting into violence.

Other violence was criminal, as city streets became the scene of holdups, stabbings, and other assaults. A huge increase in the use of addictive drugs lay behind much of this crime. Introduction of the birth control pill in 1960 with its more reliable contraception encouraged freer sexual relationships. Still, there was a noticeable increase in venereal disease and in illegitimate births. Whether cause or consequence, welfare was not far behind.

A War on Poverty

Responding to the loss of farm jobs due to automation, 1.4 million blacks left the South for northern cities in the 1960s. The struggle of black citizens for civil rights had its first major redress in the twentieth century with the 1954 Supreme Court order to desegregate public schools. Both the Eisenhower and Kennedy administrations took steps, though not aggressively, to enforce this decision, Eisenhower in Little Rock, Arkansas, and Kennedy at the University of Mississippi. The 1950s also saw the beginning of scattered efforts by black activists to break down segregation in the South on public transportation and at moderately priced eating facilities. The federal government responded with several laws to enforce voting rights, each containing stiffer enforcement provisions. Most dramatically, in August 1963, the civil rights movement came north to Washington and, 200,000 strong, marched behind the Reverend Martin Luther King, Jr., to demand "jobs and freedom." Other marches followed—Selma, Alabama; Chicago. New organizations, the Congress for Racial Equality (CORE) and the Student Non-Violent Coordinating Committee (SNCC), more confrontational than the long-established Urban League or the National Association for the Advancement of Colored People (NAACP), were organized. In August 1967 the National Welfare Rights Organization was founded.

During the years 1965–1968, racial violence erupted and lasted for several days in the ghettos of nearly all large cities. The 1965 riot in the Watts district of Los Angeles cost twenty-eight black deaths and $200 million in property damage. The 1967 Detroit riot caused forty deaths and over two thousand injuries. The assassination of King on April 4, 1968, set off riots in 125 cities in twenty-nine states. President Johnson's Commission on Civil Disorders, headed by Governor Otto Kerner of Illinois, concluded that white racism was the chief cause of black violence, and warned that the country was moving toward separate, unequal societies. Only by unprecedented levels of funding and dedicated action, the commission concluded, could this wrongful outcome be reversed.

A great many blacks were poor, though they worked long and hard. A great many blacks couldn't find jobs at all. The black middle class was composed of a thin layer of professionals—ministers, doctors, lawyers, teachers—and a larger layer of skilled workers. The semi-skilled and a mass of laborers, many of them farm laborers, made up the bulk of the black population. The high relative number of blacks on welfare compared with their numbers in the population as a whole said a great deal about the social condition of the race. Black families made up 40.4 percent of the AFDC rolls in 1961. Twelve years later, black families accounted for 45.8 percent.[1]

The Civil Rights Law of 1964, a landmark bill, barred discrimination in public accommodations; authorized the attorney general to institute suits to desegregate schools and other public facilities; and forbade discrimination in employment on the basis of race, color, religion, sex, or national origin.

In a number of vital reforms, President Lyndon B. Johnson picked up Kennedy's plans and intentions, using his own long-practiced cajoling and arm-twisting to persuade Congress to pass an avalanche of social legislation. Personally empathetic to the downtrodden because of boyhood deprivation and personally constituted to wield power happily and effectively, Johnson found such action natural. In his first State of the Union address on January 8, 1964, he called for a "War on Poverty." Eight months later, on August 30, he signed the Economic Opportunity Act, which authorized $947.7 million initially for ten separate programs, most having a strong work-training focus. The Office of Economic Opportunity (OEO), which administered the act, was allowed ample money to evaluate the program and to conduct comprehensive social experiments.

Wilbur Cohen, who as assistant secretary for legislation at HEW dropped out of planning meetings at an early stage, considered the War on Poverty a "mish-mash"—a crash effort designed for a broad spectrum of political support at minimal cost. Convinced that effective results were a product of permanent programs inscribed in law, Cohen called unsuccessfully for more attention to poor children and their deserted mothers, presumably in direct support of AFDC. Cohen rightly sensed, however, that the old ways were discredited by the new breed of reformers. The social scientists, not the social workers or the entrenched bureaucrats of any persuasion, would call the tune for this round of reform. Rest assured, it would be a new tune. For the first time ever, the poor, through OEO, were given federally financed legal aid. And the children were to be better prepared for school by a pre-kindergarten program called "Head Start."

In his State of the Union message of January 1965, Johnson called for creation of the "Great Society." Not only would the war on poverty be waged with doubled funds, he told the American people, but crippling and killing disease would be attacked through the National Institutes of Health, educational aid increased, recreational facilities enhanced. Determined to rebuild the rotting, crime-ridden inner cities, to answer calls for law and order, and offer better housing to disadvantaged families, Johnson sponsored establishment of the Department of Housing and Urban Development in 1965.

It goes without saying that all these measures were of potential help and, in many instances, of immediate practical help to those poor who were on welfare and those poor not receiving welfare whose incomes were at or a little above the $3,000 poverty line. Certainly the housing measures helped the poor, for although much has been justly criticized about the ill-effects of concentrations of welfare recipients in public housing projects, it would never do to declare that the crumbling, rat-infested shelters occupied by the rest of the poor were preferable either for them or for the surrounding community.[2]

But among all the Great Society programs, increased access to medical care stands out as the greatest achievement, the greatest benefit to American society. The Social Security Administration had never given up on health insurance, but its policymakers had changed their minds about how to bring it about. For the near future, at least, they had ruled out any try for national health insurance. Since Truman's day, health insurance coverage by business and industry arrangement, either through labor union contracts or otherwise, had become widespread. As a result, though far from universal, a great many persons in their working years were apt to be medically covered by private insurance. The group that most needed help with medical care was the aged, who had more severe health problems and more of them, and were likely to have little or no coverage. The Social Security Administration had drawn up detailed plans for insuring the aged, the survivors, and the disabled who were covered under Title II.

Medicare and Medicaid (Titles XVIII and XIX of the Social Security Act) were signed into law on July 30, 1965. Title XVIII, the Medicare title, provided inpatient hospital services for persons aged sixty-five and over who were entitled to receive old age insurance and to the entitled disabled. The hospital of the patient's choice would be paid by the federal government from the proceeds of a tax on wages, just as in Title II, OASDI. Persons sixty-five and over (whether or not entitled to old age or disability insurance) were also offered outpatient physician's care upon payment of a modest premium. Medicare relieved the welfare agency of some medical vendor payments, those entailed by persons whose social insurance was being supplemented.

But Title XIX, Medicaid, did a great deal more. The Medicaid program picked up all those whose medical bills had been paid by the welfare agency—the indigent aged, AFDC mothers and children, the needy blind and disabled. States were urged by the Welfare Administration to set up procedures to satisfy deductibles for hospital care and premiums for outpatient care in order to be ready to go on July 1, 1966, when the program became operative.

For its part the federal government would provide open-end matching with a national average rate of 55 percent, reaching 83 percent for states with the lowest per capita income. Medical vendor payments were to be terminated no later than December 31, 1969. Moreover, Medicaid did not stop with coverage of public assistance recipients, but reached out to those whose incomes were so low they could not afford to pay for medical care—the so-called medically indigent. Here too the federal government stepped in to match state expenditures. Medicaid offered a tremendous lifting of costs to the states. Medical vendor payments totaled $1.3 billion in 1964. Medicaid totaled $32.3 billion in 1983. As it happened, Medicaid was to be the last generous action of the Ways and Means Committee in regard to AFDC for a very long time. Included in the 1965 amendments were increases in welfare payments averaging $2.50 monthly for the adult programs and $1.25 monthly for AFDC.[3]

Work Incentives

Once Secretary Gardner had pocket-vetoed the report of the Advisory Council on Public Welfare and Winston had resigned, Mills of Ways and Means felt free to pursue his own ideas for cutting back AFDC. HEW, in the persons of Cohen and Joseph Meyers, acting commissioner of welfare, was not entirely left out of the legislative action, but Mills orchestrated the process. Beginning with changes in the definition of services in the preamble of Title IV, Ways and Means added words concerning "work." Joined to the 1958 goal of preserving and strengthening family life was a new objective to attain "maximum self-support . . . consistent with . . . parental care and protection." Specifically states were to ensure "that each appropriate relative, child and individual will enter the labor force and accept employment." The care of children by mothers in the home, the original raison d'être for AFDC, was thus bluntly repudiated.

A new Part C added to Title IV established a work incentive program (WIN), effective no later than July 1, 1969. Referrals of recipients were to be made by the state/local welfare agency to the Department of Labor's field offices. Only children under sixteen and those attending school, the elderly, ill, or incapacitated, or persons required to care for another member of the household were exempt from referral to work. The presence of young children should not ordinarily keep a mother at home, because the legislation called for large increases in day care facilities under the auspices of the Children's Bureau.

For its part, the Department of Labor was to establish WIN agencies in each political subdivision containing a large number of AFDC recipients. WIN aimed high. A WIN placement meant real work—a job in private industry or the government—not "made work." Those unprepared for real work were to receive needed training. Recognizing that the pay offered for many jobs would be less than the AFDC grant, a working mother would be allowed to keep $30.00 plus one-third of her earnings before her welfare check could be cut. Refusal to work or train without "good cause," however, could result in termination of assistance.[4] In order to make sure everyone knew he meant business, Mills announced a "freeze" on AFDC. States were to control AFDC recipient growth and costs or the federal government would not match the expenditure.[5]

Just about the time the Mills reforms went to the floor of the House, on August 15, 1967, Secretary Gardner announced a major reorganization and change in the leadership of welfare programs. The new agency merged the Welfare Administration with the Vocational Rehabilitation Administration to form the Social and Rehabilitation Service (SRS). Mary E. Switzer, then head of Vocational Rehabilitation, was named administrator.

A native of Boston and a Democrat, Switzer had been actively involved in Social Security programs since the days of the Federal Security Agency. In 1923, two years after graduation from Radcliffe College, Switzer received a civil service appointment to the Treasury Department. At Treasury she worked in the Office of the Secretary, clipping newspapers and articles as background information for reports on speeches and gradually assuming responsibility for drafting much of the correspondence. When she transferred to FSA in 1939, it was as an expert on the Public Health Service.

At the FSA Switzer became one of two assistants to Administrator McNutt and, when the other employee's health failed, she became the de facto assistant. It will be recalled that these were hard days for Altmeyer. His administrative power was diminished as he reported through McNutt's successor, Oscar Ewing, to President Truman. Altmeyer's control over the unity of Social Security programs was further eroded after the board was eliminated and funds for the administrator's central office were drastically cut.

Although Switzer could not be blamed for Truman's methods of operation, she had a great deal to do with allocating money to the detriment of Altmeyer's central office. The Public Health Service and the Social Security Administration had been forced to work together in drafting legislation for national health insurance. After its disastrous defeat in 1947–1948, the two agencies were at each other's throats. Through thick and thin, Switzer stuck with her old friends in Public Health.

In 1950 Ewing, who was greatly impressed with Switzer's ability, secured her a presidential appointment to head the Vocational Rehabilitation Administration. She proceeded to take this agency from a little-known, indifferently funded, poorly staffed program into one that was professionally staffed and well supported, with an exceptionally good press and an excellent reputation on the Hill. Vocational Rehabilitation was not a large program, and its funding, unlike welfare, was by closed-end appropriation. Its critics faulted it for "creaming," that is, for selecting cases most likely to succeed; its supporters pointed to its consistent high-quality results.

As a Democrat, Switzer could hope to ride the success of her leadership in vocational rehabilitation to a program of greater scope. In the early days of the Kennedy administration she made it known that she would like a big job in the pending welfare reorganization. She sought appointment as commissioner of rehabilitation and welfare, merging the functions of the VRA with those of the Children's Bureau and the Bureau of Family Services. Cohen dutifully passed this wish on to the White House, but without recommendation. Although Cohen thought Switzer a competent person who could attract support on the Hill, he was wary of her tendency to lay down "myriads of conditions" rather than allow a serious hearing for the ideas of others. Cohen doubtless also had unhappy memories of the days at the FSA.

With Winston's resignation as commissioner of welfare and the social work approach discredited, Switzer again let it be known that she was in the running for a job as commissioner of rehabilitation and welfare. This time she had the added advantage of standing at the centerpiece of the new thinking that saw work as the key welfare reform. Work, after all, was what vocational rehabilitation was all about. Switzer had long sold its program on the idea of restoring dependent disabled persons to independent status as taxpayers. Her appointment was just about irresistible. Everyone was for it—Secretary Gardner, important congressmen and senators, and after a final push or so, now Undersecretary Wilbur Cohen.[6]

Everyone, that is, except the social workers in the BFS, who knew immediately that their dominance in public welfare would be greatly curtailed if not ended. Switzer brought her VRA staff with her to the new Social and Rehabilitation Service (SRS). Divisions, branches, and sections and the persons in charge stayed much as they had been. Where functions overlapped, as in financial management or research, Vocational Rehabilitation officials were placed in the higher positions within merged offices. Gone were the separate enclaves for personnel. Where the Welfare Administration had allowed units in the BFS and the Children's Bureau, SRS soon had but one Division of Personnel. Although the Children's Bureau transferred to SRS intact, within two years its child health functions went to the National Institutes of Health and its research functions to a new Office of Child Development located in the Secretary's Office. It would not be incorrect to say that the SRS reorganization completed much of the unfinished business expected from, but not accomplished by, the Welfare Administration.

The BFS was decimated sooner rather than later, in spirit and in letter. The entire rationale for social services under the 1962 amendments had centered on counseling by the family caseworker. The SRS leadership killed this concept promptly and mercilessly by separating eligibility determination from all other social services. To be sure, Switzer and her advisors in the Secretary's Office were responding to criticism that counseling, sometimes leading the recipient toward drastic changes in lifestyle, amounted to bargaining for the money payment and therefore constituted a violation of the recipient's rights.[7]

Early in 1970, and again the following year, some 2,425 AFDC mothers living in ten cities were interviewed by National Analysts, under contract to SRS. Matching closely the characteristic pattern of AFDC, about one-third of the families were small, having one or two children; another third were medium-sized with three or four children. The rest were large families, with five or more children. Most significantly, but also typically, almost 60 percent of the women interviewed had very young children—no matter what the total family size.

At the time of both interviews, work experience was reported as about the same, even though WIN had been operative for about eighteen months when the second interview occurred. In early 1970 and in early 1971, 25 percent of recipients were working either full or part time and another 20 percent were looking for employment. The picture was a little better when work activity was considered over the period as a whole. During the past eighteen months, 35 percent had earned something—15 percent in full-time and 20 percent in part-time work.

With few exceptions, though, the work performed was unskilled. Almost 60 percent had held service jobs, with 16 percent of these in household service. Clerical jobs or light factory work accounted for the other employment. Thus the quality no more than the quantity of jobs held showed little or no improvement under WIN. Most of those who were working had not left the welfare rolls. Eighty-five percent of those working full time and 88 percent of those working part time were still dependent, although some only partially so.

Two-thirds of those interviewed reported illness, surgery, accident, or physical disability as the reason for not working. These women sounded like the elderly instead of persons in prime working years. They had heart disease, arthritis, tuberculosis, female disorders, hypertension, varicose veins. Many were overweight to the point of obesity. Ills such as these were directly attributable to a life of poverty. Though nearly all could be treated, such illnesses were not conducive to achievement in the typical service jobs that required standing upright for long periods and rather heavy physical exertion.[8]

Half of those who declared themselves unable to work said they were needed at home to care for their children. Day care for children had not been guaranteed by WIN. The situation was conditional—no mother of young children would be referred for work unless day care were available. Although an AFDC mother who was anxious to work was free to choose informal care with relatives or friends, formal care offered by the welfare worker must meet the high standards of a licensed facility—located in a safe, clean building, staffed with specialized personnel. In 1967 there were 10,400 licensed day care centers, the vast majority under private auspices. Altogether they had a capacity for 393,300 children. Expansion was clearly called for, with federal aid to states just as clearly indicated. But day care was not forthcoming in anything like the quantity or quality desired. Day care had also been an important component of the 1962 services amendments—a three-year authorization for $25 million had been approved. But appropriations were less than half that amount, just $8.8 million over the period. No wonder expansion was not rapid. By 1969 day care centers numbered 13,600; capacity, 518,000. Family day care homes added another 120,000 child spaces, for a total capacity of 638,000. The discrepancy between day care spaces and numbers of AFDC children made realistic planning for WIN laughable. At that time there were 1.5 million children under six on the AFDC rolls. Another 2 million were ages six to twelve, in school but apt to need some afternoon supervision.[9]

For all these reasons the first phase of the WIN program (WIN I, running from July 1, 1969 to July 1, 1972), if not an outright failure in terms of the working-off-welfare objective, was close to it. In the eyes of Congress, which had put its faith in workfare when social services fell into disrepute, WIN was yet another disaster.

A total of 385,100 persons, only about 10 percent of the adult caseload, had been enrolled in WIN I. Men accounted for a much larger proportion of referees than their representation in the caseload. Still, only 3 percent of those enrolled had been placed in employment by July 1, 1972. Many women dropped out because of illness, pregnancy, or lack of day care for their children. Some were still in training. Jobs obtained by women continued to be in service occupations, with earnings usually too low to take them off welfare.

Tightening Work Requirements

Responding to bitter bipartisan attacks on HEW and Labor Department administrators, Congress acted to tighten up work requirements in the WIN program to ensure that it more nearly satisfied congressional intent, that is, to get significant numbers of AFDC mothers and fathers working and off the welfare rolls. The new program—WIN II—became effective July 1, 1972. Under WIN II, welfare agencies were all but stripped of their discretionary power. Hitherto, the caseworker could decide whether referral of a given mother was "appropriate." The result was a low referral rate and, of course, a less than evenhanded performance. References to "appropriate" were deleted in the new law. Instead, as a condition of eligibility, all applicants for and recipients of AFDC were, with certain specified exemptions, required to register for WIN II.

Four exemptions specified in WIN I remained in force under WIN II:

1. Children under age sixteen or any child attending school.
2. Persons with illness, incapacity, or advanced age.
3. Persons living at great distance from a work or training project.
4. Persons whose continuous presence in the home was needed because of the illness or incapacity of another member of the household.

These exemptions would seldom prove applicable to AFDC mothers. Rather, they were included to protect children and elderly recipients of welfare from exploitation. However, WIN II specifically exempted women caretakers of children under age six, although these women could volunteer for WIN if they wished. WIN II also exempted women caretakers if the father was in the home and eligible for participation. Under penalty of possible loss of funds, states were required to refer at least 15 percent of recipients to the Department of Labor's manpower agency.

The law also stipulated the order in which persons were to be served. Highest priority was to be given to unemployed fathers; then to volunteer mothers; third, other mothers and pregnant teenagers (under age nineteen); and fourth, nonexempt dependent children and relatives.

Emphasis was on immediate referral to existing jobs in industry or public service. Formal institutional training, which had been stressed even to include the offer of college under some projects in WIN I, was discouraged under the new rules. Not less than one-third of WIN II funds had to be spent for on-the-job training and public service employment. Employers were allowed tax credits for hiring WIN participants and were reimbursed for on-the-job training.

So far as participants and job placements were concerned, WIN II showed immediate impressive results. During its first full year of operation—July 1, 1973, to July 1,1974—WIN enrolled 354,000 persons—almost as many as had been enrolled in the preceding three-and-a-half years. Placements in unsubsidized employment totaled 137,000, again more than had been so placed during the entire course of WIN I. Institutional training was greatly reduced, while on-the-job training, confined largely to men because of employer insistence, increased.

Yet WIN II failed to score significantly in relation to the program's main goal—to substitute workfare for welfare, to cut the AFDC rolls. Although participation was higher, the number of persons represented only 12 percent of the adult caseload. Of these only 4 percent were placed in jobs. More than one-third of the participants dropped out and returned to the welfare rolls because of a change in their situation that made them exempt from participation. Almost half of the participants left both WIN and welfare on their own, for reasons unrelated to WIN.

Of the 65,235 men and women who were placed in a job and held it for ninety days, 52 percent earned enough to get off welfare. But the women, who continued to be placed in service jobs, clerical and sales work, or textile factories, were not nearly as successful as the men. With a participation rate of 70 percent women, only 14,502 (41 percent) of those with a job became independent of welfare. The number of men going off welfare was 20,221 (59 percent). Part of the male "success" was undoubtedly a factor of WIN regulations themselves. Unlike women, men became ineligible for further welfare payments when they worked more than 100 hours a month, a regulation that recognized the usual male-female wage differential. Conversely, the earnings disregard regulations as applied to women tended to reduce the numbers terminated from AFDC because of employment. In states with relatively high assistance payments, the family income of a working mother could go quite high before reaching the break-off point. In Michigan, for example, with a basic grant of $316 for a family of four, gross earnings could reach $663 monthly, whereas previously the break-off point would have been $395. Since the earnings of AFDC women in the WIN I program averaged $353, many remained on the rolls, though with reduced welfare grants.

One of the seldom-mentioned barriers to AFDC mothers' working their way off welfare was their sex itself. Low-paying service jobs were the lot of hundreds of thousands of women who had never cashed a welfare check. But these women, often with children, had working husbands living at home. The wives were secondary wage earners, helping their husbands support their families. These families were part of a large group referred to as the working poor. Often it was the wife's earnings that kept the family off welfare.

Granted that the low educational attainment of AFDC mothers was a major reason for consigning them to low-paying jobs, men were able to earn considerably more, even though they had little schooling. Heavy manufacturing and construction jobs were usually reserved for men because a good deal of physical strength and endurance was required. Such jobs paid more because of the skill requirements and because of a high degree of unionization.

As the 1970s advanced, WIN II agencies became ever more interested in concentrating on job-ready participants and referring them directly to known openings. WIN II more nearly resembled a placement service than an agency created for the special purpose of fitting low-skilled, socially inadequate welfare mothers into decent jobs. The rehabilitation ideal, to prepare or restore the handicapped to job readiness, was sharply curtailed. The creaming notable in Switzer's VRA never approached the lengths resorted to by managers of WIN II. Screened out were all the hard-core recipients—those with less than an eighth grade education, those with large families, those who had been on welfare for a long time, those "too old," as well as the obese, the disfigured, and those who had difficulty expressing themselves.[10]

The huge gap between the number of registrants and the number of participants continued as an outstanding characteristic of WIN II. During fiscal year 1973, 1.2 million persons registered, 510,000 were appraised, 353,000 participated, and 136,800 were placed in jobs. Only 34,300 (0.9 percent) left welfare. Registrations were down in 1974 and 1975 to somewhat over 800,000, with participation around 500,000. Possibly because of more intensive creaming, the numbers who left welfare increased to about 52,000, or 10 percent of those participating. The shift away from even a pretense of employment training is clear from the numbers placed directly in jobs—over 70 percent in 1974 and 1975. What training there was consisted of that given on the job and, for reasons already mentioned, was doubtless mostly for men.

Sometimes it was claimed that WIN served a strong deterrent role. The increasing practice of converting welfare applicants into WIN participants before they ever got on welfare certainly skewed the data toward a possible undercount of those going off welfare. It is just as true, however, that these job-ready persons would likely have found something on their own initiative.

Pacific Consultants, after analyzing the impact of WIN II in light of the expectations of the program, concluded:

WIN is not economically cost effective in serving those who are likeliest to succeed on their own (i.e., those with recent employment experience), but attains reasonably high levels of cost effectiveness when it serves less experienced welfare recipients. . . . While this attainment benefits society as a whole, taxpayers as a class often assume a narrower perspective, weighing public expenditures against public receipts. From this perspective the WIN program is not cost effective and indeed could not be in view of the work incentive provisions built into the AFDC system [the $30 + ⅓ disregard].[11]

Exemptions written into the law itself account for a very large segment of recipient mothers not touched by WIN. With 2.7 million adult caretakers in the AFDC program, the blanket exemption of mothers with children under age six constituted a major gap in WIN coverage. Children under six made up 59.2 percent of AFDC children. Because some AFDC mothers had more than one child under six, those exempted on this ground did not make up quite one-third of the total. But the number exempted for this reason was high, accounting for 73.8 percent of total exemptions. Illness or incapacity made up 14.0 percent among women, while for men this reason was a not-unexpected 66.1 percent.

In 1973, when the National Center for Social Statistics reported its biennial study of AFDC, 16.1 percent of mothers were working—9.8 percent full and 6.3 percent part time. Twelve years earlier, when a similar biennial characteristics study was reported, 14 percent were working—5 percent full and 9 percent part time. Thus a small gain had been made over the decade, particularly among those women holding full-time jobs. Probably the WIN program had something to do with this change in work patterns. But it was not a large change and certainly was not large enough to suggest a trend. Research had shown that it would be extremely difficult to make a significant impact upon AFDC dependency. It might well be done, provided the government was prepared to make a long-term and costly investment. As it turned out, the government wasn't even willing to underwrite sufficient day care. In sum, the WIN program, introduced with such fanfare in 1969, did little to advance what Switzer had announced as the "top priority" for SRS—a reduction in the number of AFDC recipients.[12]

By the end of 1970, the year of Switzer's retirement, AFDC families numbered 2.5 million for a total of 9.6 million recipients. The growth in number of recipients had been more than 6 million in a decade. Expenditures in 1970 for AFDC payments to families reached $4.9 billion for a 10-year increase of more than $3 billion. The cost of fringe benefits could be added: public housing, food stamps, and Medicaid, for example.[13]

A Cap on Social Services

Unexpectedly and "uncontrollably," to use Martha Derthick's descriptive term, expenditures for social services grants exploded too, but not as a direct result of the exploding caseload. Although the counseling relationship typified by the BFS social workers' interpretation of the 1962 amendments was all but ignored by the new leadership in the SRS, the 75 percent matching rate for services continued to exist, its presence beckoning like an open drawer in an unguarded cash register.

The practice, begun under Hoey, of relying on State Letters to convey federal policy was immediately formalized under Switzer. Gone were separate sections in State Letters stating mandatory actions and the follow-up of suggested strategies and justifying philosophy that supposedly pulled states along in a liberal direction. Henceforth states would receive guidance through federal regulation. The change brought welfare into the same book—the *Code of Federal Regulations*—as other federal grant-dispensing programs. The system was more democratic than the clubby approach of State Letters. Preliminary "Regs" were announced as ready for comment and, after hearings, were published in final form in the *Federal Register*.

New regulations on services, issued in 1969, focused on new needs— day care, work training, treatment for alcohol and drug abuse. Since counseling by social workers had come to be regarded as one of the failed "old ways," requirements for advanced training, even for college graduates to staff intake and to follow up recipient families, were eliminated. The standard of sixty families per worker, intended to guarantee the counseling function, also went by the wayside.

As was usual for a Republican administration, President Nixon announced his interest in getting as much government as possible out of Washington and into the hands of state and local administration—the New Federalism. The Intergovernmental Cooperation Act of 1968 encouraged access to federal funds by authorizing waivers of the requirement that a single state agency administer a federal grant. In this spirit, the 1969 SRS regulations strongly encouraged the purchase of services, no matter whether from public or private sources. No specific barriers were raised to prevent purchase of services heretofore assumed by the states themselves. Gone and forgotten were the cautions earlier voiced by the BFS, where staff with long experience watched for manifestations of state greed.

Purchase of services received strong support from Switzer and staff of the Vocational Rehabilitation Administration. They had operated this way for years, albeit with a closed-end appropriation. When John D. Twiname, a public-spirited, affable businessman new to government, succeeded Switzer on her retirement in March 1970, it is probable he had given no thought to the dangers of the open-end appropriation when combined with uncontrolled purchase.

Agencies on the level of SRS are often saved from themselves by superiors at a higher level in the Secretary's Office. But in the matter at hand, that is, purchase of services in the years 1969–1972, the Secretary's Office contained key persons who were ready and willing, even anxious, to use open-end purchase for all it was worth. Nixon's first HEW secretary was Robert Finch of California, who brought with him John Veneman as undersecretary. Veneman stayed through the tenure of Finch's successor, Elliot Richardson, that is, about four years. Though a Republican himself, Veneman in turn recruited Thomas C. W. Joe, a Democrat who had worked for the California legislature, to assist in the administration of welfare programs, particularly social services. Under a grant from the APWA, Joe had written a paper, "Finding Welfare Dollars," in which he argued for maximum use of federal-state welfare programs to help the poor. Joe's door at HEW was open to state and local officials who were faced with high costs and reluctant taxpayers. Joe called his visitors' attention to open-end services grants as a probable solution to their difficulties.[14]

Federal grants to the states for social services were quite modest during the first few years of the allowable 75 percent match and purchase. In fiscal year 1967 (when social services grants were first separated from administration and training) expenditures came to $2.9 million. For the next two years, expenditures rose according to normal expectations. By 1970, however, social services grants reached over $500 million. By 1972, when Congress called a halt, expenditures had risen to $1.6 billion.

California pioneered in "finding welfare dollars" by imaginative use of the high open-end services matching rate. Long before Nixon was elected, California had arranged for attendants in day care centers for children and the elderly to be drawn from the recipient population so they could be supported at the 75 percent instead of the 50 percent rate. As early as 1967, California was receiving a 25 percent share of total services grants. In 1968, the state received a 30 percent share, the following year, 36 percent, then dropped back somewhat to 28 percent in 1971.

Once the states caught on to the immense possibilities inherent in the loosely worded 1962 services amendment, they were quick to forward proposals to a receptive HEW staff. During the early years, most of the grants funded the much-needed day care associated with WIN and other jobs programs. Then Illinois and New York began to follow California's lead. Illinois, with a liberal Republican governor, expected a large deficit, but wanted nevertheless to avoid welfare cuts or a tax rise. After discovering the services grants loophole, the state sought about $75 million, proposing to purchase services from ongoing programs in drug abuse, alcoholism, mental illness, mental retardation, and juvenile and adult corrections. Waivers of the single-state-agency rule were granted by Secretary Richardson. After much wrangling, including the intervention of the White House and Congress, Illinois did better than expected, receiving $102 million in services grants. New York's request for services grants in 1972 entailed large purchases from state offices outside the welfare agency, including health, mental hygiene, education, corrections, narcotics addiction, youth, and aging.

A contractor called in by the SRS to evaluate the explosion in expenditures for social services grants concluded that monies were being spent for activities that states had previously funded without this federal contribution. The services paid for in this way were neither new nor more plentiful.

When it became clear that state fiscal relief rather than more and improved social services for the poor was the center of this very costly enterprise, officials in HEW's Comptroller's Office, in OMB, and in Congress began to pay attention. Initial attempts to seize control by putting a cap on the appropriation were uncoordinated and unsuccessful. But in the summer of 1972, the media caught on. State estimates of $4.7 billion for fiscal 1973, up from $1.7 billion the previous year, engendered plenty of publicity.

Congress took advantage of the administration's revenue-sharing bill to cap the runaway costs of services grants. There was no good reason why the states should have both, the argument ran. In October 1972, in the State and Local Fiscal Assistance Act, services grants were capped at $2.5 billion annually, limiting a state's share to its percentage of the national population.[15]

Despite protests from state governments, including several lawsuits, as well as pressure from Community Chest agencies, the situation rocked along without new regulations for more than two years. By this time there was yet another team in charge at HEW and SRS. Casper W. Weinberger, known at OMB as "Cap the Knife," replaced Elliot Richardson as secretary. As SRS administrator, Weinberger selected James S. Dwight, Jr., an accountant and management expert. Dwight's deputy was John A. Svahn. All three came from Governor Ronald Reagan's administration in California, where welfare had become the centerpiece of partisan politics. It was Svahn who worked with Ways and Means to devise an acceptable change in the services grants legislation.

Title XX, enacted in December 1974, marked a drastic departure from all previous welfare titles of the Social Security Act. Federal matching was completely eliminated. Under a cap of $2.5 billion, states would receive block grants based on population. Specified services fell clearly within traditional social work or closely allied practices, such as protective services for children and adults, day care, and services related to management and maintenance of the home. Particular emphasis on workfare was spelled out in listing training and employment services. Family planning was also listed, as were services directed toward the physically and mentally handicapped, alcoholics, and drug addicts.[16]

The tenor of the 1960s and 1970s, with blacks, women, and youth demanding their rights, be they for political representation, for jobs, for life in the counterculture, or for welfare, had had both positive and negative fallout. The Johnson administration stretched a long way in civil rights legislation and its war on poverty to correct some of the evils of race and gender discrimination. This much being done, and having offered the elderly and the poor generous medical care, the executive branch was not inclined to buck Congressman Mills and Senator Long in their drive to put AFDC mothers to work. Although the WIN program fell far short of making a dent in welfare rolls, the strong pro-work statement included in the Social Security Act would lend itself to modification—not repeal—as time went on.

Beyond workfare was the social workers' fall from favor. Hard services replaced counseling, and after the states attempted a raid for fiscal relief, the 75 percent match was replaced by block grants under an overall cap.

11

Welfare Reform

THE ELECTION OF 1968 had been a cliff-hanger—Richard M. Nixon, the moderate Republican, against Hubert H. Humphrey, the liberal Democrat, with a third party contender, the conservative George C. Wallace. Fortified with standard Republican principles—a shift of power from Washington to the states, law and order in the cities, workfare for welfare, and vague hints about peace in Vietnam, Nixon won, but without a clear mandate. The Democrats continued to control Congress: in the House, 243–192; in the Senate, 58–42.[1]

The Family Assistance Plan

Even as the Republicans assumed control of the executive branch, the poverty issue emerged anew, this time as a "hunger" issue. The prevalence of hunger was never estimated with any exactitude, but unquestionably, in poor areas of the country and in rich areas with poor people in them, hunger and malnutrition existed. Robert Kennedy invoked this issue during his tragically aborted run for the Democratic nomination in 1968, various television specials supplied drama, and Senator George McGovern of South Dakota (to be the Democratic nominee for President in 1972) kept the matter alive during Nixon's first term.[2]

Nixon was inclined to attack hunger and, to the greatest extent feasible, even poverty, with food stamps and surplus commodities—relief in kind à la Newburgh. The budgeted authorization for food stamps in fiscal year 1969, the first year of his administration, was about double that for the last Johnson year. Then for 1971 Nixon budgeted $1.25 billion; and for 1972, $2.5 billion. The Department of Agriculture, which administers food stamps and commodities programs, has registered far more enthusiasm about them than welfare administrators at HEW and in the states, however. The subsidy to farmers aside, food stamps have had a low participation rate. Welfare recipients, required to buy stamps on a monthly basis in order to realize the savings, usually receive such low monthly payments that they cannot afford this lump sum expenditure. The welfare monthly payment is eaten up by rent, clothing, and other necessities.[3]

Revenue sharing, a major Nixon effort to transfer federal money to the states with no strings attached, offered the possibility of something for the needy. Moreover, OEO was still in business, although the last Johnson budget contained a cutback in deference to mounting costs in Vietnam. More cuts impended. With some exceptions—Head Start, legal aid, welfare reform experiments—the war on poverty was judged by Republicans and conservative Democrats to have been an extravagant failure to be phased out as soon as possible.

In sum, neither food stamps nor revenue sharing nor fragments of the war on poverty signified welfare reform in the sense of specific action to lower the scope and cost of categorical assistance programs, particularly AFDC. Instead, reformers sought something more direct, something with a distinctly Republican label, something the Democrats would have a hard time turning down. That something turned out to be the Family Assistance Plan (FAP), a proposal to supplement incomes of the working poor, to ensure equity in welfare payments, and to further encourage workfare.

One road leading to FAP began when Kennedy's Council of Economic Advisors, in January 1964, adopted the Orshansky poverty index ($3,000 for a family of four) as the standard floor of economic distress. The idea of subsidizing the working poor—the centerpiece of FAP—had begun twenty years before. In 1943, while doing a stint at the Treasury Department, the economist Milton Friedman noted income tax inequities and work disincentives faced by low-income persons. He proposed that the working poor be allowed to claim, on tax form 1040, a refund equal to the amount the family income fell below a specified floor. When a family had a good year, the taxpayer paid; when it had a bad one, he or she got a refund. Friedman's "negative income tax" (NIT) was known to fellow economists, but the idea was not introduced to a wider audience until the publication of his influential book, *Capitalism and Freedom*, in 1962. By

1968 Friedman was a tenured professor at the University of Chicago. A conservative Republican, he had been an advisor to Barry Goldwater in his futile campaign against Lyndon Johnson.[4]

A NIT or some form of guaranteed income appealed to those reformers who rejected the services approach characterized by the 1962 amendments and the war on poverty. Led by five social scientists, some 1,200 academics endorsed a "national system of income guarantees and supplements" as the preferred way to welfare reform. This endorsement, which was addressed to Congress well before the 1968 election, did not specify a NIT. An "income guarantee" left any future plan open to other strategies, such as the well-tried European system of children's allowances.[5]

Additional support for an income guarantee came from government analysts at HEW and OEO. In an effort to control the planning and policymaking hitherto widely scattered among HEW's constituent agencies, Secretary Gardner created a Planning and Evaluation unit in the Office of the Secretary. Its staff members were social scientists rather than practitioners. Those assigned to study social insurance and welfare were asked to measure their efficiency and effectiveness in relation to their impact on poverty. In a report completed in 1966 the analysts concluded that at least 60 percent of the needy received no benefits at all from OASDI, OAA, or AFDC. This despite the fact that average incomes of the aged poor fell 10 percent below the poverty line, and family incomes of poor children were deficient by 44 percent. The working poor constituted a large segment of those needy, particularly families with children.

When Undersecretary Cohen reviewed this damning report, he saw thirty years of conscientious, often bold, effort poured down the drain. He refused to sign off on the document and, according to those in his office, threw it in the waste can. Fresh from his triumph in Medicare-Medicaid legislation, which certainly should have been counted as immeasurably helpful to the aged and to children, Cohen was also privy to ongoing research for generating higher OASDI benefits.[6]

Goals for increased benefits were announced by Social Security Commissioner Robert Ball in the spring of 1966. Ball was not obliged to consider the poverty of welfare recipients or, indeed, the poverty of the working poor. If these needy could be assured a minimum income through improvements in welfare payment standards or a guaranteed income, well and good. But surely, Ball argued, Social Security could do better than that for its present and future beneficiaries. Ball sought Congressional action to (1) increase benefits and (2) to increase the amount of the wage base on which benefits were calculated. He argued further that replacement rates should be sufficiently high at all income levels to obviate recourse to private insurance. Put simply, Social Security, given a few increases in benefit levels, in the wage base, and in financing (perhaps with general revenues), could become the nation's unchallenged system for retirement income, no longer a mere "floor of protection."

With Ball's policy planning in mind, Cohen recommended a 10 percent increase in benefits to the President. Johnson, always receptive to raising income for the elderly, upped the increase to 15 percent. The Congress cut it back to 13 percent, but assisted future beneficiaries by increasing the wage base from $4,800 to $7,800.

This 1967 increase, which covered 81.7 percent of earnings in covered employment, was just a beginning. During the Nixon presidency Congress consistently topped the administration's modest requests: in 1969 granting a 15 percent increase; in 1971, 10 percent; and, in 1972, a whopping 20 percent. Along with the 20 percent windfall came indexing. Henceforth benefits would rise with prices and the wage base with earnings. By 1975 the replacement rate for married men with average wages was 67 percent, and for a married man earning the federal minimum wage it was 92 percent, up from 50 percent and 67 percent just prior to the expansion. So much for Social Security. The program so long supplemented by OAA to bring benefits to subsistence levels had now been set on a course to take most of the elderly out of poverty in a dozen or so years.[7]

Indifferent to the lack of encouragement from Cohen, social scientists at OEO and HEW continued to analyze and to devise welfare reform packages against the day when a guaranteed annual income would be welcomed. Sargent Shriver, director of OEO, encouraged such activities as wholly compatible with the agency's mission to develop new tactics and strategies to wage the war on poverty. In the spring of 1967, Shriver persuaded President Johnson to approve funding for a three-year guaranteed income experiment covering about one thousand poor families in New Jersey. Families in the study group, most of whom were working, were guaranteed a minimum cash income regardless of a change in circumstances. Control families received food stamps as token payment for reporting. The main object of the New Jersey experiment was to find out what subsidized families did with their extra money.[8]

By the time Nixon assumed office in January 1968 the guaranteed income concept had moved into the foreground, if only because more conceptual and experimental work had been produced as compared, say, with children's allowances. The latter, however, was still a viable antipoverty concept. In addition to France and other European countries, nearby Canada had a successful children's allowance system. The United States's progressive income tax already allowed children's deductions to those sufficiently well off to pay taxes. Why not allow those too poor to pay taxes to claim a children's allowance on the 1040?

About the same time that Friedman first developed his NIT, a group of academics began to push for children's allowances. In the 1960s, this group resurfaced, adding several intellectuals from government, including Lisle Carter, an assistant secretary at HEW; Mitchell Ginsberg, head of New York City's welfare agency; Alvin Schorr, then working with Carter at HEW; Mollie Orshansky, Social Security Administration; and Daniel P. Moynihan, then director of the Harvard University–Massachusetts Institute of Technology Joint Center for Urban Studies.[9]

Arguing the case for "a new and imaginative distributive strategy," the Yale economist James Tobin, formerly on Kennedy's Council of Economic Advisors, objected to children's allowances because most families did not need them. Tobin favored a guaranteed income, spelling out a suggested system (including abolition of welfare) in the fall 1966 issue of the neoconservative journal, *The Public Interest*. Replying by invitation in the winter issue, Schorr showed that a host of poor persons would be excluded entirely or would get a little something but still remain in poverty under Tobin's scheme. Schorr thought it impossible to abolish the welfare system so long as his analysis held. He favored improvements in Social Security programs and universal children's allowances.

Tobin took the lead in playing down these differences. All were agreed on three elements of reform, he argued: increasing coverage of the needy, increasing program uniformity nationwide, and enhancing work incentives. He emphasized the importance of goals as against "the details of different schemes." He hoped "no one will think there are deep conflicts among 'income guarantees,' 'negative income taxes,' and 'family allowances.' " Nor among their proponents. It was merely "an intramural debate," insisted one attendant at a Brookings Institution conference convened in October 1968. "If they say we have got to get together on one horse . . . we will get together." Subsequently, when the Nixon administration chose an income guarantee as its way to welfare reform, the children's allowance advocates were told to quash their preference, to get on track.[10]

By this time Moynihan, a Democrat, had gone to work at the Republican White House. He was brought in by President Nixon in December 1968 as an assistant for urban affairs. Shortly after the inauguration, he was appointed executive secretary of the newly formed Urban Affairs

Council, which was to develop a national policy to deal with crime, unemployment, and other social deviance characteristic of an inner-city underclass. To this end, welfare was deemed a central factor.

Moynihan was young at the time of his appointment—just forty-one years old. He was well educated, having a B.A. and a Ph.D. from Tufts University. Although his Ph.D. was in the international field, he early gravitated to American politics, working in the Albany office of Governor Averell Harriman in the late 1950s. Moynihan came to Washington with the coterie of intellectuals who joined the Kennedy administration, heading the Department of Labor's policy planning staff through the Johnson years. Doubtless he had joined a Republican White House with a recommendation from Governor Nelson Rockefeller of New York. In March 1967 Rockefeller had convened a conference of businessmen and scholars to examine new ways to deal with public welfare. At that conference, Moynihan had presented the argument for children's allowances; Milton Friedman, for a NIT.[11]

During his years at Labor, Moynihan became a well-known figure, in some ways a controversial one. In addition to his intellectual abilities, he was a prolific writer, publishing the results of his research, his observations, and his experiences in books, articles, and speeches. He didn't always make friends. Along the way he managed to alienate the professional social workers, the black middle class, and the extreme liberal wing of the Democratic party. The support of each of these groups was important, though not necessarily indispensable, to the success of any welfare reform initiative.

Professional social workers were put off by Moynihan's lack of enthusiasm for casework. He seemed deficient in the very faith so valued by social workers—faith in individual rejuvenation through patient one-to-one counseling. Like Wilbur Cohen, Moynihan had been critical of much of the war on poverty, labeling as fanciful the belief that the poor could organize and manage local programs as anticipated by the "maximum feasible participation" clause of the law. Instead of a multiplicity of programs within programs, Moynihan—partly because of his position at Labor— had argued for a large jobs program. Once the decision was made for multiplicity, however, he had chipped in and done his best to help draft the war on poverty legislation.[12]

The black middle class, as represented by such moderate civil rights organizations as the Urban League and the NAACP, joined with the more radical CORE to denounce a Moynihan report on the black family. In the winter of 1964–65, Moynihan, preparing a forecast of growth patterns in

AFDC, noted with alarm the high rates of family breakup and illegitimacy among blacks. He also noted the strong expected correlation with increases between black male unemployment and growth in AFDC during the late 1940s through 1950s. Then he was stopped short by an unexpected reverse pattern. In the early 1960s, black male unemployment was decreasing (though still comparatively high) from 12.5 percent in 1962 to 8 percent in 1965. But despite this favorable trend, AFDC rolls were rising.

The Moynihan report, *The Negro Family: The Case for National Action*, had been prepared for inner consumption at the Johnson White House. Its blunt opening sentence—"The United States is approaching a new crisis in race relations"—was arresting and ominous. Were the trends not reversed, Moynihan warned, a black underclass would dominate the inner cities where welfare would become a way of life. Moynihan pounded away at the importance of the family: "The role of the family in shaping character and ability is so pervasive as to be easily overlooked. The family is the basic social unit of American life; it is the basic socializing unit. By and large, adult conduct in life is learned as a child."

He quoted alarming social statistics: almost 25 percent of black women living in cities who had been married were divorced, separated, or living apart from their husbands. The comparable number for white women was 7.9 percent. The impact on welfare was apparent. In 1965, 14 percent of black children were on AFDC while only 2 percent of white children were. Over the long run, 56 percent of black children had received AFDC at some time, as against only 8 percent of white children. In the period 1940–1963, the number of illegitimate children per 1,000 live births increased by 11 among whites but by 68 among blacks. Sounding somewhat old-fashioned and a lot like the Catholic clergy who testified before Congress in 1949, Moynihan deplored the inability of black fathers to support their children and the resulting pressure on black mothers to go out to work. "This dependence on the mother's income undermines the position of the father and deprives the children of the kind of attention, particularly in school matters, which is now a standard feature of middle-class upbringing." Moynihan recommended (though he didn't say how) that a national effort be made to strengthen the black family to enable it to raise and support its members like their white counterparts. In a moving address at Howard University on June 4, 1965 (the "We Shall Overcome" speech), President Johnson drew on the Moynihan report for a brief discussion of the importance of black family stability.

Moynihan regarded his report as social science—facts, not emotions. He developed his theme from black roots in slavery and Reconstruction to the modern migration from farms to cities and the industrial wage system. He wanted to underscore the Labor Department's conviction that black male unemployment and underemployment was inordinately high and to lay the groundwork for some kind of income guarantee to underpin black family life. In the wake of the first black riot in the Watts district of Los Angeles (August 11–16, 1965), as if to say "I told you so," the Johnson White House released the Moynihan report. The result? A tremendous backlash. Black leaders—appalled at the violence in Watts—could not swallow what they perceived as an attack on their own parentage. However correct Moynihan's predictions about AFDC rolls and however benign his intentions regarding black male unemployment, all parties, including the White House, turned away from the Moynihan report and its implications.[13]

Dissatisfied with the services pattern of response to social problems, Moynihan aligned himself with a group of intellectuals who styled themselves "neoconservatives." The group was against big government, looked to families to teach children how to behave and take a responsible place in society, believed that parents should demand and receive a major role in decisions about public school curricula (no black English) and methods of instruction, and argued that the streets should be made safe from crime, period. The group's journal, *The Public Interest*, began publication in July 1965.[14]

In several background memos, including conclusions from his own report on the black family, Moynihan prepared President Nixon for consideration of major welfare reform. He pointed out, for example, that "the bulk of AFDC recipients are now made up of persons not associated with husbands or fathers with an attachment to the labor market. They are drawn from a population that is rapidly growing in size. As a result changes in the labor market no longer affect the number of AFDC recipients." He drew on studies by Perry Levinson, a sociologist, and Thomas S. Langner, a psychiatrist, which were published in the March–April 1969 issue of *Welfare in Review*. Levinson showed that children from AFDC families presented many more serious behavioral problems—dropping out of school, delinquency, premarital pregnancy—than non-AFDC families, however poor. Langner found similar comparative differences— in speech, sight, and hearing development—between welfare and non-welfare children. The psychiatrist also noted that welfare children "seem to have a higher incidence of serious disorders such as psychosis and appear to be more isolated, mistrustful, and anxious than the nonwelfare children." Genevieve Carter summed up the results: "Children in families receiving public assistance suffer from more social and emotional problems than children in families not receiving public assistance, however low their income."[15]

When the Urban Affairs Council's Committee on Welfare met at the White House on March 24, 1969, its chairman, Secretary of HEW Finch, submitted a guaranteed income proposal prepared by Worth Bateman, HEW deputy assistant secretary for program analysis (Income Maintenance and Social Services Programs), assisted by James Lyday of OEO and Greg Barlous of the Bureau of the Budget (BOB). Using the $3,000 poverty level as a cutoff for a family of four, families with earnings of $1,500 would qualify for cash benefits of $750 plus $325 worth of food stamps for a total income of $2,575.

Bateman and company, no less than Friedman, promoted a strictly limited income maintenance program, one that: "keeps those who can't work out of poverty . . . supplements the earnings of those who do work without destroying incentives . . . does not stigmatize persons receiving aid or meddle in their lives . . . strictly separates income assistance from the provision of social and rehabilitation services."

Where did this leave WIN or a similar work requirement? In general, FAP planners knew a work requirement was politically necessary but hoped to soften the sound of compulsion somewhat. After all, the centerpiece of FAP was an income supplement for persons already working. Secretary of Labor George Shultz, however, regarded FAP as an opportunity to beef up WIN and other manpower and training programs already in place in his department. When the work programs were added in, FAP shed the simplicity and low cost of Friedman's NIT and Bateman's guaranteed income plan.[16]

In this spirit President Nixon presented FAP in a television address to the nation on August 8, 1969. He attacked welfare as "a colossal failure" that stifled enterprise and prolonged dependency whose "mounting costs are bringing states and cities to the brink of disaster." Turning specifically to AFDC, he charged that the program "breaks up homes, often penalizes work, and robs recipients of dignity." Recipients suffered, too. Payment levels were grossly unequal, averaging around $263 monthly in the highest-paying state to $19 in the lowest. As a result, thousands of persons (many of whom were black) migrated to crowded inner cities, "as unprepared for city life as they are for city jobs."

Even as he assured welfare recipients that their payments would not be cut, the President assured taxpayers that the program called "Aid to Families with Dependent Children—the program we all normally think of

when we think of 'welfare'—would be done away with completely." As
to the immediate future, this statement was defensible only if one were to
argue that changing a name abolished a substance. As was his wont, the
President came on strong for work: "Any system which makes it more
profitable for a man not to work than to work, or which encourages a man
to desert his family rather than to stay with his family, is wrong and inde-
fensible." FAP would rest on three principles: equality of treatment, a
work requirement, and a work incentive. After spelling out the benefits
designed for those on welfare and the working poor, Nixon summed up:
1"In the final analysis, we cannot talk our way out of poverty; we cannot
legislate our way out of poverty; but this nation can work its way out of
poverty. What America needs now is not more welfare, but more 'workfare.' "[17]

First-year costs, including child care and job training, were now estimated at $4 billion, about twice as much as had been estimated before the
jobs-training segment was added by Shultz. Along the way, Shultz had
reached an estimate as high as $6.6 billion. But Nixon chose a lower BOB
figure of $4 billion in his appeal to the nation. The $4.0 billion figure cost
out as follows:

Benefits to families	$2.5 billion
Adult minimum standards	.4 billion
Training and day care	.6 billion
Other: administration, etc.	.5 billion
Total	$4.0 billion

This was new money. When old money, that is, projected expenditures for
ongoing categorical welfare programs was counted, an additional $4.20
billion brought the grand total to $8.20 billion. Benefits to families, based
on a family of four, were spelled out as in Table 11.1. Larger families
would receive larger benefits, up to $5,720 for a family of seven. A work-
related disregard of $60 a month was allowed.

Because AFDC payments were so low in sixteen to eighteen southern
and southwestern states, FAP would take over entirely in these areas.
While each state was required to spend at least 50 percent of what was
spent in the base year for AFDC and the adult categories, no state was
required to spend more than 90 percent of that amount, leaving a bonus of
at least 10 percent for high-paying states like New York.[18]

Immediately following the presidential address, Cohen appeared on
NBC to support FAP. He claimed, despite the shadow of Friedman but not

TABLE 11.1. Proposed Benefit Schedule (excluding state benefits)

Earned income	New benefit	Total income
$ 0	$1,600	$1,600
500	1,600	2,100
1,000	1,460	2,460
1,500	1,210	2,710
2,000	960	2,960
2,500	710	3,210
3,000	460	3,460
3,500	210	3,710
4,000	0	4,000

SOURCE: Social Security Administration, "Welfare Reform Fact Sheet, Background Material," Appendix to Chapter 2, Daniel Patrick Moynihan, *The Politics of a Guaranteed Income* (New York: Random House, 1973), 235.

entirely without justification, that "Nixon's good deed" was part of the Democratic agenda. Cohen was thereafter helpful in rounding up votes and lobbying for the legislation both in Congress proper and with interested individuals and groups.

Labor unions remained more or less neutral, probably perceiving that the group of casual workers whose wages would be supplemented posed no threat to its constituency. This was a time of white backlash. Among other signs of incipient racism was the emergence of "hard hats," the unionized construction workers who opposed admission of blacks to the skilled trades. No one said so out loud, but it might have been comforting to such white workers to imagine that blacks might be kept "in their place" and out of the competition if assured a supplement to low wages. Blacks also might find it advantageous to stay in the South instead of migrating north only to overload the welfare rolls.[19]

It was welfare mothers themselves who opposed FAP most vehemently. Many of these mothers—mostly black—had been organized by George Wiley into the National Welfare Rights Organization (NWRO). Wiley, a black and a professor of chemistry at Syracuse University, took up the welfare rights cause at the urging of Richard Cloward, the opportunity theorist, and Frances Fox Piven, his collaborator at the Columbia University School of Social Work. Piven and Cloward, frustrated by local political attacks on community action centers, had devised a strategy of counterattack that would utilize welfare recipients and would-be recipients to gain attention from the federal government. They hoped to create a crisis by so loading the welfare rolls as to make governors and mayors and other political leaders at the local level turn with increasing apprehension to Washington, demanding intervention and reform in the welfare system, possibly along the lines of a national minimum income. The May 2, 1966, issue of *The Nation* carried their platform. That same month Wiley drew a few local welfare mothers' organizations together and opened a Poverty Rights Action Center in Washington. In August 1967, a founding convention named itself the National Welfare Rights Organization.

NWRO membership was never large, only about 25,000–35,000 of a potential 1.3 million AFDC mothers. Nevertheless, NWRO was represented in thirty-five states and, most important, could count six hundred locals. It was the locals, particularly in the large cities, that gathered up many times their membership for a protest march or demonstration to counter, say, a cut in benefits.[20]

In pursuing these concrete objectives—for example, forcing the New York City welfare department to comply with its own regulations to grant clothing and furniture allowances—NWRO was not only successful but inspired a good deal of admiration, both inside and outside the department. Why shouldn't welfare mothers have charge accounts? After all, they had a steady income. A charge account would help them budget the little they had. Who could object to a peaceful march from Cleveland to Columbus, Ohio, to protest a cut in welfare payments? Or to the marching song:

> We feed our children bread and beans
> While rich folks ride in limousines.
> After all, we're human beings,
> Marching down Columbus Road.[21]

But Wiley soon shed his middle-class model, adopting the sixties' style of confrontation and disruption. It was NWRO that "occupied" Finch's office at HEW, Wiley in a dashiki and beat-up shoes, feet propped up on the secretary's desk. He and the welfare mothers were arrested at closing time. Immediately thereafter, nevertheless, Finch was brought down and a more thick-skinned Elliot Richardson was sent to replace him. A photo of Wiley at the HEW sit-in was reproduced nationwide. The "ladies," as they were referred to within NWRO, perhaps belied their title, even when testifying before Congress. To be sure, they came well-dressed, wearing hats, having skimped and saved in order to look good for their appearances in Congress. The middle-class blacks around NWRO thought they looked too good—not poor enough. But the ladies were loud and threatening, one of them announcing to Senator Long: "We are going to disrupt this Senate, this country, this capital, and everything that goes on."

But were all their respondents gentlemen? Long himself called them "brood mares," who had better be cleaning the streets of dead dogs and rats than testifying before his committee. Perhaps more telling, a number of black leaders were also unsympathetic, cautioning Wiley it was dumb to tangle with Long and unwise to make an issue of welfare.[22]

As soon as a guaranteed income left its theoretical base and became part of the FAP proposal, NWRO declared its base too low. Using the Bureau of Labor Statistics' lower-level budget, which was $5,915 for an urban family of four, NWRO held out for a minimum standard of $5,500. Wiley was quick to persuade attendants at the White House Conference on Hunger and Malnutrition, including its distinguished leader, Dr. Jean Maier, to endorse the $5,500 figure. NWRO found catchy slogans to shout and paint on signs: "ZAP FAP!" "$5,500 or FIGHT!" "Fight" was doubtless the most frequently used word in the NWRO vocabulary. *The Welfare Fighter* carried the news. The October 1971 issue featured a cartoon showing two charladies, one white, one black. The white asks the black: "What's that FAP mean?" The black answers: "Fuck America's Poor!"[23]

Moynihan has criticized Wiley for insisting on a $5,500 benefit level rather than accepting the given $2,400 as a beginning. Estimates from the Bureau of the Budget indicated a total eligibility of 150 million workers at the $5,500 level compared with only 13 million at the $2,400 FAP level. The cost would have jumped from the modest $4.0 billion to an enormous $71 billion. Conservatives were already warning about the dangers of a work disincentive inherent in a guaranteed income. It appeared certain that many moderates would join them if coverage were made applicable to thousands more families. Moderates as well as conservatives were also beginning to worry about costs. Was FAP just a beginning upon which to build, as Moynihan hoped, or was it a ceiling as the minimum wage had turned out to be?

It is true, nevertheless (as Moynihan also points out) that many, if not most, of Wiley's constituency were already receiving about $5,500 from AFDC in the high-paying states. States where payments averaged $3,000–$5,000 were to get fiscal relief, but were not required to pass on these savings to recipients. Only in the South would welfare recipients get more. It is hardly surprising that NWRO stood its ground.[24]

FAP did, however, receive a boost from social science. After some discussion with Moynihan, John O. Wilson, an economist then assistant director for planning, research, and evaluation, OEO, arranged to break into the data from the ongoing New Jersey graduated work incentive experiment. A memo, distributed to the Cabinet on February 18, 1970, based, as stated, on "preliminary data," contained the positive statements:

> There is no evidence that work effort declined among those receiving income support payments. On the contrary, there is an indication that the work effort of participants receiving payments increased relative to the work effort of those not receiving payments.
>
> Another important question is whether an increase in income would decrease the divorce, separation, and desertion rate among families. While the experiment was not designed to specifically address this question, data . . . suggest that an increase of income of the levels examined in the experiment has little impact on family stability.

Although the report was subsequently to boomerang when the GAO characterized it as "premature" and Senator Williams of Delaware denounced it as a fraud and hoax, it could not have been other than a comfort to Moynihan and the stalwarts in the administration in early 1970.[25]

NWRO's opposition to FAP went far beyond its immediate constituency, adding another dimension to the opposition of social work professionals. Alvin Schorr, at this time editor of *Social Work*, the journal of the AASW, retained a decided preference for children's allowances. Both Schorr and Elizabeth Wickenden were also wary of Nixon's emphasis on workfare evidenced in his television address. Sharing their unease were the leaders of black social agencies, such as the Urban League.

In contrast, early newspaper reports and editorials as well as public opinion polls were quite favorable to FAP. Welfare reform at last, it seemed. John Gardner's Urban Coalition announced support that continued unwavering. The churches and synagogues were initially in favor but became lukewarm or opposed as black Protestants lined up with their own welfare mothers. The U.S. Conference of Mayors was positive but hardly crusading. The National Governors Conference agreed, but wanted more fiscal relief. The National Association of Manufacturers was noncommittal, but the Chamber of Commerce was dead set against FAP on the ground that many small businesses, forced to pay inordinately high wages, would simply have to shut down.

Where was the South in all this? The South was due to receive the lion's share of benefits. From that region came sullen silence. Moynihan argues, with a good deal of justification, that FAP was a radical proposal, a proposal that would have brought about some redistribution of wealth, however small. As such, it would seem that FAP needed some vocal, crusading proponents. These it did not have.[26]

Against this background Ways and Means held brief hearings beginning October 15, 1969. Chairman Mills, at first undecided about FAP, responded favorably by the time it mattered, managing the "Family Assistance Act of 1970" under a closed rule. All was smooth sailing. The House approved FAP 243–135 on April 16, 1970.[27]

In the Finance Committee the going got rough. It was chaired by Senator Long, who had had his fill of protesting welfare mothers. Six of the ten Democratic members were from the South, including Herman E. Talmadge of Georgia and Harry F. Byrd, Jr., of Virginia, veteran defenders of states' rights, particularly in welfare and labor matters. Though the Democrats counted six liberals, only Ribicoff of Connecticut came from a densely populated industrial state where welfare presented a major problem. The seven Republican senators were even farther removed from northeastern ghettos and southern sharecroppers. They represented Arizona, Utah, Nebraska, Iowa, Idaho, Wyoming, and one technically from the South, John J. Williams of Delaware.[28]

So far as the elderly were concerned, Long had been a stalwart supporter of higher welfare payments, even to the extent of posing a threat to the supremacy of social insurance. His sympathies did not extend to AFDC, a population that he considered belonged in the work force. "Who will iron my shirts?" he cried, viewing FAP's income guarantee as a threat to his region's way of life. In a backhanded way, the southern states could be said to be supplementing low wages already when recipients were allowed to keep earnings up to the welfare standard. Where was the welfare reform in a bill that would add fourteen million persons to the rolls? With all this talk about workfare, why not put some real teeth into the WIN program, a reform passed just three years ago? The devastating detailed questions were left to Williams of Delaware, virtually a company-owned state where welfare payments were among the lowest in the nation. Using tables prepared at his behest by HEW, Williams used worst-case scenarios to show that workers would be losers under FAP. Following administration promises to produce a revised bill, Long recessed the hearings on May 1, 1970.[29]

Throughout the FAP debate, President Nixon did little beyond delivering an occasional pep talk. He refrained from entering the fray. Not even his legislative representative lobbied the bill, let alone the President himself. Yet some might have said that Nixon's distancing himself from his "good deed" was more helpful than not. For it was as true in 1970 as in 1973–1974 that people, even a good many who had voted for him, distrusted Richard Nixon. It was widely assumed that FAP was part of the so-called southern strategy, which was designed, through racist maneuvering, to bind the

South to the Republican party at the national level. However idle it is to speculate on what might have been Nixon's game, the fact is that no politician was led to believe that he or she would be helped or hurt by any position taken on FAP. In fact, H. R. Haldeman, a Nixon press officer, recorded in his diary that the President instructed him to "be sure it's [FAP] killed by Democrats and that we make a big play for it, but don't let it pass, can't afford it." To give Nixon the benefit of the doubt, however, Richard Nathan suggests that as the conflict over FAP's passage dragged on, Nixon came to recognize this fact, so far as he and his party were concerned, and simply lost interest.[30]

The Finance Committee proved unimpressed with the requested FAP revision, voting the measure down 10–6 on November 20. The 91st Congress consequently died minus FAP as well as "Social Security" increases. Yet Mills did not give up. H.R. 1, introduced on January 22, 1971, raised the FAP guarantee level to $2,400 while eliminating food stamps. Five months later, on June 22, 1971, the House passed FAP for the second time, 288–132. But FAP was not to be. The Finance Committee held further hearings early in 1972 and again rejected it 10–4.

Something important was salvaged, nevertheless. Under Long's tutelage, the adult categories (OAA, AB, and APTD) were transferred to SSA for administration and their recipients awarded a federal floor of assistance. Treated more like the beneficiaries of OASDI, applicants and recipients of Social Security Income (SSI) would, as well, rise above the shame and stigma of welfare.[31]

Quality Control

Meanwhile, work processes at SRS had been confined to the most elementary routines. John Twiname, the administrator, had ordered a holding pattern within the Assistance Payments Administration (APA) pending enactment of FAP. A loyal Nixon appointee, Twiname was also personally enthusiastic about FAP. In order to keep APA staff from contamination by critics of the proposal and vice versa, Twiname moved the entire staff into rented space in nearby Maryland. A halt was called to further research and policy development. Research had been completed. FAP *was* welfare reform.[32]

Shortly after FAP's final defeat and early in Nixon's second term, however, a new and far less liberal team took over at SRS. The President himself, having won more than 60 percent of the vote, felt free to pursue a tougher welfare policy. To a reporter, Nixon called for tight restraints on giveaways: "Another thing this election is about is whether we should move toward more massive handouts to people, making the people more and more dependent, or whether we say, no, it is up to you."[33] Still without Republican control of Congress, Nixon eschewed new legislation, adopting instead welfare reform via administration.

At SRS, James S. Dwight, Jr., succeeded Twiname. Dwight was a professional accountant who had been deputy director of the California Finance Department during the Reagan governorship. Dwight's appointment as administrator put an unmistakable fiscal management stamp upon SRS. Although he lost no time in bringing APA back from Maryland to the Switzer Building, the move was hardly because he wanted the staff's help.[34]

The newly created Office of Financial Management, located on the west side of the building, balanced Administrator Dwight's office on the east. Francis DeGeorge, a fellow accountant, was placed in charge of quality control with the goal of making the system yield a significant reduction in the rates of ineligibility and overpayment. If nothing else, DeGeorge was determined and ambitious about results. Asked about his goals in establishing "error rates," he replied, in *Federal Register* language, that the approved rate was "3 percent for ineligibility or 5 percent for overpayment." He added, "We might want to reduce it down from 3 percent to something lower if practicable, recognizing it is probably physically impossible to get to zero." Later Administrator Dwight denied any intention to inflict penalties on the states. But DeGeorge was serious: "I not only anticipated [taking the allowance]—I fought to make it happen. . . . I don't want there to be any doubt that my personal intention was to take a penalty. It was not a bluff," he testified. The first year's operation of the aggressive QC initiative showed average error rates of 10.2 percent for ineligibility and 2.8 percent for overpayment. Once it was clear that SRS might take penalties, the eleven states most affected formed the Urban Coalition, hired a top Washington law firm, and filed suit. These states won, the court finding that tolerance levels had been decided "in an arbitrary and capricious manner." Weinberger's successor at HEW, Ford-appointed F. David Mathews, did not appeal. As a longtime member of Congress, Ford was not as ready as Nixon to withhold money from the states.[35]

Making Fathers Pay

Second only to QC on the welfare reform agenda was child support enforcement. It will be recalled that an increased effort to make fathers pay had been one of Ribicoff's administrative reforms in 1962. In 1967, as part of the Social Security amendments, child support enforcement became a major responsibility for state welfare agencies. The new legislation required each state to establish a single organizational unit dedicated exclusively to establishing paternity and collection of support from fathers of AFDC children. States were also required to enter into reciprocal agreements with other states and to enter into cooperative agreements with appropriate courts and law enforcement officials. Yet, after a decade, the enforcement effort remained small in scale and showed little progress. Asked by Congress to investigate in 1972, the GAO reported a lack of commitment, not only in the several states studied, but also within HEW and, by implication, within SRS itself.[36]

Under the leadership of John Svahn, deputy administrator, SRS, and with the enthusiastic approval of Senator Long, child support enforcement legislation, this time with a strong federal role, was shepherded through Congress and signed by President Ford on January 4, 1975. Breaking all precedents, Title IV-D reached into state administration of Title IV-A by making certain actions incumbent upon the applicant-recipient. As a condition of eligibility, each applicant for or recipient of AFDC was required to assign support rights to the state and to cooperate, if need be, in establishing paternity and securing support from the father. Cooperation in locating the father and other steps in the support process could be waived only if such activities were found not to be in the best interests of the child. The burden of proof of prior violence or abuse, however, lay with the mother. Certainly no room was made for allowing social workers time to reconcile the family. Having to pay, it was thought, might be a more powerful tool in reconciliation than counseling.

Once a family was accepted for AFDC, all child support payments were to be paid to the state, not to the family. If collections were insufficient to take the family off welfare, the family received its full welfare grant. Any money in excess of this amount was retained by the state as reimbursement for present or past welfare payments. Services to collect support were also available to women not receiving AFDC—women who had enough money to get by but who were at risk for welfare if their circumstances changed. The match for child support enforcement services was set at 75 percent. To assist the states in locating absent fathers, a federal Parent Locator Service was established. Social Security numbers and information exchange were used to assist in apprehending runaway fathers.

Although the IV-A agency located in state and local welfare departments handled intake, the applicant-recipient was also interviewed by the separate IV-D agency in order to assist in child support action. At the federal level also, the IV-D agency—the Office of Child Support Enforcement (OCSE)—was placed directly under the deputy director, SRS, who was initially, John Svahn. OCSE's first director was Louis B. Hays, a young lawyer from the Los Angeles County welfare department. Hays proved to be an able and knowledgeable administrator, favorably impressing Republicans and Democrats alike. When OCSE was transferred to SSA during the Carter administration, Hays was kept on.[37]

The payoff in child support is, of course, the dollar size of collections. In this respect, the impact of child support legislation was immediate and impressive. In 1976, the start-up year, collections totaled $511.6 million. In 1980 they reached nearly $1.5 billion. Of these totals, collections on behalf of AFDC families amounted, in 1976, to $203.5 million; in 1980, to $603.2 million. Collections for non-AFDC families were even higher, in 1976, $308.1 million; in 1980, $874.5 million.[38]

Not all these millions and billions were pure gain. Child support enforcement was very expensive to administer. Collections exceeded expenditures by $3.31 to $1 in 1985. If the cost-effective ratio seemed slim (one highly respected research contractor deemed the program *not* cost-effective), certain intangibles could be counted. The term "cost avoidance" came to be used to describe and estimate such actions as failure to apply for AFDC, voluntary dropout, or voluntary reporting of child support. Although it was difficult to put a figure on deterrence, deterrence was doubtless present to some degree. And how about the man who had run but decided to pay up before he was caught by the Parent Locator Service? Or the putative father seeking to escape a blood test?

The Republican version of welfare reform was unsuccessful in the sense that it failed to reduce AFDC rolls. For whatever reason, however, the rolls began to level off at about eleven million recipients in the 1970s.[39] The Republicans also failed to institute a guaranteed income as an alternative to AFDC. This was probably not a bad thing. All four of the social experiments, including the first one in New Jersey, showed seriously high rates of work disincentive and family breakup. The quality control effort was marred by overzealous leadership and ignorance of the danger and futility of pushing the states around. The HEW leadership should have remembered Herbert Hoover's "loans" to states. Nevertheless, QC put the fear of God into those states that had become indifferent to fraud and abuse and consequently to maintaining the integrity of the caseload. In contrast, the child support enforcement program was a success, even if not a spectacular one, and deservedly popular with a public that deeply resented paying taxes to support other people's children.

12

To End Welfare as We Know It

JUST TWO WEEKS after the election of 1992, Senator Daniel Patrick Moynihan challenged President-elect William Jefferson Clinton to keep his campaign promise "to end welfare as we know it." Both politicians were, of course, referring to AFDC. At the start of the Clinton moment, recipients of AFDC—at least the mothers—were held uniquely reprehensible among beneficiaries of the welfare state.

The Welfare State at Sea

By contrast, Social Security, that program for elderly retirees who had worked steadily for thirty to forty years and paid in a portion of their wages, seemed sacrosanct. Speaking at Bryn Mawr College in December 1993, Clinton emphasized the obvious: "There are people who believe they are literally entitled to receive something back that they paid into. . . . Thirty-four million people go to see a doctor or get medical care, because of the Medicare program. Social Security has changed what it means to be old."[1] The media unfailingly tagged the elderly "a powerful lobby." A canard, the President countered. "It's not just organized interest groups," he ventured. Still, the chairman of Ways and Means, Dan Rostenkowski, was not apt to forget the "helpless" old folks pushing away his limo with their canes. Their displeasure centered on an amendment that would tax them at a high rate for coverage of catastrophic illness. The despised amendment was repealed before it became effective.[2]

It was possible, however, that in 1993 Social Security was simply riding a wave of popularity. Only ten years before, early in the Reagan presidency, Social Security had weathered what Edward Berkowitz identifies as its second major crisis, the first having been successfully resolved in 1939. It will be recalled that in 1939, the trust fund was pared down in response to fears of political raiding and potential damage to the economy. In 1939, Social Security shifted to pay-as-you-go. The second crisis was for the opposite reason. In late 1982 to early 1983, Social Security "hysteria" typically warned that the "Old age fund could go bust" and that "Social Security is headed for a crash."

The worst was not allowed to happen. President Reagan honored the compact made by the Eisenhower administration that established Social Security as the kingpin of America's welfare state. Under the 1982 agreement, Senator Robert Dole, chairman of Finance, worked with Moynihan on a National Committee on Social Security Reform. At Dole's statesmanlike insistence, the committee confined itself to the immediate fiscal crisis. Consequently, not just political rivals but also bureaucratic enemies circled the wagons. Robert Myers, the dissident actuary who in the 1950s had predicted just such trouble, directed the 1980 committee staff—joining Robert Ball, who had let him go for making just such predictions. The crisis faded quickly once these knowledgeable parties found a fix. Beneficiaries swallowed a one-time "diet cola" (one year's cost of living allowance); the retirement age was raised to sixty-seven effective sometime after the year 2000; and, for the first time, one-half of Social Security income became reportable for income tax purposes.

Faith in Social Security was severely shaken nevertheless. Baby boomers discovered that they were paying more in Social Security taxes than in income taxes and began to doubt out loud that they would live to get their money back. Some listeners noted that it was Sam Donaldson, not the more conservative George Will, who wondered on "This Week," "Why don't they just give it to people that need it?" "The problems of Social Security," wrote an official at the American Enterprise Institute, "are the result of the transformation of the system from a simple safety net to an intergenerational Ponzi scheme."

At the same time, a nonpartisan half-dozen or so former secretaries of the Treasury began to speak up. The elderly should know that they got back in very short order whatever they had paid in; thereafter, they were living off the taxpayers, just like people on welfare. The Treasury secretaries' major concern, though, was the drain on savings and investment caused by the high rate of Social Security taxation.

That Social Security benefits were funded by regressive taxes no one contested. Redistribution was arguable. Most economists believed the system was at best neutral; a few thought it was mildly redistributive. But there was no question that Social Security was popular with the elderly and near elderly. And no wonder. Sometimes retirees were better off than they had been while working and supporting a family. They needn't move in with their children. If they took nice vacations, who could object? The tourist business and the gambling casinos flourished. As liberal Democrats and Republicans pointed out pridefully, Social Security had lifted the elderly out of poverty. In the 1960s, when the poverty index had been developed, about 50 percent of those aged sixty-five and over were counted poor. By 1986 only 14 percent of the elderly had incomes below the poverty line. Whatever the future might hold, there was no indication in 1993 that Social Security was immediately threatened.[3]

In stark contrast to those receiving their old age pensions, female-headed families receiving welfare through AFDC were by definition at or below the poverty line. In her pioneering analysis of 1962 census data, Mollie Orshansky focused on childhood deprivation. She noted that the vast majority of American children—87 percent—were growing up in adequately supported two-parent households. For the small number—8.5 percent—who lived with their mothers alone, about 61 percent had incomes below the $3,000 poverty level. Included were those on AFDC, where annual incomes ranged from $1,344 to $1,680. By 1966 the number of children growing up in poverty had decreased, but one-fourth of the nation's children remained poor. Twenty-five years later the picture was much the same. Even while the elderly, helped immeasurably by Social Security, had left poverty behind, and even while for all households in 1990, the incidence of poverty was down to 11 percent, 42 percent of women with children who had divorced, separated, or who were widowed were impoverished. For never-married mothers, the rate was even higher—44 percent.[4]

Although social scientists who watched annual poverty counts found them useful, they criticized their "snapshot" methodology as an inadequate picture of economic mobility. In 1968, the Office of Economic Opportunity funded the Panel Study of Income Dynamics. Under its design, five thousand families were to be interviewed annually and comprehensively for ten years. The results would substitute a motion picture for a snapshot. The first and most important finding of the panel study was to affirm, though not dramatically, "the promise of American life." Analysts found that "economic well-being fluctuated markedly" for individuals over the ten-year period—with many shifting upward and others going down. Moreover, the one factor having the greatest influence on up or down movement was change in family composition. The destructive effect of death, divorce, and separation on the economic well-being of women and their dependent children was confirmed. Conversely, remarriage brought an improved standard of living.

A large number of families—almost 25 percent of the sample—received income from welfare at least once during the ten-year period, 1969–1978. For half of them (12.3 percent), the duration of their welfare episode was under two years. Others (8.5 percent) stayed on longer, from three to seven years. The rest (4.4 percent)—deemed persistent welfare dependents—received aid in eight or more years. From such figures, the University of Michigan economist Greg J. Duncan concluded that "the picture of need in U. S. society . . . is largely one of many people in temporary need . . . while others may need temporary assistance." This motion picture sharply challenged the Stanford University economist Martin Anderson's view, based on snapshots, that the "welfare system had created a new caste of Americans—perhaps as much as one-tenth of this nation . . . almost totally dependent on the state, with little hope or prospect of breaking free." Rural poverty, with its overlapping poverty among blacks in the South, turned out to be a great deal more prevalent than urban poverty. Rural families accounted for one-third of the persistently poor. However, long-term welfare dependents—55 percent of the persistent poor—were concentrated in urban areas. At any single point in time, 50 percent of all welfare recipients were in the midst of long-term dependency. These long-term welfare users, concentrated in city ghettos, accounted for most of the cost and characterized most of the AFDC load.[5]

Americans are extremely reluctant to admit the presence of an "underclass." Indeed the very idea seems un-American. But in 1980 social scientists led by Isabel V. Sawhill identified 880 underclass neighborhoods where 2.5 million persons lived. Underclass neighborhoods were full of school dropouts, female-headed families with children (averaging 60 percent of the population), joblessness or irregular employment among adults, and welfare dependency. Drinking, drug abuse and dealing, theft, stabbing, and shooting were the day-to-day occupations of all too many. These ghettos were almost 60 percent black, with Hispanics a significant but much smaller group at just over 10 percent. In the old days of rigid neighborhood segregation, in Harlem, for example, the black middle class with its professionals and its skilled and semi-skilled workers would have been present as models. Now, thanks to the civil rights movement and to Great Society programs, the hard-working, upwardly mobile fathers and mothers had moved to the suburbs.

Moynihan continued to settle upon absent fathers as the most potent cause of social pathology. Children, particularly male children, needed a father to provide not only money for food and clothing but discipline and example to lead the young toward attainment of a decent life, Moynihan argued. He referred with alarm to the disintegration of the black family, pausing to note that the white family, though holding up better so far, was also quite unstable. In 1992, 15 percent of white women aged eighteen to forty-four were unmarried mothers, an increase from 7 percent in 1982. For black women the rate rose from 49 percent in 1982 to 56 percent in ten years. For Hispanic women the rate rose from 23 to 33 percent. Unmarried motherhood characterized more than one-half the AFDC caseload in 1986, up from about one-third in 1973. Divorced or separated women made up 31.7 percent in 1986, about the same as in 1973. Blacks, who were only 12 percent of the population, constituted over 40 percent of the caseload; Hispanics about 15 percent.[6]

Just as the black family was too often fatherless, so too many of its children spent too much time on welfare, and by definition spent too much time in poverty. Of all children born between 1967 and 1969, more than 72 percent of black children spent some time on welfare before age eighteen. Almost one-third (29.8 percent) of these children had been short-term recipients; another one-third (28.1 percent) had been on for seven to twelve years; the remainder for most of their lives (thirteen to eighteen years). Only 16 percent of the rest of the nation's children had ever been on welfare at all, and most (12.1 percent) of this dependency was short-term.[7]

The cost of maintaining the fourteen million recipients on AFDC totaled $20 billion in 1992. Although Clinton didn't dwell on it in his address at Bryn Mawr, he made the same point often made by Moynihan—that welfare expenditures amounted to only about 1 percent of the total federal budget and only about 2 percent of all entitlements.[8]

Social Security for the old and welfare for the young were the most talked about but by no means the only entitlements under fire. Disability insurance and Aid to the Disabled—both administered by the Social Security Administration—were said to harbor many malingerers, including alcoholics and drug addicts. In the 1960s, alcohol and drug abuse had been newly defined as illnesses. Users were subject to cure rather than punishment or reform. Release of thousands of the mentally ill from hospitals with the new miracle drugs in hand left many on the street when community facilities failed to materialize. Year after year the federal government picked up the tab for unemployed persons whose unemployment compensation had run out. Technically, these individuals were kept off welfare, but the "compensation" paid them was all tax monies, none of it offset by employer contributions. On some of the finest streets in the most prosperous cities, the homeless confronted business-bent pedestrians. Not all of these beggars were drunks, druggies, or crazies, as was commonly asserted. On closer examination the members of this group were more properly identified as victims of chronic poverty fallen through the safety net.[9]

Even as President Clinton tried to close the last big gap in America's welfare state with universal health care, he persisted in his effort to shut down AFDC. Under the Clinton reform, welfare mothers would be schooled or trained for as long as two years and then go "off to work," either in private industry or community projects. The reform would build upon the Family Support Act of 1988 and the Earned Income Tax Credit Act of 1975. The earned income tax credit for the working poor—Milton Friedman's NIT and a favorite of Moynihan—was expanded with Clinton's enthusiastic approval in 1993, giving payments up to $3,370 a year for families with incomes under $11,000. The Family Support Act, drafted largely by Moynihan, emphasized child support enforcement and workfare. Like WIN before it, however, the Family Support Act has never been sufficiently funded to ensure child care or work training. Since Clinton had promoted the Family Support Act while a member of the Governors' Conference, it was thought he meant business on welfare reform now that he was President.

By the winter of 1993–94, the goal of "ending welfare as we know it" was giving its supporters pause. The prospect of creating well over a million jobs—almost as many as the WPA—raised knotty questions about costs versus savings arose. Hard upon the questions came signs of equivocation as the planners talked of "scaling back," "phasing in," and "savings in the long run." Meanwhile, Moynihan threatened to hold health care hostage to welfare reform. Leaks from the all-too-secret welfare reform task force in mid-March 1994 described "final sticking points" such as dropping the subsidy to grandmother caretakers and assistance to needy immigrants altogether. With the group's report for the President only days away, birth control, foster care, and help for the homeless were costed out.

Others, objecting to cuts as "misguided, hubristic, or mean," were told the American public had to be shown that welfare mothers were "getting off their duffs." Phasing in did seem to be the order of the day. With a budget of about $15 billion, it was predicted that only about 130,000 of the five million heads of families would be enrolled in a work program at the end of five years.[10]

The More Welfare Changes . . .

What went wrong? First let it be said that many things went right. The social insurance and social welfare programs instituted under the Social Security Act of 1935 embodied long-sought reforms designed to temper the inequities of industrial capitalism. Vital as these programs were in and of themselves, the great beauty of the Social Security Act lay in its over-arching federal power. To be sure, except for old age insurance (and subsequently survivor's and disability insurance) federal power was shared with the states. But federal authority buoyed by the carrot of matching money could be expected to shake the liberal stick with confidence undreamed of when assistance to the needy was a local affair.

To the New Dealers who designed and then administered it, the Social Security Act carried a guarantee, a "never again!" to the devastating hardships of the Great Depression. In planning, the preference had been for social insurance, but the immediacy of destitution necessitated some federally aided welfare. Moreover, gaps in the insurance coverage were evident. Confined to wage earners in commerce and industry, the large agricultural areas of the country would find most of their workers unprotected when they were out of work or got old. Conceiving the act as a developmental platform, the Social Security Board carefully laid the groundwork for future amendments that would cover, in addition to agricultural labor, the disabled, the self-employed, and household workers.

Pending extension of social insurance coverage, the board expected categorical welfare programs to rise above poor laws, private charity, and emergency relief practices of the past to establish and maintain standards of health and decency. Until well into the 1950s, Old Age Assistance, Aid to Dependent Children, and Aid to the Blind were seen as integral to social security in the larger sense, defined by Altmeyer as the prevention or amelioration of "the hazards causing economic insecurity."[11]

The choice of professional social workers to administer categorical assistance proved crucial to the direction taken. The fledgling profession was on the one hand trying to shed relief-giving for psychoanalytic casework, while on the other faulting the Roosevelt administration for its failure to finance a general relief program similar to that of the FERA. Yet, the shortage of social workers persisted despite all efforts. How then were the dispensers of welfare to be distinguished from mere clerks? Casework in the style of the private agencies had been ruled out by Josephine Brown at the FERA: eligibility would be established by applicant and agency representatives working together. Hoey and her staff in the Bureau of Public Assistance hit upon "individualization" as the distinctive mark of the social worker in welfare administration.

Hoey's opposition to flat grants in the pension states and insistence on family budgeting had its justification largely in the social worker's faith in the merit of intervention. Perhaps it is too much to assert that the social worker presence preserved Social Security through its rocky years until its big boost in the 1950s. But once "need" was made an absolute condition of eligibility and "income and resources" had to be considered in determining need, states were constrained to put a brake on their generosity to the elderly. This allowed time for Social Security payments to begin and the contributory concept to take hold. This being said, flat grants would have been far simpler to administer and, as Board member Bigge was to argue in vain, would have obviated the means test. The larger the welfare program became, the more difficult it was to retain equity when so much discretion remained in the hands of the caseworker. Family budgeting, in ADC as well as OAA, led to noncompliance and compounded the error rates that necessitated the quality control system.

In the administration of ADC a monumental break with the past occurred. Contrary to assumptions made by the Children's Bureau, the Bureau of Public Assistance refused to confine ADC to the "nice families." A fateful decision, perhaps, but for its time and circumstance, a decent and logical decision. In concurring, the Social Security Board underscored its position that whatever the model (in this case mother's pensions), public welfare programs were not a prisoner of the past.

Acknowledging the difficulty of popularizing a program in which need arose largely from social deviance, the BPA encouraged more adequate assistance payments, arguing with some justification that poverty itself was a major cause of deviance. The bureau, following the advice of consultants and again with the board's concurrence, recommended that ADC be scrapped for general assistance. Presumably this action would sweep family breakup and illegitimacy under the rug. But general assistance would cover the chronically unemployed, which, not unreasonably, aroused fears of institutionalizing a dole and therefore was turned down by Congress.

Granted Congress had reserved a great deal of power to the states, the bureau failed, in many ways, to use the power it had effectively. At the outset its reviews of state plans show careful attention to ensure sound and equitable methods of operation. Because of her desire to ensure staffing by social workers, Hoey at first resisted the board's desire to secure early adoption of personnel merit systems. After she finally went along, she pronounced herself satisfied with the outcome. Foot-dragging on the merit system, however, is an excellent example of poor management by case-work method. Rather than "force" unwanted procedure, the social workers thought it preferable to discuss and persuade the "backward states," even after the 1939 amendments encouraged federal approval of the state welfare agency's personnel system.

Direction by persuasion was the rule long after most federal agencies adopted more formal systems. As early as 1935 the Bureau of the Budget began a codification of federal regulations. Had the BPA adopted this means of communication with the states, mandates would perforce have been clear and required actions presented without qualification. The State Letters that substituted for "Regs" were replete with suggestions regarding the wisdom of talking things over and getting agreement rather than a directive for necessary action. The State Letter on the required Notice to Law Enforcement Officers regarding child support enforcement pointed out every possible loophole to evade compliance, including a recommendation that the states not make the grant conditional on the mother's cooperation. The bureau's position was strongly opposed by the APWA as well as by several welfare-burdened states.

When conditions of eligibility in state plans became more restrictive, they were nevertheless approved in Washington. Louisiana's cutoff of over six thousand families with over twenty-three thousand children in 1960 should have surprised no one. Plan after plan had contained language narrowly defining a suitable home or substitute father in such a way as to deny assistance. Many children in many states had been dropped from the rolls, though not so many all at once. Was a man-in-the house really a substitute father—that is, responsible for support of another man's children? Widows on Social Security received support for children regardless of their subsequent relationships with men. Were special investigators warranted to ferret out fraud and abuse? It was one thing to call for a halt to unreasonable searches and seizures (if indeed they existed). It was another to shrug off the idea of abuse altogether.

The administrative review, begun to replace the case audit, quickly lost focus. A careful check for accurate determination of eligibility and amount of payment with a concise evaluation of performance was essential. Instead, the administrative review became an opportunity for additional state counseling, with elaborate recommendations for fixing this or that, here and there. While reports piled up unread, outside investigators were finding, as in the District of Columbia, intolerably high rates of ineligibility. Although managers of the quality control system later overreached in their zeal to punish the states for errors, the objectives and methods of the system were clear and were properly directed.

In the 1960s when Social Security took over the financial needs of those not expected to work, OAA, AB, APTD, and the segment of widows with young children in ADC declined markedly. Welfare as we know it emerged in full view, almost 50 percent black and stripped of its supposedly "worthy" cases. Black Americans had been overrepresented in the caseload from the beginning of the program, but until they became visible in the inner cities outside the South, this caused little comment. Indeed the BPA had allowed the southern states to regulate the size of the black caseload by approving the less egregious forms of suitable homes policy. The southern practice of paying less than the standard while allowing earnings up to that standard was deplored in Washington but excused because of the region's low per capita income. Inequitable as it was, everyone was more or less content with this situation: household labor was subsidized, mothers had a little more to live on, day care came from relatives. In retrospect this treatment of household labor seems less shameful than the apparently common practice of avoiding payment of Social Security taxes for faithful employees—male and female—who ended up on welfare because there was no record of their having worked.[12]

Once up north and in the ghettos, blacks began to draw unfavorable attention. It was said that AFDC was made to order for their allegedly loose family structure. The Moynihan report on the black family made a comeback as the black man was portrayed as forever on the run, leaving illegitimate children or leaving the mother and children of a bona-fide or common-law marriage to go on welfare. When the Newburgh code and the Byrd report erupted in the early 1960s, the public's response was unmistakably racist.

With the concept of a poverty level rather than indigence the new measure of deprivation, AFDC was battered by Great Society reformers because of its low standards and assistance payments. The Welfare Administration, though it encouraged child support enforcement and quality control, understood the 1962 amendments as an endorsement of casework. The administrative reorganization, however long it had been desired by social workers, divorced welfare from the more popular Social Security. Stripped of its protective cover and with the rolls rising, AFDC faced a hostile citizenry.

A series of reforms, begun in 1967 and continuing into the Clinton administration, offered workfare as a centerpiece. So far these efforts have fallen far short of expectations. The reasons for this outcome are many, not the least of which is the failure to fund day care with any degree of adequacy. In all these reforms, cost is the shocker. Collecting child support is very expensive, driving the program to the edge of cost-effectiveness. Keeping a teenager in high school and preparing her for a job is also costly. In today's economy, it is doubtless realistic to plan another year or two of education so she can command enough salary to become self-supporting. Insofar as black men are irresponsible parents, attention must be paid, not least by keeping them in school and helping with job preparation. State experimentation with new approaches should be encouraged provided it is responsible experimentation—not just mean-spirited cost-cutting or racist. Vigilance, best exerted at the federal level to ensure some measure of equity, is a must. As shown by this history, once the public assistance titles of the Social Security Act were in place fundamental change was slow. It was 1967 before AFDC was amended to include the Work Incentive Program (WIN).[13] Because work (with the higher the earnings, the better) is what merits respect, the Moynihan-sponsored reforms that underlie President Clinton's proposals are headed in the right direction.

That these reforms are not all-inclusive or moving in the fast lane has led some welfare critics to demand immediate drastic action. Charles Murray, a white conservative moralist and writer, argued in his book *Losing Ground* (1984) that AFDC is the *cause* of dependency. In his view, from the welfare program spring all its attendant ills—unmarried motherhood, teenage pregnancy, school dropouts, and so forth. To abolish welfare would, Murray claims, not only save money but greatly reduce the number of out-of-wedlock births and encourage additional good news. Although *Losing Ground* is larded with statistics to bolster its case, experts in statistical analysis have questioned the validity of Murray's conclusions.

As of 1994, Murray has partly shifted his attention to studying I.Q.'s and their relationship to race, class, and genes.[14] There are precedents aplenty for the adoption of unproven theories in the hope of miraculous cures. Highly trained and experienced persons of earlier times have grasped at solutions later undercut by evidence. *The Jukes: A Study in Crime, Pauperism, Disease, and Heredity* (1877) by the criminologist Richard Louis Dugdale; the teaching of the Italian physician-criminologist Cesare Lombroso, who traced crime to a distinct anthropological type, a product of degeneracy; and phrenology, "the science of the mind," developed by a Viennese brain physiologist, Johann Gaspar Spurzheim, in the 1820s, were all embraced as scientific saviors of society.[15]

Murray's prescriptions for welfare reform are currently being promoted by a group of Republican office-seekers, among them William Kristol, Dan Quail's erstwhile campaign manager; William Bennett, Ronald Reagan's secretary of education and President Bush's drug czar; and Jack Kemp, Bush's secretary of housing and urban development, with some middle-of-the-road Republicans, such as columnist Charles Krautheimer, joining in.[16]

Earnest, well-meaning folk discuss the reestablishment of orphanages, not simply to care for handicapped premature babies but also to lock up promiscuous teenagers. Unfortunately, some unrepentant liberals have countered Murray's prescriptions with a "leave 'em alone" attitude.[17] The underclass urban ghetto is not, however, just a bad headache. To do what is necessary to abolish its evils requires cohesion of all races and classes to confront the unsavory combination of welfare, crime, and educational decline.

Questioned at a press conference on October 22, 1994, Clinton confessed he hadn't read the Murray book but emphasized his disbelief in "the proposition that there are inherent racially based differences in the capacity of the American people to reach their full potential." Showing a sure grasp of the larger social issues spawned by the underclass, the President posed the familiar rhetorical questions. "What can the government do about it?" "What can the President do about it?" He had tried to offer opportunities "to give hope to people . . . left behind." "But," he concluded, "to rebuild a society that has been pressured both in our inner cities, our isolated rural areas, for a generation now . . . is going to take a concerted effort that starts with parents, churches, community groups, private business people, and people at the local level. The federal government cannot be the salvation of that. We have to rebuild the bonds of society."[18]

To assist this effort it may be timely to recall the ancient precept that "poverty is not a kind of crime," as well as to consider how best to give welfare recipients a place at the boardroom table.[19]

Notes

1. This Business of Relief

1. Galbraith, *The Great Crash*, 88–90, 168, 174; Morison, *The Oxford History of the American People*, 941–944; Morris, *Encyclopedia of American History*, 751; Geddes, "Trends in Relief Expenditures, 1910–1935"; Bernstein, *History of the American Worker*, 59; Smiley, "Recent Unemployment Rate Estimates for the 1920s and 1930s," 488.
2. Schlesinger, *The Age of Roosevelt*, I, *Crisis of the Old Order*, 77–89, 163–64; Brandes, "Hoover, Herbert Clark," in *Dictionary of American Biography*, supp. 7, 357–360; Morison, *Oxford History of the American People*, 945; Burner, *Herbert C. Hoover: A Public Life*, 248; Wilson, *Herbert Hoover: Forgotten Progressive*, 137–138, 142.
3. Burner, *Hoover*, 259–261; Brown, *Public Relief*, 68–73; Schlesinger, *Crisis of the Old Order*, 235–238.
4. Schlesinger, *Crisis of the Old Order*, 224.
5. Galbraith, *The Great Crash*, 77, 173–174, 177; Link et al., *The American People: A History*, II, 731–732.
6. Coll, *Perspectives in Public Welfare: A History*, chaps. 2, 4; Lubove, *Professional Altruist*, 108–117. Cities without public outdoor relief, which represented ten out of twenty-one with a population over 200,000, were New York, Philadelphia, Brooklyn, St. Louis, Baltimore, San Francisco, New Orleans, Washington, Kansas City, and Louisville. Coll, *Public Welfare*, 58n.
7. Brown, *Public Relief*, 14, 28, 277–278; Lurie, "The Drift to Public Relief," 214–219.
8. Brown, *Public Relief*, 3–4, 13–14, is more critical of the poor laws and poor law administration. My own conclusions were reached after reviewing a great many of the reports cited by Brown, pp. 483–485, as well as additional ones. A bibliography of these sources, covering some fifteen states in all, is available in Coll files.
9. Clague, *Seventeenth-Century Poor Relief in the Twentieth Century*, 5. This pub-

lication is based on *Poor Relief Administration in Pennsylvania*, State Department of Welfare Bulletin no. 61, 1934.

10. Brown, *Public Relief*, chaps. 1, 2, pp. 78–79; Coll, *Public Welfare*, chaps. 2, 3; Ford, "Federated Financing," 327–328; Coll, "Social Welfare: History," and Leiby, "Social Welfare: History of Basic Ideas," 1503–1529.

11. Wilson, *Hoover*, 142.

12. Ibid.; Schlesinger, *Crisis of the Old Order*, 167–172; Brown, *Public Relief*, 65–66.

13. Brown, *Public Relief*, 65–66, 71–72; Burner, *Hoover*, 263–265; Hamilton, "Herbert Hoover and the Great Drought of 1930," 850–875.

14. Brown, *Public Relief*, 68–70, 74; Burner, *Hoover*, 265–266; Schlesinger, *Crisis of the Old Order*, 169–170.

15. Brown, *Public Relief*, 74, 76–77; Burner, *Hoover*, 266.

16. Swift, "The Future of Public Social Work," 451–452; Brown, *Public Relief*, 80–83.

17. Brown, *Public Relief*, 89–90.

18. Ibid., 90, 94–95; Burner, *Hoover*, 267–268.

19. Brown, *Public Relief*, chap. 5.

20. Ibid., 118–123.

21. Hopkins, *Spending to Save*, 74–77.

22. Brown, *Public Relief*, 124–125, 128, quotation at 124.

23. Ibid., 126–130; Burner, *Hoover*, 313.

24. Brown, *Public Relief*, 126; Hopkins, "The Developing National Program of Relief," 67; interview, Frank Bane w/James Leiby, 1965, University of California Oral History Office, Berkeley, California.

25. Schlesinger, *Crisis of the Old Order*, 242, 256–265; Burner, *Hoover*, 267, 309–312; Brown, *Public Relief*, 69.

26. Schlesinger, *Crisis of the Old Order*, 314; Morison, *Oxford History of the American People*, 951–953; Cook, *Eleanor Roosevelt*, I, *1884–1933*, 338–380.

27. Morris, *Encyclopedia of American History*, 402.

28. Brown, *Public Relief*, 129–130; Federal Emergency Relief Administration, "Final Statistical Report," 23 National Archives, WPA Collection.

29. Brown, *Public Relief*, 429.

30. Schlesinger, *Crisis of the Old Order*, 302, 391–392, 433.

31. Quoted in Kurzman, *Harry Hopkins and the New Deal*, 72; Schlesinger, *Crisis of the Old Order*, 391, 433.

32. Trout, "Perkins, Frances," in *Notable American Women: The Modern Period*, 535–539; Freidel, *Franklin D. Roosevelt*, 3, *The Triumph*, 195; Schlesinger, *Crisis of the Old Order*, 391–393; Burner, *Hoover*, 253–254, 258.

33. Brown, *Public Relief*, 136–142; Martin, *Madam Secretary: Frances Perkins*, 247–248, 257–258; Kurzman, *Hopkins*, 72–73; Huthmacher, *Senator Robert F. Wagner and the Rise of American Liberalism*, 139.

34. Carothers, *Chronology of the Federal Emergency Relief Administration*. Hereafter FERA Chrono.

35. Sherwood, *Roosevelt and Hopkins*, 14–19, 21–29, 44–45, 59–60, 62–63; FERA Mo. Rpt. 1933, May, 22, June, 38; Hopkins press conference, Nov. 9, 1934, 29, FDR Library, Hopkins Papers; Hellman, "House Guest," 25, 30; Perkins, Oral History Memoir, III, Columbia University Oral History Collection (CUOHC).

36. Sherwood, *Roosevelt and Hopkins*, 46–47; interview, Bane w/Leiby; interview, Bane w/Peter Corning, 1965, CUOHC; Brown, *Public Relief*, 85–89, 119–120, 135. From its founding in 1930 until 1932, the APWA was called the Association of Public Welfare Officials.

37. FERA Conference, Staff, Field Reps., and Field Statisticians, Sept. 5–8, 1933, FDR Library, Hopkins Papers, 25, Rpt., Minutes on Conf. re State Set-Up; Brown, *Public Relief*, 192, 196–197, 201, 274; interview, Bane w/Corning; Sherwood, *Roosevelt and Hopkins*, 48–49.

38. Brown, *Public Relief*, 192–196, 199–201; FERA Conference, Sept. 5–8, 1933; FERA Chrono., May 3, 1934, 56; "Ladies of the FERA," 271.

39. Hopkins, "The Developing National Program of Relief," 68–69; FERA, "Final Statistical Rpt." 23, 41, 77; FERA Mo. Rpt., May 22–June 30, 1933, 3.

40. Telegram, Hopkins to Govs., May 31, 1933, FERA Chrono., 3; Brown, *Public Relief*, 149–151.

41. Emilia E. Martinez-Brawley, "From Countrywoman to Federal Emergency Relief Administration: Josephine Chapin Brown, A Biographical Study," unpublished MS, n.d., in Coll file through kindness of Professor Martinez-Brawley; Martinez-Brawley, "Brown, Josephine Chapin," in *Biographical Dictionary of Social Welfare in America*; 1961 Bryn Mawr Alumnae Survey, Bryn Mawr College Archives; Davenport and Davenport, "Josephine Brown's Classic Book Still Guides Rural Social Work," 413–419; interview, Dorothy Mohler w/Coll, Nov. 18, 1985, Coll files; interview, Mary Flynn w/Coll, May 9, 1986, Coll files; interview, Elizabeth Wickenden w/Coll, May 28, 1986, Coll files.

42. Hopkins, "The Developing National Program of Relief," 68–69; FERA, "Final Statistical Rpt.," 23, 41, 77; FERA Mo. Rpt., May 22–June 30, 1933, 3; FERA Chrono., May 31, 1933, quotation at 4; telegram, Hopkins to Govs., FERA Chrono., May 31, 1933, 3.

43. FERA Mo. Rpt., May 22–June 30, 1933; Kurtz, "Two Months of the New Deal in Federal Relief," 284–285.

44. M. Smith, "Public Welfare, Local Agencies," 393–394; Brown, *Public Relief*, 179–181.

45. Interview, Bane w/Leiby; Sherwood, *Roosevelt and Hopkins*, 47; Brown, *Public Relief*, 184–186, Hopkins speech, NCSW, *Proceedings*, June 1933, quotation at 66–67.

46. FERA Rules and Regulations no. 1, Governing Expenditures of Federal Emergency Relief Funds, June 23, 1933; FERA Chrono., 5; Brown, *Public Relief*, quotation at 185–186.

47. Dunham, "Pennsylvania and Unemployment Relief, 1929–1934," 257–276; Hopkins speech, NCSW, *Proceedings*, June 1933, quotation at 70–71.

48. FERA Rules and Regulations no. 3, "Administration of Public Agencies," July 11, 1933, FERA Chrono., 7–8.

49. Brown, *Public Relief*, 220–221; Lubove, *Professional Altruist*, 127; FERA Rules and Regulations no. 3, July 11, 1933, FERA Chrono., 7.

50. Brown, *Public Relief*, 221, 277–282; Springer, "Social Workers—What Now?" 291.

51. FERA Chrono., May–June 1933, 3–5, Nov. 8–15, 1933, 27–30, Feb. 2, 1933–Apr. 4, 1934, 41–53; Brown, *Public Relief*, 156–169.

52. Telegram, Hopkins to Govs., May 11, 1933, FERA Chrono., 3.

53. Letter, Hopkins to Govs. and State Relief Administrators, Jul. 20, 1933, FERA Chrono., 12; Kurtz, "Two Months of the New Deal in Federal Relief," 285–286; Kurtz, "On the Governors' Doorsteps," 344–345.

54. Brown, *Public Relief*, 204.

55. E. Abbott, "Public Welfare and Politics," 32, 37–40; Colcord and Kurtz, "Unemployment and Community Action," *Survey Midmonthly*, June 1935, 183–184.

56. Brown, *Public Relief*, 211–215; Kurtz, "Unemployment Relief," 522; Colcord

and Kurtz, "Unemployment and Community Action," *Survey Midmonthly*, Mar. 1934, 90.

57. Colcord and Kurtz, "Unemployment and Community Action," *Survey Midmonthly*, Dec. 1933, 422; Colcord and Kurtz, "Unemployment and Community Action," *Survey Midmonthly*, Mar. 1934, 90; Brown, *Public Relief*, 208–209.

58. Letters, Davey to Hopkins, Mar. 4, 1935, and Hopkins to Davey, Mar. 8, 1935, FDR Library, Roosevelt papers, OF 4, OF 444 Jan.–Jul. 1935; *Cleveland Plain Dealer*, Mar. 17, 1935, 1, May 25, 1935, 6; Colcord and Kurtz, "Unemployment and Community Action," *Survey Midmonthly*, Apr. 1935, 118.

59. *Cleveland Plain Dealer*, May 25, 1935, w/letter, Kathryn Goodwin, FERA, to Stephen Early, May 28, 1935, FDR Library, OF 7, OF 444 FERA Misc. 1933–34; Colcord and Kurtz, "Unemployment and Community Action," *Survey Midmonthly*, Apr. 1935, 118; "Social Workers on the Spot" in "The Common Welfare," *Survey Midmonthly*, Apr. 1935, 111; Colcord and Kurtz, "Unemployment and Community Action," *Survey Midmonthly*, May 1935, 150.

60. White House, press release, Feb. 28, 1934, FERA Chrono., 46–47.

61. FERA Chrono., WD-3, Mar. 20, 1934, 51; FERA, "Final Statistical Rpt.," 20–21; FERA Mo. Rpt., Jan. 1–31, 1935, 16–17, 21.

62. FERA, "Final Statistical Rpt.," 45–47.

63. Ibid., 40, 169–70.

64. Ten states exceeded the average payment in July 1933, July 1934, and January 1935: Massachusetts, New York, Maine, Maryland, Rhode Island, California, Connecticut, Illinois, Michigan, and Wisconsin. In addition, eleven states and the District of Columbia exceeded the average on at least one of these dates: District of Columbia, New Jersey, Vermont, Delaware, Ohio, Washington, Colorado, New Hampshire, Minnesota, Nevada, Pennsylvania, and Montana. Table VII, Average Amount of General Relief Extended by Case, by State, Monthly, July 1933–Mar. 1937, FERA, "Final Statistical Rpt.," 169–170.

65. Brown, *Public Relief*, app. L, Average Mo. Relief Benefits per Family, May 1933–May 1935, 466.

66. Brown, "Social Services Division," FERA Mo. Rpt., Mar 1–31, 1936, 6–9, 254–255.

67. Derived from: table 1, Number of Applications for Relief Received and Number Accepted for Care under the General Relief Program, Monthly, Feb. 1934–Nov. 1935, FERA, "Final Statistical Rpt.," 16; table 4, Total Number of Cases, Number of Families and Single Persons Receiving General Relief, Monthly, Jan. 1935–Mar. 1937, FERA, "Final Statistical Rpt.," 23.

68. Hauser, "Workers on the Public Unemployment Relief Rolls in the United States, March 1935."

69. Smith, "The Negro and Relief," 10–15.

70. Quoted in Colcord and Kurtz, "Unemployment and Community Action," *Survey Midmonthly*, Jan. 1935, 23–24.

71. Schlesinger, *Coming of the New Deal*, 273–276; Colcord and Kurtz, "Unemployment and Community Action," *Survey Midmonthly*, Jan. 1935, 23–24.

72. Franklin D. Roosevelt, *Annual Message*, Jan. 4, 1935, FERA Chrono., 70.

2. From the Cradle to the Grave

1. Brown, *Public Relief*, 165–166; Roosevelt, *Public Papers and Addresses*, 1934.

2. Schlesinger, *Age of Roosevelt*, II, *The Coming of the New Deal*, 303–304, III,

The Politics of Upheaval, 16–28, 31–33, 46–48, 53–56, 62–68, 249, 338–41, 555–559; Witte, *Development of the Social Security Act,* 6–7; Executive Order 6757, June 29, 1934, reprinted in Social Security Board (SSB), *Social Security in America,* 515; Morison, *Oxford History of the American People,* 970–974; Brinkley, *Voices of Protest: Huey Long, Father Coughlin, and the Great Depression,* passim.

3. F. Perkins, *The Roosevelt I Knew,* 151–152; Martin, *Madam Secretary,* 240–241; Witte, *Development of the Social Security Act,* 65–66; interview, Thomas Eliot w/Peter Corning, 1965, CUOHC; Altmeyer, "If," 8.

4. Executive Order 6757, June 29, 1934, in SSB, *Social Security in America,* 515; Witte, *Development of the Social Security Act,* 9; Altmeyer, *Formative Years of Social Security,* 7.

5. Witte, *Development of the Social Security Act,* 17–20, 24–25, 40–41; SSB, *Social Security in America,* 521–523, 525–530.

6. Lubove, *Struggle for Social Security,* 25–90; Security Employment—A Part of a Program of National Economic Security, 5, Hopkins Papers, 48, Economic and Social Security, Roosevelt Library; *Rpt. of the Committee on Economic Security,* Jan. 15, 1935, 24–25, reprinted in Pifer and Chisman, eds., *Report . . . Security of 1935,* 50th anniversary edition; "Old Age Security," in SSB, *Social Security in America,* 154.

7. Witte, *Development of the Social Security Act,* 7, 17–18; Edwin E. Witte, "Possible General Approaches to the Problem of Economic Security," Aug. 16, 1935, National Archives, Record Group (RG) 47, Committee on Economic Security, General.

8. Perkins, *Roosevelt I Knew,* 280–281.

9. Preliminary Outline of the Work of the Staff of the Committee on Economic Security, submitted to the Technical Board, Aug. 10, 1934, and Informally Agreed Upon as Basis for Beginning Work, National Archives, RG 47, Committee on Economic Security, General; Witte, *Development of the Social Security Act,* 11–12, 18; Schlesinger, *Politics of Upheaval,* 325; Schlabach, *Edwin E. Witte: Cautious Reformer,* 106.

10. Preliminary Outline . . . submitted to Technical Board, Aug. 10, 1934. Brown, *Public Relief,* 164, states: "No account was taken of dependent children or any other unemployable persons or of any other type of disability until the committee was approached in late summer and early fall by the Federal Children's Bureau, the United States Public Health Service and the Office of Education. In response to special requests made by these agencies, the problems dealt with in four titles of the present social security act were finally taken under consideration after the original studies were well under way." This statement must be compared with evidence in the Preliminary Outline of August 10, 1934, which includes in the fields of social insurance to be studied "retirement annuities, survivors' insurance, family endowment and maternity benefits" and lists among studies planned "the problem of maternity and child welfare in relation to economic security," adding, "a person of the caliber of Grace Abbott [former chief of the Children's Bureau] is needed for this study; perhaps someone in the Children's Bureau can be drawn in." See also Preliminary Report of the Staff of the Committee on Economic Security, presented to the Committee on Economic Security and the Technical Board on Economic Security, Sept. 1934, Social Security Administration Library, U.S. Committee on Economic Security, Reports, vol. 9.

11. "Old Age Security," in SSB, *Social Security in America,* 141, 167, 172–180, and table 36 facing 160, 162–165; Lubove, *Struggle for Social Security,* 114–116, 127–130, 133–134, 137–141. (Lubove's figures on the aged differ slightly

from the earlier source); Coll, *Public Welfare*, 81. Twenty-eight states had old age pension legislation as of December 1934: Maine, New Hampshire, Massachusetts, New York, New Jersey, Pennsylvania, Delaware, Maryland, Minnesota, Iowa, Wisconsin, Michigan, Indiana, Ohio, West Virginia, Kentucky, North Dakota, Nebraska, Washington, Oregon, California, Nevada, Arizona, Montana, Idaho, Utah, Colorado, and Wyoming. "Old Age Security," in SSB, *Social Security in America*, table 37, facing 160.

12. Preliminary Report of the Staff of the Committee on Economic Security, Sept. 1934, 52–56, SSA Library, Comm. on Economic Security, Reports, vol. 11; Douglas, *Social Security in the United States*, 28–29, 31–33; interview, Thomas Eliot w/Corning, CUOHC, 1965.

13. Coll, *Public Welfare*, 76–80; Leff, "Consensus for Reform: The Mothers' Pension Movement in the Progressive Era," reprinted in Breul and Diner, eds., *Compassion and Responsibility*, 245–247, 251–260; "Security for Children," in SSB, *Social Security in America*, 234–236, 241; Bell, *Aid to Dependent Children*, 1–19.

14. Preliminary Outline . . . submitted to Technical Board, Aug. 10, 1934; Parker and Carpenter, "Julia Lathrop and the Children's Bureau," 60–63, 73–74; Trattner, *From Poor Law to Welfare State*, 182–184; "Security for Children," in SSB, *Social Security in America*, 239–240, 246–248; Security for Children, Summary of Recommendations of the U.S. Children's Bureau prepared at the request of the Committee on Economic Security, in cooperation with the Advisory Committee on Child Welfare, National Archives, RG 47, Advisory Council, Misc., includes quotations; Witte, *Development of the Social Security Act*, 162–163; interview, Katharine Lenroot w/Peter Corning, 1965, CUOHC.

15. Witte, *Development of the Social Security Act*, 38–39; First Tentative Draft of the Preliminary Recommendations of the Technical Board to the Committee on Economic Security, prepared by Edwin E. Witte, for the Executive Committee Meeting, Sept. 29, 1934, National Archives, RG 47, Committee on Economic Security Technical Board Reports; Preliminary Report of the Technical Board to the Committee on Economic Security, Oct. 1934, National Archives, RG 47, Technical Board Reports.

16. Letters, Perkins to Kahn, Nov. 16, 1934, and Kahn to Perkins, Nov. 19, 1934, National Archives, RG 47, Committee on Economic Security; Public Employment and Public Assistance: Informal Report of a Special Committee Advisory to the President's Committee on Economic Security, Nov. 24, 1934, signed by Dorothy Kahn and Walter West, National Archives, RG 47, Committee on Economic Security, Public Employment and Public Assistance, Minutes of Meetings; Brown, *Public Relief*, 304–306.

17. *Rpt. of the Committee on Economic Security*, Jan. 15, 1935, 7; Brown, *Public Relief*, quotation at 163–165.

18. *Rpt. of the Committee on Economic Security*, Jan. 15, 1935, passim; Witte, *Development of the Social Security Act*, 174, 182, 187–188.

19. Interview, Thomas Eliot w/Corning, 1965, CUOHC; Altmeyer, *Formative Years of Social Security*, 3–4; Witte, *Development of the Social Security Act*, 79.

20. Schlesinger, *Politics of Upheaval*, 29–37, 40–41; Douglas, *Social Security*, 27, 69–71, 73; Witte, *Development of the Social Security Act*, 46–47, 78–79; Holtzman, *Townsend Movement*, 48–49.

21. "Old Age Security," in SSB, *Social Security in America*, 196–197; Witte, *Development of the Social Security Act*, 143–144.

22. "Security for Children," in SSB, *Social Security in America*, 293; Witte, *Development of the Social Security Act*, 163–164.

23. Witte, *Development of the Social Security Act*, 145; House, Committee on Ways and Means, *The Social Security Bill*, Report to Accompany H.R. 7260, House Rpt. 615, 74th Cong. 1st sess., 4, 18; Social Security Act, Titles I, IV, X.
24. Schlesinger, *Coming of the New Deal*, 312.

3. Planning Welfare Programs

1. Witte, *Development of the Social Security Act*, 145–148, 162–165; Altmeyer, *Formative Years of Social Security*, 15–37; House, Committee on Ways and Means, *Economic Security Act*, Hearings on H.R. 4120, 74th Cong., 1st sess., Jan.–Feb. 1935, 8. The Children's Bureau, Department of Labor, was to administer the programs covering Child Welfare Services and Maternal and Child Health and Crippled Children's Services. The Public Health Service, Treasury Department, was to administer Title VI, covering increased funds for public health work. The Bureau of Vocational Rehabilitation, Office of Education, Department of the Interior, was to administer increased grants to States for Vocational Rehabilitation. The Department of Labor retained control of the U.S. Employment Service. Witte, *Development of the Social Security Act*, 165.
2. Memo, Perkins to the President, with attachments, Aug. 15, 1935, Roosevelt Library, OF 8, OF 1710a; Altmeyer, *Formative Years of Social Security*, vii–x, 100; interview, Maurine Mulliner w/Peter Corning, 1967, CUOHC.
3. Altmeyer, *Formative Years of Social Security*, 43–45; McKinley and Frase, *Launching Social Security*, 18–22; Schlesinger, *Politics of Upheaval*, 337.
4. McKinley and Frase, *Launching Social Security*, 389–392; interview, Frank Bane w/Leiby, 1965, 185–188; interview, Mulliner w/Corning; SSB, Minutes, Nov. 1934–Dec. 1935; interview, Frank Bane w/Corning, July 19, 1965, CUOHC; Frank Bane, "Administrative Problems and Progress of the Social Security Board," address at the Brookings Institution, Apr. 6, 1937, Health and Human Services (HHS) Departmental Library.
5. McKinley and Frase, *Launching Social Security*, 180–181; Witte, *Development of the Social Security Act*, 71, 162–163; Altmeyer, *Formative Years of Social Security*, 36–37.
6. Brown, *Public Relief*, 151, 229; Colcord and Kurtz, "Unemployment and Community Action," *Survey Midmonthly*, Jul. 1935, quotations at 217–218.
7. Gill, "How Many Are Unemployable?" 4–5.
8. Lubove, *Professional Altruist*, 127, 131–137; Steiner, *Social Insecurity: The Politics of Welfare*, 178–182; Brown, *Public Relief*, 279–280, 282–286; Etzioni, ed., *The Semi-Professions and Their Organization*, 93–95, 102–109, 111–115, 120–125; Leighninger, *Social Work: Search for Identity*, chap. 5; McKinley and Frase, *Launching Social Security*, 22, 30–31, 40–41, 85–88, 98–99, 407–416, 424–425, 428, 431–432, 480–483, 504–505; Bane, "Administrative Problems and Progress of the Social Security Board," Apr. 6, 1937; "Notes and Comment," *Social Service Review*, Sept. 1937, 490–492, article unsigned but in the style of Edith Abbott, who was on the journal's editorial board.
9. Brown, *Public Relief*, 218–219, 273–295.
10. The job had previously been offered to Josephine Roche and to Robert T. Lansdale, a trained social worker, both of whom turned it down, Lansdale on the ground that he would not have sufficient authority to run the program. Social Security Board, Minutes, Dec. 12 and 17, 1935, and Jan. 7, 1936.

11. Coll, "Hoey, Jane Margueretta," *Notable American Women: The Modern Period*, 341–343; vita, Jane M. Hoey, Roosevelt Library, OF 1, OF 1710—1935–37; interview, Wilbur Cohen w/Coll, Oct. 25, 1985. Additional information on Hoey in Coll files.

12. Lubove, *Struggle for Social Security*, 171–178; Schlesinger, *Politics of Upheaval*, 33–35, 40–41; Holtzman, *Townsend Movement*, 49, 88–89, 101.

13. Dewhurst and Schneider, "Objectives and Social Effects of the Public Assistance and Old Age Provisions of the Social Security Act," 394–403.

14. AASW, *This Business of Relief: Proceedings of Conference*, Feb. 14–16, 1936.

15. West, "The Present Relief Situation," 439–440.

16. Brown, "Present Relief Situation in the United States," 429–431.

17. Williams, "Works Progress Administration," in AASW, *This Business of Relief*, 135–137; Williams, "Progress and Policy of the W.P.A.," 443–453; Williams, *Survey Midmonthly*, May 1936, 166.

18. Costin, *Two Sisters for Social Justice*, 159–161; G. Abbott, "Social Workers and Public Welfare Developments," in AASW, *This Business of Relief*, 23; E. Abbott, "Public Assistance—Whither Bound?" 6–8.

19. Springer and Lerrigo, "Social Work in the Public Scene," 165–67.

20. Brown, *Public Relief*, 313; Schlesinger, *Coming of the New Deal*, 273–278, 317; Bane, "Administrative Problems and Progress of the Social Security Board," Apr. 6, 1937.

21. Bane, "Administrative Problems and Progress of the Social Security Board," Apr. 6, 1937; McKinley and Frase, *Launching Social Security*, 145–146; Social Security Act, Title I, Sec. 2. Identical language in Titles IV and X.

22. Frank Bane, "Development of a Sound State and County Welfare Organization," July 16, 1936, SSB, Addresses by Frank Bane, nos. 1–10, 1936–1938, HHS Library; Bane, "Administrative Problems and Progress of the Social Security Board," Apr. 6, 1937; memo, Mary E. Austin to Regional Representatives, Sept. 30, 1936, sub.: Suggested State Legislation for Social Security, National Archives, RG 47, Social Security Administration, Central Files, 610, Dec. 1937.

23. McKinley and Frase, *Launching Social Security*, 140–145; Submittal of State Plan, c. Dec. 1935 w/attachment, Outline-Description, National Archives, RG 47, SSA, Central file 621, Dec. 1935; SSA, Administrative Order no. 2 (revised 5/36), sub.: Procedure for Handling State Plans Submitted for Approval by the Board under Titles I, IV, and X . . . , May 27, 1936, SSB Doc. 211, HHS Library.

24. Wisconsin State Plan for OAA and Recommendations regarding Wisconsin State Plan—SSB, c. Dec. 1935; telegram, Bane to Keith, Supervisor of Pensions, Wisc., Dec. 20, 1935, and Keith to Bane, Dec. 21, 1935; telegram, Oscar Powell, Exec. Dir., SSB, to Gov. Julius P. Heil, Wisc., Aug. 15, 1939, National Archives, RG 47, Doc. 15, Commissioner's Action Meeting Documents, Welfare Administration.

25. Letter, Winant to Keith, Supervisor of Pensions, Wisc., Dec. 27, 1935, National Archives, RG 47, Doc. 15, Commissioner's Action Meeting Documents, Welfare Administration.

26. McKinley and Frase, *Launching Social Security*, 146–147; SSB, Minutes, Dec. 20, 23, 31, 1935; memo, Public Assistance Div. to SSB, Dec. 30, 1935, sub.: Alabama Plans for OAA and ADC and letter, Winant to State of Alabama, Jan. 4, 1936, National Archives, RG 47, Doc. 32, Commissioner's Action Meeting Documents, Welfare Administration.

27. Memo, BPA and GC to SSB, Dec. 28, 1935, sub.: Recommendations upon Missouri Plan for OAA, w/letter, Chm., SSB, to W. Ed Jameson, Pres., State Eleemosynary Institutions Bd., Jan. 6, 1936, National Archives, RG 47, 67A 1930, SSA 4325; memo, Hoey to W. L. Mitchell, Acting Exec. Dir., SSB, Mar. 9, 1939, sub.: Missouri—Legislative Amendments, National Archives, RG 47, 67A 1930, SSA 4325; McKinley and Frase, *Launching Social Security*, 146, 157–158.

28. SSB, Administrative Order no. 2 (revised 5/36), sub.: Procedure for Handling State Plans Submitted for Approval by the Board under Titles I, IV, and X of the Social Security Act, May 27, 1936; memo, BPA to SSB, Mar. 30, 1936, sub.: Status of State Plans submitted to the SSB but not yet approved, RG 47, SSA Central Files, 621.

29. Doc. 422, memo, BPA (Ivan Asay) to Exec. Dir., Jul. 15, 1936, sub.: Status of Pending Plans, Louisiana; Doc. 441, Rpt. on Pending Plans, Louisiana, July 1936; Doc. 134, memo, BPA to SSB, Mar. 30, 1936, sub.: Status of State Plans Submitted to the SSB but Not Yet approved, Massachusetts, OAA, AB, ADC, National Archives, RG 47, SSA Central Files, 621, Dec. 1935; memo, Hoey to Bane, Jan. 10, 1938, sub.: Mo. Rpt. for BPA (Dec. [1937]) file 317.2/21/2.

30. McKinley and Frase, *Launching Social Security*, 166–168.

31. Ibid., 169–174; SSB, Informal Minutes, Feb. 18, Mar. 24, Mar. 26, 1936; "Major Findings of Study of Administration of OAA in Ohio," Mar. 28, 1936, including, for quotations, letter, Bane to Davey, Mar. 28, 1936, BPA file, 061.11; Chm., SSB, to H. J. Berrodin, Chief, Div. of Aid for Aged, Columbus, Ohio, Mar. 31, 1936, same file; Resolution of the Board under Provisions of Title I, Section 4 of the Social Security Act—Providing for the Resumption of Payments to the State of Ohio under Its Plan for Old Age Assistance, Nov. 30, 1938, RG 47, Commissioners Action Meeting Documents.

32. McKinley and Frase, *Launching Social Security*, 174–176; memo, BPA to SSB, Mar. 11, 1936, sub.: Colorado State Plans for OAA, AB, and ADC, National Archives, RG 47, Doc. 106, Commissioner's Action Meeting Documents, Welfare Administration; memo, Herman McKaskle to Hoey, Mar. 12, 1936, sub.: Official Colorado State Relief Committee, same file; SSB, Minutes, Mar. 13, 1936; letter, Chm., SSB, to Ed C. Johnson, Governor of Colorado, Mar. 16, 1936, same file; letter, John C. Winant to the President, Mar. 17, 1936, with attachments, telegrams, Ed C. Johnson to the President, Mar. 12, 1936, for quotation and suggested reply, same file.

33. McKinley and Frase, *Launching Social Security*, 183–187; memo, BPA to SSB, Mar. 23, 1936, sub.: Illinois Plan for OAA, National Archives, RG 47, SSA, Commissioner's Action Meeting Documents, Doc. 195; SSB, Informal Minutes, Mar. 24, 1936; memo, Eliot to Members of the Board, May 5, 1936, sub.: Illinois OAA Plan; memo, Eliot to Members of the Board, May 7, 1936, sub.: Illinois OAA Plan, same file.

34. Quotation, SSB, Informal Minutes and Minutes, July 30, 1936; memo, Arnie Solem to Merrill G. Murray (Bureau of Unemployment Compensation), Aug. 21, 1936, sub.: Approach of BPA toward Qualifications and Standards of Experience of State Personnel, SSA Central Files, Box 233, 631–301.

35. SSB, *Annual Rpt., FY 1936*, 26; quotation, Bane, "Administrative Problems and Progress of SSB," Apr. 6, 1937, HHS Library.

36. McKinley and Frase, *Launching Social Security*, 147, 163–165; SSB Minutes, Apr. 7, 1936; SSB, *Annual Rpts., FY 1936*, 72, *FY 1937*, 96, *FY 1939*, 193.

298   *Notes to Pages 81–89*

4. The Unsettling Question

1. *Historical Statistics of the United States,* Series D 85–86, Unemployment: 1890–1970, 135.
2. Memo, Altmeyer to the President, Sept. 11, 1937, sub.: Amendments to the Social Security Act, reprinted in Altmeyer, *Formative Years of Social Security,* app. 3, 295–297.
3. Holtzman, *Townsend Movement,* 48–49, 88–89, 101–105; Brinkley, *Voices of Protest: Huey Long, Father Coughlin, and the Great Depression,* 79–80, 144–145, 154–155, 168.
4. SSB, *Annual Rpts., 1936,* 29, 35, 37, *1937,* 27, 28, 32, 36.
5. SSB, *Annual Rpts., 1936,* 29, 35, 37, *1937,* 27–28, 32–33, 36; remarks, Josephine Brown, BPA Field Staff Luncheon, Dec. 8, 1936, BPA file 321.22, Field Staff Conferences, Dec. 7 to Dec. 22, 1936.
6. Lansdale et al., *Administration of Old Age Assistance,* 115, 121–122.
7. SSB, *Annual Rpt., 1936,* 9–10, 25–26; SSB, Informal Minutes, Mar. 26, 1936.
8. Memo, Eliot to Bane, Dec. 6, 1935, RG 47, Social Security Admn. Executive File Unit, 600.
9. SSB, *Annual Rpt., 1936,* 31; Altmeyer, "If," 13–14.
10. Memo, Eliot to Exec. Dir., sub.: Need of Applicant as Condition of Approval of Plans for Public Assistance, May 3, 1937, RG 47, SSA Central Files, 621.1.
11. SSB, *Annual Rpt., 1936,* 31.
12. Lansdale, *Administration of OAA,* 83–84; SSB, *Annual Rpt., 1938,* 102–103; memo, Hoey to John J. Corson, Acting Exec. Dir., SSB, sub.: Monthly Rpt. for BPA, Dec. 7, 1937, BPA file 317.2/21–2, Oct 1937– .
13. Burns, *Social Security and Public Policy,* 21–25; Lansdale, *Administration of OAA,* 86–88; Meriam, *Relief and Social Security,* 33–34.
14. Memo (rough draft), Hoey to John J. Corson, Acting Exec. Dir., SSB, sub.: Monthly Rpt. for BPA (Nov.), Dec. 7, 1937, BPA file 317.2/21.2, Oct 1937– .
15. Lansdale, *Administration of OAA,* 83–85; Hoey to Corson, Dec. 7, 1937, sub.: Monthly Rpt. for BPA, BPA file 317.2/21–2, Oct 1937– .
16. SSB, Informal Minutes, May 4, 1937, BPA file 47–79–56; memo, Office of the General Counsel (Eliot) to Exec. Dir., May 3, 1937, sub.: Need of Applicant as Condition of Approval of Plans for Public Assistance, RG 47, SSA Central Files, 621.1; memo, Hoey to Oscar M. Powell, Exec. Dir., June 28, 1939, sub.: Grant Request for the Month of July 1939, RG 47 SSA 67A 1930, no. 4761A.
17. Memo, Office of the General Counsel (Eliot) to Exec. Dir., May 3, 1937; Burns, *Social Security and Public Policy,* 23; Property and Income Provisions in Approved State Plans for OAA, Nov. 20, 1937, RG 47, SSA Chairman's Files, 632.13, Payments; memo, Gertrude Gates, Chief, Div. of Plans and Grants, BPA, to Chief, Div. of Public Assistance Research and Statistics, Bureau of Research and Statistics, Nov. 23, 1940, sub.: Rpts. on Consideration of All Resources, BPA file 621, July 1940.
18. "Analysis of Grants to 586,000 Recipients of Old Age Assistance," 13, 15–17.
19. Property and Income Provisions in Approved State Plans for OAA, Nov. 20, 1937, RG 47, SSA Chairman's Files, 632.13, Payments; memo, Gertrude Gates, Chief, Div. of Plans and Grants, BPA, to Chief, Div. of Public Assistance Research and Statistics, Nov. 23, 1940, sub.: Reports on Consideration of All Resources, file 621, July 1940; transcript, Luncheon Meeting with Altmeyer and Bigge, Hoey and Staff, Dec. 14, 1938, file 321.2.2, Dec. 14, 1938, Conference.
20. SSB, Informal Minutes, May 4, 1937, file 47–79–56, California.

21. Transcript, Luncheon Meeting with Altmeyer and Bigge, Hoey and Staff, Dec. 14, 1938, Conference, including quotations; Burns, *Social Security and Public Policy*, 20–21.

22. Memo, Hoey to Bane, Oct. 15, 1936, sub.: Amendments to Social Security Act, RG 47, SSA Chairman's files, 011.1 Public Assistance.

23. Derthick, *Policymaking for Social Security*, 232–234, quotation at 232; Altmeyer, "If," 12; Altmeyer, *Formative Years of Social Security*, 108–110, 295–296.

24. Derthick, *Policymaking for Social Security*, 90–91; memo, Altmeyer to the President, Sept. 11, 1937, sub.: Amendments to the Social Security Act, reproduced in Altmeyer, *Social Security*, 295–296 (original in FDR Library, OF 1, 1710, 1935–1937).

25. Memo, Altmeyer to the President, Sept. 11, 1937, sub.: Amendments to the Social Security Act, in Altmeyer, *Formative Years of Social Security*, 295–296.

26. Memo, Altmeyer to the President, Sept. 11, 1937; Altmeyer, *Formative Years of Social Security*, 91; letter, Roosevelt to Altmeyer, Apr. 28, 1938, with notation attached, FDR Library, OF 2, 1710, Social Security Board 1938–39.

27. "Final Report of the Advisory Council on Social Security," reprinted in House, Ways and Means, "Social Security," Hearings Relative to the Social Security Act Amendments of 1939, 76th Cong., 1st sess., 1939, 26–27.

28. Rpt. of the Social Security Board, House Document no. 110, Jan. 16, 1939; "Social Security Act Amendments of 1939," House Rpt. no. 728, 1938; Altmeyer, *Formative Years of Social Security*, 101–103, 106, 111, 113; Derthick, *Policymaking for Social Security*, 232–237; Berkowitz, "The First Advisory Council and the 1939 Amendments," in Berkowitz, ed., *Social Security after Fifty*, 60–61.

29. Memo, Thomas I. Emerson to J. J. Corson, Dec. 28, 1936, no sub., with attachment, letter, Chairman, Social Security Board (Winant) to Daniel W. Bell, Dir., Bureau of the Budget, Jan. 5, 1937, RG 47, Social Security Administration, Executive Director's File Unit, and RG 47 SSA, Central files, 622.2; Altmeyer, *Formative Years of Social Security*, 105; "Social Security Act Amendments of 1939," House Rpt. no. 728, 1938, 10.

30. The three states outside the South and Southwest were Vermont, Delaware, and Nebraska. Virginia had no public assistance programs at this time. SSB, Informal Minutes, Mar. 26, 1936.

31. SSB, *Annual Rpt., FY 1938*, 104, and *FY 1939*, 115; Lansdale, *Administration of Old Age Assistance*, for quote, 182–189; memo, A. D. Smith, Office of the General Counsel, to Hoey, Oct. 7, 1938, sub.: Public Assistance Waiting Lists, RG 47, SSA Central files, 632.1, 1937–1939.

32. Memo, Wilbur J. Cohen, to W. R. Williamson, Actuarial Consultant, Mar. 17, 1941, sub.: Justification for Proportionate Grants to States, RG 47, Social Security Administration, Central Files, 622; Gerig, "Financial Participation of the Federal Government in State Welfare Programs," 22–23.

33. Gerig, "Financial Participation of the Federal Government in State Welfare Programs," 23–24; "Analysis of Grants to 586,000 Recipients of Old Age Assistance," 15.

34. Memo, Hoey to Bane, Oct. 15, 1936, sub.: Amendments to the Social Security Act; memo, Eleanor Lansing Dulles and Daniel Gerig, Research and Statistics, to Altmeyer, Dec. 15, 1936, sub.: Public Assistance Grants, Query as to Type of Plan and General Aims to be Furthered and Memo, Altmeyer to Dulles, Dec. 16, 1936, same sub., RG 47, Social Security Administration, Chairman's files, 011.1, Public Assistance.

35.   Duncan and Shelton, *Revolution in United States Government Statistics, 1926–1976,* 76–78, 81–82.
36.   Altmeyer, *Formative Years of Social Security,* 98, 104–107, 111–113; BPA, Joint Field Staff Meeting with Field Staff of the Bureau of Unemployment Security, Oct. 2, 1939, sub.: 1939 Amendments to the Social Security Act, BPA files, 011.1.
37.   Altmeyer Testimony, House, Ways and Means, *Social Security Act, 1939 Amendments Hearings,* Feb. 1–22, 1939, 2254, 2282, 2393–95, 2407, 2416–17; Mar. 29, 1939, 2253, 2256, 2394, 2407; Altmeyer quotations, Feb. 1–22, 1939, 2394, and Mar. 29, 1939, 2394; McCormack quotation, Feb. 1–22, 1939, 2382.
38.   BPA, Joint Staff Meeting with Field Staff of the Bureau of Unemployment Security, Oct. 2, 1939, sub.: 1939 Amendments to the Social Security Act, BPA files 011.1.
39.   *Congressional Record,* House, June 6, 1939, 6708–6709, 6850, 6859, 6877, 6897, 6901, 6907, 6913.

5. An Orphan Program

 1.   SSB, *Annual Rpts., FY 1938,* 99–101, *FY 1939,* 11, 15, 95–99; Witte, *Development of the Social Security Act,* 162–165; Social Security Act, Title IV–Grants to States for Aid to Dependent Children, Sec. 406, Approved Aug. 14, 1935, reprinted in Pifer and Chisman, eds., *Rpt. of the Committee on Economic Security of 1935,* 50th anniversary edition, 85.
 2.   SSB, *Social Security in America,* 248–249; (2) Security for Children, Summary of the Recommendations of the U.S. Children's Bureau . . . , Dec. 1, 1934, RG 47, Committee on Economic Security, Advisory Council–Misc; *Rpt. of the Committee on Economic Security,* 36.
 3.   SSB, *Annual Rpts., 1936,* 30, *1938,* 76; Hoey and Franklin, "Aid to Dependent Children," 30.
 4.   Hoey and Franklin, "ADC," 30–31; SSB, *Annual Rpt., 1939,* 96–97; *Historical Statistics of the U.S.,* Series A 160–171; B 28–35, 216–220; memo, McGuire to Austin, Dec. 7, 1938, sub.: Compilation of Material on ADC, RG 47, SSA, Exec. File Unit, 600.
 5.   Hoey and Franklin, "ADC," 31; House, Ways and Means, Hearings on HR 4120, *Economic Security Act,* 496.
 6.   Hoey and Franklin, "ADC," 31–32; FSA, SSB, BPA, *Aid to Dependent Children: A Study in Six States,* PA Rpt. no. 2, Nov. 1941, 58–59, 62.
 7.   Memo, Helen R. Jeter, Chief, Div. of Public Assistance Statistics, to Ewan Clague, Dir., Bureau of Research and Statistics, sub.: Memo on Suggested Amendment to Definition of Dependent Child in Title IV, Oct. 27, 1937, w/attachment, same sub., Oct. 25, 1937, BPA file 011.1; House, Ways and Means, *The Social Security Bill,* Rpt. to Accompany H.R. 7260, House Rpt. 615, 74th Cong., 1st sess., 18, 23, including quotations.
 8.   Memo, Jeter to Clague, Oct. 27, 1937, w/attach., Oct. 25, 1937; E. Abbott, "Public Assistance—Whither Bound?" 6–8; SSB, *Annual Rpt., 1940,* 14–15, 119.
 9.   Hoey and Franklin, "ADC," 34.
10.   SSB, *Annual Rpt., 1939,* 11.
11.   Memo, Jeter to Clague, Oct. 27, 1937, w/attach., Oct. 25, 1937; remarks, Alvin Roseman, BPA Luncheon Conference, Oct. 4, 1938, BPA file, 321.22.

12. Remarks, Roseman, BPA Luncheon Conference, Oct. 4, 1938.
13. Memo, Jeter to Clague, Oct. 27, 1937, w/attach., Oct. 25, 1937; remarks, Roseman, BPA Luncheon Conference, Oct. 4, 1938; SSB, Rpt., House Doc. 110, Jan. 16, 1939.
14. Social Security Act, Amendments of 1939, H.R. 6635, approved Aug. 1939, reprinted in Pifer and Chisman, eds., *Rpt. of the Committee on Economic Security of 1935*, 50th anniversary ed., 211–213, 228–229.
15. Remarks of Congressman Treadway, *Congressional Record,* House, June 6, 1939, 6697, 6700; Altmeyer remarks at BPA Joint Field Staff Meeting, Oct. 2, 1939, sub.: 1939 Amendments to the Social Security Act, BPA file 011.1; memo, Hoey to Staff, Sept. 13, 1939, sub.: Mo. Rpt., BPA, Aug. 1939, BPA file 317.2/21–2, Jan. 1940.
16. Altmeyer remarks at . . . Meeting, Oct. 2, 1939.
17. BPA Staff Meeting, Sept. 29, 1938, RG 47–53A118, file 321.2.2.
18. BPA, *Aid to Dependent Children: A Study in Six States,* PA Rpt. no. 2, Nov. 1941, 1, 3; BPA, *Families Receiving Aid to Dependent Children,* Oct. 1942, pt. I, 31–35, 41.
19. BPA, *ADC in Six States,* Nov. 1941, 19–23; BPA, *Families Receiving ADC,* Oct. 1942, pt. I, 31–35, 41.
20. BPA, *ADC in Six States,* Nov. 1941, 11; BPA, *Families Receiving ADC,* Oct. 1942, pt. I, 26–27.
21. BPA, *ADC in Six States,* Nov. 1941, 11–17; BPA, *Families Receiving ADC,* Oct. 1942, pt. I, 26–31, 41.
22. BPA, *ADC in Six States,* Nov. 1941, 39–41, 60. In explaining the more liberal interpretation of suitability of the home, the BPA also noted pressures due to lack of or inadequacy of general assistance or available foster care. Ibid., 41.
23. BPA, *ADC in Six States,* Nov. 1941, 7, 13, 47, 58–59; BPA, *Families Receiving ADC,* Oct. 1942, pt. I, 11–12, 31, 41, table 22.
24. BPA, *Families Receiving ADC,* Oct. 1942, pt. I, 3–4.
25. BPA, *ADC in Six States,* Nov. 1941, 35, 37, 63.
26. BPA, *ADC in Six States,* Nov. 1941, 48; Series H 346–367, Public Assistance—Payments, Recipients, and Average Monthly Payments, 1936–1970, *Historical Statistics of the U.S.,* 356; BPA, *Families Receiving ADC,* Oct. 1942, pt. I, 7, 30.
27. BPA, *Families Receiving ADC,* Oct. 1942, pt. I, 42, pt. II, 2.
28. Submittal for Board Consideration, BPA to Exec. Dir., Oct. 14, 1944, sub.: Reappraisal of ADC as a Category, w/attachments, memo, Hoey to Powell, same date, same sub., and statement by Marcus, no date, BPA file 607, Jun.–Dec. 1944; Marcus, "Reappraising Aid to Dependent Children as a Category," 3–5. The addition of alcoholism and venereal disease are mine in order to name two common causes of debility found in welfare caseloads.
29. Marcus, "Reappraising ADC as a Category," 4.
30. Title IV, Social Security Act, Sec. 402 (a) (15), *Compilation of the Social Security Laws,* House Doc. no. 93–117, vol. I, 192.

6. The Main Stem

1. Altmeyer, *Formative Years of Social Security,* 117–124.
2. Interview, Bigge w/Abe Bortz, 1965, SSA Historian's Office; Bigge obituary, *Washington Post,* Dec. 6, 1977; SSB, *Annual Report, FY 1939,* 6.

3. Altmeyer, *Formative Years of Social Security.* 122–123; Cates, *Insuring Inequality,* 54–58.
4. Altmeyer, *Formative Years of Social Security,* 126, 128, 130; Cates, *Insuring Inequality,* 59–70; Holtzman, *Townsend Movement,* 49.
5. BPA, Bureau Circular no. 9 (Preliminary), State Administration, pt. I, Plan of Operations, June 18, 1938, 104, 106, 106.4, 109, HHS Library, Archives.
6. "What the Social Security Act Is Doing to Aid the Needy," a discussion by Frank Bane and Jane M. Hoey, Mutual Broadcasting Co., Jan. 23, 1936, in U.S. Social Security Board, Addresses of Frank Bane, nos. 1–10, 1936–1938, HHS Library.
7. Perkins, "The Outlook for Economic and Social Security in America," 62; Key, *Administration of Federal Grants to States,* 265–266; Klein, *Civil Service in Public Welfare,* 41–46.
8. Memo, Technical Consultant on Personnel, Div. of Standards and Procedures, BPA, to Albert Aronson, Chief, State Technical Advisory Service, Sept. 12, 1938, sub.: Study of Personnel in a Selected Group of State Plans for Public Assistance, w/attachment, Sept. 8, 1938, same sub., BPA file, 631.3.
9. SSB, Informal Minutes, Dec. 14, 1937, RG 47-79-56; BPA Mo. Rpt., Dec. 1937; Jan. 10, 1938, BPA file, 317.2/21.2.
10. SSB, Informal Minutes, Dec. 2, 1938; SSB, minutes, Dec. 2, 1938.
11. Standards for Personnel Administration in State Unemployment Compensation and State Public Assistance Agencies, adopted by the SSB, Dec. 17, 1938, BPA file 631, 301, Jan. 1939–Apr. 1939; Standards for Personnel Administration in State Public Assistance Agencies, adopted by SSB, Dec. 23, 1938, same file; SSB Informal Minutes, Dec. 14, 1937.
12. Memo, Hoey to Altmeyer, Apr. 24, 1939, sub.: State Situations Which Illustrate the Need for Merit System Requirements in Federal Act, BPA file, 631.31. The other states named were Arkansas, Colorado, Indiana, Kentucky, Nebraska, Ohio, and Tennessee.
13. Ibid.
14. BPA, Joint Staff Meeting w/Field Staff, Bureau of Employment Security, Oct. 2, 1939, sub.: Amendments to the Social Security Act, BPA file, 011.1.
15. Standards for a Merit System of Personnel Adminstration in State Unemployment Compensation, State Employment Service, and State Public Assistance Agencies Adopted by the SSB, Oct. 1939, SSA Submittals, Doc. 4062–0.
16. Memo, Hoey to Regional Directors, Apr. 28, 1941, sub.: Development of Merit System in State Public Assistance Agencies, BPA file 631.301, May 1941–June 1941.
17. "Personnel in State and Local Public Assistance Agencies, June 1949," 1–9.
18. Epler, "Public Assistance Employees: Their Education," 13–21, 31.
19. SSB, Minutes, Dec. 23, 1937; memo, BPA to Exec. Dir., Dec. 10, 1937, RG 47, SSA Commissioner's Action Meeting Documents, Docket 2520.
20. Leighninger, *Social Work: Search for Identity,* 125–127; Brown, *Public Relief,* 282–298.
21. Leighninger, *Social Work,* 127; Steiner, *Social Insecurity,* chap 7.
22. Letter, Hoey to Wisner, Feb. 8, 1938, BPA file, 631.34.
23. Draft Report, AASSW, "Education for the Public Social Services, A Report of the Study Committee," Oct. 1, 1940, BPA file 64, AASSW Committee on Study Training Needs in Public Social Services; AASSW, *Education for the Public Social Services.* The Library of Congress copy is stamped "Received Jul 18, 1942, Copyright Office."
24. AASSW, *Education for the Public Social Services,* 18–19, 22–23.

25. Leighninger, *Social Work,* 131.
26. Emilia E. Martinez-Brawley, "From Countrywoman to Federal Relief Adminis-trator: Josephine Chapin Brown, A Biographical Study," 13–15, MS article in possession of its author. The letters quoted are: Wisner to E. Abbott and E. Abbott to Wisner, Oct. 29, 1937 and Nov. 3, 1937, respectively, AASSW files, U.S. Committee on Training and Personnel; E. Abbott to Leona Masoth, AASSW, Apr. 29, 1943, Council on Social Work Education Coll., Social Welfare History Archives, University of Minnesota. See also Davenport and Davenport, "Josephine Brown's Classic Book Still Guides Rural Social Work." For the Brown-Lenroot friendship, *see* interview, Lenroot w/Peter Corning, 1965, CUOHC.

    Despite her many publications, which include two major books, and her pioneer-ing contributions to public welfare, including teaching the subject at Catholic Uni-versity's School of Social Work where she had obtained the M.A., Brown never was accorded so much as a mention in the *Encyclopedia of Social Work.* However, Walter Trattnor's *Encyclopedia of Social Work and Social Welfare* contains a bio by Martinez-Brawley, and a bio by me for the *American National Biography.* is forth-coming.

27. Leighninger, *Social Work,* 125–126, 133–143; Hollis and Taylor, *Social Work Education in the United States,* passim.
28. Leighninger, *Social Work,* chap. 5, p. 35.
29. Memo, Hoey to Powell, Mar. 7, 1941, sub.: Staff Development Programs in State Public Assistance Agencies—Revised, with attachment, same sub., BPA file 631.39, Jan. 1941; SSB, Minutes, Mar. 14, 1941.
30. These conclusions draw on Steiner, *Social Insecurity,* chap. 7; Etzioni, ed., *The Semi-Professions and Their Organization*; and my own recollections of the staff and practices in the Family Welfare Association, Baltimore, where I worked as a stenographer, 1935–1940.
31. Rachel B. Marks, "Towle, Charlotte Helen," *Notable American Women: The Modern Period,* 695–697.
32. Minutes of Executive Staff Meeting of the bureau, Nov. 30, 1944, to discuss Document on Public Assistance Service by Grace Marcus, BPA file 670.
33. Grace Marcus, *Nature of Service in Public Assistance Administration,* Public Assistance Rpt. no. 10, 1946, 3–4, 20, 32, quotation at 31; Executive Staff Meeting, Nov. 30, 1944; memo, Van Driel to Turner, July 12, 1944, sub.: Ms. on Public Assistance Service, BPA file, 670.
34. Marcus, *Nature of Service in Public Assistance Administration,* iii.
35. Towle, *Common Human Needs,* 15, 145, quotation at 79.
36. ADC Characteristics Studies, 1942 and 1948; *Historical Statistics of the U.S.,* Series H 346–367, 356. The case analysis is mine.
37. Memo, Goodwin, Act. Dir., BPA, to Regional Directors, Sept. 13, 1945, Attn. PA Reps., sub.: *Common Human Needs* by Charlotte Towle, BPA file, 658.
38. "Personnel in State and Local Public Assistance Agencies, June 1949," 7–12.
39. Epler, "Public Assistance Employees: Their Education," 14.
40. *Social Security Bulletin, Annual Statistical Supplement,* 1983, tables 5.3, 248, and 5.6, 254.
41. Memo, Hoey to Powell, July 26, 1939, sub.: Request for Additional Funds for BPA to Permit Bureau to Assume Responsibility for Verification of Eligibility of Recipients of Public Assistance, RG 47, SSA Executive Director's file unit, 622.2, Jan.–Dec., 1939; memo, Altmeyer to Powell, July 31, 1939, same file; memo, Staten to W. L. Mitchell, Asst. Exec. Dir., Dec. 22, 1939, sub.: Public Assistance Audit, RG 47, SSA Central Files, 620, Jan. 1939; SSB, Minutes, Dec. 22, 1939.

42. Review of State and Local Administration, 1940–1942, 24–25, BPA file, 630, Administrative Review 1940–1942; Goodwin, "Administrative Review in Public Assistance," 6.

43. Memo, Hoey to Powell, July 22, 1940, sub.: Family Budgeting, RG 47, Submittals for Meetings, no. 3950c.

44. Letter, Bane, to H. J. Early, Dir. Emergency Relief Admin., Louisiana, Oct. 27, 1936, RG 47, Submittals for Meetings nos. 3950–3963; SSB, Informal Minutes, Aug. 2, 1940, Mar. 24, 1942; letter, Hoey to Howard L. Russell, APWA, Sept. 4, 1944, BPA file, 672.11. Hoey's words were: "The Board has recognized that certain practical difficulties are involved for the States administering categorical programs. It was the recognition of these practical difficulties that induced the Board as early as 1936 to construe the Act broadly in relation to the expenses involved in household operation." Ibid.

   Jerry Cates, in his book *Insuring Inequality* (1983), 119–134, does not mention the early liberal decision of 1936 covering general household expenses. This omission leads him to discuss family budgeting as if born anew and devoid of precedent in 1940. The position taken by the board members Bigge, Dewson/Woodward, even Altmeyer, in the course of discussion, therefore becomes skewed toward illiberality. The accuracy of Cates's discussion is not helped by his failure to take account of what is contained in the Informal Minutes of Board Meetings—the notes taken and preserved by Maurine Mulliner, the secretary of the Social Security Board. Worse still, Cates ignores the formal, official Minutes of the Social Security Board. For example, he states that the board entered a "formal admonition" to the BPA regarding unwarranted, informal guidance by regional public assistance staff to state staff. Cates cites the Informal Minutes of Board Meetings to prove that a "formal admonition" was taken. This is incorrect. To be sure, the board discussed an admonition as a possible step on October 15, 1943, but decided, after a vote, *not* to take this step. A note in Maurine Mulliner's handwriting reads "No" and directs the reader to the directive adopted. Because there was no formal admonition, the Board Minutes of October 15, 1943, are silent. My files, which are open for examination, contain many more examples of Cates's omissions/commissions. Cates's sweeping charge that a "fundamental conflict of interest existed for the SSB/SSA during the period under study: that given the SSB's overwhelming commitment to the primacy of conservative social insurance, it did not do an equitable job of developing America's public assistance system," is hereby challenged.

45. BPA Conference of Regional Representatives, May 26–29, 1941, 23. Peter Kasius, the lead staffer on family budgeting, is speaking.

46. General assistance figures from *Historical Statistics of the U.S.*, Series H 346–367.

47. Memo, Hoey to Powell, July 22, 1940, sub.: Family Budgeting, Submittals for Board Meetings, 3950–C; SSB, Informal Minutes, June 29, 1940.

48. Memo, Hoey to Powell, May 19, 1941, sub.: Establishment of Need and Determination of Payments to Applicants for Public Assistance, with attachment, Hoey to Powell, May 19, 1941, same sub. Submittals for Board Meetings, no. 3950m; SSB, Minutes, July 2, 1941.

49. BPA Conference for Regional Representatives, May 29, 1941, BPA file, Edited Transcripts of Field Staff Meetings, May 26–29, 1941.

50. SSB, Informal Minutes, Mar. 24, 1942.

51. SSB, Informal Minutes, May 15, 1943; SSB, Minutes, May 15, 1943; memo, Bigge to Altmeyer, Oct. 13, 1943, sub.: Family Budgeting—PA Memo of Oct. 9, 1943, for Board Consideration, BPA file, 672.111.

52. SSB, Informal Notes, Oct. 15, 1943; SSB, Minutes, Oct. 15, 1943; cf. Cates, *Insuring Inequality,* 118–132.
53. SSB, Informal Minutes, Dec. 3, 1943; SSB, Minutes, Dec. 3, 1943.
54. Memos (2), Gates, Act. Dir. BPA, to Powell, Apr. 5, 1944, sub.: Federal Matching of Assistance Payments in Which the Need of the Individual Is Affected by the Presence in the Household of Persons Essential to His Well-Being, Submittals for Board Meetings, no. 3950aa.
55. SSB, Informal Minutes, Apr. 14, 1944; SSB, Minutes, May 16, 1944.
56. Letter, Howard L. Russell, Director, APWA, to Hoey, Aug. 4, 1944, and Hoey to Russell, Sept. 4, 1944, BPA file 672.11.
57. Bigge, "Looking Ahead in Public Assistance," 4–8.
58. Altmeyer, *Formative Years of Social Security,* 119.
59. Bell, *Aid to Dependent Children,* 191; Derthick, *Uncontrollable Spending for Social Services Grants,* 22.

7. The Safety Net

1. *Historical Statistics of the U.S.,* I, Series D 85–86, Unemployment: 1890–1970, 135; ibid., I, Series D 927–939, Labor Union Membership, by Affiliation; 1935–1970, 177; Bureau of the Budget, *United States at War,* 431–432.
2. Altmeyer, *Formative Years of Social Security,* chap. 5; Sherwood, *Roosevelt and Hopkins,* 230–231, 361.
3. Quoted by President Harry S. Truman, "Special Message to Congress," Sept. 6, 1945, *Public Papers and Addresses,* 1945, 279–280; Perkins, *The Roosevelt I Knew,* 283–284; Altmeyer, *Formative Years of Social Security,* 133–138, 141–144; Morris, *Encyclopedia of American History,* 350.
4. *Historical Statistics of the U.S.,* Series D, 85–86, Unemployment: 1890–1970, 135; Morison, *Oxford History of the American People,* 1046–60, 1065–67, 1074–76; Link et al., *American People,* II, 832–849; McCullough, *Truman,* 550–553.
5. Truman, "Special Message to Congress," Sept. 6, 1945, *Public Papers and Addresses,* 1945, no. 128; Link, et al., *American People,* II, 829.
6. Altmeyer, *Formative Years of Social Security,* 153–154, 158–160, 162–163, 171; Posner, "Charlotte Towle: A Biography," Ph.D. diss., University of Chicago, 1986, 234, University Microfilm Pub. no. 8703812.
7. Altmeyer, *Formative Years of Social Security,* 164–165, 175–178; Posner, "Charlotte Towle," 228–229.
8. Altmeyer, *Formative Years of Social Security,* 173–175; "Public Assistance Goals: Recommendations of the Social Security Board," 2–8; "Issues in Social Security," 3–9.
9. Interview, Cohen w/Coll, Oct. 25, 1985; letter, Eloise Cohen, to Coll, Oct. 28, 1989; interview, Wickenden w/Coll, May 28, 1986; Derthick, *Policymaking for Social Security,* 52–55.
10. House, Ways and Means, *Social Security Act Amendments of 1949,* Hearings, 82, 110, 225, 230–231.
11. *Historical Statistics of the U.S.,* Series H 48–56, Civilian Labor Force and Workers Covered Under Government Social Insurance Programs: 1934 to 1970, 342; Series H 230–237, Old Age, Survivors, Disability, and Health Insurance—Number and Average Monthly Benefits in Current-Payment Status, by Selected Family Groups, 1940 to 1970, 350; Series H 346–367, Public Assistance—Payments, Recipients, and Average Monthly Payments: 1936 to 1970, 356.

12. Altmeyer, *Formative Years of Social Security*, 169–170; Elizabeth Wickenden, APWA, Testimony, House, Ways and Means, *Social Security Act Amendments of 1949*, Hearings, 225.

13. *Historical Statistics of the U.S.*, Series H 346–367, Public Assistance—Payments, Recipients, and Average Monthly Payments: 1936 to 1970, 356.

14. Altmeyer, *Formative Years of Social Security*, 185; Cohen and Myers, "Social Security Act Amendments of 1950: A Summary and Legislative History," 7.

15. Altmeyer testimony, House, Ways and Means, *Social Security Act Amendments of 1949*, 103; Wickenden testimony, same hearings, 225.

16. "Public Welfare Platform—Objectives for Public Welfare Legislation in 1949," House, Ways and Means, *Social Security Act Amendments of 1949*, Hearings, 230.

17. Wickenden testimony, House, Ways and Means, *Social Security Act Amendments of 1949*, Hearings, 1949, 230.

18. *Historical Statistics of the U.S.*, Series H 346–367, Public Assistance—Payments, Recipients, and Average Monthly Payments: 1936 to 1970, 356; Altmeyer testimony, House, Ways and Means, *Social Security Act Amendments of 1949*, Hearings, 1949, 76; Altmeyer, *Formative Years of Social Security*, 134, 152, 155.

19. House, Ways and Means, *Social Security Act Amendments of 1949*, Hearings, 7, 76–78, 84–85, 100–101.

20. Ibid., 171; House, Rpt. no. 1300, *Social Security Act Amendments of 1949*, 53.

21. Altmeyer, *Formative Years of Social Security*, 153–157; Murray, "Social Security Act Amendments of 1946," 2–3; Senate, Finance, Rpt. no. 1862, *Social Security Amendments of 1946*, 1946; House, Ways and Means, Rpt. no. 2526, *Social Security Act Amendments of 1946*, pt. 2, 1–4.

22. *Social Security Bulletin, Annual Statistical Supplement*, 1983, 47; Altmeyer, *Formative Years of Social Security*, 163.

23. Cohen and Myers, "Social Security Act Amendments of 1950: A Summary and Legislative History," 5; State Letter no. 129, Sept. 26, 1950; State Letter no. 274, Aug. 20, 1956; Charles I. Schottland, "Social Security Amendments of 1956: A Summary and Legislative History."

24. House, Ways and Means, Rpt. no. 1300, Aug. 22, 1949, 44.

25. Elizabeth Wickenden, "Social Welfare Law: The Concept of Risk and Entitlement," *University of Detroit Law Journal* 43 (1966): 517; Interview, Wickenden with Coll, 1986.

26. ADC Characteristics Study, "ADC in a Postwar Year," June 1948, 8; House, Ways and Means, Rpt. no. 1300, Aug. 22, 1949; Steiner, *Social Insecurity*, 94–96, 114–118; BPA, State Letter no. 160, June 11, 1951, sub.: Handbook of Public Assistance Administration—pt. IV, chap. 8100, "Notice to Law-Enforcement Officials—Aid to Dependent Children."

27. Steiner, *Social Insecurity*, 90–96.

28. House, Ways and Means, *Social Security Act Amendments of 1949*, Hearings, 228, 233.

29. Hoey, "The Federal Government and Desirable Standards of State and Local Administration," 442; BPA Staff Meeting, Sept. 29, 1938; Hoey, "Next Steps in Public Assistance," 158–159.

30. Hoey testimony, House, Ways and Means, *Social Security Act Amendments of 1949*, Hearings, 401–404, 407–410.

31. John O'Grady, Testimony, House, Ways and Means, *Social Security Act Amendments of 1949*, Hearings, 540–541; Cohen and Myers, "Social Security Act Amendments of 1950: A Summary and Legislative History," 8.

32. House, Ways and Means, *Social Security Amendments of 1949*, Rpt. no. 1300, Aug. 22, 1949, 55.

33. Steiner, *Social Insecurity*, 21–23, 26, 34–35, 71–72; House, Ways and Means, *Social Security Act Amendments of 1949*, Hearings, 103; House, Ways and Means, *Social Security Act Amendments of 1949*, Rpt. no. 1300, 37–38.

34. *Historical Statistics of the U.S.*, Series H 346–367, Public Assistance—Payments, Recipients, and Average Monthly Payments: 1936 to 1970, 356.

35. Hoey testimony, House, Ways and Means, *Social Security Act Amendments of 1949*, Hearings, 398.

36. Senate debate on House Bill no. 6000, June 12, 1950, *Congressional Record*, 8767; Altmeyer, *Formative Years of Social Security*, 273.

37. Derthick, *Policymaking for Social Security*, 67–68; Leiby, *Charity and Correction in New Jersey*, 376–377; Miles, *The Department of Health, Education, and Welfare*, 36, 310–311; Berkowitz and McQuaid, *Creating the Welfare State*, 173–175, 179–188; Sanford M. Jacoby, "Employees and the Welfare State: The Role of Marion B. Folsom," 525–526.

38. Derthick, *Policymaking for Social Security*, 151–153; Altmeyer, *Formative Years of Social Security*, app. 1, 282–285.

39. Mugge, "Concurrent Receipt of Public Assistance and Old-Age, Survivors, and Disability Insurance," 12–14, 17–18.

40. Derthick, *Policymaking for Social Security*, 304–315; Edward D. Berkowitz, *Disabled Policy*, chaps. 2 and 3.

41. Div. of Administrative Surveys, BPA, "Some Aspects of the Administration of Aid to the Blind," Apr. 1943, BPA file 606, 1943–1948; Hill, "Aid to the Permanently and Totally Disabled," 12–13, 15; memo, Hoey to Powell, Oct. 11, 1943, sub: Definition of Incapacity in Aid to Dependent Children in Relation to Definition of Disability in Old-Age and Survivors Insurance, BPA file, 672.72.

42. *Historical Statistics of the U.S.*, I, table H 346–367, Public Assistance—Payments, Recipients, and Average Monthly Payments: 1936 to 1970, 356; Mugge, "Concurrent Receipt of Public Assistance and Old-Age, Survivors, and Disability Insurance," 12.

43. In June 1948, the percentage of families receiving ADC due to incapacity of the father was 26.6; in November 1953, it was 21.3 (Alling and Leisy, "Aid to Dependent Children in a Postwar Year: Characteristics of Families Receiving ADC, June 1948," Div. of Statistics and Analysis, BPA, June 1950, 8, 28; BPA, "Characteristics of Families Receiving Aid to Dependent Children, November 1953," Nov. 1953, 15).

44. BPA, State Letter no. 129, Sept. 26, 1950, sub.: Conference of State Administrators—Washington, D.C., Sept. 11–13, 1950—Supplemental Information.

45. Hill, "Aid to the Permanently and Totally Disabled," 11, 14, 15; Hoey testimony, House, Appropriations, *Department of Labor–Federal Security Agency Appropriation*, Hearings, 1953, pt. 1, 269.

46. Cohen and Myers, "Social Security Amendments of 1950," 3.

8. The Welfare Mess

1. Steiner, *Social Insecurity*, 91–93, 97–98; *U.S. News and World Report*, Oct. 19, 1951, 26–27.

2. *Historical Statistics of the U.S.*, table VII, Requirements for Filing Individual Income Tax Returns: 1913–1970, 1093; table VIII, Federal Individual Income

Tax Exemptions and First Top Bracket Rates, 1913–1970, 1095, Series Y 652–670, State and Local Government Revenue by Source: 1902–1970, 1125–26.

3. See, for example: Rufus Jarman, "Detroit Cracks Down on Relief Chiselers," *Saturday Evening Post,* Dec. 10, 1949; Paul Molloy, "The Relief Chiselers Are Stealing Us Blind," *Saturday Evening Post,* Sept. 8, 1951; "In Biggest Boom—Millions on Relief," *U.S. News and World Report,* Oct. 19, 1951; Jacob Panken, "Relief Can Mean Ruin," *Reader's Digest* (excerpts from the *Saturday Evening Post*); W. T. Brannon, "Chicago's Relief Revolution," *Reader's Digest,* Feb. 1952 (condensed from *Kiwanis Magazine*); Jerome Beatty, "A New Trap for Runaway Husbands," *Saturday Evening Post,* Apr. 19, 1952. RG 363, BPA file 607, Criticisms of Program, contains the above articles and others. Harold Silver, Director, Jewish Social Service Bureau of Detroit, "The Current Threat to Relief Standards," a paper delivered at Family Service Association of America Board Members Institute, Mar. 18, 1950. Same file.

4. Henry F. and Katharine Pringle, "The Case for Federal Relief," *Saturday Evening Post,* July 19, 1952.

5. Memo, Elizabeth Wickenden to Members of the APWA Committee on Welfare Policy and Services to Children, Mar. 15, 1950, sub.: Desertion across State Lines, APWA files, Social Welfare History Archives, University of Minnesota; memo, Jules H. Berman to Hoey, Aug. 9, 1951, sub.: Interstate Support Legislation, BPA file, 610 Council of State Governments, 1949– ; Jerome Beatty, "A New Trap for Runaway Husbands," *Saturday Evening Post,* Apr. 19, 1952.

6. Posner, "Charlotte Towle," 224–225, quotation at 225.

7. Posner, "Charlotte Towle," 226–228, 240–246, 250–251; letter, Hoey to Towle, May 31, 1951, BPA file, 321–2.1, PA Rpt. no. 8; letter, Hoey to Helen R. Livingston, Legislative Ref., LC, Mar. 26, 1952, with enclosures, same file. In his answer to Towle, Ewing noted that *Common Human Needs* was being reprinted by the NASW. In the 1957 edition published by NASW, the offending sentence reads: "Social Security and public assistance programs are a basic requirement for the development of the mature personality, a state of being essential if democracy as a way of life is to be realized in full measure." *Common Human Needs,* 1957 ed., 74.

8. Steiner, *Social Insecurity,* 48, 97; Cohen, "Social Security Amendments of 1952," 3, 8–9; Cohen, Ball, and Myers, "Social Security Act Amendments of 1954: A Summary and Legislative History," 3, 15; Schottland, "Social Security Amendments of 1956: A Summary and Legislative History," 3, 10–11; Cohen, "The Social Security Amendments of 1958: Another Important Step Forward," Subcommittee on Income Maintenance and Social Security of the Coordinating Committee on Social Welfare Research, School of Social Work, University of Michigan, Oct. 17, 1958, 4–7, Social Welfare History Archives, University of Minnesota, APWA Collection; Schottland, "Social Security Amendments of 1958: A Summary and Legislative History," 3–13.

9. Steiner, *Social Insecurity,* 50–57; Derthick, *Policymaking for Social Security,* 40–43.

10. Cohen, "The Social Security Act Amendments of 1958: Another Important Step Forward," 11–12; Long quotation, *Congressional Record,* S, June 25, 1959, 1958–63.

11. *Congressional Record,* S, June 25, 1959, 10860, 10862; E. Perkins, "State and Local Financing of Public Assistance, 1935–1955," 5. Long omitted ADC from his package in proposing an amendment in 1958. Steiner, *Social Insecurity,* 54–55. Interview, Cohen w/Coll, Oct. 19, 1985, Coll files.

12. Katz, *Poverty and Policy in American History*, 18–54; Richmond, *Friendly Visiting among the Poor*, 73–74.
13. Draft, Handbook of Public Assistance Administration, pt. IV, Eligibility and Payments to Individuals, 2/12/52, attachment to letter to Frank Bane et al., Mar. 3, 1952, BPA file, 672.71 NOLEO.
14. Letter, Dunn to Altmeyer, Apr. 22, 1952, BPA file 672.71 NOLEO.
15. Letter, Schottland to Altmeyer, Mar. 18, 1952, BPA file 672.71 NOLEO.
16. BPA, State Letter no. 177, June 26, 1952, sub.: Notice to Law Enforcement Officials—Aid to Dependent Children; Recommendations and Report on Final Meeting of the Advisory Group.
17. State Letter no. 198, Feb. 24, 1953, sub.: Requests to Bureau of Old Age and Survivors Insurance for Addresses of Deserting Parents.
18. Memo, Jules H. Berman, Acting Chief, Division of Program Standards and Development, to Jay L. Roney, Director, BPA, Dec. 29, 1945, sub.: Mr. Schottland's Interest in the Development of State Programs for Family Desertion, with attachment, Schottland to Roney, Dec. 14, 1954, sub.: Development of State Programs on Problem of Family Desertion, BPA file, 672.71.
19. Kaplan, "Support from Absent Fathers in Aid to Dependent Children," 3–13; Jules H. Berman, interview w/Coll, Aug. 20, 1987, Coll files.
20. Memo, w/attachments, John J. Hurley, Chief, Div. of Program Operations to Regional Representatives, PA, Sept. 18, 1959, sub: Amendment to BOASI Regulation no. 1 to Provide for Release of Information from BOASI Records about Deserting Fathers in Administration of the ADC Program, BPA file 664.4121 Deserting Fathers, 1959; State Letter no. 402, Mar. 19, 1960, sub.: Referrals to Bureau of Old Age and Survivors Insurance for Addresses of Deserting Parents.
21. Bell, *Aid to Dependent Children*, 29, citing Ways and Means Committee, Rpt. no. 615, 24.
22. Ibid., 29.
23. Ibid., 74, 77–78.
24. Ibid., 50–51; State Letter no. 46, Mar. 5, 1945, sub.: "Suitable Home" Provisions of State Plans for Aid to Dependent Children.
25. Bell, *Aid to Dependent Children*, 93–94. The states were: Arkansas, Connecticut, Florida, Georgia, Illinois, Iowa, Louisiana, Michigan, Mississippi, New Jersey, New York, Oregon, South Dakota, Tennessee, Texas, Vermont, Virginia, and Wisconsin. Ibid., 51, 58.
26. Ibid., 96–98.
27. Ibid., 124–130. Tennessee had a similar law. Ibid., 124–125, 133–134.
28. Ibid., 111–117.
29. *Historical Statistics of the U.S.*, Pt. I, Series D 42–48, Civilian Labor Force as Percent of Civilian Noninstitutional Population, by Race and Sex, 1940 to 1970; Series D 49–62, Marital Status of Women in the Civilian Labor Force: 1890 to 1970, pt. 1, 133.
30. *Historical Statistics of the U.S.*, Series D 63–74, Married Woman (Husband Present) in the Labor Force, by Age and Presence of Children: 1948 to 1970, 134.
31. *Historical Statistics of the U.S.*, Series H 236–367, Public Assistance . . . 1936–1970, I, 356.
32. Quoted in Alvin Schorr, "Problems in the ADC Program," w/attachment, Kathryn Goodwin to Reg. Reps., July 8, 1959, BPA file 607, Alvin Schorr's Paper.

33. Schorr paper citing Margaret Greenfield, *Self-Support in Aid to Dependent Children, the California Experience.*

34. Cox, "The Employment of Mothers as a Means of Family Support," 15.

35. Blackwell and Gould, *Future Citizens All,* 50–51, 57; Burgess and Price, *An American Dependency Challenge,* 26, 160; BFS, Characteristics of Families Receiving AFDC, Nov.–Dec. 1961, table 23, Status of Mother in AFDC Families, by State within Census Divisions, for a selected month, Nov.–Dec. 1961. Eighteen states had maximums: Alabama, Arkansas, Delaware, Florida, Indiana, Iowa, Kansas, Louisiana, Maine, Mississippi, Missouri, Nebraska, North Carolina, South Carolina, Tennessee, Texas, Vermont, and Virginia.

36. Coll, "How Work Incentives Affect Welfare Rolls," 12.

37. Handwork of Public Assistance Administration, pt. IV, Eligibility and Payments to Individuals, 12/8/61, w/attachment, Development of Policies and Procedures Relating to Recipient Fraud in Public Assistance, Dec. 1961, transmitted by State Letter no. 540.

38. George E. Bigge, Federal Audit of State Eligibility, Nov. 12, 1952, Coll files.

39. Memo, Saya S. Schwartz, C, Div. of State Administrative and Fiscal Standards, to Goodwin, Mar. 8, 1957, sub.: Attached Draft Materials on Special Investigating Units; memo, Schwartz to Roney, Oct. 31, 1957, sub.: Development of Materials Relative to the Inquiry on Special Methods of Investigation in Public Assistance Agencies, BPA file 671.4, 1954; Bell, *Aid to Dependent Children,* 158.

40. Bigge, Federal Audit of State Eligibility, Nov. 12, 1952, Coll files.

41. Bureau Committee on Reconsideration of the Administrative Review, Minutes, Sept. 27, 1943, BPA file 620.6, 1944–45.

42. Chart, Major Developments in the Continuing Review of State and Local Public Assistance Administration by the Bureau of Public Assistance, 1940–1952, attachment to memo, Mary E. Austin, Chief, Div. of Prgm. Opns., to Regional Directors, Mar. 23, 1953, BPA file 620.6 General 1944–1955; Bell, *Aid to Dependent Children,* 190–191; Goodwin, "Administrative Review in Public Assistance," 9; interview, Jules H. Berman w/Coll, Aug. 20, 1987, Coll files; Derthick, *The Influence of Federal Grants: Public Assistance in Massachusetts,* 88.

43. Interview, Charles Schottland w/Peter Corning, CUOHC, 1965; Title IV, Social Security Act 1935 and 1956; Schottland, "Social Security Amendments of 1956: A Summary and Legislative History," 3–4, 10–11; Steiner, *Social Insecurity,* 40–42, 75–76.

44. Interview, Alvin L. Schorr w/Coll, June 12, 1987, Coll files.

45. Alvin L. Schorr, "Problems in the ADC Program," Preliminary Draft, May 19, 1959, attachment to memo, Goodwin to Regional Representatives, July ? 1959, sub.: Aid to Dependent Children Program—Analysis of Some Problems by Alvin Schorr, BPA file, 607, Alvin Schorr's Paper.

46. Berman to Schorr, Feb. 27, 1959, no sub., BPA file 607 Alvin Schorr's Paper; memo, Mitchell to Roney, Mar. 20, 1959, sub.: Rpt. on "Problems in the ADC Program," Mar. 20, 1959, same file; memo, Roney to Mitchell, Mar. 26, 1959, sub.: Publication of Mr. Schorr's report, "Problems in the ADC Program," same file.

47. Memo, George K. Wyman, to Roney et al., June 23, 1959, sub.: Meeting to Discuss Paper on "Problems in the ADC Program," w/attachments, including Comments of Marion K. Craine, staff of the Welfare Council of Metropolitan Chicago, June 5, 1959; letter, Cohen to Mitchell, June 8, 1959; and Wickenden to Mitchell, BPA file 607, Alvin Schorr's Paper.

48. Memos, Mitchell to Goodwin, Dec. 24, 1959, sub.: Publication of Paper on "Problems in the ADC Program"; Goodwin to Mitchell, Jan. 18, 1960, sub.: Publication of Mr. Schorr's Paper on ADC—Your Memorandum of Dec. 24, 1959; Mitchell to Goodwin, Feb. 2, 1960, sub.: Publication of Mr. Schorr's Paper.

49. BPA, ADC Characteristics Study, 1956; E. Perkins, "Old Age Assistance and Aid to Dependent Children, 1940–50," 11–15, 29; Steiner, *Social Insecurity,* 92–93.

50. Blackwell and Gould, *Future Citizens All,* xxii–xxviii, 37, 77–79, 95, 114–115, 136–138.

51. Burgess and Price, *An American Dependency Challenge,* vii, 4, 6–7, quotation at 6. Eight states—Alaska, Arkansas, California, Georgia, Maryland, New Mexico, Oregon, and Tennessee—with about 18 percent of ADC families, did not participate.

52. *Historical Statistics of the U.S.,* Table H 346–367, p. 356. Actual figure, 1960: $1,056 billion.

53. Burgess and Price, *An American Dependency Challenge,* xi, 18, 22–25, 33–34, 42–43, 48–50, 59–60, 66–67, 70–71, 94–97, 107–114, 157–159, 182, 191.

9. More Than a Salvage Operation

1. Memo, Vocille M. Pratt to Jules Berman and Dr. McKneely, Mar. 26, 1958, BPA file 600.15/41.

2. Janowitz, *The Last Half-Century,* 138; *Historical Statistics of the U.S.,* Series H 1–31, Social Welfare Expenditures under Public Programs, 1890–1970, 340.

3. Steiner, *Social Insecurity,* 169–172; "Public Assistance: Report of the Advisory Council," *Social Security Bulletin,* Feb. 1960, 10–22.

4. "Health and Social Security for the American People, A Report to President-Elect John F. Kennedy," Jan. 10, 1961, Kennedy Library, Pre-Presidential Transition Files, Task Force Reports, Box 1071, Health and Social Security Task Force Report. Hereafter cited as Cohen Task Force Rpt.

5. Ibid.

6. "Public Assistance: A Report of the Findings and Recommendations of the Advisory Council on Public Assistance," Jan. 1960, *Social Security Bulletin,* Feb. 1960, 11–12.

7. Interview, Ivan Nestingen w/Peter Corning, 1965, CUOHC.

8. Cohen interview w/Coll, Oct. 19, 1985; Bell, *Aid to Dependent Children,* 148–149.

9. Bell, *Aid to Dependent Children,* 137, 142–148; Miles, *The Department of Health, Education, and Welfare,* 38–41.

10. Cohen interview w/Coll, 60–61; Miles, *Department of HEW,* 40–41; P.L. 87–31, May 8, 1961.

11. P.L. 87–31, May 8, 1961; Wickenden and Bell, *Public Welfare: Time for A Change,* 38–39. The FERA was signed into law on May 12, 1933.

12. Hailey, "Newburgh Facing Crisis over Relief."

13. *New York Times,* June 24, 1961.

14. Ibid.

15. Steiner, *Social Insecurity,* 110–112; *New York Times,* June 11, 1961, July 8, 1961, July 20, 1961.

16. *New York Times,* July 8, 1961.

17. *New York Times,* June 13, 1961, July 11, 1961, July 19, 1961, July 20, 1961; memo, H. Hagen to L. Dunn, APWA, July 14, 1961, sub.: Newburgh Situation, Social Welfare History Archives, Univ. of Minn., APWA Coll.; editorial, "The Meaning of Newburgh," *Nation,* July 29, 1961, 42; *Wall St. Journal* quoted in Rollins and Lefkowitz, "Welfare à la Newburgh," 157.

18. *New York Times,* June 24, 1961, July 13, 1961. The *Times* contains numerous articles during this period quoting Mitchell as determined to put the plan into effect. On December 21, 1961, the court made the injunction permanent. *New York Times,* Dec. 21, 1961.

19. Ribicoff testimony, House, Ways and Means, *Hearings,* "Extended Unemployment Compensation," 1961, 105.

20. Ibid., 103; Steiner, *Social Insecurity,* 36–37; Ad Hoc Committee on Public Welfare, *Report to the Secretary of Health, Education, and Welfare,* 1–3 (hereafter Ad Hoc Committee rpt.); George K. Wyman, *A Report for the Secretary of HEW,* Aug. 1961 (hereafter Wyman rpt.).

21. Wickenden and Bell, *Public Welfare.*

22. Steiner, *Social Insecurity,* 37–38; Ad Hoc Committee Rpt., 2–3; Wyman Rpt., appendix; Wickenden and Bell, *Public Welfare,* 5–6.

23. Wyman rpt., 26–27.

24. Ad Hoc Committee rpt., 13, 16, 26.

25. Wickenden, *Public Welfare,* 20–21; Ad Hoc Committee rpt., 10, 21–22, 25–27; Wyman Rpt., 4, 6, 11, 22–25, 34, 38–39. Only 4 percent of public assistance workers as against 30 percent of child welfare workers had the MSW degree.

26. Wyman rpt., 16–20; Wickenden and Bell, *Public Welfare,* 17–19, 42–44, 81–95, 121–123; Ad Hoc Committee rpt., 18.

27. Katherine Lenroot, "Comments on Suggestions for Possible Family and Child Welfare Aid Programs and Alternative Suggestions," Dec. 17, 1960; Wickenden and Bell, *Public Welfare,* 121–122.

28. Wyman rpt., 8, 27, 42–43; Ad Hoc Committee rpt., 20.

29. Wyman rpt., 9, 29–30; *New York Times,* July 12, 1961; "Notes and Comments," *Social Service Review,* Mar. 1962.

30. Ad Hoc Committee rpt., 16–17. Prevailing wages were paid construction workers under the Davis-Bacon Act of 1931, 46S194.

31. Wyman rpt., 28–29, 31–32, 44–45; Ad Hoc Committee rpt., 18–19.

32. Wickenden and Bell, *Public Welfare,* 19; Wyman rpt., 27.

33. Memo, Ribicoff to Mitchell, Dec. 6, 1961, sub.: Administrative Actions Necessary to Improve Our Welfare Programs, BPA file, 620, 69–A-5829 no. 17.

34. Kennedy message, Feb. 1, 1962, quoted in Cohen and Ball, "Public Welfare Amendments of 1962," 5; Ad Hoc Committee rpt., 5.

35. Cohen and Ball, "Public Welfare Amendments of 1962," 9–10.

36. Ibid.; Cohen interview w/Coll, Oct. 19, 1985.

37. Berkowitz, *Disabled Policy,* 157–163; Hill, "Aid to the Permanently and Totally Disabled," 14–15.

38. Cohen and Ball, "Public Welfare Amendments of 1962"; Steiner, *Social Insecurity,* 45.

39. Steiner, *Social Insecurity,* 45–47; House, Ways and Means, *Hearings,* "Public Welfare Amendments of 1962," passim.

40. House, Ways and Means, *Hearings,* "Public Welfare Amendments of 1962," 165–168, 410–415, 441–442.

41. Informal Note, Feb. 16, 1962, JFK Library, 997 WE Welfare, 1/20/61–4/22/61.

42. Rpt., Meeting of Members of Executive Committee of Council of State Public

Welfare Administrators, Aug. 6–7, 1962, BFS file 620.1, Aug.–Dec. 1962; Steiner, *Social Insecurity*, 47.
43. *Congressional Record*, Sept. 28, 1962, 21190–21201 (quotations at 21195–96); Steiner, *Social Insecurity*, 157–158.
44. ADC Characteristics Study, 1956.
45. Memo, Ribicoff to Mitchell, Dec. 6, 1961, sub.: Administrative Actions Necessary to Improve Our Welfare Programs, BFS file 620.
46. The ten low-ineligibility percentage states were: California, Florida, Georgia, Illinois, Michigan, New York, Oklahoma, Pennsylvania, Texas, and West Virginia.
47. U.S. Department of Health, Education, and Welfare, "Eligibility of Families Receiving Aid to Families with Dependent Children: A Report Requested by the Senate Appropriations Committee," July 1963. The high states were: Connecticut, 11.0; Delaware, 10.2; Georgia, 16.4; Kentucky, 12.8; Mississippi, 11.6; Nevada, 12.4; South Carolina, 13.4; Tennessee, 14.3; and West Virginia, 17.3.
48. Interviews with Coll: Cohen, Oct. 19, 1985; Wickenden, May 28, 1986; Ball, Feb. 2, 1988.
49. Altmeyer, *Formative Years of Social Security*, 167–168; interviews w/Coll: Wilbur Cohen, Oct. 19, 1985, Wickenden, May 28, 1986, and Ball, Feb. 12, 1988; for administrative organization, *see* Miles, *Department of Health, Education, and Welfare*; personal recollections. Research contracts could be awarded under Sec. 1110, and demonstration projects under Sec. 1115 of the Social Security Act.
50. Interview, Ellen Winston w/Coll, Sept. 13, 1982, Women in the Federal Government Project, Library for the History of Women in America, Radcliffe College.
51. For the number of drafts, see Gilbert, "Policy-making in Public Welfare: The 1962 Amendments," 21.
52. State Letter no. 606, Nov. 30, 1962, sub.: Social Services and Cost Allocation.
53. Pauline L. Bushey, "Public Assistance Agencies (Social Work Practice in)," *Encyclopedia of Social Work*, 1965, 600; Alan Keith-Lucas, *Decisions about People in Need*, passim.; State Letter no. 606, para. 1230 and 1241.
54. State Letter no. 682, sub.: Rpt. of Meeting on Coordination in the Location of Absent Parents of Children Receiving AFDC, Sept. 17, 1963, with encl. U.S. HEW, WA, BFS, Coordination in the Location of Absent Parents . . . , May 28 and 29, 1963; State Letter no. 732, sub.: Rpt. of Second Meeting on Location of Absent Parents of Children Receiving AFDC, May 12, 1964; House, Ways and Means, "Public Welfare Amendments of 1962," Hearings, 410.
55. State Letter no. 670, sub.: Control of Eligibility Determination—A Program for Administrative Control of the Processes and Validity of Eligibility Determination, July 10, 1963; State Letter no. 685, sub.: QC no. 2, Quality Control of Case Actions—Schedules and Instructions for AFDC, Sept. 24, 1963; State Letter no. 696, sub.: QC no. 4—Quality Control of Case Actions—Schedules and Instructions for Adult Categories, Oct. 28, 1963; State Letter no. 704, sub.: QC no. 5—Quality Control of Case Actions—Issuance of Consolidated Materials for Carrying Out QC, Dec. 18, 1963.
56. Memo, Winston to Cohen, Jan. 3, 1964 (revised 3/18/64), sub.: Major Achievements under the Public Welfare Amendments of 1962, WA file 011.1, 1-28-63–69-A-5691 no. 1.
57. Swenson, "Provisions for Social Services: Characteristics of State Public Assistance Plans."
58. Advisory Council on Public Welfare, *Having the Power, We Have the Duty*, June 29, 1966, 13.

59. Ibid., xi, 52.
60. Ibid., 76–83; Szaloczi, "Closing the Gap in Social Work Manpower," 13–17; Steiner, *Social Insecurity*, chap. 7.
61. Advisory Council on Public Welfare, *Having the Power, We Have the Duty*, 47–54; Bushey, "Public Assistance Agencies (Social Work Practice in)," 600.
62. Orshansky, "Children of the Poor," 3–13; Orshansky, "The Aged Negro and His Income," 3–13; Orshansky, "Counting the Poor: Another Look at the Poverty Profile," 3–26; Council of Economic Advisors, "The Problem of Poverty in America," reprinted from *The Economic Report of the President*, 1963.
63. Advisory Council on Public Welfare, *Having the Power, We Have the Duty*, xiii, 15, 23, 26, 33–34. Along with "safety net," Elizabeth Wickenden should be credited with introducing the term "entitlements" into the language of the Welfare State. See Wickenden, "Social Welfare Law: The Concept of Risk and Entitlement."
64. " 'Having the Power We Have the Duty,' " *Welfare in Review*, Dec. 1966; Steiner, *The State of Welfare*, 107–108, 111; interview, Winston w/Coll, Sept. 13, 1982; interview, Cohen w/Coll, Oct. 19, 1985; Coll recollections of speculations at the time; interview, Wickenden w/Coll, May 28, 1986.
65. House, Appropriations Committee, Sub-Committee on Labor and HEW, *Hearings*, 1965, 798–799.
66. Steiner, *State of Welfare*, 25; Meyer and Borgatta, *Girls at Vocational High*.
67. *Historical Statistics of the U.S.*, Series H 346–367, Pubic Assistance—Payments, Recipients, and Average Monthly Payments, 356.

10. Workfare

1. Katz, *In the Shadow of the Poor House: A Social History of Welfare in America*, 252–261; Link et al., *American People*, II, 868–886; *Encyclopedia of American History*, 528–530; HEW, Welfare Administration, BFS, Characteristics of Families Receiving AFDC, Nov.–Dec. 1961, table 3; HEW, SRS, BFS, Findings of the 1973 AFDC Study, pt. 1, table 9.
2. Patterson, *America's Struggle against Poverty, 1900–1980*, 136–141; Steiner, *State of Welfare*, chaps. 4 and 5; Notes on Meeting with President Johnson, Nov. 23, 1963—by Walter Heller, JFK Library, Heller, Box 13, 11-16-63—11-30-63; Wilbur J. Cohen, interview w/James Sargeant, Mar. 18–19, 1974, Kennedy Library; Wilbur J. Cohen, interview w/Peter Corning, July 20, 1966, CUOHC.
3. *Welfare in Review*, Statistical Supplement 1965 ed., table 8, Payments for Vendor Medical Bills . . . , 7; *Social Security Bulletin: Annual Statistical Supplement, 1983*, ii; Hawkins, "Welfare and Child Health Provisions of the 'Medicare' Act"; Winston, "Medical Assistance under Title XIX of the Social Security Act"; "Welfare Provisions of the 1965 Social Security Amendments: A Brief Guide for State Action," 1–16; HR Doc. no. 93–117, vol. I, 93d Cong., 1st sess., *Compilation of the Social Security Laws*, vol. I, Titles XVIII and XIX.
4. "The Social Security Amendments of 1967 (P.L. 90–248): Legislative History and Summary of the Welfare and Child Health Provisions," 1–34; *Compilation of the Social Security Laws*, vol. I, Title IV, Sec. 401 and Sec. 402 (19).
5. Steiner, *State of Welfare*, 43–50.
6. Walker, *Beyond Bureaucracy: Mary Elizabeth Switzer and Rehabilitation*, 68–69, 74, 104, 176–177; Coll, "Switzer, Mary Elizabeth," *Dictionary of American*

Biography, supp., vol. 9; Berkowitz, *Disabled Policy: America's Programs for the Handicapped*, 170–180; note, Cohen to Sorenson, July 31, 1962, sub.: Important Policy Issues for Your Consideration, Kennedy Library, Sorenson Subject Files, Box 34, Folder HEW 7–19–62; Cohen interview w/Coll, 1985; Derthick, *Uncontrollable Spending for Social Services Grants*, 15.

7. Derthick, *Social Services Grants*, 19–20, 37; personal recollections.
8. Coll, "How Work Incentives Affect Welfare Rolls."
9. Ibid.; Steiner, *State of Welfare*, 51–54, 62; HEW, SRS, BFS, findings of the 1969 AFDC Study, pt. 1, Demographic and Program Characteristics, table 39, AFDC Recipient Children by Age, 1969.
10. Pacific Consultants, "The Impact of WIN II: A Longitudinal Evaluation of the Work Incentive Program (WIN)," Rpt. MEL 76–06, Contract no. 53-3-013-06, Sept. 1976; Coll, "Work Incentives."
11. Pacific Consultants, "Impact of WIN II," 185–186.
12. HEW, SRS, Center for Social Statistics, Findings of the 1973 AFDC Study, pt. 1, Demographic and Program Characteristics, 6, 8, 42–44, 83; Pacific Consultants, "Impact of WIN II," 26; "Aid to Families with Dependent Children: Initial Findings of the 1961 Report on the Characteristics of Recipients, 12; Steiner, *State of Welfare*, 50–51.
13. *Historical Statistics of the U.S.*, table H 346–367, Public Assistance: Payments, Recipients, and Average Monthly Payments: 1936–1970, 356.
14. Derthick, *Social Services Grants*, 19–20, 22, 24–28, 33, 35–36, 129n10.
15. Derthick, *Social Services Grants*, 8, 29–30, 43ff., 72–76, 86–88, 98–99, 101.
16. Derthick, *Social Services Grants*, 102–104; Title XX—Block Grants to States for Social Services, *Compilation of the Social Security Laws*, vol. I, [Ways and Means] Committee Print, 102d Cong., 1st sess., 1243–48.

11. Welfare Reform

1. Link et al., *American People*, II, 971–973.
2. Moynihan, *Politics of a Guaranteed Income*, 118–121.
3. Steiner, *State of Welfare*, chap. 6.
4. Council of Economic Advisors, "Problem of Poverty in America," *Economic Report of the President*, chap. 2; Moynihan, *Guaranteed Income*, 50–51; Steiner, *State of Welfare*, 8.
5. Steiner, *State of Welfare*, 96–97.
6. Burke and Vee Burke, *Nixon's Good Deed*, 14–16.
7. Derthick, *Policymaking for Social Security*, 339–345, 350–368.
8. Moynihan, *Guaranteed Income*, 58, 191; Burke and Burke, *Nixon's Good Deed*, 21–22.
9. Steiner, *State of Welfare*, 7–8, 97–98.
10. Tobin, "The Case for an Income Guarantee"; Schorr, "Against a Negative Income Tax"; Tobin, "A Rejoinder"; Steiner, *State of Welfare*, 98–100.
11. Moynihan, *Guaranteed Income*, 56–58, 73–75, 79–80; office of Senator Daniel Patrick Moynihan, biographical sketch.
12. Steinfels, *The Neo-Conservatives, passim*; Moynihan, *Maximum Feasible Misunderstanding: Community Action in the War on Poverty, passim*; Moynihan, *Guaranteed Income*, 54–55, 240–245.

13. Moynihan, *Guaranteed Income*, 82–83, 328–330; Kotz and Kotz, *A Passion for Equality: George Wiley and the Movement*, 163–164.
14. Steinfels, *Neoconservatives*, chap. 6, *passim*.
15. Moynihan, *Guaranteed Income*, 86, 89–91; Levinson, "The Next Generation: A Study of Children in AFDC Families"; Langner, et al., "Psychiatric Impairment in Welfare and Nonwelfare Children"; Carter, "Introduction." 1–21.
16. Burke and Burke, *Nixon's Good Deed*, 53–56; Moynihan, *Guaranteed Income*, 128–129, 135–139.
17. "Toward a Full Opportunity for Every American: The President's Proposals for Welfare Reform," 1–16; Moynihan, *Guaranteed Income*, 220–226. The President's speech was written by William Safire. Ibid., 218.
18. Social Security Administration, *Welfare Reform Fact Sheet*, Aug. 1969, quoted in Moynihan, *Guaranteed Income*, 229–235.
19. Moynihan, *Guaranteed Income*, 321–322; Burke and Burke, *Nixon's Good Deed*, 123–125.
20. Kotz and Kotz, *A Passion for Equality*, 182–183, 185–188, 199–200, 212, 215; Steiner, *State of Welfare*, 284–285.
21. Steiner, *State of Welfare*, 281–282, 286–287; Kotz and Kotz, *Passion for Equality*, 189–190.
22. Moynihan, *Guaranteed Income*, 334–336; Kotz and Kotz, *Passion for Equality*, 212, 218, 230, 233–234, 250, 268–269.
23. Moynihan, *Guaranteed Income*, 226, 247; Kotz and Kotz, *Passion for Equality*, 266, 268, 275; Burke and Burke, *Nixon's Good Deed*, 138.
24. Moynihan, *Guaranteed Income*, 247–249, 333–334.
25. Ibid., 191–193, 509–512.
26. Moynihan, *Guaranteed Income*, 250–325.
27. Burke and Burke, *Nixon's Good Deed*, 152; Moynihan, *Guaranteed Income*, 428, 437–438.
28. Moynihan, *Guaranteed Income*, 455–456.
29. Ibid., 456–458, 464–483; Kotz and Kotz, *Passion for Equality*, 218; Burke and Burke, *Nixon's Good Deed*, 153–157.
30. Moynihan, *Guaranteed Income*, 352–353, 365–366, 372–375, 422–423, 427, 483, 487–490, 519–524, 529–530; Burke and Burke, *Nixon's Good Deed*, 183–185.
31. Moynihan, *Guaranteed Income*, 531–535.
32. Personal recollections.
33. Garnett D. Horner, *Washington Star-News*, Sept. 9, 1972, quoted in Randall, "Presidential Power versus Bureaucratic Intransigence: The Influence of the Nixon Administration on Welfare Policy," 797.
34. Randall, "Presidential Power," 797–798; personal recollections.
35. House, Appropriations, Subcommittee on Labor, HEW Oversight, 1974, pt. 5, 269–280; Randall, "Presidential Power," 798.
36. HEW, OCSE, "Child Support Enforcement Program, First Annual Rpt.," June 30, 1976, 5.
37. Ibid., 1–3; personal recollections.
38. Child Support Enforcement Statistics, FY 1985, Dept. of Health and Human Services, OCSE, 10th Ann. Rpt., 1985, 1; Maximus, Inc., "Evaluation of the Child Support Enforcement Program," Apr. 1983, also contains a number of recommendations for improving cost-effectiveness. See OCSE, Annual Rpt., 1983, 17.
39. John K. Maniha, "The Welfare 'Explosion' of the 1960s, and Caseload Dynamics: A Literature Survey," June 30, 1978, mimeo, Coll files.

12. To End Welfare as We Know It

1. Moynihan, "A Landmark for Families"; Friedman, "Clinton Speaks of Need for U.S. Entitlements."
2. Pear, "Clinton Fails to Get Endorsement of Elderly Group on Health Plan."
3. Berkowitz, "The First Advisory Council and the 1939 Amendments," in Berkowitz, ed., *Social Security*, 55; Berkowitz, *America's Welfare State: From Roosevelt to Reagan*, 72–87; Makin, "Social Security: Nothing but a Ponzi Scheme."
4. Orshansky, "Children of the Poor" (the larger figure includes additional income, e.g., food stamps, income from part-time work, and so on); Orshansky, "The Shape of Poverty in 1966"; *New York Times*, Feb. 20, 1994.
5. Duncan et al., *Years of Poverty, Years of Plenty*, 1–5, 18–22, 28, 34–35, 48–49, 76–78, 80–81; Duncan and Hoffman, "The Use and Effects of Welfare: A Survey of Recent Evidence," 241.
6. Sawhill, "The Underclass: An Overview," 3, 5–10; Moynihan, "Defining Deviancy Down," 21–26; *New York Times*, July 14, 1993; Hacker, "Getting Rough on the Poor," 13.
7. Toner, "Politics of Welfare: Focusing on the Problems," uses figures from the University of Michigan Survey Research Center.
8. Friedman, *New York Times*, Dec. 14, 1993.
9. Berkowitz, *Disabled Policy*, 122–127; Investigative Staff Report of Senator William J. Cohen, *Tax Dollars Aiding and Abetting Addiction: Social Security Disability and SSI Cash Benefits to Drug Addicts and Alcoholics*, Feb. 7, 1994, Senate Special Committee on Aging, Senate Subcommittee on Oversight of Government Management; Butterfield, "New Yorkers Turning Angry with More Beggars on Street"; DeParle, "Report to Clinton Sees Vast Extent of Homelessness."
10. Tolchin, "Congress Leaders and White House Agree on Welfare"; Clymer, "Moynihan Preparing for a Role on a Wider Stage"; Verhovek, "Expansion of Aid for Working Poor Is Tied to Budget"; DeParle, "Clinton Aides See Problem with Vow to Limit Welfare"; Nathan, "Reform Welfare? What For?"; DeParle, "Change in Welfare Is Likely to Need Big Jobs Program"; DeParle, "Clinton Advisors Urge Tough Line on Welfare"; DeParle, "Gauging Workfare's Employability."
11. Altmeyer, *Formative Years of Social Security*, 167.
12. "Addressing Nannygate."
13. See above, Chapter 10; Offner, "Welfare: Still Dreaming about Reform."
14. DeParle, "Daring Research or 'Social Science Pornography'?" 48, 50–51.
15. Benét, ed., *The Reader's Encyclopedia*, 571, 647; Schwartz, "Samuel Gridley Howe as Phrennologist."
16. DeParle, "Daring Research or 'Social Science Pornography'?" 62.
17. Abramovitz and Piven, "Scapegoating Women on Welfare." *Inside Washington*'s October 22, 1994, pre-planned segment focused on Murray's new book, *The Bell Curve*, rather than on welfare per se. It was Evan Thomas of *Newsweek* who suggested that Murray and his group were out to kill the welfare state.
18. Clinton Press Conference, October 21, 1994, *New York Times*, October 22, 1994.
19. Brian Tierney, *Medieval Poor Law*, quoted in Coll, *Perspectives in Public Welfare*, 8.

Bibliography

Abbott, Edith. "Public Assistance—Whither Bound?" *National Conference of Social Work, Proceedings* 1937.
———. "Public Welfare and Politics." *National Conference of Social Work, Proceedings* 1936.
Abbott, Grace. "Social Workers and Public Welfare Developments." In American Association of Social Workers, *This Business of Relief.*
Abramovitz, Mimi, and Frances Fox Piven. "Scapegoating Women on Welfare." *New York Times.* September, 2, 1993. Op-Ed. page.
"Addressing Nannygate." Editorial. *New York Times,* March 30, 1994.
Ad Hoc Committee on Public Welfare. *Report to the Secretary of Health, Education, and Welfare.* September 1961.
Advisory Council on Public Welfare. *Having the Power, We Have the Duty: Report to the Secretary of Health, Education, and Welfare.* June 29, 1966.
Altmeyer, Arthur J. *The Formative Years of Social Security.* Madison: University of Wisconsin Press, 1966.
———. "If." *Social Security Conference, Proceedings.* Ann Arbor: University of Michigan, 1960.
American Association of Schools of Social Work (AASSW). *Education for the Public Social Services.* Chapel Hill: University of North Carolina Press, 1942.
American Association of Social Workers (AASW). *This Business of Relief: Proceedings of the Delegate Conference, February 14–16, 1936.* New York: AASW, 1936.
"Analysis of Grants to 586,000 Recipients of Old Age Assistance." *Social Security Bulletin* (November 1938).
Annual Statistical Supplement. *Social Security Bulletin* (1983).
Beatty, Jerome. "A New Trap for Runaway Husbands." *Saturday Evening Post,* April 19, 1952.
Bell, Winifred. *Aid to Dependent Children.* New York: Columbia University Press, 1965.
Benét, William Rose, ed. *The Reader's Encyclopedia: An Encyclopedia of World Literature and the Arts.* New York: Thomas Y. Crowell Co., 1948.
Berkowitz, Edward D. *America's Welfare State: From Roosevelt to Reagan,* Baltimore: Johns Hopkins University Press, 1991.

———. *Disabled Policy: America's Programs for the Handicapped*. New York: Cambridge University Press, 1987.

———. "The First Advisory Council and the 1939 Amendments." In *Social Security after Fifty*, ed. Berkowitz.

———, ed. *Social Security after Fifty: Successes and Failures*. New York: Greenwood Press, 1987.

Berkowitz, Edward D., and Kim McQuaid. *Creating the Welfare State: The Political Economy of Twentieth-Century Reform*. New York: Praeger, 1980.

Bernstein, Irving. *A History of the American Worker, 1920–1930: The Lean Years*. Boston: Houghton Mifflin, 1960.

Bigge, George E. "Looking Ahead in Public Assistance." *Social Security Bulletin* (September 1944).

"Bigge, George E." (Obituary). *Washington Post*. December 6, 1977.

Blackwell, Gordon W., and Raymond F. Gould. *Future Citizens All*. Chicago: American Public Welfare Association, 1952.

Brandes, Joseph. "Hoover, Herbert Clark." *Dictionary of American Biography*. Supplement 7, 1961–1965. New York: Scribner's.

Brannon, W. T. "Chicago's Relief Revolution." *Reader's Digest* (February 1952).

Brinkley, Alan. *Voices of Protest: Huey Long, Father Coughlin, and the Great Depression*. New York: Alfred A. Knopf, 1982.

Brown, Josephine Chapin. "Present Relief Situation in the United States." *National Conference of Social Work, Proceedings* (1936).

———. *Public Relief: 1929–1939*. 1940. Reprint. New York: Octagon Books, 1971.

———. "Social Services Division." *U.S. FERA Monthly Report* (March 1936).

Bruel, Frank R., and Steven J. Diner, eds. *Compassion and Responsibility: Readings in the History of Social Welfare Policy in the United States*. Chicago: University of Chicago Press. 1980.

Burgess, M. Elaine, and Daniel O. Price. *An American Dependency Challenge*. Chicago: American Public Welfare Association. 1963.

Burke, Vincent J., and Vee Burke. *Nixon's Good Deed: Welfare Reform*. New York: Columbia University Press, 1974.

Burner, David. *Herbert C. Hoover: A Public Life*. New York: Alfred A. Knopf, 1979.

Burns, Eveline. *Social Security and Public Policy*. New York: McGraw-Hill, 1956.

Bushey, Pauline L. "Public Assistance Agencies (Social Work Practice in)." In *Encyclopedia of Social Work*, vol. 15, ed. Lurie.

Butterfield, Fox. "New Yorkers Turning Angry with More Beggars on Street." *New York Times*, July 29, 1988.

Carothers, Doris. *Chronology of the Federal Emergency Relief Administration*. Research Monograph 6. Washington, D.C.: U.S. Works Progress Administration, Division of Research, 1937.

Carter, Genevieve W. "Introduction." *Welfare in Review* (March–April 1969).

Cates, Jerry R. *Insuring Inequality: Administrative Leadership in Social Security, 1935–54*. Ann Arbor: University of Michigan Press, 1983.

Clague, Ewan. *Seventeenth-Century Poor Relief in the Twentieth Century*. Philadelphia: Joint Committee on Research of the Community Council of Philadelphia and the Pennsylvania School of Social Work, 1935.

Clymer, Adam. "Moynihan Preparing for a Role on a Wider Stage." *New York Times*, December 6, 1992.

Cohen, Wilbur J. "The Social Security Act Amendments of 1958: Another Important Step Forward." Ann Arbor: Subcommittee on Income Maintenance and Social Security, Coordinating Committee on Social Welfare Research, School of Social Work, University of Michigan, October 17, 1958.

————. "Social Security Amendments of 1952." *Social Security Bulletin* (September 1952).

Cohen, Wilber J., and Robert M. Ball. "Public Welfare Amendments of 1962." *Social Security Bulletin* (October 1962).

Cohen, Wilbur J., Robert M. Ball, and Robert J. Myers. "Social Security Act Amendments of 1954: A Summary and Legislative History." *Social Security Bulletin* (September 1954).

Cohen, Wilbur J., and Robert J. Myers. "Social Security Act Amendments of 1950: A Summary and Legislative History." *Social Security Bulletin* (October 1950).

Cohen, William J., Investigative Staff Report. *Tax Dollars Aiding and Abetting Addiction: Social Security Disability and SSI Benefits to Drug Addicts and Alcoholics.* Washington, D.C.: Senate Special Committee on Aging, Subcommittee on Oversight of Government Management. February 7, 1994.

Colcord, Joanna, and Russell H. Kurtz. "Unemployment and Community Action." *Survey Midmonthly,* various issues, 1933–1935.

Coll, Blanche D. "Hoey, Jane Margueretta." In *Notable American Women: The Modern period,* ed. Sicherman et al.

————. "How Work Incentives Affect Welfare Rolls." *Social and Rehabiliatation Record* (May 1974).

————. *Perspectives in Public Welfare: A History.* Washington, D.C.: U.S. Department of Health, Education, and Welfare, 1969.

————. "Social Welfare: History." In *Encyclopedia of Social Work,* vol. 17, ed. Turner.

————. "Switzer, Mary Elizabeth." In *Dictionary of American Biography.* Supplement 9, March 1994. New York: Scribner's.

Committee on Economic Security. *Report to the President.* January 15, 1935. Reprinted in Alan Pifer and Forrest Chisman, eds., *The Report of the Committee on Economic Security of 1935 and Other Basic Documents . . . 50th anniversary* edition. Washington, D.C.: National Conference on Social Welfare, 1985.

Cook, Blanche Weisen. *Eleanor Roosevelt.* Vol. 1, *1884–1933.* New York: Viking, 1992.

Costin, Lela B. *Two Sisters for Social Justice: A Biography of Grace and Edith Abbott.* Urbana and Chicago: University of Illinois Press, 1983.

Council of Economic Advisors. "The Problem of Poverty in America." *The Economic Report of the President.* 1963.

Cox, Irene. "The Employment of Mothers as a Means of Family Support." *Welfare in Review* (November–December 1970).

Davenport, Joseph III, and Judith A. Davenport. "Josephine Brown's Classic Book Still Guides Rural Social Work." *Social Casework* (September 1984).

DeParle, Jason. "Change in Welfare Is Likely to Need Big Jobs Program." *New York Times.* January 10, 1994.

————. "Clinton Advisors Urge Tough Line on Welfare." *New York Times.* March 3, 1994.

————. "Clinton Aides See Problem with Vow to Limit Welfare." *New York Times,* July 21, 1993.

————. "Daring Research or 'Social Science Pornography'?" [Charles Murray]. *New York Times Magazine.* October 9, 1994.

————. "Gauging Workfare's Employability." *New York Times,* March 6, 1994.

————. "Report to Clinton Sees Vast Extent of Homelessness." *New York Times.* February 17, 1994.

Derthick, Martha. *The Influence of Federal Grants: Public Assistance in Massachusetts.* Cambridge: Harvard University Press, 1970.

————. *Policymaking for Social Security*. Washington, D.C.: Brookings Institution, 1979.

————. *Uncontrollable Spending for Social Services Grants*. Washington, D.C.: Brookings Institution, 1975.

Dewhurst, Frederick, and Margaret Grant Schneider. "Objectives and Social Effects of the Public Assistance and Old Age Provisions of the Social Security Act." *National Conference of Social Work, Proceedings* (1936).

Douglas, Paul H. *Social Security in the United States*. New York: McGraw-Hill, 1936.

Duncan, Greg J., and Saul D. Hoffman. "The Use and Effects of Welfare: A Survey of Recent Evidence." *Social Service Review* (June 1988).

Duncan, Greg J., et al. *Years of Poverty, Years of Plenty: The Changing Economic Fortunes of American Workers and Families*. Ann Arbor: Institute for Social Research, University of Michigan, 1984.

Duncan, Joseph W., and William C. Shelton. *Revolution in United States Government Statistics., 1926–1976*. Washington, D.C.: U.S. Department of Commerce, 1978.

Dunham, Arthur. "Pennsylvania and Unemployment Relief, 1929–1934." *Social Service Review* (June 1934).

Epler, Elizabeth. "Public Assistance Employees: Their Education." *Social Security Bulletin* (February 1952).

Etzioni, Amitai, ed. *The Semi-Professions and Their Organization*. New York: Free Press, 1969.

"Final Report of the Advisory Council on Social Security." Reprinted in U.S. Congress, House of Representatives, Committee on Ways and Means, *Social Security*. Hearings Relative to the Social Security Act Amendments of 1939, 76th Cong., 1st sess., 1939.

Ford, Lyman S. "Federated Financing." In *Encyclopedia of Social Work*, vol. 15, ed. Lurie.

Freidel, Frank. *Franklin D. Roosevelt*. Vol. 3, *The Triumph*. Boston: Little, Brown, 1952.

Friedman, Thomas L. "Clinton Speaks of Need for U.S. Entitlements." *New York Times*. December 14, 1993.

Galbraith, John Kenneth. *The Great Crash: 1929*. Boston: Houghton Mifflin, 1954; 50th Anniversary Edition, 1979.

Geddes, Anne E. "Trends in Relief Expenditures, 1910–1935." Washington, D.C.: Works Progress Administration, 1937.

Gerig, Daniel S., Jr. "The Financial Participation of the Federal Government in State Welfare Programs." *Social Security Bulletin* (January 1940).

Gilbert, Charles E. "Policy-making in Public Welfare: The 1962 Amendments." *Political Science Quarterly* (June 1966).

Gill, Corrington. "How Many Are Unemployable?" *Survey Midmonthly* (January 1935).

Goodwin, Kathryn D. "Administrative Review in Public Assistance." *Social Security Bulletin* (October 1943).

Greenfield, Margaret. *Self-Support in Aid to Dependent Children: The California Experience*. Berkeley: University of California Press, 1956.

Hacker, Andrew. "Getting Rough on the Poor." *New York Review of Books*. October 13, 1988.

Hailey, Foster. "Newburgh Facing Crisis over Relief." *New York Times*. June 11, 1961.

Hamilton, David E. "Herbert Hoover and the Great Drought of 1930." *Journal of American History* (March 1981).

Hauser, Philip M. "Workers on the Public Unemployment Relief Rolls in the United States, March 1935." *U.S. FERA Monthly Report* (April 1936).

Hawkins, Charles E. "Welfare and Child Health Provisions of the Medicare Act." *Welfare in Review* (September 1965).

Hellman, Geoffrey T. "House Guest." *New Yorker*. August 7, 1943.

Herrnstein, Richard J., and Charles Murray, *The Bell Curve: Intelligence and Class Structure in American Life*. New York: Free Press, 1994.

Hill, Phyllis, "Aid to the Permanently and Totally Disabled." *Social Security Bulletin* (December 1950).

Hoey, Jane M. "The Federal Government and Desirable Standards of State and Local Administration." *National Conference of Social Work, Proceedings* (1945).

———. "Next Steps in Public Assistance." *National Conference of Social Work, Proceedings* (1945).

Hoey, Jane M., and Zilpha Franklin. "Aid to Dependent Children." *Social Work Yearbook* (1939).

Hollis, Ernest V., and Alice L. Taylor. *Social Work Education in the United States*. 1951. Reprint. Westport, Conn.: Greenwood Press, 1971.

Holtzman, Abraham. *The Townsend Movement: A Political Study*. New York: W. W. Norton, 1936.

Hopkins, Harry L. "The Developing National Program of Relief." *National Conference of Social Work, Proceedings* (1933).

———. *Spending to Save: The Complete Story of Relief*. New York: W. W. Norton, 1936.

Huthmacher, J. Joseph. *Senator Robert F. Wagner and the Rise of American Liberalism*. New York: Atheneum, 1968.

"In Biggest Boom—Millions on Relief." *U.S. News and World Report*, October 19, 1951.

"Issues in Social Security." *Social Security Bulletin* (February 1946).

Jacoby, Sanford M. "Employees and the Welfare State: The Role of Marion B. Folsom." *Journal of American History* (September 1993).

Jarmon, Rufus. "Detroit Cracks Down on Relief Chiselers." *Saturday Evening Post*. December 10, 1949.

Kaplan, Saul. "Support from Absent Fathers in Aid to Dependent Children." *Social Security Bulletin* (February 1958).

Katz, Michael B. *In the Shadow of the Poorhouse: A Social History of Welfare in America*. New York: Basic Books, 1986.

———. *Poverty and Policy in American History: A Social History*. New York: Academic Press, 1983.

Keith-Lucas, Alan. *Decisions about People in Need: A Study of Administrative Responsiveness in Public Assistance*. Chapel Hill: University of North Carolina Press, 1957.

Key, V. O., Jr. *The Administration of Federal Grants to States*. Chicago: Public Administration Service, 1937.

Klein, Alice Campbell. *Civil Service in Public Welfare*. New York: Russell Sage Foundation, 1940.

Kotz, Nick, and Mary Lynn Kotz. *A Passion for Equality: George Wiley and the Movement*. New York: W. W. Norton, 1977.

Kurtz, Russell H. "On the Governors' Doorsteps." *Survey Midmonthly* (October 1933).

———. "Two Months of the New Deal in Federal Relief." *Survey Midmonthly* (August 1933).

———. "Unemployment Relief." *Social Work Yearbook* (1935).

Kurzman, Paul A. *Harry Hopkins and the New Deal*. Fairlawn, N.J.: R. E. Burdick, 1974.

"Ladies of the FERA." *Survey Midmonthly* (August 1934).

Langner, Thomas S., et al. "Psychiatric Impairment in Welfare and Nonwelfare Children." *Welfare in Review* (March–April 1969).

Lansdale, Robert T., et al. *The Administration of Old Age Assistance*. Chicago: Public Administration Service for Social Science Research Council, 1939.

Leff, Mark H. "Consensus for Reform: The Mothers' Pension Movement in the Progressive Era." *Social Service Review* (September 1973).

Leiby, James. *Charity and Correction in New Jersey: A History of State Institutions*. New Brunswick: Rutgers University Press, 1967.

———. "Social Welfare: History of Basic Ideas." In *Encyclopedia of Social Work*, vol. 17, ed. Turner.

Leighninger, Leslie. *Social Work: Search for Identity*. Westport, Conn.: Greenwood Press, 1987.

Levinson, Perry. "The Next Generation: A Study of Children in AFDC Families." *Welfare in Review* (March–April 1969).

Link, Arthur S., ct al., *The American People: A History*. Vol. 2, *Since 1965*. Arlington Heights, Ill.: AHM Publishing, 1981.

Lubove, Roy, *The Professional Altruist: The Emergence of Social Work as a Career. 1880–1930*. Cambridge: Harvard University Press, 1965.

———. *The Struggle for Social Security, 1900–1935*. Cambridge: Harvard University Press, 1968.

Lurie, Harry L. "The Drift to Public Relief." *National Conference of Social Work, Proceedings* (1931).

Lurie, Harry L., ed. *Encyclopedia of Social Work*. Vol. 15. New York: National Association of Social Workers, 1965.

McCullough, David. *Truman*. New York: Simon & Schuster, 1992.

McKinley, Charles, and Robert W. Frase. *Launching Social Security, 1935–1937*. Madison: University of Wisconsin Press, 1970.

McWilliams, Carey. Editorial. *Nation*, July 29, 1961.

Makin, John H. "Social Security: Nothing but a Ponzi Scheme." *New York Times*, October 8, 1988.

Marcus, Grace M. *The Nature of Service in Public Assistance Administration*. Washington, D.C.: U.S. Federal Security Agency, Social Security Administration, Bureau of Public Assistance, Report no. 10, 1946.

———. "Reappraising Aid to Dependent Children as a Category." *Social Security Bulletin* (February 1945).

Marks, Rachel B. "Towle, Charlotte Helen." In *Notable American Women: The Modern Period*, ed. Sicherman et al.

Martin, George. *Madam Secretary: Frances Perkins*. Boston: Houghton Mifflin, 1976.

Martinez-Brawley, Emilia E. "Brown, Josephine Chapin." In *Biographical Dictionary of Social Welfare in America*, ed. Trattner.

Maximus, Inc. "Evaluation of the Child Support Enforcement Program." April 1983.

Meriam, Lewis. *Relief and Social Security*. Washington, D.C.: Brookings Institution, 1946.

Meyer, Henry Joseph, and Edgar F. Borgatta. *Girls at Vocational High*. New York: Russell Sage Foundation, 1965.

Miles, Rufus E. *The Department of Health, Education, and Welfare*, New York: Praeger, 1974.

Morison, Samuel Eliot. *The Oxford History of the American People*. New York: Oxford University Press, 1965.

Morris, Richard B., ed. *Encyclopedia of American History*, 6th ed. New York: Harper & Row, 1982.

Moynihan, Daniel Patrick. "Defining Deviancy Down." *American Scholar* (Winter 1993).
———. "A Landmark for Families." *New York Times,* November 16, 1992.
———. *Maximum Feasible Misunderstanding: Community Action in the War on Poverty.* New York: Free Press, 1972.
———. *The Politics of a Guaranteed Income: The Nixon Administration and the Family Assistance Plan.* New York: Random House, 1973.
Mugge, Robert H. "Aid to Families with Dependent Children: Initial Findings of the 1961 Report on the Characteristics of Recipients." *Social Security Bulletin* (March 1963).
———. "Concurrent Receipt of Public Assistance and Old-Age, Survivors, and Disability Insurance." *Social Security Bulletin* (December 1960).
Murray, Angela J. "Social Security Act Amendments of 1946." *Social Security Bulletin* (September 1946).
Murray, Charles. *Losing Ground: American Social Policy 1950–1980.* New York: Basic Books, 1986.
Nathan, Richard P. "Reform Welfare? What For?" *New York Times,* October 7, 1993.
"Notes and Comments." *Social Service Review* (March 1962).
"Notes and Comment." *Social Service Review* (September 1937).
Offner, Paul. "Welfare: Still Dreaming about Reform." *Washington Post.* October 11, 1994.
"Old Age Security." In *Social Security in America,* U.S. Social Security Board. 1937.
Orshansky, Mollie. "The Aged Negro and His Income." *Social Security Bulletin* (February 1964).
———. "Children of the Poor." *Social Security Bulletin* (July 1963).
———. "Counting the Poor: Another Look at the Poverty Profile." *Social Security Bulletin* (January 1965).
———. "The Shape of Poverty in 1966." *Social Security Bulletin* (March 1968).
Pacific Consultants. *The Impact of WIN II: A Longitudinal Evaluation of the Work Incentive Program (WIN),* September 1976.
Panken, Jacob. "Relief Can Mean Ruin." *Reader's Digest* (November 1951). (Excerpts from *Saturday Evening Post,* September 30, 1950.)
Parker, Jacqueline K., and Edward M. Carpenter. "Julia Lathrop and the Children's Bureau: The Emergence of an Institution." *Social Service Review* (March 1981).
Patterson, James T. *America's Struggle against Poverty, 1900–1980.* Cambridge: Harvard University Press, 1981.
Pear, Robert. "Clinton Fails to Get Endorsement of Elderly Group on Health Plan." *New York Times,* February 25, 1994.
Perkins, Ellen J. "Old Age Assistance and Aid to Dependent Children, 1940–50." *Social Security Bulletin* (November 1951).
———. "State and Local Financing of Public Assistance, 1935–1955." *Social Security Bulletin* (July 1956).
Perkins, Frances. "The Outlook for Economic and Social Security in America." *National Conference of Social Work, Proceedings* (1935).
———. *The Roosevelt I Knew,* New York: Viking Press, 1946.
"Personnel in State and Local Public Assistance Agencies, June 1949." *Social Security Bulletin.* April 1950.
Pifer, Alan, and Forrest Chisman, eds. *Report of the Committee on Economic Security of 1935 and Other Basic Documents . . .* 50th anniversary edition. Washington, D.C.: National Conference of Social Welfare, 1985.
Posner, Wendy Beth. "Charlotte Towle: A Biography." Ph.D. diss., University of Chicago, 1986; University Microfilm Pub. no. 8703812.

Pringle, Henry F., and Katharine Pringle. "The Case for Federal Relief." *Saturday Evening Post,* July 19, 1952.

"Public Assistance: Report of the Advisory Council." *Social Security Bulletin* (February 1960).

"Public Assistance: A Report of the Findings and Recommendations of the Advisory Council on Public Assistance, January 1960." *Social Security Bulletin* (February 1960).

"Public Assistance Goals: Recommendations of the Social Security Board." *Social Security Bulletin* (November 1944).

Randall, Ronald. "Presidential Power versus Bureaucratic Intransigence: The Influence of the Nixon Administration on Welfare Policy." *American Political Science Review* 73 (1979).

Richmond, Mary E. *Friendly Visiting among the Poor.* New York: Macmillan, 1899.

Rollins, William B., and Bernard Lefkowitz. "Welfare à la Newburgh." *Nation,* September 16, 1961.

Roosevelt, Franklin D. "Annual Message to Congress, January 4, 1935." *Public Papers and Addresses.* Washington, D.C.: GPO, 1935.

Roosevelt, Franklin D. *Public Papers and Addresses.* Washington, D.C.: GPO, 1934.

Sawhill, Isabel V. "The Underclass: An Overview." *Public Interest* (Summer 1989).

Schlabach, Theron F. *Edwin E. Witte: Cautious Reformer.* Madison: State Historical Society of Wisconsin, 1969.

Schlesinger, Arthur M., Jr. *The Age of Roosevelt.* Vol. 1, *The Crisis of the Old Order, 1919–1933.* Boston: Houghton Mifflin, 1957.

———. *The Age of Roosevelt.* Vol. 2, *The Coming of the New Deal.* Boston: Houghton Mifflin, 1959.

———. *The Age of Roosevelt.* Vol. 3, *The Politics of Upheaval.* Boston: Houghton Mifflin, 1960.

Schorr, Alvin L. "Against a Negative Income Tax." *Public Interest* (December 1966).

Schottland, Charles I. "Social Security Amendments of 1956: A Summary and Legislative History." *Social Security Bulletin* (September 1956).

———. "Social Security Amendments of 1958: A Summary and Legislative History." *Social Security Bulletin* (October 1958).

Schwartz, Harold. "Samuel Gridley Howe as Phrenologist." *American Historical Review* 57, no. 3 (April 1952).

"Security for Children." In *Social Security in America,* U.S. Social Security Board.

Sherwood, Robert E. *Roosevelt and Hopkins: An Intimate History.* New York: Harper & Brothers, 1948.

Sicherman, Barbara, et al., eds. *Notable American Women: The Modern Period.* Cambridge: Harvard University Press, 1980.

Smiley, Gene. "Recent Unemployment Rate Estimates for the 1920's and 1930's." *Journal of Economic History* (June 1983).

Smith, Alred Edgar. "The Negro and Relief." *U.S. FERA Monthly Report* (March 1936).

Smith, Mary Phlegar. "Public Welfare, Local Agencies." *Social Work Yearbook* (1935).

"The Social Security Amendments of 1967 (P.L. 90-248): Legislative History and Summary of the Welfare and Child Health Provisions." *Welfare in Review* (May–June 1968).

"Social Workers on the Spot." *Survey Midmonthly* (April 1935).

Springer, Gertrude. "Social Workers—What Now?" *Survey Midmonthly* (October 1935).

Springer, Gertrude, and Ruth A. Lerrigo. "Social Work in the Public Scene." *Survey Midmonthly* (May 1936).

Steiner, Gilbert Y. *Social Insecurity: The Politics of Welfare*. Chicago: Rand McNally, 1966.

———. *State of Welfare*. Washington, D.C.: Brookings Institution, 1971.

Steinfels, Peter. *The Neo-Conservatives: The Men Who Are Changing America's Politics*. New York: Simon & Schuster, 1979.

Survey Midmonthly. New York: Survey Associates, 1902–1948.

———. Swenson, Eleanor V. "Provisions for Social Services: Characteristics of State Public Assistance Plans." *Welfare in Review* (June–July 1966).

Swift, Linton B. "The Future of Public Social Work." *National Conference of Social Work, Proceedings* (1931).

Szaloczi, Jean K. "Closing the Gap in Social Work Manpower." *Welfare in Review* (May 1966).

Tierney, Brian. *Medieval Poor Law: A Sketch of Canonical Theory and Its Application in England*. Berkeley and Los Angeles: University of California Press, 1959.

Tobin, James. "The Case for an Income Guarantee." *Public Interest* (December 1966).

———. "A Rejoinder." *Public Interest* (December 1966).

Tolchin, Martin. "Congress Leaders and White House Agree on Welfare." *New York Times*, September 27, 1988.

Toner, Robin. "Politics of Welfare: Focusing on the Problems." *New York Times*, July 5, 1992.

"Toward a Full Opportunity for Every American: The President's Proposals for Welfare Reform." *Welfare in Review* (September–October 1969).

Towle, Charlotte. *Common Human Needs*. Bureau of Public Assistance Report no. 8. September 1945.

Trattner, Walter I., ed. *Biographical Dictionary of Social Welfare in America*. Westport, Conn.: Greenwood Press, 1986.

———. *From Poor Law to Welfare State: A History of Social Welfare in America*. New York: Free Press, 1974.

Trout, Charles H. "Perkins, Frances." In *Notable American Women: The Modern Period*, ed. Sicherman et al.

Truman, Harry S. "Special Message to Congress, September 6, 1945." *Public Papers and Addresses*. Washington, D.C.: GPO, 1945.

Turner, John B., ed. *Encyclopedia of Social Work*. Vol. 17. New York: National Association of Social Workers, 1977.

U.S. Bureau of the Budget. *The United States at War: Development and Administration of the War Program by the Federal Government*. Washington, D.C.: GPO, 1947.

U.S. Congress. Social Security Act, Titles I, IV, and X. 1935.

U.S. Congress, House of Representatives. *Congressional Record*. June 6, 1939.

———. "Social Security Act Amendments of 1939." House Report no. 728, 1938.

U.S. Congress, House of Representatives, Committee on Appropriations. *Department of Labor and Health, Education and Welfare, Hearings*. 1965.

———. *Department of Labor–Federal Security Agency Appropriation Hearings, 1953*. Part 1, 1952.

U.S. Congress, House of Representatives, Committee on Appropriations, Subcommittee on Department of Health, Education and Welfare Oversight, 1974.

U.S. Congress, House of Representatives, Committee on Ways and Means. *Compilation of the Social Security Laws*. 93rd Cong., 1st sess., Document no. 93-117. 1973.

———. *Compilation of the Social Security Laws*. Committee Print, 1991.

———. *Compilation of the Social Security Laws*. Vols. 1 and 2. Washington, D.C.: GPO, 1992.

————. *The Economic Security Act*. Hearings on H.R. 4120, 74th Cong., 1st sess., January–February 1935.

————. "Extended Unemployment Compensation." *Hearings*. 1961.

————. "Public Welfare Amendments of 1962." *Hearings*. February 1962.

————. "Public Welfare Platform—Objectives for Public Welfare Legislation in 1949." *Social Security Act Amendments of 1949, Hearings*, March 1949.

————. *Social Security Act Amendments of 1946*. Report no. 2526.

————. "Social Security Act Amendments of 1949." *Hearings*, March 1949.

————. *Social Security Amendments of 1949*, Report no. 1300. August 22, 1949.

————. *Social Security Act Amendments of 1950*. Report no. 2771, Conference Report.

————. *The Social Security Bill*. Report to Accompany H.R. 7260, House Report 615, 74th Congress, 1st sess., 1935.

U.S. Congress, Senate. *Congressional Record*. June 25, 1959.

————. "Debate on House Bill No. 6000." *Congressional Record*. June 12, 1950.

————, Committee on Finance. *Social Security Amendments of 1946*. Report no. 1862.

U.S. Department of Commerce, Bureau of the Census. *Historical Statistics of the United States: Colonial Times to 1970*. Bicentennial Edition. 93rd Cong., 1st sess., House Document no. 93-78, vols. 1 and 2.

U.S. Department of Health and Human Services, Office of Child Support Enforcement. *Annual Report 1983*.

————, Social Security Administration. *Social Security Bulletin: Annual Statistical Supplement*, 1983.

U.S. Department of Health, Education, and Welfare. "Eligibility of Families Receiving Aid to Families with Dependent Children: A Report Requested by the Senate Appropriations Committee." July 1963.

————, Office of Child Support Enforcement. *First Annual Report, 1976*.

————, Social and Rehabilitation Service, Bureau of Family Services. *Findings of the 1969 Aid to Families with Dependent Children Study*. Part I, "Demographic and Program Characteristics."Social and Rehabilitation Service, Bureau of Family Services. *Findings of the 1973 Aid to Families with Dependent Children Study*.

————, Social Security Administration, Bureau of Public Assistance. *Characteristics of Families Receiving Aid to Dependent Children, November 1953*. September 1955.

————, Social Security Administration. *Characteristics of Families Receiving Aid to Families with Dependent Children. November–December 1961*.

————, Welfare Administration. "Statistical Supplement." *Welfare in Review* (1965).

U.S. Federal Emergency Relief Administration. *Chronology May 12, 1933–December 31, 1935. See* Carothers, Doris.

U.S. Federal Security Agency, Social Security Administration, Bureau of Public Assistance. *Aid to Dependent Children in a Postwar Year*. June 1948.

U.S. Federal Security Agency, Social Security Board, Bureau of Public Assistance. *Aid to Dependent Children: A Study in Six States*. Public Assistance Report no. 2, November 1941.

————. *Families Receiving Aid to Dependent Children: October 1942*. Public Assistance Report no. 7, Part I.

U.S. Social Security Board. *Annual Reports,* Fiscal Years 1936–1952 (July 1, 1936–June 30, 1952).

————. Report. House Document no. 110, January 16, 1939.

————. *Social Security in America: The Factual Background of the Social Security Act as Summarized from Staff Reports to the Committee on Economic Security*. Washington, D.C.: Social Security Board, 1937.

Verhovek, Sam Howe. "Expansion of Aid for Working Poor Is Tied to Budget." *New York Times,* July 26, 1993.

Walker, Martha Lentz. *Beyond Bureaucracy: Mary Elizabeth Switzer and Rehabilitation.* Lanham: University Press of America, 1985.

"Welfare Provisions of the 1965 Social Security Amendments: A Brief Guide for State Action." *Welfare in Review* (September 1965).

West, Walter. "The Present Relief Situation." *National Conference of Social Work, Proceedings* (1936).

Wickenden, Elizabeth. "Social Welfare Law: The Concept of Risk and Entitlement." *University of Detroit Law Journal* 43, no. 6 (April 1966).

Wickenden, Elizabeth, and Winifred Bell. *Public Welfare: Time for a Change.* New York: Columbia University School of Social Work, 1961.

Williams, Aubrey. "Progress and Policy of the Works Progress Administration." *National Conference of Social Work, Proceedings* (1936).

———. "The Works Progress Administration." In American Association of Social Workers, *This Business of Relief.*

Wilson, Joan Hoff. *Herbert Hoover: Forgotten Progressive.* Boston: Little, Brown, 1975.

Winston, Ellen. Interview with Blanche D. Coll, September 13, 1982. *Women in the Federal Government Project.* Cambridge: Radcliffe College Library, 1983.

———. "Medical Assistance under Title XIX of the Social Security Act." *Welfare in Review* (September 1965).

Witte, Edwin E. *The Development of the Social Security Act.* Madison: University of Wisconsin Press, 1962.

Wyman, George K. *A Report for the Secretary of Health, Education, and Welfare* (August 1961).

Index

About the Author

BLANCHE COLL, the author of *Perspectives in Public Welfare: A History* holds a Master of Arts in History from The Johns Hopkins University. She entered service with the federal government in 1946, and has researched, supervised, and published studies about labor, industrial mobilization, and social welfare history. Retired from the Department of Health and Human Services in 1979, she resides in Washington, D.C.